(continued from front flap)

recounts how both Long's and Coughlin's initial support for Roosevelt waned and gradually turned into strident opposition. Finally, he depicts the constellation of events and forces—the inherent weaknesses of their organizations, Coughlin's increasing demagoguery, Long's assassination in 1935, and Roosevelt's landslide victory in 1936—that led to the collapse of popular dissidence.

Brinkley succeeds in giving us vivid portraits of two major figures of a troubled time, the social programs and reforms they espoused, and their genius for articulating—and manipulating—the needs and hopes of ordinary men and women ruined by the Depression.

Alan Brinkley graduated from Princeton University in 1971 and received his M.A. and Ph.D. degrees from Harvard University. He is currently an assistant professor of history at the Massachusetts Institute of Technology.

VOICES OF PROTEST

VOICES
OF PROTEST

Huey Long,
Father Coughlin,
and the
Great Depression

ALAN
BRINKLEY

Alfred A. Knopf   New York   1982

THIS IS A BORZOI BOOK

PUBLISHED BY ALFRED A. KNOPF, INC.

Library of Congress Cataloging in Publication Data
Brinkley, Alan.   Voices of protest.
Includes bibliographical references and index.
1. United States—Politics and government—1933–1945.
2. Long, Huey Pierce, 1893–1935. 3. Coughlin, Charles
Edward, 1891–   . 4. United States—Social conditions
—1933–1945. 5. United States—Economic policy—1933–
1945. I. Title.
E806.B75   973.91′6   81–48121
ISBN 0–394–52241–9   AACR2

Manufactured in the United States of America

FIRST EDITION

To Anita Gordon

CONTENTS

Illustrations follow page 112

PREFACE

THIS IS A BOOK about two remarkable men—Huey P. Long, a first-term United States Senator from the red-clay, piney-woods country of northern Louisiana; and Charles E. Coughlin, a Catholic priest from an industrial suburb near Detroit. From modest origins, they rose together in the early years of the Great Depression to become the two most successful leaders of national political dissidence of their era.

This is also a book about the nature of political protest in modern America. It is an examination of the imposing political movements that Long and Coughlin led; of the millions of men and women from all regions of the country who admired and supported them; of the organizations they formed, the alliances they forged, and the ideas they espoused. Long and Coughlin presided over a popular insurgency more powerful than any since the populist movement of the 1890s. As such, they gave evidence of the extent and the limits of popular willingness to challenge the nation's economic and political system.

These latter concerns help to explain why I have chosen to treat Long and Coughlin together in this study. The two men were not personal friends or formal political allies. Indeed, they viewed each other with much suspicion and some contempt. But despite the tenuousness of their personal relationship, their political movements were closely—in fact, inextricably—linked. Long and Coughlin drew from similar political traditions and espoused similar ideologies. And as time went on, their constituencies increasingly overlapped and merged. Politicians and journalists in the 1930s saw nothing inconsistent about discussing these two movements as part of a common phenomenon; they did so constantly. There is good reason to do so again.

Anyone attempting to assess the public impact of Long and Coughlin confronts several obstacles from the start. The first is the personalities and careers of the two men themselves, the powerful and ominous images that both

continue to evoke. For more than seven years, Huey Long wielded a control
of the government of his native Louisiana so nearly total, so antithetical to
many of the nation's democratic traditions, that there was some justification
for popular characterizations of him as a "dictator." Mention of his name
decades later brings to mind a vision of ruthless, brutal power, of the reckless
ambition of Robert Penn Warren's Willie Stark, of the specter of despotism.
Father Coughlin, for his part, became after 1938, in the last years of his public
career, one of the nation's most notorious extremists: an outspoken anti-
Semite, a rabid anti-communist, a strident isolationist, and, increasingly, a
cautious admirer of Benito Mussolini and Adolf Hitler. Those who recall him
almost invariably remember a man of hysterical passion and hatred, a harsh
and embittered bigot.[1]

Such images are not altogether false, but neither are they complete.
Long's remarkable accumulation of power was largely a local phenomenon,
of concern to few outside Louisiana. Coughlin's bigotry was late in appearing;
and those who heard him before 1938—by which time he was already in
decline as a public figure—were generally unaware of and unaffected by it. It
is always difficult to separate the character of a political movement from the
characters of those who lead it. At times, perhaps, it is also inappropriate to
do so. In the cases of both Long and Coughlin, however, controversial personal careers have tended to obscure and distort a larger political significance.

A second obstacle to the assessment of these movements is a shortage of
evidence. Neither the leaders themselves nor their organizations left any
papers or records of significance. Both movements existed in an era before
modern opinion-polling. Only after both had in large measure collapsed did
either face the test of a national election. Many avenues to an evaluation of
their strength, behavior, and character, therefore, are closed. I have attempted
to compensate for the absence of more systematic records by relying upon a
wide range of other, often fragmentary sources: the letters and writings of
supporters of Long and Coughlin; national and local press reports of the
activities of the two movements; speeches and publications of the two leaders;
and observations of their impact by other political figures of the time.*

There is, finally, a third obstacle to the study of these movements: the
legacy of nearly five decades of harsh ideological debate over the nature of
mass politics. Few scholarly issues have proven so sharply divisive, so capable
of evoking passionate commitment and strident disagreement. The polariza-

---

*Because some of the material cited in this study is the work of men and women of limited education,
errors in spelling, punctuation, and grammar appear in many of the quoted passages. I have left the
language in its original form and have used the notation "sic" only sparingly, when it has been necessary
to avoid confusion.

tion of opinion that has resulted has done much to shape and, in the end, distort analysis of the Long and Coughlin movements.

On one side of the argument have stood those to whom mass politics represents the most frightening tendencies of modern society: the loss of individualism, the primacy of uncontrolled emotions, the triumph of crude prejudices—the victory of the dark forces that have in this century produced fascism, Stalinism, and other terrors. To some such critics, the Long and Coughlin phenomena have appeared as menacing examples of irrational or semi-rational mass behavior, a challenge to American traditions of tolerance and individual freedom, portents of an ominous collective future.[2]

Other historians and social scientists—particularly in the last two decades—have taken a far more sympathetic view of mass behavior. Collective protest and even violence, they have argued, are not necessarily irrational or anti-democratic. They can, rather, be rational and entirely justified responses to oppression and injustice. Few scholars have attempted to apply this view directly to the Long and Coughlin movements. But the most important study of Huey Long—T. Harry Williams's exhaustive and justly honored biography —has adopted the model explicitly. Williams describes Long as neither fascist nor demagogue, but as a "good mass leader," a crusading force for progressive change who challenged powerful, reactionary elites. Long's mission, Williams claims (quoting Jacques Maritain), was "to *awaken* the people, to awaken them to something better than everyone's daily business, to the sense of a supra-individual task to be performed." Others might make the same case for Coughlin.[3]

My own inquiry into these movements has produced a picture at odds with both views. Long and Coughlin were not the leaders of irrational, anti-democratic uprisings. Neither, however, were they the vanguards of a great, progressive social transformation. Instead, they were manifestations of one of the most powerful impulses of the Great Depression, and of many decades of American life before it: the urge to defend the autonomy of the individual and the independence of the community against encroachments from the modern industrial state. Followers of Long and Coughlin yearned for no shining collective future. They called, rather, for a society in which the individual retained control of his own life and livelihood; in which power resided in visible, accessible institutions; in which wealth was equitably (if not necessarily equally) shared.

Such visions had often been difficult to sustain in the first decades of the twentieth century, as large, national, highly bureaucratic institutions had expanded their hegemony over the nation's industrial economy. The Great Depression, however, called the modern corporate structure into question once again, enabling men and women who had long vaguely resented the impersonal forces governing their lives to translate that resentment into concrete, economic terms. What had in the 1920s been a diffuse localism producing a wide range of disconnected cultural protests became in the 1930s a powerful challenge to the nature of the industrial state.[4]

It was, however, a challenge that fell far short of toppling or even seriously threatening the structure of the modern economy. And the Long and Coughlin movements, the most powerful manifestations of that challenge, are thus as significant for their failure as for their successes. On the one hand, they gave evidence of the survival in the 1930s of the long American tradition of localism. On the other hand, they gave equally compelling evidence of the enfeeblement of that tradition. The battle against centralized wealth and power continued in the Great Depression; but the war, the outcome of the Long and Coughlin movements suggests, was already lost.

MY WORK ON THIS BOOK has left me indebted, both personally and professionally, to many people. I relied heavily during my research upon the assistance of archivists and librarians in many places, and my first thanks, therefore, should go to them. In particular, I owe much to the staff of the Franklin D. Roosevelt Library in Hyde Park (and to my friend William Emerson, its director); to the staff of the Department of Manuscripts and Archives at Louisiana State University, to the Manuscripts Division of the Library of Congress, and to the Harvard University libraries.

I was fortunate to receive generous financial support at crucial stages of my work. Grants from the Charles Warren Center for Studies in American History at Harvard and from the Harvard Department of History helped sustain my initial research. An Old Dominion Fellowship from the Massachusetts Institute of Technology and an American Council of Learned Societies Fellowship (funded in part by the National Endowment for the Humanities) made it possible for me to spend an uninterrupted year completing the final version of the manuscript.

Two men closely associated with one of the subjects of this study deserve particular thanks. Senator Russell B. Long kindly shared with me some of his memories of his father and offered useful observations of Louisiana and national politics, and of Huey Long's impact upon both. The late T. Harry Williams, author of the definitive biography of Long, was unfailingly generous with advice and encouragement in the early stages of my work. He disagreed with many of my conclusions, but he was never less than gracious and constructive in his comments.

Leo Ribuffo generously shared with me some of the results of his as yet unpublished research into extremist movements of the 1930s, and Glen Jeansonne did likewise with his work on the life of Gerald L. K. Smith. Ned Lamont and Charles Seigel permitted me to read their illuminating senior honors essays (written for Harvard University and the University of Chicago respectively) and to profit from their own research into the careers of Long and Coughlin. Gale Halpern typed an early draft of the manuscript, offering numerous helpful corrections and suggestions along the way; and Ruth Spear cheerfully and efficiently typed a later version.

Most of all, I am deeply grateful to those friends and colleagues who consented to read various versions of this study and whose comments and suggestions have been of more value than I can say. They include Thomas N. Brown, Robert Coles, Richard N. Current, William A. Henry III, Robert J. Manning, Ernest R. May, Leo Ribuffo, Susan Ware, and Nancy J. Weiss. Charles S. Maier brought the benefit of his knowledge of European history and his critical insight to bear on several chapters. Roy Rosenzweig read through the entire manuscript with great care and insight and provided a valuable criticism of my analysis of the social bases of the two movements. Ashbel Green and others at Alfred A. Knopf provided both valuable substantive suggestions and excellent editorial assistance.

Pauline Maier committed so much time and energy to her reading of this study, and commented so intelligently and usefully upon it, that it would be difficult for me to exaggerate the importance of her contribution to the result. Frank Freidel kept a watchful eye on this project throughout the more than five years of its life, and on its author for more years than that. His insight into the history of the 1930s, his constant support and his warm and generous friendship have contributed immeasurably not only to this book, but to my professional growth.

I would like, finally, to thank a number of people who were not directly involved in my work on this study but who made the process of researching it far more agreeable through their friendship and hospitality: Edmund and Virginia McIlhenny, Louise McIlhenny and Hugh Riddleberger, Luther and Virginia Munford, and Sheldon and Lucy Hackney in New Orleans; Kevin and Deedee Reilly, Kevin Reilly, Jr., and Nick and Margaret Dalrymple in Baton Rouge; the McLean family in Charlottesville, Virginia; Jim, Mary, and T. L. Larew in Iowa City; and Mark and Barbara Wine in Minneapolis. To thank my family for their support during my years of work on this project would be to acknowledge only the least of my debts to them.

—ALAN BRINKLEY

Cambridge, Massachusetts
September 1981

VOICES OF PROTEST

Prologue

THE SIXTH WINTER of the Great Depression was much like those that had preceded it and those that would follow. Conditions were better early in 1935 than they had been two years before, when, with banks failing and relief efforts collapsing, the American social edifice had seemed about to crumble. They were better than in the previous winter, when only a desperate infusion of federal funds had prevented thousands from starving. But conditions were not good. National income remained more than 40 percent lower than six years earlier. Farm prices continued to languish far beneath their 1929 levels, which had themselves been uncomfortably low. Ten million people, 20 percent of the workforce, remained unemployed. The Depression was not over, and there was no end in sight. So it had been for over four years. So it would continue for four years more.

For all the sameness, however, the winter of 1934–35 was also different. Throughout the past two years, during some of the Depression's darkest hours, most Americans had looked to Franklin Roosevelt as a source of energy and hope. Now, however, the New Deal seemed to be losing both its spirit and its strength. It had been months since the President had proposed any major new initiative. He had concentrated instead on shoring up existing programs, many of which remained in disarray. Despite an overwhelming Democratic victory in the 1934 elections, the Administration had been notably unsuccessful in its dealings with Congress, where New Deal measures floundered in both houses in the face of determined opposition. "Once more," wrote Walter Lippmann in a much quoted column, "we have come to a period of discouragement after a few months of buoyant hope. Pollyanna is silenced and Cassandra is doing all the talking." By early March, *Time* noted, there "had come a change in spirit so marked that no Washington observer could miss it. The general morale of the Administration seemed at a new Roosevelt low." Eighteen months later, Franklin Roosevelt would win re-election by an

3

unprecedented margin, and it would become easy to forget the discouragement and unease of 1935. At the time, however, the grip of the New Deal upon
the loyalties of the public seemed far from secure; and new political forces
began to compete with the President for popular acclaim.[1]

During the first years of the crisis, the specter of dissident politics had
been a mere flicker on the horizon, a sullen murmur barely heard. By early
1935, it had grown and darkened until it clouded the political landscape.
Strident voices, challenging existing leaders and demanding drastic changes,
were becoming increasingly powerful. Insurgent organizations, threatening
loudly to supplant the two major parties, were spreading widely. At no time
since the Depression began had the prospects for political upheaval seemed
greater. At no time had the future seemed more uncertain.

In this troubled atmosphere, on the 4th of March, 1935, a group of the
nation's most successful and influential men gathered in New York, in a
private dining room of the Waldorf-Astoria Hotel. Bernard Baruch, financier
and advisor to Presidents; Owen Young, chairman of the board of General
Electric; Rexford Tugwell, one of Franklin Roosevelt's most intimate advisors; John L. Lewis, the most powerful labor leader in the country; other men
of wealth, of power, of public renown: all sat comfortably, dressed in evening
clothes, sipping champagne, puffing cigars, radiating the contentment and
self-assurance of success. Yet there was also an air of tense expectancy this
evening. In part, it was a result of the general feeling of political discouragement, which cast a pall over many a public occasion. In greater part, however,
it was a result of the identity of the guest of honor. For sitting at the center
of the head table was General Hugh S. Johnson, one of the most controversial
and flamboyant figures in American public life.[2]

Nearly two decades had passed since Johnson had burst into public
prominence as the highly visible and surprisingly effective director of the
Selective Service during World War I. After retiring from the Army as a
brigadier general, he had in the 1920s embarked upon a successful business
career. And in 1933, he had answered a summons from Franklin Roosevelt to
become the director of the most prominent of the early New Deal experiments:
the National Recovery Administration. For a year and a half, Johnson had
infused the agency with his own restless, driving energy. It had been he who
had conceived the famous Blue Eagle to symbolize the NRA and who had
composed the agency's slogan, "We Do Our Part." And it had been he who,
storming back and forth across the country in an Army airplane, had implored, exhorted, and browbeaten thousands of employers and virtually all of
the big ten industries into accepting NRA wage and price codes, all within
an astounding three months of his appointment. It was a remarkable performance, and for a time it had made Johnson one of the most celebrated and

popular figures in a much celebrated and highly popular new government.

But his moment of glory had been brief. The nearly universal enthusiasm for the NRA of the fall of 1933 soured in the first months of the following year, as economic conditions failed to improve and as criticism grew from all quarters. A special review board, appointed by the President, agreed that the agency was not working and laid much of the blame on Johnson. Exhausted, overworked, increasingly befogged by alcoholism, the General did not respond well. He replied to his critics with belligerent defiance and compounded his problems with violent displays of temper and provocative public statements. By midsummer, the President and Johnson's own subordinates within the NRA were quietly shoving him aside; and on September 24, his position finally untenable, he unhappily resigned.[3]

For five months, Johnson maintained a conspicuous public silence as he worked on a volume of memoirs. But on the occasion of this banquet in his honor, hosted by *Redbook* magazine (which was about to publish excerpts from his forthcoming book), he had chosen finally to speak. No topic had been announced, but Johnson's reputation (and the presence of microphones from the NBC radio network) had created high expectations. Shortly after dinner, he rose from his seat and moved slowly to the dais. His once powerful blue eyes were sunken and bloodshot. His once firm, leathery face was flabby, ravaged by drink. But it was clear after only a few sentences that his gruff voice was as commanding as ever and that his thirst for controversy remained unquenched.

Johnson's subject was one that every public figure in the room had pondered but that few had dared publicly discuss: the increasing recalcitrance and growing popularity of Senator Huey P. Long and Father Charles E. Coughlin. Only a week before, Long had launched his most spirited attacks to date on the Roosevelt Administration, capped by loud demands for an official investigation of Postmaster General James Farley's financial transactions. Coughlin, in his most recent Sunday radio sermon, had described the first two years of the New Deal as a series of failures and disappointments and had spoken particularly harshly of the NRA. The time had come, Johnson had decided, for the friends of the Administration to reply. "Two years ago this morning," he began, "in a national gloom surely as deep as that of the days when Washington stood in the snow at Valley Forge," Franklin Roosevelt had taken the oath of office that "placed upon his back as heavy a freight of human hopes as ever was borne by any man." Now "shadows have fallen athwart that faith—and it is my purpose here—with what force God has given me—to smash at two of them."

For more than an hour, in language no less melodramatic than his opening words, Johnson smashed at Long and Coughlin with rising fervor.

"They speak," he claimed, "with nothing of learning, knowledge nor experience to lead us through a labyrinth that has perplexed the minds of men since
the beginning of time." They were offering paths that would lead inevitably
"to chaos and destruction." They were appealing to men and women on
society's "emotional fringe," people easily seduced and misled. "These two
men are raging up and down this land preaching not construction but destruction—not reform but revolution." They had, moreover, entered into an "open
alliance" with each other. "You can laugh at Father Coughlin," he barked;
"you can snort at Huey Long—but this country was never under a greater
menace."[4]

The response from the audience at the Waldorf, Roosevelt admirers all,
was predictably enthusiastic, and Johnson sat down almost visibly glowing
with triumph. For days afterward, he basked in the praise of an admiring
press. The speech had come, Walter Lippmann wrote, at just the right moment, for it had exposed the "desperate and disreputable" plans of these
dangerous men while there was still time to do something about them. Its
effect in Washington, columnist Arthur Krock reported, was "epochal." Public officials "who have feared to breathe a word against the Louisiana dictator
and the radio priest" were now emboldened to speak out. The unofficial veil
of censorship that had protected Long and Coughlin for months had been
lifted. It was, the *New York Times* commented, "like the break-up of a long
and hard Winter."[5]

From other quarters, however, the response to Johnson's attack was
notably less rapturous. The White House, on whose behalf the General had
allegedly spoken, reacted with a profound and, some thought, chilly silence.
Many believed that Roosevelt himself had prompted Johnson to make the
speech. Whether or not this was true (and there was no evidence that it was),
most members of the Administration decided rapidly that the incident had
created more problems than it had solved. Long and Coughlin had been
troubling enough when most public officials had attempted to ignore them.
Now, thrust into a public controversy that newspapers were calling "the battle
of the century," they were reaping a harvest of publicity far greater than either
could have hoped to produce on his own.[6]

For weeks, stories about the Long-Coughlin-Johnson controversy dominated the front pages of the country's newspapers. National magazines and
radio newscasters publicized it further. Coughlin appeared on the cover of
Newsweek a few days after the Johnson speech. Long and Coughlin were the
subject of the lead article in *Time* the same week. H. V. Kaltenborn, the
popular CBS commentator, devoted an entire weekly broadcast to them. And
although most of this attention was hostile, the net result was to raise public

awareness of and thus to strengthen the Long and Coughlin movements significantly.[7]

By the time the fervor subsided several weeks later, most critics of Long and Coughlin were looking upon the whole affair with undisguised frustration. The Johnson attack, Raymond Gram Swing wrote in the *Nation,* had been "a demonstration of political feeble-mindedness." Not only had it provided Huey Long and Father Coughlin with a huge new audience of the curious when they took to the air for their replies (on time provided free by NBC). It had served to encourage what critics of both men most feared: a merging of the two movements into one. Long and Coughlin themselves had taken no formal steps toward amalgamation, but Johnson's speech had helped to link them in the public mind, had "performed the miracle of combining an excommunication with a public wedding." It had served as official confirmation of what was already becoming clear. "Huey Long and Father Coughlin, as the result of the last ten days of stupidity, are now designated to be the leaders of protesting America."[8]

Only a few years earlier, both men had been virtually unknown. Now, in 1935, they stood at the head of movements of popular protest that even their harshest critics feared might alter the face of American politics.

The bleak Depression winter continued. For the President, it was a time of anxious uncertainty. For leaders of both major parties, it was a time of dire forebodings. For Huey Long, for Father Coughlin, and for the millions of Americans who were rallying to their banners, it was a season of fervent hopes and frenzied expectations.

1

The Kingfish Ascending

EARLY in Huey Long's adult life, before he had become a political figure of any significance, well before he had accumulated the remarkable power that would make him a national phenomenon and that would ultimately destroy him, he sent a letter to the editor of the New Orleans *Item.* "A conservative estimate," he wrote, "is that about sixty-five or seventy per cent of the entire wealth of the United States is owned by two per cent of the people . . . wealth is fast concentrating in the hands of the few." He complained further, "What do you think of such a game of life, so brutally and cruelly unfair, with the dice so loaded that the child of today must enter it with only fourteen chances out of a thousand in his favor of getting a college education?" And he concluded, "This is the condition, north, east, south and west; with wealth concentrating, classes becoming defined, there is not the opportunity for Christian uplift and education and cannot be until there is more economic reform."[1]

Several years earlier, when he was not yet twenty, he had made a frank and startlingly brash prophecy about his own future. He would, he told the young woman who was soon to become his wife, run for election first to a secondary state office in Louisiana, then for governor, then for United States Senator, and finally for President. He expected to win them all. "It almost gave you cold chills to hear him tell about it," Rose McConnell Long later recalled. "He was measuring it all."[2]

It was this combination—the compassion for the downtrodden combined with the steely cold, ruthless ambition—that enabled Huey Long for a period of seven years utterly to dominate and lastingly to transform the state of Louisiana, and to develop a national following of such potential strength that it disturbed even Franklin Roosevelt. Between his election as Governor of Louisiana in 1928 and his death by assassination seven years later, Long erected a structure of power in the state unprecedented in American history.

He terrorized the legislature into doing his bidding almost at will. He intimidated the courts and virtually destroyed their independence. He dominated the state bureaucracy so totally that even the lowest level of government employees served only at his pleasure. And when in 1932 he left Louisiana to take a seat in the United States Senate, he placed in the governor's chair a political ally so loyal and so docile that Long was able to control the state from Washington as effectively as he had while serving as its chief executive.

Journalists from around the country marveled at his strength, referring to him routinely in their newspapers as "the dictator of Louisiana," almost as if it were an official title. His followers were equally blunt. To them, he was simply "the Kingfish." Long himself made no effort to disguise his power. Once, while he was busy ramming bills through his obedient legislature, one of his few remaining opponents walked up to him, thrust a volume in his face, and shouted, "Maybe you've heard of this book. It's the Constitution of the State of Louisiana." Long brushed him aside. "I'm the Constitution here now," he replied.[3]

To his enemies in Louisiana, Long's power was a dangerous and frightening thing, and they came, before it was over, to harbor an almost obsessive hatred of the man. They formed secret organizations, armed themselves, even staged a brief and ineffectual insurrection. And while there is no evidence to link his assassination in 1935 to anyone besides the young man who fired the shots, many of Long's enemies celebrated the event openly and without shame. A few even proposed erecting a monument to his assassin.[4]

The power and the hatred were only one side of the Huey Long phenomenon. The other was the record of accomplishment he created during his years in control and the unwavering support, even adulation he received from the plain people who formed the vast majority of the state's population. It was for them, he claimed, that he built hundreds of miles of paved highways, provided free textbooks, constructed bridges, hospitals, schools, and a major university. It was for them that he revised the state tax codes, for them that he railed against the oil companies and utilities that had dominated Louisiana for decades. The people responded by resoundingly electing Long and his candidates to office time and time again. And some, like Theodore Buckner, expressed admiration in more personal ways. Sitting in the bleak confines of a parish jail, where he was imprisoned for a minor crime, Buckner wrote in 1935 an awkward, nearly illiterate song, which he sent to Long for approval:

> *Just walking in the moon light*
> *For the night so long*
> *If yo wants to meat A Real man*
> *Meat H. P. Long*

Some People are glad Some People are so
But he will bring the baken back where Ever He go
And if yo wants to be Reborn
Just keep on voten for H. P. Long
Dont Pull up your Cotton Crop
Give the kids an Edecasion and bring them to the top.

Now this Song is coming to an end
So stick to H. P. Long He is yo only Friend.[5]

II

LONG BURST into the consciousness of Louisianans so suddenly that to many it must have seemed as though he had emerged from nowhere. Indeed, Long himself once commented that he defied normal classification—that he was, as he put it, "sui generis." Yet there was much in his early life, both in its events and its location, that helped to determine the kind of man and the kind of politician he would later become.[6]

Winn Parish, where Long was born in 1893, had always been something of an anomaly in the state. It was one of the last areas of Louisiana to be settled, one of the last of the state's parishes to be formally incorporated. While it was not as desperately poor and infertile as Long liked to claim, it was a region of only modest physical endowments and of limited wealth. Located between fertile lands to the north and east and the even richer lands of the Mississippi Delta to the south, Winn Parish consisted largely of red clay hills and dense pine forests that prevented the emergence of a thriving plantation economy. There were some slaves in ante-bellum Winn—more than 1,300 in 1860, or nearly a quarter of the entire population. But more than half of these lived in farm units of ten slaves or less, a proportion markedly lower than in the rest of the state. The total value of agricultural property in the parish, $950,000 in 1860, was the lowest of any agrarian parish in Louisiana, a distinction Winn could continue to claim twenty years later.[7]

When the Louisiana secession convention met early in 1861, the delegate from Winn, following the emphatic instructions of his constituents, was one of only seventeen to vote against secession and one of only seven to refuse to sign the ordinance after it had overwhelmingly passed. Many Winn residents, including Huey Long's grandfather, refused to enlist in the Confederate Army; a few fought openly for the Union. But the anti-secession sentiment of the parish was most clearly expressed by the seventy-three Winn farmers who in the fall of 1863 sent a petition to General Ulysses S. Grant, pledging their allegiance to the Union and asking for aid in resisting the "aristocratic" and "oppressive" Confederate government. Their specific complaint: a 10 percent "tax in kind" that the Confederacy had recently imposed on their crops.[8]

Winn continued its political contrariness after the war, becoming the home of one of the state's strongest Farmers' Alliances in the 1880s and, in 1890, the birthplace of the People's Party in Louisiana. Alliance men bought the parish's only newspaper shortly thereafter, renamed it the *Comrade,* and transformed it into the state's leading populist journal. Populist sentiment faded quickly in Louisiana as elsewhere after the 1896 election; but it lasted longer in Winn than it did in the rest of the state. At the Louisiana Constitutional Convention of 1898, only one delegate represented a party other than the Democrats or Republicans: B. W. Bailey, a populist from Winn.[9]

During the first decade of the new century, as socialist sentiment spread into the uplands of Louisiana from New Orleans, transforming itself in the process into a new form of agrarian radicalism, Winn Parish once again played a prominent role in challenging political orthodoxy. Socialism never attracted the following that populism had, never approached dominating the parish the way the People's Party briefly had done. But over 35 percent of Winn's voters supported Socialist Presidential candidate Eugene V. Debs in 1912, the highest percentage in the state. And several Socialist candidates actually won election to local offices, including the party's entire slate of municipal officials in the county seat of Winnfield.[10]

It was into this environment of nagging poverty and recurrent political radicalism that Huey Pierce Long, Jr., was born on August 30, 1893. Yet Long's own family was neither particularly poor nor particularly radical. Huey was indeed, as he often boasted, born in a modest log cabin; but he was only one year old when the family moved into a more comfortable farmhouse. And by the time he entered high school, his father had constructed an imposing colonial home, one of the biggest in the town of Winnfield. Huey P. Long, Sr., had known poverty in his life, had worked hard and suffered many frustrations in his youth and young adulthood. But by the time his children were born, he had become one of the community's more prosperous citizens and one of its largest landowners.

Nor had the senior Long ever been much of a radical. Years later, at the peak of his son's career, he was reported to have remarked, "There wants to be a revolution, I tell you. I seen this combination of capital for years." But in his prime he gave little evidence of such radicalism and never joined or even consorted much with either the populist or the socialist parties in the parish. If Huey P. Long, Jr., was, as he liked to claim, influenced by poverty and leftist politics during his youth, they were influences from outside his own family.[11]

Huey's childhood was in fact, a reasonably comfortable one. He developed an early aversion to farmwork (" . . . the rows were long; the sun was hot; there was little companionship," he recalled in his autobiography). But with eight brothers and sisters to help with the chores, he was able to avoid all but an occasional stint in the fields. He attended school in Winnfield, played sandlot baseball, went to church intermittently, worked at an occasional part-time job, and on the surface led a life in many ways not much different from countless other youths in small Southern towns.

Yet even as a child, his friends and relatives noticed, he was markedly unlike the boys around him. He was bright, outspoken, opinionated, restless (he ran away from home for the first but not the last time at the age of ten), and intensely, consumedly self-centered. He read widely. He became a champion debater on the Winnfield High School team, even winning a small college scholarship after a debating contest at Louisiana State University (too small, as it turned out: his father, having fallen temporarily on difficult times, was unable to pay for his living expenses, and Huey was forced to turn it down). And he began very early to take an active interest in politics. At the age of fourteen, he helped his older brother Julius work in the primary campaign of a gubernatorial candidate, and he recalled later of the experience, "All I remember is that the first time I knew anything about it, I was in it."[12]

Despite his brashness and selfishness, his insulation from the privations of rural poverty, Huey was not insensitive to the problems of his community. The character of the Winnfield of his youth—the fabric of community life and the increasing external challenges to it—was of crucial importance in creating Long's political outlook. What he remembered about Winnfield years later, when he described it in his autobiography and when he reminisced about his childhood, was the community's sense of its own organic structure. Neighbors helped neighbors; the prosperous assisted the poor; the community was an autonomous unit, and within it each individual had a clear sense of where power resided and where assistance, when needed, could be found. Long liked to recall carrying baskets of food from his mother to needy families, and he spoke frequently of the spirit of sharing, of communal responsibility that pervaded the town of his childhood.

The image was a romanticized one, no doubt, and Long may have exaggerated further for political purposes. But certain aspects of life in Winnfield he did not distort. Never, for example, did he try to argue that the community's social or economic structure was egalitarian. Some men owned far more property than others; some wielded significantly more power; and that was as it should be. Long's own father, after all, was an unusually prosperous landowner through much of Huey's youth. His uncle owned the town's leading bank. His older brother was a modestly successful attorney. But the Long family's steady, Snopes-like advance had occurred within limits. Successful citizens of Winnfield had prospered within the framework of community life; they had remained part of a network of local associations and responsibilities; they had not accumulated power and wealth to the detriment of their neighbors.

It was not the community's internal inequalities that disturbed Long. It was the encroachments upon it from without. In 1900, the first railroad line was extended into Winnfield. With it came lumber mills, increased population, and new commercial pressures. Long was horrified in 1901 or 1902 when he saw his first farm foreclosure. A crowd had gathered to watch the sheriff auction off the property, and the dispossessed owner stood on the steps of the courthouse begging his neighbors not to bid on his home. At the last minute, one of Huey's cousins bought the land, and Long never forgot his reaction. "I thought that was the meanest thing I ever saw in my life," he told an interviewer years later, "for my cousin to buy that poor man's farm when he didn't need it." In his autobiography, he was more blunt. "It seemed criminal," he wrote.[13]

Long's formal education ended, for the most part, when he left high school in 1910, still without a diploma. For the next several years, he traveled around the South and parts of the Midwest working as a door-to-door salesman and selling, among other things, Cottolene, a cottonseed-oil substitute for cooking lard. He was very persuasive. When necessary, he would walk into the kitchen of a startled housewife, tie on an apron, and bake a cake with his product. On other occasions, he would pull out a Bible and cite the Old Testament injunction against using the products of swine (i.e., lard) in food. The series of sales jobs he held did not make him rich, but they did provide him with a modest living and even allowed him to attend classes part-time at the University of Oklahoma one year.[14]

After four years of selling, however, Huey had saved virtually nothing and was ready to abandon his uncertain profession. He now had a wife—Rose McConnell, whom he had met at a pie-baking contest sponsored by Cottolene in 1911 and had married two years later. More importantly, he had decided he wanted to study law. Borrowing money from his brother Julius and a Winnfield friend, he and Rose moved into a tiny apartment in New Orleans, where Long enrolled in law school at Tulane. He was not a full-time student. Most of his time he spent cramming privately, and after less than a year in New Orleans he petitioned for a special bar examination, which he passed with apparent ease. In May of 1915, at the age of twenty-one, he moved with Rose back to Winnfield and prepared to practice law.[15]

For a while, Huey shared an office with Julius, an established and relatively prosperous attorney; but the brothers soon had a bitter falling out.

Huey's brashness, arrogance, and lack of deference toward his older brother (as when he took a brief prepared by Julius, pronounced it "not worth a damn," and tore it up) made the arrangement intolerable. Thrown on his own resources, Huey moved into a tiny one-room office above his Uncle George's bank; and there, equipped with a pine table, two kitchen chairs, a kerosene lamp, and three lawbooks, he hung out a painted tin sign and waited for clients. A shoe store next door handled his telephone calls. So meager was his business that after several months he was forced to work part-time again as a traveling salesman in order to feed himself and his family and to pay the four-dollar monthly rent on his office. It was, as he later described it, "a little 'chip and whet-stone' practice," and for more than a year it seemed to hold little future for him.[16]

Gradually, however, Long's prospects improved. In 1916, he agreed to handle the apparently hopeless case of a Winnfield widow who was suing the local bank over some long-lost insurance money. To the surprise of nearly everyone, Long won—largely by attacking the bank for its callousness and building up public sympathy for his client. The fee barely covered his expenses, but the publicity he received greatly enhanced his reputation as a lawyer. He did not quickly become rich, but he never again had to worry about paying his rent.[17]

Over the next several years, Long handled a wide variety of cases, many of them in the relatively new field of "compensation law"—helping laborers and their families win compensation from employers for work-related injuries. "Always," he later claimed, "my cases in Court were on the side of the small man—the under-dog." This was not quite true. He did occasionally take on corporate clients, but almost always the cases involved smaller companies suing larger ones. Long was telling the truth when he wrote in 1933, "I had never taken a suit against a poor man and have not done so to this day." He was, according to almost everyone who worked with or against him, a lawyer of unusual ability, a lawyer whose future in the profession seemed almost limitless. But it was not in the law that Huey envisioned his future; it was in politics. Even as he was building up a successful practice, even as he was leaving Winnfield to open a law office in the much larger city of Shreveport, he was preparing to begin a political career that would soon almost totally supplant his legal one.[18]

III

POLITICS IN LOUISIANA in the first decades of the twentieth century was in many respects much like that in the rest of the South. The state had emerged from Reconstruction in the control of a tight, jealous oligarchy of planters, merchants, and professionals, and it had remained under their myopic rule ever since. Like its neighbors, Louisiana had seen its black citizens legally disenfranchised and its poor whites, except for an occasional, ineffectual uprising, ignored because politically inert. It was, in a popular phrase, a "government by gentlemen." And if, as the new century progressed, this circle of gentlemen began to include new elements—industrialists, railroad and utility magnates, and representatives of the fast-growing oil industry—the changes only strengthened the oligarchy in its smug and comfortable ways.

Yet Louisiana was also different, both from the rest of the South and from the rest of the nation. Perhaps in no other state did politics attain the same dazzling, almost Byzantine complexity. Politicians in Louisiana had to take into account the same racial and class divisions, the same rural-urban tensions that existed throughout the South. But they had to deal as well with a fundamental cultural and religious schism: between the Catholics of French descent in the Delta region and the Protestant Anglo-Saxons of the north. Louisiana, alone in the South, possessed a large and powerful city machine: the Old Regulars organization of New Orleans. Under the supervision of its boss Martin Behrman, the machine controlled the city for decades through a combination of philanthropy and corruption. Louisiana politics was, in short, a morass of warring factions "of an intensity and complexity," a Northern reporter observed as late as 1960, "matched, in my experience, only in the republic of Lebanon."

The intense factional rivalry did not much alter the final result. Whatever the outcome of the elections—and they were nearly always bitterly fought and closely watched—the winners continued to serve the ruling oligarchy, continued to ignore the great mass of poor blacks and whites, continued to truckle to the business interests and particularly to the great Standard Oil Company. It was this, in fact, that most distinguished Louisiana politics. While most of the South had experienced oligarchic rule in the decades since Reconstruction, no state had suffered such total domination by venal and short-sighted leaders.

In other Southern states, the "governments by gentlemen" had occasionally faced and occasionally lost battles with new leaders claiming to represent the voice of the common people. In Georgia, there had been Tom Watson and Hoke Smith; in South Carolina, Ben Tillman and Cole Blease; in Mississippi,

Jim Vardaman and Theodore Bilbo. And if most of these new leaders had failed, once in power, to do anything concrete for the people who had elected them, they had at least given voice to the welling resentments of the poor, and had provided them with some temporary hope.[19]

In Louisiana, there had been no such challenges. The state's active populist movement had been crushed with a speed and ferocity unmatched in other parts of the South. Occasionally, politicians had emerged who promised to battle the "interests" on behalf of the people, but few had attained real stature or significance. The clearest evidence of the ineffectuality of political protest in Louisiana came from the one significant "popular" victory: the election of John M. Parker to the governorship in 1920. Parker had campaigned on a pledge to limit the power of the corporations and the entrenched conservatives, to serve the "people" rather than the "interests." But while he compiled a modest record of "progressive" physical achievements in office, from the beginning he, like all his predecessors within recent memory, lacked both the strength and the will to mount a genuine challenge to the existing political structure. Subdued, gentlemanly, ineffectual, Parker stood in marked contrast to the standardbearers of discontent in other Southern states. Politics in Louisiana, in short, lacked not only the reality but the rhetoric of class conflict. It subsisted instead on airy platitudes, patriotic homilies, barbecues, and country music.[20]

The result was a state in which public needs remained unmet and in which social pressures could quietly and inexorably grow. Louisiana ranked near the bottom among all states in services to its citizens. Its roads were abominable, its hospitals inadequate, its tax system insufficient and obsolete. It was far behind the rest of the nation in providing such basic comforts as electricity and piped water to its citizens. Its schools were so bad that only one other state had a higher illiteracy rate. Louisiana suffered, as V. O. Key once observed, from "a case of arrested political development," a problem the more striking because the state, while far from wealthy, was better endowed with natural resources and more advanced economically than much of the rest of the South.[21]

It was into this retarded political environment that Huey Long began to move almost as soon as he was old enough to vote. In 1916, at the age of twenty-two, he began a "state-wide agitation," as he wrote in his autobiography, against a new law limiting the amount of money a worker could recover from his employer for an injury incurred on the job. "State-wide agitation" was a somewhat inflated term for a relatively private effort, but Long did make himself heard. Drafting a series of amendments he thought would improve the law, he persuaded his friend State Senator S. J. Harper of Winnfield to introduce them before the legislature. Long appeared before the Committee on

Capital and Labor to speak on their behalf. His blunt and combative remarks won him few friends among the legislators; and the condescension he received from the committee members did little to raise his opinion of them. ("It was my first time to have seen a legislature in session," he later recalled. "The formalities, mannerisms, kow-towing and easily discernible insincerities surrounding all of the affairs of the session were, to my mind . . . disgusting.") But the Harper amendments were ultimately approved, and Long claimed a large share of the credit for the victory.[22]

Less than a year later, S. J. Harper provided Long with another opportunity to gain the ear of the public. The United States had finally entered the First World War. (Huey, as a husband, a father, and a notary public, claimed exemption from service; "I wasn't mad at anybody," he later explained.) And Harper, an aging, cantankerous socialist who opposed the war as a financiers' plot, published a small book denouncing American involvement. When a grand jury indicted him for violations of the Espionage Act, Long agreed to handle the defense. He first released a bristling statement to the New Orleans papers accusing the prosecution of attempting "to coerce a reputable official of this State, whose views are not in accord with the war profiteers." He then proceeded to win the case in characteristically unorthodox fashion. Carefully identifying the potential jurors he considered most hostile to Harper, Long conspicuously engaged them in conversation in full view of the prosecutors —conversation unrelated to the case, although the opposition predictably believed otherwise. The prosecutors quickly exhausted their challenges dismissing men they had seen talking with Long. And the friendly jury Huey then assembled acquitted Harper on all counts.[23]

In the meantime, Long was considering his own prospects for political office. He was not a patient man. At twenty-three, he was legally ineligible for most state offices, but, unwilling to wait, he began to look anyway. He thought he had secured appointment as an Assistant United States Attorney in Shreveport, but at the last minute the offer was withdrawn. "Probably that was my evil day," he later wrote. "Once disappointed over a political undertaking, I could never cast it from my mind. I awaited the opportunity of a political contest."

In 1918, he found the opportunity. Noting that the state constitution, probably because of an oversight, failed to specify a minimum age for election to the Railroad Commission, he announced his candidacy for commissioner from the North Louisiana District. In the campaign that followed, he made use of techniques that would characterize his political activities throughout his career: heavy use of circulars and posters, harsh attacks on the opposition, extensive travel through rural areas in an automobile he purchased for the purpose (he ignored the advice of older politicians who warned that country

people would be offended by this symbol of wealth). He also used the campaign to compile an extensive mailing list, make contacts, win allies—to
establish the beginnings of a political organization. By the narrowest of mar-
gins, he defeated the incumbent commissioner, and at the age of twenty-five
he assumed his first political office.[24]

At first glance, the Railroad Commission (or Public Service Commission,
as it was soon renamed) appeared to be an unpromising place to begin a
political career. The three-man body had done virtually nothing for years;
many of its members were no more than aging incompetents biding their time
until retirement. Yet the state constitution gave the commission broad powers
over the rules and rates not only of railroads, but of telephone and telegraph
companies, pipelines, and other utilities. Long, who had spent much of his
campaign attacking these interests, began almost immediately to exploit the
potential of his new office. For the next six years, and after 1922 as chairman
of the commission, he worked incessantly and often successfully to limit the
powers of the utilities and to reduce rates and improve services. His favorite
target, as it would be throughout much of his public career, was the Standard
Oil Company. The commission under Long had only modest success in curb-
ing Standard's power, but that it made the effort at all won for Huey valuable
political capital for the future.[25]

Long had served on the commission only a few years before it became
clear to politicians throughout the state that he was a figure to be reckoned
with. His efforts to force the large oil companies to make their pipelines
common carriers (carriers, in other words, of the products of smaller companies as well as their own); his success in rolling back several exorbitant
telephone rate increases; his constant pressure on the railroads to improve
facilities and extend service to rural areas; and his continual harping on the
need for a tax structure that would place a larger burden on the corporations
—all received prominent attention in newspapers throughout the state and in
the conversations of courthouse politicians and rural sheriffs. In 1920, he
played a prominent role (a decisive role, he liked to claim) in the election of
the "progressive" John M. Parker as governor. But when Parker proved
unable to secure the reforms he had promised, Long turned on him with what
was to become a characteristic ferocity. So bitter did the controversy become
—Long calling Parker and the legislators "chattel" of the corporations,
the administration calling Huey a "liar" and a scoundrel—that the Governor
and his allies in 1921 first backed a movement to impeach Long and remove
him from the commission, then sued him for libel. They failed at both.
The matter dragged on for months, winning valuable publicity for Long
and drawing attention to Parker's failure to deal effectively with the corporations.[26]

By 1923, Long decided he was ready to run for governor and entered the Democratic primary. He was thirty years old. For months before the election, he stumped the state tirelessly, handing out thousands of circulars, nailing posters to trees and signposts, sending literature to his ever-growing mailing list, and, as always, attacking and attacking. He assailed the Parker administration as a fraud and a tool of the corporations; he denounced Standard Oil as a corrupt predator; he attacked his opponents as allies of Parker and the old guard; and virtually everywhere he went, he found out the name of the local political boss and attacked him, too. It was the campaign of an outsider opposing the oligarchy in all its forms, and at times it was devastatingly effective.[27]

It was not, however, effective enough. Long ran third in the January 1924 primary and found himself eliminated from the race. Henry L. Fuqua, a Protestant, picked up enough of Huey's first-round support to defeat his Catholic opponent in the run-off, even though Long refused to endorse either man. But the real story of the 1924 campaign was not Fuqua's victory, but Long's surprising strength. Even the most generous estimates had predicted that Long would receive only a few thousand votes. Yet when the returns were in, Huey had polled almost 74,000, barely 10,000 fewer than the leader and 31 percent of the total. He had carried twenty-eight parishes, more than either of his opponents; and he had virtually swept the poor hill parishes of the north and central sections of the state. He had even made inroads into poorer areas of the south.

Long liked to claim that if a heavy rain on election day had not kept many rural voters from the polls, he would have won the election. In fact his defeat was a result of other problems: his rather clumsy attempt to straddle the heated Ku Klux Klan issue during the campaign, alienating voters on both sides, and his all but total failure to make inroads into the important urban vote in the New Orleans area (he won only 12,000 votes, 17 percent of the total, there). Yet whatever his failures in the campaign, he had established himself as a substantial power in state politics.[28]

Long was a candidate in the 1928 gubernatorial election, he later admitted, almost from the moment the 1924 ballots were counted. He spent the next four years preparing single-mindedly for the campaign, attempting to hold on to his existing support and add new strength elsewhere. In the fall of 1924, and again in 1926, he actively supported Louisiana's incumbent United States Senators for re-election. Both were Catholics; both were popular in the south; both won difficult contests, in large part because of Long's assistance. Huey could not have liked either man's politics, but he was willing to ignore ideological differences in exchange for added support from the lower parishes. He even made inroads in New Orleans, winning the backing of the New Regulars, a splinter group that had recently broken with the Behrman machine, and of one of the city's three major newspapers, the *States*. And he sought further popularity in the city by denouncing the construction of a toll bridge across Lake Pontchartrain. "Go build that bridge," he warned, "and before you finish it I will be elected governor and will have free bridges right beside it. You are building the most expensive buzzard roost that has ever been constructed in the United States."[29]

By the time Long formally announced his candidacy in July of 1927, his campaign had already gathered almost irresistible momentum. Even his opponents appeared to sense it. The Old Regulars staged an elaborate convention in Alexandria to anoint their candidate, Congressman Riley Wilson; but Wilson was almost overlooked as the delegates chanted anti-Long slogans and waved signs that read "It Won't Be Long Now." The issue of the campaign was clearly drawn. It was the issue that would dominate Louisiana politics for decades to come, one that would permanently change the face of the state. The issue was Huey Long.[30]

Long himself did not behave like a man who sensed he had the election won. If anything, he campaigned even more frantically than he had four years earlier. Large crowds gathered wherever he spoke—in auditoriums and at rural crossroads, in town squares and at church picnics, before bandstands or around Long's own dusty Ford. Waving above them were banners proclaiming Huey's new campaign slogan: "Every Man a King, But No One Wears a Crown," a phrase adapted from William Jennings Bryan. And from the rapt audiences came applause and cheers—"Pour it on 'em, Huey! Rub their noses in it!"—as the candidate, dripping with sweat, attacked the "thieves, bugs and lice" who opposed him. It was a harsh, even a savage campaign, unprecedented in the state's political history, and it left Long's opponents stunned. "Huey P. Long," wrote one incredulous observer, "who would not have been allowed to live a week if the code duello had still been in force, had made the conservatives ridiculous with unavenged insults."[31]

Yet it was not all ridicule and invective. Long tapped not only the anger and resentment, but the hopes that lay just beneath them. Standing beneath the famous Evangeline Oak in the heart of Cajun country, he spoke simply and movingly of his vision of the future:

> And it is here under this oak where Evangeline waited for her lover, Gabriel, who never came. This oak is an immortal spot, made so by Longfellow's poem, but Evangeline is not the only one who has waited here in disappointment.
>
> Where are the schools that you have waited for your children to have, that have never come? Where are the roads and the highways

that you send your money to build, that are no nearer now than ever before? Where are the institutions to care for the sick and disabled? Evangeline wept bitter tears in her disappointment, but it lasted through only one lifetime. Your tears in this country, around this oak, have lasted for generations. Give me the chance to dry the eyes of those who still weep here![32]

There was momentary suspense on election night as the New Orleans vote, which came in first, disclosed that Long had only slightly increased his totals in the city over 1924. Riley Wilson led him by nearly 21,000 votes. But as returns from the country rolled in, it quickly became clear that it would be Huey's night after all. Long piled up his expected huge majorities in the rural parishes of the north, and he swept many of the southern parishes as well —winning two-thirds of the vote and more from some of the Cajun Catholic districts that had defeated him four years earlier. In the end, he received over 126,000 votes, 44 percent of the total—almost as many as his two major opponents combined—and carried forty-seven of the state's sixty-four parishes. It was the largest total vote and the largest margin of victory ever recorded in a Louisiana primary. Riley Wilson, who finished second, declined to enter a run-off; the desiccated Republican Party offered no opponent for the general election. At the age of thirty-five, Huey Long stood elected Governor of Louisiana.

The 1928 election revealed a pattern new to Louisiana politics, a pattern startling and disturbing to those members of the old guard who could perceive what had happened. Political divisions in the state had traditionally followed ethnic and religious lines: Protestant against Catholic, Anglo-Saxon against Creole, north against south. Suddenly, everything had changed. Huey Long, who had lost the election four years earlier at least in part because of cultural and religious issues brought to the fore by the Ku Klux Klan, had now assembled a majority coalition that reflected the sharp economic divisions in the state.

The distribution of Long's rural vote was relatively simple. Small farmers voted for him, and wealthy planters did not. In the cities, the divisions were not quite so clear, for Long's agrarian image troubled many urban workers who might otherwise have turned against the old guard. Still, the support Long did attract in cities reflected economic rather than regional or cultural divisions. Except for New Orleans, where he fared worse than anywhere else, Long won about as many votes in northern urban areas as he did in the south. Similarly, Long accumulated majorities as strikingly large in the poor rural areas of southern Louisiana as he did in his own northern hill country. Of the sixteen parishes in which he received 62 percent of the vote or more, eight were in the northern half of the state, eight in the south. It no longer seemed to matter whether the parish was Protestant or Catholic, northern or southern. What mattered was its wealth, or lack of it.

That Long carried the state's poorest parishes did not mean that he attracted the state's poorest voters. Black citizens were almost completely disenfranchised. Many poor whites similarly found themselves effectively barred from the ballot because they could not afford to pay the poll tax. Concentrated in the fertile delta parishes, impoverished tenants, sharecroppers, and farm laborers either did not vote at all or cast ballots at the direction of local patriarchs, who paid the tax for them and watched them carefully at the polls. Long and his allies at times actually feared large turnouts of poor voters in wealthy parishes, because such voters were, they believed, under the firm control of their landlords and employers. Huey relied instead upon the independent farmers who, although they lived in economically troubled regions, at least owned their own lands.[33]

Yet if Long's victory was not a stark reflection of the sharpest class divisions in the state, it remained a clear indication of the political power of economic grievances. Only one Louisiana election within the memory of 1928 voters had produced an even remotely similar pattern. In 1896, John Pharr had run for governor on the Populist-Republican ticket, voicing many of the same economic laments that Long later exploited. And while Pharr had lost by a larger margin than the one by which Long had won, the distribution of his support was strikingly similar to the vote in 1928. The politics of economic protest, which had made a brief and ineffectual appearance in the 1890s, had re-emerged and triumphed in the person of Huey P. Long.[34]

It was little wonder, then, that the lobby of the Roosevelt Hotel in New Orleans, Long's campaign headquarters, was a scene of pandemonium and exultation on election night. Crowds jammed every corner; campaign workers slapped one another on the back, whooping in triumph. And slowly through the crush moved Huey Long, shirt open at the neck, hair tousled, eyes bloodshot, face red. As he reached for the eager hands pressing at him from all sides, his tired, hoarse voice expressed his confidence in the future: "We'll show 'em who's boss. . . . You fellers stick by me. . . . We're just getting started."[35]

IV

THE MONTHS BETWEEN the January primary and Long's inauguration in May gave conservative Louisianans a chance to examine the stranger who was about to become their governor. They saw a man five feet eleven inches in height, weighing about 175 pounds, with curly reddish-brown hair, brown eyes, and skin, a Northern reporter once noted, "the color of a sunburn coming on." His features looked almost as if they were molded out of putty: a bulbous, slightly upturned nose, puffy jowls, a sagging chin with a pronounced cleft. He had an appearance of perpetual agitation, head, arms, or body always moving, with untamable hair falling constantly across his forehead. To some, he looked almost comical, but most who saw him carried away a different, if somewhat diffuse impression—of a man of power, a man driven, a man with a sense of mission.[36]

Still, the old guard had reason to hope that they could make peace with Long. In other Southern states, common men had stirred up class antagonisms, won election, and then quietly sold out to the vested interests, pacifying their followers with heated rhetoric and race-baiting. And Long himself had shown no aversion to the accumulation of personal wealth. In the years between his two gubernatorial races, he had developed a highly profitable legal practice. He had built a $40,000 home in a fashionable district of Shreveport. He had begun to wear expensive tailored suits. And he had, if some reports were to be believed, accepted large campaign contributions from some of the same special interests he had attacked in public.[37]

Thus encouraged, conservative Louisianans tried to win Long over. They entertained him at lavish banquets and showered him with flattery and gifts. They promised conciliation and reasonableness. And if Huey occasionally responded harshly and crudely, as at a formal dinner when he swept an elegant place setting to the floor and demanded a plain knife and fork, he was only, they could tell themselves, posturing for his public.[38]

The old guard could draw scant comfort, however, from the scene at Long's inauguration. From all over Louisiana, thousands of Huey's followers poured into Baton Rouge—in cars and buggies, on mules and on foot— passing before the neat homes of the city's middle class. Baton Rouge residents peeked through their shutters in horror at the tobacco-chewing, red-gallused farmers and their plainly dressed, sunbonneted wives. On the grounds around the old gingerbread-Gothic state capitol, Long had erected a dance pavilion for country-music and jazz bands and had placed buckets of water with tin dippers. It was the largest (and surely the least genteel) crowd ever to attend a Louisiana gubernatorial inauguration. Many observers were tempted to compare it to Andrew Jackson's famous inaugural levee in 1829.[39]

Long had been governor only a few months before it finally became clear that he was not to be simply another Southern "demagogue" receptive to the ruling interests once in office. Almost immediately, he began to do two things that no Louisiana governor had ever done before. He consolidated unprecedented personal power over all levels of the state government, and he forced through the legislature a program of progressive legislation, fulfilling his campaign promises to the common people of the state.

Long used many political techniques, from the conventional to the unsavory. But the key to his future, he realized, was patronage; and he acted first to maximize the jobs and favors at his disposal. Through pressure and chicanery, he won control of one after another of the state's administrative commissions: the Hospital Board, the Highway Commission, the Levee Board, the Dock Board, and others. He fought the Old Regulars for control of the Democratic State Central Committee and won. He studied the state constitution and legal code, seeking out long-forgotten powers officially invested in the governor. By skillfully using the patronage thus acquired and by ruthlessly brandishing his increasing political power, he cajoled or intimidated a majority of the legislature into supporting most of his program.

His legislative record in 1928 was impressive. He won approval of a measure to provide free textbooks for Louisiana students (in both public and private schools). He pushed through a bond issue to finance the speedy construction of a network of paved highways to replace the painfully inadequate roads that the "pay-as-you-go" policy of the old guard had imposed upon the state. He helped force the piping of cheap natural gas into New Orleans, despite the adamant opposition of the city's electric company and the tame public officials who supervised rates. He managed to revise the state tax codes, redefining the severance tax (the tax on natural resources "severed" from the land) so as to increase the burden on wealthy oil and gas interests while lessening the state's reliance on the burdensome property tax. His opponents subjected virtually every Long accomplishment to court tests, but Huey (who was also slowly increasing his influence over the judiciary) defeated them there almost every time. It was a good beginning, and it was with the smugness and self-confidence of victory that Long's allies, Long himself, and finally his public began now to refer to him, simply and frankly, as "the Kingfish of the Lodge."[40]

Huey's opponents, long confirmed in their courtly and conservative ways, found themselves virtually helpless to counter the new Governor as he trampled upon them these first few months. Shellshocked and demoralized, they fumed and sputtered, tried futilely to block him in the legislature, attacked him in their newspapers, and made a few ineffectual efforts to thwart him with their financial leverage. Early in 1929, however, Long took a step that goaded his enemies into more concerted and forceful action. Calling a special session of the legislature to deal with an unexpected budget deficit, Long proposed the enactment of a new "occupational license tax" of five cents on every barrel of petroleum refined in the state. Standard Oil and the rest of the petroleum interests had been irritated by some of Long's earlier efforts to tax them, but now, faced with the imposition of an unprecedented levy that might lead to an ever increasing burden of taxation, they displayed some of their old strength. Conservatives in the legislature managed to vote down the license tax decisively, inflicting Long with his first major defeat as governor. Emboldened by their success, they talked of impeachment; and Huey, realizing he was on dangerous ground, prepared to retreat. It was too late.[41]

A tumultuous meeting of the House of Representatives, thrown into chaos by an excessively hasty attempt to adjourn the special session by Long's Speaker of the House, and involving a jammed voting machine, hysterical shouting and swearing, flying fists, thrown inkwells, and the bloodying of a Long opponent by a Long ally (through a wound inflicted accidentally with a diamond ring or intentionally with brass knuckles, depending on who was telling the story), galvanized the opposition. The now enraged anti-Long faction quickly drew up an exhaustive list of impeachable offenses, accusing the Governor of everything from bad manners to attempted murder. ("You can impeach for anything," one of the opposition leaders later explained. "Impeachment is a political move.") A mass meeting in Baton Rouge, with music by the Standard Oil Company band, helped mobilize what popular support the movement had; and within the next few weeks, the House of Representatives voted to impeach Long on eight separate charges.[42]

For a moment in the midst of the crisis, Huey seemed on the edge of despair. His older brother claimed later to have found him lying sobbing on his bed, and other associates heard him speak darkly of giving up. But it was not long before he started to fight back. He held a mass meeting of his own, on the same site his opposition had used; an enormous crowd flocked to Baton Rouge from all over the state, and he told it that the impeachment was simply a plot by Standard Oil and its allies to thwart his program for the people. Circulars helped spread his message to the rest of the state, and slowly the influence of the Long organization and of Long's popular following began to be felt in the capital. How strongly it was felt became clear during the trial. Having survived a vote in the Senate on the first and weakest impeachment charge, Long produced a "Round Robin" signed by fifteen senators (one more than necessary for acquittal) who said they would not vote to convict on any of the remaining counts no matter what the evidence, because the charges had been voted by the House after the official expiration of the special legislative session. No one knew what inducements Long had offered the senators, but it mattered little. The impeachment effort dissolved, and the legislators straggled home. Never again was Long to face so potent a challenge in Louisiana.[43]

"I used to try to get things done by saying 'please,' " Long remarked after the impeachment crisis. "That didn't work and now I'm a dynamiter. I dynamite 'em out of my path." Huey had not, of course, ever been much for saying "please," and the impeachment struggle probably only hastened the development of his inclination for dynamiting. But, whatever the impetus, Long moved in the months and years after the 1929 special session to erect a structure of personal power in Louisiana unprecedented in its extent and often frightening in its implications.[44]

Patronage—the giving and taking away of jobs—remained the cornerstone of the Long machine. Inexorably, he seized control of virtually every government position in the state—from high-ranking cabinet officers to lowly road workers, clerks, and janitors. Local political bosses, once important as dispensers of jobs and favors, gradually vanished in the face of this political centralization—vanished, or themselves became part of the Long organization, albeit with vastly diminished power. As important as the giving of patronage was the withdrawal of it. Even the slightest hint of disloyalty or opposition could cost a government employee his job. And it was not just Long's enemies who suffered; it was their brothers, nephews, cousins, and friends. A bridge tender in Plaquemines Parish lost his job when Huey, passing through, discovered he was a friend of a wealthy state senator who had turned against the Long organization. No foe was too weak, no job too unimportant to receive attention. Even the courts, once thought by some to be sacrosanct, were slowly brought into the fold, through persuasion, pressure, and gerrymandering.

What jobs could not accomplish, bravado often did. When conservative opponents threatened to block Long's plan to tear down the old Governor's Mansion so that a new one could be built, Huey simply assembled several dozen convicts from the state prison, led them to the mansion, and personally supervised its destruction. When members of the legislature dragged their feet on a bill authorizing construction of a new capitol building, Long had a hole drilled in the leaky roof of the old statehouse so that rain would gush in on the head of one of his most vehement opponents. When Sam Irby, a disgruntled and unstable former member of the Long entourage, threatened to defect to the opposition on the eve of a crucial election, Huey had him kidnapped, spirited away to a remote island, and later brought to New Orleans. There, after unknown inducements, Irby explained benignly over the radio that the Governor had merely been protecting him from the Old Regulars.[45]

Long quickly realized that he could expect little favorable attention from the establishment press in Louisiana—the "lying newspapers," as he routinely called them. So he created his own system of communications. He made heavy use of the radio. He built an expensive sound truck—he liked to brag it was the first of its kind in the country—so he could tour the state and speak to impromptu crowds (crowds often drawn as much to see the truck as to hear Huey). And he began in March of 1930 to publish his own journal, the sometimes weekly, sometimes monthly *Louisiana Progress,* which, despite its pretensions to being a legitimate newspaper, was an outspoken (and often effective) propaganda organ for the Long regime.[46]

Nor did Huey overlook the visible trappings of power. He traveled everywhere in sleek, chauffeured automobiles, accompanied by obsequious aides and favor-seekers. He dressed impeccably, if at times flamboyantly. "I wanted those folks to think I was something," he once explained, "and they did." He surrounded himself constantly with police and armed bodyguards—hard, occasionally brutal men who insulated Long from the masses whose adulation he sought. Huey had always been a physical coward. As a child, he had often let his brother Earl do his fighting for him. He was still afraid, not only of assassination but of the jostling and shoving, of the impassioned responses from friends and enemies that naturally accompanied his public appearances.[47]

Of course, power of such magnitude required money—money for the radio time, the newspaper, the thousands of printed circulars, the bodyguards; money to pacify political enemies and reward friends. The Long machine seldom lacked for it. In the summer of 1932, the Treasury Department sent a few men to New Orleans for a week to look into Huey's finances, and the agents reported back incredulously, "Louisiana is crawling. Long and his gang are stealing everything in the state." But it was not primarily covert graft that oiled the Long machine; it was a brazenly open system of deductions from the salaries of state employees, deductions collected automatically every month and kept—in cash—under Long's personal control. The "deduct box," as it was known, was rumored to contain up to one million dollars at a time.[48]

The most remarkable evidence of Long's power in Louisiana was that he did not even have to be governor to exercise it. Barred by law from succeeding himself in the statehouse in 1932, he announced in 1930 his candidacy for the United States Senate against the conservative incumbent Joseph Ransdell (whom Huey had helped to elect six years before). After a campaign of unusual viciousness on both sides, Long won by a decisive margin. He waited over a year before assuming his new office, to prevent the lieutenant governor, a political enemy, from becoming governor. Having arranged finally for a suitably servile successor, Long left for Washington secure in the knowledge that he would continue to control the state as firmly as ever. Indeed, the new governor, Oscar K. Allen, a boyhood friend of Long and former Highway Commissioner, popularly known as "O.K.," proved so slavishly loyal, so clearly without a mind of his own, so helpless to withstand the public humiliations that Long constantly inflicted upon him ("Oscar, you sonofabitch, shut up!" Huey shouted on the rare occasions when the Governor attempted to intervene in caucus meetings), that he was soon little more than a statewide joke. "A leaf once blew in the window of Allen's office and fell on his desk," Earl Long liked to say. "Allen signed it."[49]

Increasingly in the early 1930s, journalists from around the country and the world were drawn to Baton Rouge to witness one of the most remarkable spectacles in American politics: the sessions of the Louisiana legislature. There, in the solemn splendor of the new state capitol, amidst gleaming marble, polished wood, shining brass, and rich carpeting, the elected representatives of the people of Louisiana assembled to transact the public business. And there, running it all, moving incessantly from committee meeting to committee meeting, from House to Senate, was a man with no official standing in the state government: United States Senator Huey P. Long. Marching uninvited into virtually every important committee meeting, Long explained in a few vague words the substance of the bills he wanted enacted. Then, often without even calling for a vote, he declared them approved and sent them to the full House or Senate for consideration.

In the larger chambers, he was equally brazen. The clerk would mumble a few words of a bill; Long, standing just below the podium and bellowing instructions at his floor leaders, would call for a vote; and the legislators, often not even knowing what they were voting for, would dutifully pass it. The opposition, increasingly demoralized and with each passing election fewer in numbers, rarely intervened. Even Long's supporters, who surely chafed at their lack of opportunities to posture and expound, seldom dared to speak, knowing that a curt "Shut up" or "Sit down" from Huey would almost certainly cut them off. On one occasion, the state Senate passed forty-four bills, introduced for the first time only the night before, in a little over two hours, or at an average of fewer than three minutes each. "The end justifies the means," Long explained of his tactics. "I would do it some other way if there was time or if it wasn't necessary to do it this way."[50]

"Louisiana lay entangled in a cruel web of intimidation," one anguished conservative wrote of the new regime. The state's citizens were, wrote another Long opponent, "guinea pigs in the first American experiment with the authoritarian state." Even many of Huey's allies admitted that the Louisiana government had become a virtual dictatorship. Yet Long himself disagreed. Louisiana was, he liked to claim, a "perfect democracy," because alone among the states its government responded directly and fully to the people's will. In one sense, he was right; for if the Long machine maintained its power in part by ruthless political maneuvering, it survived primarily because of the impressive majorities it received from the voters of the state.[51]

Long's 1930 Senate race against Ransdell was the first test of his popularity after his ascent to the governorship; and his legislative program was the major campaign issue. Two years earlier, against relatively weak opposition, he had won 44 percent of the vote and carried thirty-eight parishes by a majority; now, against a formidable foe, he received more than 57 percent of the ballots and a majority in fifty-three parishes. The 1932 gubernatorial race of Oscar K. Allen gave similar evidence of Huey's political strength. Allen captured more than 56 percent of the vote and fifty-four of the sixty-four parishes. And several months later, Long backed his friend John Overton in a primary for the other United States Senate seat against incumbent Edwin S. Broussard. Overton ran away with the election, winning more than 59 percent of the vote and receiving a majority in forty-eight parishes.[52]

Much of this success reflected the demoralization of the opposition as much as the fervor of Long's supporters. After the impeachment drive collapsed in 1929, Long's enemies grew desperate and ineffectual. They formed organizations: the Constitutional League, the Square Deal Association, the Women's Committee. They filed court suits. They traveled to Washington and badgered government officials, demanding federal intervention in Louisiana. They even staged a ludicrous comic-opera insurrection in Baton Rouge, crushed with pathetic ease by the National Guard. But only occasionally and temporarily were they able to present anything approaching a credible threat to Long at the polls.[53]

At the same time, Long was evoking an almost religious adulation from many of the poor and struggling throughout the state, not just on farms and in the small towns but in urban factories and warehouses, on coastal shrimp boats and oil rigs. The intensity of his support was everywhere evident. A visitor to the shabby home of a small farmer noticed Long's picture and autobiography lovingly placed on the mantel, next to a crucifix and the Bible. A traveler stopping at a gas station between Baton Rouge and New Orleans was surprised to hear the attendant talk casually about Huey as if he were a relative or a close friend. In a small northwestern town, a crowd twice as large as the population gathered before dawn to catch a glimpse of Long as he passed through on a campaign trip, and they stood spellbound, almost visibly transported, as he mounted a cotton bale and spoke to them while the sun rose behind him. "They do not merely vote for him," a St. Louis reporter wrote in 1935. "They worship the ground he walks on. He is part of their religion." Louisiana voters were saying much the same thing. "He is a God-sent, God-fearing, God protect man. He is like Jesus," one woman wrote several months later. Said another, "He is . . . an angel sent by God."[54]

Even in 1940, five years after Long's death and soon after the exposure of widespread corruption in his organization, 55 percent of the Louisiana voters questioned in a Gallup poll called Long a good influence on the state. Only 22 percent judged him "bad." "Huey Long was the bestest man we ever had," a New Orleans woman told a pollster. Said a factory worker, "He did more for us poor folks in a day than all the others did in all the years." And in 1974, when a Louisiana newspaper polled citizens asking them who had been the greatest governor in the history of the state, the vast majority chose Huey Long.[55]

What did Louisianans get from Long in return for their support? That question has preoccupied both critics and defenders of the Long regime for more than forty years. There is as yet no general agreement about the answer. Some have argued that nothing Long did could justify his subversion of the democratic process in his state, that his violence to constitutional procedures outweighed any social good he may have accomplished. Others offer an even more damning indictment: that Long not only debased the institutions of government in Louisiana, but failed to use his power effectively to address the real needs of the state. There is some evidence to support their claim.

It is true, for example, that Long often seemed excessively concerned with physical monuments, many of which served little purpose beyond glorifying his regime. The new state capitol, topped by a thirty-four-story office tower and including Huey's profile in bronze on the elevator doors; the new Governor's Mansion, designed to resemble the White House; the elaborate athletic facilities at Louisiana State University, including a swimming pool that at the last moment Long ordered lengthened so it would be the biggest in the country —all seemed designed as much to satisfy Huey Long's ego as to answer real needs. Even the new airport Long built for New Orleans seemed to reflect a capricious vanity. Huey named it after Levee Board Commissioner Abe Shushan, an obscure dry-goods merchant only recently appointed to state government. It was a heady honor, and Shushan recognized how fleeting might be his fame. Visitors to the new airport were startled to find on every doorknob, every window sill, every countertop, every plumbing fixture—virtually every available surface—the name or initials of the Levee Board Chairman, permanently inscribed. It would cost the state up to $100,000, Shushan boasted, if anyone tried to change the name.[56]

Yet others of Long's physical achievements struck directly at the real social needs of Louisiana. At the beginning of his administration, the state highway system comprised fewer than 300 miles of paved roads and only three bridges; by 1935, there were 3,754 miles of paved highway, forty bridges, and almost 4,000 miles of new gravel farm road. At one point, the Louisiana highway-construction program was the largest in the nation.[57]

There were other, equally valuable accomplishments. Long expanded the state's abysmally inadequate public-health facilities, improved conditions for treatment of the mentally ill, founded a major medical school. He lavished money and attention upon Louisiana State University and helped transform it from a provincial college into a respectable major university. For adults, he began night schools in an effort to lower the state's appalling illiteracy rate; and for children, he supplied not only free schoolbooks but state-supported school buses and new classroom facilities. Long was, whether he realized it or not, helping to fulfill one of the first needs of any developing society: the creation of an infrastructure, the construction of the basic services and facilities without which more complex economic progress would be impossible.[58]

Yet the "Long Revolution," as some described it, operated within very rigid limits. From the beginning, Long assailed the "trusts" and the giant oil companies, and he shifted a portion of the state's tax burden onto their shoulders through increases in the severance taxes on natural resources. But, aware of the importance of these enterprises to the Louisiana economy, he could offer no fundamental challenge to their power. Even the severance-tax increases left the corporations with a relatively light load; and Long's only real effort to enlarge that load significantly—his proposal for an "occupational license tax" in 1929—failed in the legislature. When several years later, with his control of the legislature complete, he managed finally to win passage of the same tax, he inserted a provision giving the governor discretion to set the rate where he pleased within certain limits. That rate remained low while Long controlled the state government. When asked who was to pay for the public-works projects and social programs he was instituting, Long's supporters customarily replied "the corporations." That was, however, only partially true. An even larger proportion of the bill he passed on to future generations of taxpayers through a seemingly endless series of state bond issues.[59]

Long took other steps to attempt to help poor Louisianans, but in every case there were hard limits to such efforts. He exempted low-income families from most state property taxes. He did virtually nothing, however, for tenant farmers and sharecroppers, many of whom were being driven from their land, others of whom continued to live as they traditionally had—in desperate poverty. He supported increases in workmen's compensation and openly opposed the "yellow dog" contract, winning the support of the state's tiny American Federation of Labor office as a result; but he sponsored no positive legislation to strengthen the position of labor unions or to curb labor abuses, and he used non-union labor on many state building projects. Plagued with a cruel crop-lien agricultural system, inhospitable to labor unions, ranked near the bottom in per-capita income and literacy, Louisiana remained after Long's death what it had been during his lifetime—one of the poorest and least developed states in the nation. It would remain so even thirty years later.[60]

The case for Long as an important departure from the traditional Southern "demagogue" has not rested solely on his economic accomplishments. He appeared to differ from other leaders of his region even more conspicuously in his record on the issue of race. One of the most frequent tributes to Long's career in Southern politics has been that his attitude toward blacks was relatively enlightened, that he did not rise to power at the expense of the Negro, that once in office he extended to them economic benefits almost unprecedented in a Southern state. Many Louisiana blacks seemed to accept this flattering portrait. Few of them could vote, but in some areas of the state they formed local Long organizations of their own, attempting in the only way open to them to give voice to their political loyalties. "He was fair to colored people, good to all poor people," a black worker who had lived through the Long era once recalled. "He walked the land like Jesus Christ and left nothing undone." A black leader in New Orleans claimed in 1939, "The Negro masses, as well as the white masses, were solidly behind Huey P. Long."[61]

Such tributes were not entirely unmerited. Long seldom attempted to exploit racial prejudice in his rise to power, either in Louisiana or in the nation. He rarely mentioned race at all. And an argument could be made that there were genuine active efforts to assist the black population of his state. "My educational program is for everybody, whites and blacks," he told Roy Wilkins in an interview for the *Crisis* in 1935. "I can't have my people ignorant." When black leaders in New Orleans complained that there were no jobs for their people in one of Huey's new state hospitals, Long managed to find openings for black nurses. Black workers frequently secured employment on Long's highway-construction projects. When Hiram Evans, the Imperial Wizard of the Ku Klux Klan, threatened in 1934 to campaign in Louisiana against Huey, Long responded blisteringly that "that Imperial bastard will never set foot in Louisiana," and that if he did, he would leave with "his toes turned up." Evans never came.[62]

Yet the case for Huey Long as an active friend of black Louisianans is little stronger than the case for him as an active enemy. His heralded actions on their behalf were, more often than not, either expedient or condescending, with limited results. Long's tirade against the Klan, for example, came well after the organization had ceased to wield any significant political influence. A decade earlier, when men such as Evans might indeed have found an audience in Louisiana, Long had been silent on the issue. Even in 1934, his animosity was probably more a result of his solicitude for the state's many Catholic voters than of any concern for the non-voting blacks. The jobs Long provided for blacks on highway projects paid wages so minimal that many white workers would not consider them—even low-paying New Deal relief projects offered higher salaries. When Long forced his state hospitals to hire black staff members, he made no statements on behalf of racial justice. Instead, he marched into a "colored" ward and feigned outrage that white nurses should have to care for black patients. Long made no gestures at all, not even symbolic ones, on behalf of black political rights. "I ain't gonna get into that fight," he said in an interview in 1935. "A lot of guys would have been murdered politically for what I've been able to do quietly for the niggers. But do you think I could get away with niggers voting? No siree!" His record was true to his words. When he won the Louisiana governorship in 1928, a mere 2,054 blacks were registered to vote, one half of one percent of all registrants. In 1936, just after Long's death, that already negligible number had actually declined by 11, to 2,043; and since white registration had soared in the same period (a result of Long's successful effort to abolish the poll tax), blacks now constituted only .3 percent of the state's registered voters.[63]

Long discussed racial issues so infrequently that evidence of his personal feelings is limited. His opinions seemed to differ little from those of most other Southerners of his time, and he apparently adopted, perhaps unthinkingly, conventional assumptions about the inferiority of the Negro. On the few occasions when he did discuss racial issues, he almost always referred to blacks with either condescension or contempt. In several Louisiana campaigns (in the 1928, 1930, and 1932 contests, all of which Long or his allies won with relative ease), he resorted occasionally to race-baiting of the crudest and most vicious kind. In the 1932 gubernatorial campaign, for example, he circulated leaflets attempting to link one of O. K. Allen's opponents with an insurance company that offered burial insurance to blacks, while his *Louisiana Progress* ran inflammatory stories under such screaming headlines as "His Secret Negro Partnerships Vex Dudley LeBlanc—Divided 15¢ a Head Profit on Dead Coons with Negro Partner."[64]

In later years, as he moved into national politics, Long almost entirely abandoned such offensive tactics. There were occasional lapses: using "nigger stories" to spice up a few Senate filibusters, inserting a condescending racial joke in the opening paragraphs of a radio speech in 1935. For the most part, however, he avoided the subject of race. While the *Louisiana Progress* had occasionally run racist editorials and news items, his new national journal, the *American Progress,* remained silent on the question. And if Long himself paid little heed to racial issues, his national following paid even less. A reading of several thousand letters from Long admirers—letters to the *American Progress,* to the White House, to other politicians, to Huey himself—discloses virtually none that makes even indirect reference to racial matters.[65]

This silence made it possible for Long to claim, as he did to Roy Wilkins, that he was genuinely, if quietly, committed to racial justice. "I say niggers have got to have homes and security like anybody else," he said. "Black and white, they all gotta have a chance." But the claim was not a strong one. Long refused to support the most prominent national effort to assist blacks: the campaign to secure federal anti-lynching legislation. "I can't do nothing about it. No sir," he explained. "Can't do the dead nigra no good." He showed in general no recognition that racial discrimination was itself an issue, that a solution of the problems of blacks would require special efforts to overcome the effects of bigotry. "Don't say I'm working for niggers. I'm not," he explained once. "I'm for the poor man—all poor men. . . . 'Every Man a King' —that's my slogan. That means every man, niggers 'long with the rest, but not specially for niggers."[66]

"Of the late Senator Huey P. Long," the *Crisis* observed after Huey's death, "Negro Americans may say that he was the only southern politician in recent decades to achieve the national spotlight without the use of racial and color hatred as campaign material." For that, he clearly deserved note. Few Southern popular leaders of his era could claim as much. He cannot, however, be said to have offered any positive message, either to Louisiana or to the nation, about the future of the Negro. He made few ugly appeals to racial prejudice. "But when this is said," as the *Crisis* concluded, "his story, so far as Negroes are concerned, is done."[67]

Bold, even reckless in his accumulation of political power, forceful and effective in translating "New South" visions of physical progress into reality, Long remained a moderate, even at times timid leader in matters of economic and social reform. Yet even if he had wished to move more forcefully (and there is no evidence that he did), he would have faced major, perhaps insurmountable obstacles. A state government, even one as potent as Long's, had only limited powers and limited assets. Louisiana, a poor state in the best of times, had fewer resources than most. And the years of Long's power were far from the best of times.

Louisiana had not shared very much in the booming prosperity of the 1920s, so the arrival of the Great Depression after 1929 did not affect it as immediately as it did others. Gradually, however, the Louisiana economy began to languish. For farmers, the crisis was particularly severe: in 1929, their total cash income had been $170 million; by 1932, it had fallen 65 percent, to $59 million. The cities suffered as well. In New Orleans, where repair shops advertised low-price resoling for those who had worn holes in their shoes walking the streets looking for jobs, a special committee reported early in 1930 that over 10,000 men were unemployed; and the problem only grew worse thereafter. Louisiana's already low per-capita income declined precipitously: from $415 in 1929, to $344 in 1930, to as low as $222 in 1933.[68]

Long's public-works projects, his pouring of government money into a famished marketplace, undoubtedly helped prevent an even more drastic economic decline and provided many badly needed jobs. Said one Long supporter in a 1935 letter to President Roosevelt: "If all you high up men would listen to our great man there would not be people begging the streets. . . . He has guided this state through this hard-time DEPRESSION and OPPRESSION."

But while Louisiana may have suffered less from the Depression with Huey Long than it would have without him, it suffered nonetheless. And no one was more aware of the problem than Long himself. Both because of the limits of his own vision and because of the political and economic constraints of his position, he faced a major dilemma. Having risen to power as the champion of the common man, he found himself unable to do very much to help him in his hour of greatest need. Perhaps that was why, as early as 1930, Long began to shift his focus away from Louisiana and toward the larger and more fertile pastures of national politics.[69]

2

Beyond Louisiana

LONG FIRST CAME to national attention not by winning elections or building highways, but by wearing a pair of green silk pajamas and a bathrobe to receive a German naval commander who was paying an official courtesy call on the Governor in New Orleans. After formal protests from an outraged German consul, Huey apologized by appearing on board the Commander's ship the next day carefully dressed in striped pants and tails. But the lesson he learned from the incident was less the importance of diplomatic niceties than the value of buffoonery in winning national publicity. The national press, long out of the habit of taking Southern politics seriously, delighted in the episode; and for the first time, Huey found himself on the front pages of newspapers around the country.[1]

He continued in the following months and years to cultivate a reputation as a country bumpkin and a clown. When Northern reporters called on him in the Governor's Mansion fourteen months after the green-pajamas incident to discuss some new legislative proposals, Long rummaged around in a drawer, pulled out a jew's-harp, and treated them to a few "country favorites." "Properly played," he explained, "the jew's-harp expresses the human soul." When the LSU marching band traveled to Nashville for an important football game with Vanderbilt, Huey rode with them on the train and strutted in front of the trombones and trumpets through the downtown streets to the stadium. And in the spring of 1931, Long began a national debate with an editor of the Atlanta *Constitution* over the proper method for eating cornpone and "potlikker" (the juice left in the bottom of the pan after boiling collard greens and salt pork). While Huey claimed that cornpone should be dunked in the liquid, the *Constitution* insisted it should be crumbled. The debate continued for weeks, drawing comments from personalities as diverse and illustrious as Franklin D. Roosevelt and Amos 'n' Andy (to whom Long was already indebted for his famous nickname, "Kingfish," after a character in their popular radio program). Huey reveled in the publicity.[2]

Long was not, however, content to make his way in the world through buffoonery alone. By 1931, he was ready to extend his serious political activities beyond Louisiana, and he looked first to the rest of the South. In August, he meddled, uninvited, in a Mississippi gubernatorial primary, intruding prominently enough to make his presence an issue in the campaign. The Long-endorsed candidate won decisively. At almost the same time, he began to spearhead a movement that would, if successful, profoundly affect the entire South: a movement to forbid the planting of cotton in 1932.[3]

The idea of reducing cotton production to raise prices was not a new one. Crop-reduction schemes had appeared in the South as early as 1907 and as recently as 1926. By 1931, however, the problem of excess production had taken on new urgency. The price of cotton, which had stood at 40 cents a pound in 1920 and at over 20 cents in 1927, had fallen to a new low of 5.66—a victim of enormous surpluses and shrinking world markets. Cotton farmers, after decades of struggling with fluctuating prices, found themselves finally on the verge of extinction.[4]

Long's was not the only proposal for dealing with the crisis, but it was at once the simplest and the most drastic. The legislatures of the cotton-growing states were to pass laws banning all planting for the 1932 harvest year. The halt in production would permit the distribution of the existing surplus and would force a dramatic rise in prices. With an effective cotton holiday, Long claimed, "the farmers will get more money for this year's crop alone than they would get for this and the next two cotton crops they raise."[5]

There were legitimate questions about the workability of the plan. Long produced no evidence to prove that, even with a planting moratorium, the existing surplus could be sold to the depressed world market. He gave no reason to believe that overproduction would not quickly become a problem again once planting resumed in 1933. Yet it was not the practicality of the plan that its opponents questioned almost as soon as Long announced it. It was the proposal's "hysterical radicalism," its infringement upon individual liberties and property rights, its unprecedented extension of government power. "No government can undertake to say to its citizens what they can grow and what they can not grow," editorialized a North Carolina newspaper in a typical hostile response, "without thereby assuming dictatorial powers alien to the American system."[6]

Indeed, Long had barely finished announcing the proposal before it became clear that its chances for adoption were slim. A conference in New Orleans to discuss the cotton holiday drew a large and enthusiastic crowd, but only two of the twelve or more governors Long had invited appeared. The Louisiana legislature quickly approved a planting moratorium for the state (Long signed the bill sitting on a cotton mattress and wearing a cotton night-shirt, then—once the photographers had left—changed back into his usual silk pajamas); but in many of the other cotton states, there were no signs that the governors even planned to call their legislatures into session.[7]

Most discouraging was the attitude of Texas Governor Ross Sterling. Texas produced more than a quarter of the nation's cotton crop, and its participation was essential if the plan was to have any chance for success. (The Louisiana moratorium, for example, would take effect only if states producing at least three-quarters of the national cotton crop joined in the planting ban.) Yet Sterling, a wealthy and conservative planter-businessman, was at first coolly noncommittal toward the proposal, then implacably hostile. Only be-cause of intense public pressure did he finally agree to call the Texas legislature into special session to consider the cotton holiday; and even before the session began, Sterling and his allies had worked to ensure that there would be no chance of enactment.[8]

Supporters of the plan, and Long himself, did what they could to reverse the tide. Huey sent O. K. Allen to Texas to deliver a copy of the new Louisiana bill personally to Governor Sterling. Official delegations from Arkansas and South Carolina, both of which had passed their own moratorium laws, lobbied energetically as the legislature gathered in Austin. Seven thousand farmers gathered in the capital to add to the pressure; and Long, addressing the crowd by radio, sent them into paroxysms of enthusiasm. Sterling, however, was adamant. "Radical hysteria" would not sway him, he insisted. Almost in the same breath, he lent his tacit support to a "compromise" bill that would reduce cotton acreage by half, a hypocritical gesture almost certainly intended only to weaken support for a total moratorium.[9]

Long had remained conciliatory toward Sterling while there appeared to be any chance for the holiday scheme in Texas. Once it was clear there was not, he loosed a flood of abuse at both the Governor and his legislature that actually hastened the end. Taking to the radio once again, he announced that there was only one explanation for the Texas opposition to the plan: "cash money" distributed lavishly to legislators by "speculators," Wall Street bank-ers, and the "cotton trust." Sterling and his allies had "sold the people into slavery."[10]

Sputtering with rage, members of the Texas legislature quickly passed a resolution calling Long a "consummate liar" and voted the cotton-holiday plan into oblivion. "I have met defeat in many fights," Long remarked som-berly when the struggle was over. "But in all the misfortunes of my lifetime I have never been struck to the heart as I have in the last twenty-four hours when . . . I saw the veil of doom and distress maliciously forced upon the families of two million Southern farmers." Sporadic efforts to enact acreage reductions over the next few months proved ineffective, and by June of 1932 the price of cotton had dropped to 4.6 cents a pound, its lowest since 1894.[11]

Yet if on one level the cotton-holiday episode was a political defeat for Long, on another it benefited him significantly. While elected officials spurned his efforts, farmers throughout the cotton South responded warmly to the proposal. The flood of mail Long received during the struggle, almost all of it favorable, gave evidence of how far his influence had spread. Nearly two-thirds of his letters and telegrams came from outside Louisiana—most of them from cotton states such as Texas, Alabama, Mississippi, and Georgia, but some from as far away as New York, California, Illinois. "Your radio speech talked and praised on every street corner," wired a probate judge in Alabama. Said another supporter, "You are the Moses of the cotton farmer."[12]

For three steamy weeks of the bleak Depression summer, the name of Huey Long resonated throughout the Deep South—not only in the minds of cotton farmers scratching out impassioned letters on cheap stationery, not only in the conversations of merchants and tradesmen standing in shops and on streetcorners, but in the proud, defiant, even desperate roars of crowds gathered in empty fields and in town squares to demonstrate their support for the Long plan. In Texas, nearly 12,000 farmers assembled in the space of a few days in meetings in seventy-six different towns to urge approval upon Governor Sterling. Mass meetings of "farmers, bankers, businessmen and tenants" in Alabama drew crowds of from 300 to 3,000—95 percent of them, the state agriculture commissioner claimed, in favor of a cotton holiday. There were similar scenes in countless other Southern communities—in Ocilla, Georgia; Jonesboro, Arkansas; Florence, Alabama; in Little Rock, where some observers estimated the crowd at 20,000, and in Steele, Missouri, where nearly the entire population of the tiny agricultural village turned out. Farmers around Greenville, Alabama, distributed circulars calling the Long plan "the quickest and most common sense remedy." And later, in Statesboro, Georgia, disgruntled cotton-growers met to denounce in bitter language the scuttling of the holiday by the Texas legislature. "Governor Sterling," wrote one Statesboro man to Long, "is as popular in this neck of the woods as General Sherman."[13]

The cotton-holiday plan, in spite of (or perhaps because of) its failure, had won for Long the beginnings of a regional and to some extent even a national following. He had shown himself willing to take bold, forceful action to deal with the Depression, in marked contrast to more timid and conservative Southern leaders. He had succeeded, as the Lieutenant Governor of Texas wrote him after the collapse of the movement, in "bringing to the attention [of the nation] in a way never done before, the necessity of reducing the production of cotton." And he had evoked from struggling men and women throughout the South some of the same intimate expressions of gratitude he had been receiving from Louisianans for years. "I wish that I knew you better," a Mississippi bank teller wrote him after one of his radio addresses, "and I want to invite you to come up to Woodville some Sunday and take dinner with me. I have plenty of turnip greens, chickens, eggs, and good cows in my backyard."[14]

There was more to these responses, however, than simple gratitude and approval. Running through the comments of Long's supporters were intimations of how victims of the Depression were beginning to view their world, of how they were connecting such disasters as falling cotton prices to specific villains and inequities in the economic system. It was inconceivable to many Southerners that cotton prices had simply fallen of their own accord, that overproduction was the only problem. Someone must be profiting from their distress; someone must have a vested interest in destroying the means of their salvation. "The farmers are with you, but the bankers and the newspapers controlled by them are opposed," wrote a South Carolina man to Long. An Alabama farmer complained bitterly, after the issue was settled, "Well, wall street and the money power won, as usual."[15]

For others, the problem went deeper still, to the structure of an economic system that permitted some men to accumulate vast wealth and power while others starved. "Your views regarding 'wealth fallen into the hands of the few' is both logical and sound," a Tennessee supporter wrote Long in a letter lamenting the "perversion" of capitalism. A Texas sharecropper proposed new legislation "to tax the idle money which I believe will put the idle money to work and by putting the idle money to work you put the idle men to work."[16]

Long seemed to sense this changing mood; as the Depression deepened, he, too, was considering its causes in a broader and more systematic way. During the 1920s, he had directed his fire primarily at local enemies (Standard Oil, the Old Regulars) and at specific problems (the Louisiana tax structure, inadequate highways, exorbitant utility rates). Now, he was speaking forcefully about a more general problem: the "concentration of wealth." He had made reference to this issue as long ago as 1918, and sporadically thereafter; but only in 1930 and 1931 did it begin to dominate his rhetoric, as it would for the rest of his life.

The *Louisiana Progress,* the weekly newspaper Long launched during his 1930 Senate campaign, suggested the shift in his focus. In its early issues, the *Progress* spoke primarily about the Governor's highway program and other legislative accomplishments, attacked primarily individual opposition leaders and local special interests. By the end of the year, the paper was giving more space and prominence to Long's condemnation of wealth maldistribution. In December, it inaugurated a regular monthly feature: a front-page editorial written by Long that would discuss the "great issues" of the day. And in the first article of the series, Huey wrote, under the title "Will the God of Greed Pull the Temple Down on Himself?" a lengthy description of the perils of wealth "concentrated into the hands of a few people." "The chain banks in Wall Street control money in the remotest corner of the country," he warned. "All of our businesses have been taken over by a few men." If the situation should continue, if there would ultimately be "no profitable enterprise left to anyone except them," then the inescapable result would be their own destruction. "They can await the early day when the powerful fall from the topheavy structure that has no support below, FOR THEN:—'The Abyss yawns for all.' "[17]

Ensuing issues of the *Progress* continued to press these gloomy predictions, until the question of wealth concentration came, by the time the paper ceased publication early in 1932, to dominate its pages. Yet along with the increasing pessimism, along with the emphasis upon the staggering danger confronting America came a new ray of hope: Huey P. Long might yet lead the nation out of its despair. "He may be the Moses for which the Democratic party has been waiting," predicted the *Progress* early in 1931. Several months later, the paper printed (in a special slip-out section "suitable for use as sheet music") a song written by one of its readers and "Dedicated to Governor Huey P. Long." It closed with a refrain that was, if not particularly poetic, at least explicit:

> *And as long as we shall live*
> *One thing we should try and give*
> *In return for ev'ry toil that he has spent——*
> *When we sing thru-out the land*
> *Huey has helped the common man*
> *We should give to him our vote for President.*[18]

Even before Huey Long had announced his candidacy for the Senate, those who knew him well had realized he would not forever be content to focus his energies on Louisiana alone. And as he prepared to resign the governorship (if only in name) and move on to Washington early in 1932, others of his followers were coming to a similar realization. "Please permit me to say that you are now standing on the waves crest of your political life," a supporter in Shreveport, Louisiana, wrote only months before Long left for the Senate. "If you now falter . . . you are going to be swallowed up in the trough of political disaster. If you go forward . . . you will remain standing in the light of the sun."[19]

II

"I HAD COME to the United States Senate with only one project in mind," Long wrote in his autobiography, "which was that by every means of action and persuasion I might do something to spread the wealth of the land among all the people." This commitment was not immediately apparent to his new colleagues, for Long's first session in the Senate was more remarkable for his absence than for anything else. The Seventy-second Congress had been meeting for nearly two months when Huey finally arrived to be sworn in; of the 137 days that remained, he was present for 56 of them, absent for 81. "Important business of the state of Louisiana" required his presence in New Orleans, he explained. But to his colleagues, the absences only confirmed what most of them had believed of him even before he arrived: that Huey Long had no serious interest in the work of the United States Senate.[20]

However annoying the Senate may have found Huey's absence, it soon discovered that his presence could be even more unsettling. Other members had equally spotty attendance records, but most of them at least behaved with appropriate reticence when they did appear, leaving the floor, and the limelight, to those who had been trudging faithfully through the legislative calendar. When Long appeared in the Senate chamber, however, he displayed no such restraint, proving so shameless in his pursuit of publicity, and so adept at getting it, that he was soon attracting more attention from the press and the galleries than most of the rest of his colleagues combined. Other Senators envied and resented him; some attempted futilely to restrain him; but no one seemed to have any effect. Even as a part-time Senator, Huey Long was quickly establishing himself as a nationally acclaimed phenomenon. And he was doing so, as he did so much else in his career, with a combination of style and substance.[21]

Long remembered the value of buffoonery in winning national press attention during his term as governor. Once again, he played the clown: receiving the press in his hotel room wearing lavender silk pajamas; insisting that potlikker be added to the menu in the Senate dining room; wearing flamboyant pink shirts, purple ties, and white suits to the Capitol. Northern reporters, A. J. Liebling once wrote, "couldn't figure out how he expected to get space with the same gags every time he came to town." But he did get space; and the more outrageous he became, it seemed, the more space he got.[22]

Had this been all he did, of course, the attention would have ceased as soon as the novelty faded; but no one knew better than Long himself that more was necessary. He might occasionally behave like a clown, but he could also turn deadly serious, as Senate Democratic leader Joseph Robinson of Arkansas soon discovered to his chagrin. The limited time Huey spent in Washington between January and April of 1932 was enough, apparently, to convince him that Joe Robinson, like most of the other Southern Democrats in the Senate, represented the same conservative forces that Long had been fighting for years in Louisiana. Of the thirty-seven roll-call votes to which both Robinson and Long responded during the session, they voted alike on only ten. And having grown accustomed to instant obedience and total control in his dealings with the Louisiana legislature, Long chafed at Robinson's efforts to impose party discipline upon Democratic members of the Senate.[23]

By the end of April, he had had enough. In the midst of a speech on wealth redistribution, he suddenly digressed to announce that he was sending to the desk his resignation from the three Senate committees to which Robinson had assigned him. In Louisiana, he explained, "whenever the time came that anyone who had received anything from my political organization felt that he had to go another way, I expected him to surrender whatever the organization gave him." It was a preposterous gesture. A Senate committee assignment was not equivalent to a patronage position in state government. But the resignations accomplished their purpose. In a glare of publicity, Long had broken his ties with the Democratic leadership.[24]

Two weeks later, he resumed the attack. From Martindale's legal directory, he read to the Senate the names of the major clients of Robinson's law firm in Arkansas, a list that included many of the largest power companies, banks, and railroads of the Southeast. Admonished that a Senator could not question the integrity of a colleague, Long replied with mock innocence: "I want now to disclaim that I have the slightest motive of saying, or that in my heart I believe, that such a man could to the slightest degree be influenced in any vote which he casts in this body by the fact that this association might mean hundreds of thousands and millions of dollars to him in the way of lucrative fees." The implications were unfair. Robinson had no active connection with the law firm, and there was no evidence that he profited from its operations. But his voting record and his public statements suggested a strong enough sympathy with conservative, corporate interests to give Long's charges a degree of credibility. These initial incidents were only the opening salvos in a feud that would continue for three years and grow so bitter that Robinson would at times have to be physically restrained from assaulting Long on the Senate floor.[25]

Although it was for these personal encounters that Long received the most intense publicity, his primary concern, he continually insisted, was with issues, and with one issue in particular. He waited more than a month before raising on the Senate floor the question of the unequal distribution of wealth; but when he did, in occasional brief remarks during debates in March and finally in a major speech early in April, he minced no words. "Unless we provide for redistribution of wealth in this country," he warned, "the country is doomed." And in case he had left any doubt about the urgency of the problem, he added: "I tell you that if in any country I live in . . . I should see my children starving and my wife starving, its laws against robbing and against stealing and against bootlegging would not amount to any more to me than they would to any other man when it came to a matter of facing the time of starvation." The nation faced a choice. It could act to limit large fortunes and guarantee a decent life to its citizens, or it could wait for the otherwise inevitable revolution.[26]

Long's alarmist rhetoric almost immediately won him a reputation as a crusading Senate radical. "He might be the leader of the revolution if and when," a writer for *Collier's* magazine commented. The Chicago *Tribune* pictured him in one of its political cartoons holding aloft a red flag under the caption "Patriotism vs. Communism." The newspaper of the New Llano colony, a socialist-Utopian settlement in Louisiana, praised him for raising the "real issue" of the Depression and for having "split the subject wide open."[27]

Yet there was little in Long's performance during his first session in the Senate that really merited such alarm or acclaim. He made some flamboyant speeches and some vituperative attacks, but he was largely an irritant to his Congressional colleagues, not a disruptive or galvanizing force. He spoke with great passion about wealth redistribution, but except for a single halfhearted effort to revise some tax rates, he did nothing concrete to force consideration of the issue. He displayed unusual bravado in attacking Joseph Robinson, but it was not really the maverick performance it at first appeared; his unhappiness with the Majority Leader was widely shared by other Democrats disgruntled at Robinson's apparent alliance with the Hoover White House during much of the session.[28]

Nor was Long's voting record impressive for its radicalism. Although he generally sided with Senate progressives on economic issues, he also voted consistently for such parochial measures as a tariff on imported oil to protect the Louisiana petroleum industry and against such apparently benevolent measures as federal appropriations for Howard University, a black institution in Washington. On the measures most appropriate for expressions of leftist sentiment, Long was usually silent.

In some respects, the silence was understandable. Much of the major work of the Senate session—the creation of the Reconstruction Finance Corporation, the passage of the Glass-Steagall Act to expand the currency supply, and other Administration-supported measures—was nearly done before Long arrived in Washington late in January. The rest of the session was characterized by sullen bickering and intra-party feuding, producing few significant accomplishments. Even so, Long's neglect of his Senate duties was so flagrant and consistent as to suggest little genuine interest in the issues under discussion. When the Senate became embroiled in debate over a Hoover- and Robinson-supported measure to impose a national sales tax, Huey appeared long enough to win a rousing ovation from the galleries for his denunciation of the proposal, but did not bother to remain for the final vote on the bill. When the Senate debated the major proposals for federal relief for the unemployed, the La Follette-Costigan and Wagner-Garner Acts, Long remained silent, skipping most of the crucial roll calls on the measures. When Congress considered the Patman Bonus Bill and when federal troops brutally dispersed the Bonus Expeditionary Force from its encampment in Washington, Long said nothing.[29]

In short, Long treated the Senate during these first months in Washington as a casual plaything—a toy to be used when he wanted publicity and acclaim and to be discarded when more attractive ventures presented themselves. For the moment, his indifference hardly seemed to matter. By the time the session came to an end, Huey Long, who had attended less than a third of it and had spent that third doing nothing of much importance, had emerged as one of the Senate's most closely watched and highly publicized members.

Yet if the publicity Long was receiving in Washington was in many ways undeserved, he was performing in other arenas that legitimately merited attention. The real focus of national politics in 1932, after all, was not upon Congress, but upon the approaching elections. And it was there that Long was to make his greatest mark.

III

EARLY IN MAY, Long stepped off a train in Atlanta, Georgia, and told waiting reporters that he would support Franklin D. Roosevelt for President. It was a natural choice, he claimed, for only Roosevelt had endorsed the Long proposals for redistribution of wealth.[30]

Roosevelt had done no such thing, as Long well knew. Supporting Roosevelt was, in fact, far from a natural choice to him. He had mistrusted the New York Governor from the beginning; and while he finally succumbed to the persuasive tactics of Senate progressives Burton K. Wheeler and George W.

Norris, both of whom worked to lure him into the Roosevelt camp, he did so grudgingly. "I didn't like your son of a bitch," he snarled at Wheeler when he reached his decision, "but I'll be for him."[31]

The new alliance was, however, of tremendous practical value to both Long and Roosevelt at the Democratic National Convention in June. When Huey arrived in Chicago, his Louisiana opponents were attempting to unseat his hand-picked delegation and replace it with their own. Long's persuasive and surprisingly serious speech to the convention on behalf of his cause no doubt helped; but when his delegation finally won a comfortable if less than overwhelming endorsement from the party, it was clear that much of the credit belonged to the Roosevelt floor managers. In return, the Roosevelt forces received important assistance from Long. His efforts to play a major role in the decisions of campaign organizers were often intrusive and occasionally embarrassing, but when the nomination was on the line, Roosevelt could not have asked for a more effective ally.[32]

As expected, Long kept the Louisiana delegation firmly in line. But at a crucial moment he used his influence elsewhere as well. On the fourth ballot, the Roosevelt coalition continued to lack the two-thirds majority necessary for nomination, and several important delegations began to waver. Long stormed onto the floor to help prevent a break. Elbowing his way into the middle of the Mississippi delegation, his hair tousled and his white suit wilting with sweat, Long waved a fist in the face of Senator Pat Harrison and shouted, "If you break the unit rule, you sonofabitch, I'll go into Mississippi and break you!" Harrison did not break. Nor did Joseph Robinson and his Arkansas delegation, to whom Long applied similar pressure. On the next ballot, Roosevelt captured the nomination. "There is no question in my mind," Edward J. Flynn, Democratic boss of the Bronx, later wrote, "but that without Long's work Roosevelt might not have been nominated."[33]

Long wanted to make himself equally indispensable in the fall campaign, and sometime in midsummer he appeared at Roosevelt headquarters in New York to outline for an astounded Jim Farley his ideas for further contributions to the cause. The Democratic National Committee, he proposed, should provide him with a special train equipped with loudspeakers. In it, he would cross the country speaking for Roosevelt and promising immediate payment of the soldiers' bonus. "The scheme was unthinkable," Farley later recalled, not only because Roosevelt had not endorsed the bonus proposal but because what Huey was suggesting would have made Long, not Roosevelt, the dominant figure in the campaign. Wary of antagonizing him, Farley carefully suggested a "modified" speaking tour that would take Huey only to a few relatively unimportant Midwestern states. Long knew he was "getting the runaround," and he responded crossly: "Jim, you're gonna get licked. I tried to save you, but if you don't want to be saved, it's all right with me." After fuming and sulking for a few days, however, he agreed to the plan.[34]

He not only agreed; he worked to transform what Farley had envisioned as an exercise in futility into a stunning personal success. At his own expense (or at the expense of his state organization, which was much the same thing), he sent a fleet of sound trucks and support vehicles from Louisiana to North Dakota, where he was to begin his tour. In the closing weeks of the campaign, Long himself arrived, accompanied by his customary retinue of bodyguards and aides. He was a sensation. He spoke in only four states—North and South Dakota, Nebraska, and Kansas, hardly the critical areas of the campaign; but everywhere he appeared, he attracted large and enthusiastic crowds. By the end of the tour, local political leaders were urging Farley to send Long into any doubtful regions. Huey himself displayed no modesty about his impact. He was, he told reporters, winning the Midwest for Roosevelt. "We would have lost North Dakota if I hadn't gone there and straightened things out. I have been in South Dakota and we will carry that state." By the end, Farley seemed almost inclined to agree. Had he sent Long into Pennsylvania (one of only five states Roosevelt lost to Hoover), the Democrats might have won there, too, he later speculated. "We never underestimated him again."[35]

Farley should not have been surprised at Long's October successes. The Midwestern trip was Huey's first involvement with a national campaign, but if the Democratic leadership had wished for evidence of his influence outside Louisiana, it would have had only to look at events in the state of Arkansas two months before. It was there, in a primary campaign for the United States Senate, that Long gave the most dramatic display of his political potential.

IV

WHEN UNITED STATES SENATOR Thaddeus Caraway of Arkansas died unexpectedly in November 1931, only a little more than a year remained of his term of office, a year that hardly seemed worth a major political battle. No one objected, therefore, when Governor Harvey Parnell quickly appointed Caraway's widow, Hattie, to the seat, and no one paid very much attention when state Democratic leaders agreed to support her in the special election required by law in January 1932. The regular Democratic primary, after all, was only eight months away, and the party establishment could settle on a permanent replacement then. In the meantime, Hattie Caraway would be a harmless, innocuous compromise.

The new Senator evoked a similarly patronizing response from the national press upon her arrival in Washington. She was, wrote one reporter, a "demure little woman who looks as though she ought to be sitting on a porch in a rocking-chair, mending somebody's socks." And Mrs. Caraway did little to challenge the prevailing impression that she was simply a housewife on holiday. Short, dowdy, meek, she sat impassively in the back row of the Senate day after day and never opened her mouth. "So far the men have left nothing unsaid," she explained.

Yet early in May 1932, to the surprise of her colleagues in the Senate and politicians in Arkansas, she announced that she was a candidate for re-election to a full term. It seemed a ludicrous decision. Already there were six candidates in the race for the Democratic nomination, all of them men, all of them with powerful allies. Mrs. Caraway, entering late, could expect support from no established political faction in Arkansas. She was, moreover, virtually without funds and had recently even lost her home when a bank foreclosed for non-payment on the mortgage. Democrats in factious Arkansas could agree on few things, but of one thing they seemed certain: Hattie Caraway would receive no more than about 3,000 votes out of a total of perhaps a quarter of a million: votes from a few feminists, from personal friends, from sentimental admirers of the late Thaddeus. There would be little else.[36]

It was not long before reports of her discouraging prospects reached Mrs. Caraway in Washington. At first, she refused to believe them. Finally, she turned to her neighbor in the back row of the Senate chamber, Huey Long, and asked him to investigate the situation for her. Long reported back a few days later: her position was hopeless, she should withdraw from the race. Mrs. Caraway thanked him for his trouble, returned to her seat, put her head down on her desk, and began to weep. And there the matter might have ended had not Long walked over to her the next day and offered to help. "Never mind about the campaigning," he assured her. "We can make that campaign in one week. That's all we need. That won't give 'em a chance to get over their surprise."[37]

Long's reasons for this decision were not entirely clear. Huey himself offered two explanations. Hattie Caraway was a "brave little woman" in distress, he said, and, chivalric soul that he was, it was his simple duty to help her. She was, however, also a "little woman" who had compiled a Senate voting record that accorded more nearly with Long's own than those of most of his other colleagues. She had supported Long's fleeting efforts to impose limits on individual fortunes; she had delighted Huey by voting almost as frequently as he against the senior Senator from her own state, Joseph T. Robinson. Indeed, Long's feud with the Democratic leader may have been an important reason for his intervention. Robinson had taken no public position in the contest; but if the voters of Arkansas responded enthusiastically to Huey Long, his most outspoken critic, it could not help but embarrass him.[38]

Yet there was more to Long's decision. The Arkansas campaign and even the feud with Robinson were elements of a larger strategy—a strategy that reflected Long's limitless ambition and monumental impatience and one that was only slowly becoming clear to observers outside Louisiana. The *New York Times* seemed vaguely to sense what was happening when it remarked on the eve of the Arkansas effort: "He has begun a campaign which he expects to yield him the leadership of the [Senate] minority—or perhaps the majority— after March 4, 1933." Even that did not go far enough. It was not simply leadership in Congress that Long wanted; it was leadership of the national electorate—leadership he would obtain not by working through his party or through the Senate, but by going directly to the people. Arkansas was as good a place as any to begin.[39]

Even before Long entered the state, Arkansas was aware of a new element in the Senate campaign. Beginning in mid-July, teams of advance workers from Louisiana blanketed the state with printed copies of Long's speaking schedule and with leaflets presenting his explanation of "What the Re-election of Senator (Mrs.) Caraway Means to the People of America." Arkansas voters opened their mailboxes to find garish broadsides showing the bloated figure of "Uncle Trusty" (representing the "combined power that directs the energies of the great money interests") wearing a jacket covered with dollar signs and sitting at a desk holding a pen in his pudgy fingers. He was signing an order "to my hired politicians" to "get busy day and night to see that Senator Caraway is not returned to the Senate." The Long organization printed thousands of copies of an American Federation of Labor endorsement of Mrs. Caraway and distributed them too, along with copies of some of Huey's Senate speeches.[40]

On August 1, Long himself crossed the border into Arkansas with a fleet of sound trucks and a small army of retainers. For the next week, he tore back and forth across the state at a pace some observers found difficult to believe. The schedule called for four, five, six speeches a day, but Huey frequently added an impromptu appearance at a moment's notice when he sensed he could draw a crowd. Since the rallies were usually in towns widely separated, each appearance required a frantic drive at breakneck speed along bumpy country roads just to arrive in time. Members of the entourage had no time for meals; they grabbed sandwiches on the run. Sleep was a luxury to be stolen in the back seat of a car or briefly in a cheap hotel at night. Many in the group, including Mrs. Caraway, fell victim to fevers, diarrhea, and other travel discomforts; but Long showed no outward signs of fatigue.[41]

He seemed, rather, to grow stronger as the week progressed and as the size and enthusiasm of the crowds grew. In courthouse squares, fairgrounds, and city parks, he whipped audiences into near frenzy with his denunciations of the bankers of Wall Street and their cronies in Washington, who were, he claimed, conspiring to remove this "brave little woman" from the Senate. Always there was talk of the Long proposal to limit large fortunes and of its dismal fate in the Senate: "Mrs. Caraway voted for it. I voted for it. But they killed it deader'n a doornail." Again and again there was mock chagrin at criticisms of his positions: "Why, they got me so I couldn't hardly sleep nights, thinking of this terrible thing I was proposing to do. Just think of it, my friends! Here I was actually proposing that a man had to live for a whole year of 365 days on one measly, lousy, slivery million dollars." Constantly there were warnings of the dire fate awaiting the nation if people like Hattie Caraway were driven from office: "It is nip and tuck with us, up there in the Senate. If Wall Street and their trust gang succeed in defeating enough senators who have stood with the people like this little woman senator from Arkansas has, they'll have the whip hand on you . . . you'll never be able to get anyone from this state to stand by you again."[42]

One feature of Long's message that members of his party should have found particularly ominous was his implicit rejection not only of the policies of the Republicans but of those of the Democrats as well. Long's distaste for the leaders of his party in Congress was well known, and it was hardly surprising that he had no kind words for Joseph Robinson in Arkansas. But 1932 was a Presidential year, and the Democratic Party had recently nominated, with Long's help, a Presidential candidate he claimed enthusiastically to support. It was particularly revealing, then, that during his Arkansas tour Long said nothing about Franklin Roosevelt, nothing about the virtues of the Democratic Party (he referred instead to "we progressives of both parties"), nothing to suggest that anyone but Huey Long and such allies as Hattie Caraway were offering hope to the people.[43]

As revealing as the message of the campaign was the efficiency with which Long's organization handled its mechanics. Members of his staff preceded Huey and Mrs. Caraway by several hours at every scheduled speaking site, drove around town in a sound truck announcing the time of the speech, and then set up microphones in the town square or on the courthouse lawn. If a speaker's platform or bandstand was available, they used that. If not, they set up a folding table and chairs on the roof of the sound truck itself, which was designed to serve as a podium. For an hour or so before the rally began, loudspeakers blared country music to attract a crowd. Occasionally, the audience grew so large that Long's organizers had to shift the site of the meeting at the last minute so as to be able to accommodate everyone.

Anyone attending one of the rallies who was unacquainted with the campaign might logically have assumed that Huey Long, not Hattie Caraway, was the candidate. Mrs. Caraway generally spoke first, but never for more than five minutes and, although she improved as the week progressed, without notable eloquence. "I know I can't talk like a statesman," she explained apologetically, "but I've always tried to vote like one for you." Once her fleeting appearance was out of the way, the real event began. The chairmen of the meetings, who had usually given Mrs. Caraway a brief and perfunctory introduction, now unleashed the full force of their windy eloquence, lauding the man who "comes to Arkansas as the plumed Knight of Jeffersonian democracy fighting the corrupt and sinister influence within our own party." And finally Long himself would appear, smiling and waving and ready to erupt.[44]

This combination of exuberant flamboyance and machine-like precision made the campaign profoundly effective. Scarcely had Long arrived in Arkansas when a local politician who had heard him speak sent a telegram to Little Rock: "A cyclone just went through here and is headed your way. Very few trees left standing." And as the cyclone proceeded through the state, it cleared an ever wider path. The crowds, large from the beginning, grew bigger at each stop—1,000 in Newport on Wednesday, 4,000 in Russellville on Thursday, 5,000 in Hot Springs on Friday night. In Pine Bluff, he drew more than 20,000 people, and in Little Rock, nearly 30,000, the largest political gathering in the history of the state. Even when he did not stop to make a speech, he attracted an audience. Men and women lined highways and city streets just to watch the caravan passing by, hoping to catch a glimpse of the Kingfish through the window of his blue Cadillac limousine.[45]

Many of the onlookers, no doubt, were drawn simply by curiosity, but the prevailing atmosphere at the rallies was one of enthusiastic support. Audiences roared approval at Long's attacks on the "money power" and the "Wall Street Gang," laughed uproariously as he ridiculed "Mr. Herbert Hoover, of London, England" who was "trying to balance his boodget—that's the way they pronounce it in England." Hermann Deutsch, an astute Louisiana journalist who traveled with Long in Arkansas and wrote a penetrating account of the campaign for the *Saturday Evening Post,* took note of Huey's extraordinary persuasive powers:

> . . . there were many . . . who came to scoff and who remained as prey. Farmers drove to town in their own automobiles—and no few of the cars were this year's models—in such numbers that highways were congested in every direction. Fifteen minutes after he began to talk, Huey Long would have these same farmers convinced that they were starving and would have to boil their old boots and discarded tires to have something to feed the babies till the Red Cross brought around a sack of meal and a bushel of sweet potatoes to tide them

over; that Wall Street's control of the leaders—not the rank and file
—of both Democratic and Republican parties was directly responsible for this awful condition; that the only road to salvation lay in
the reelection of Hattie W. Caraway to the Senate.[46]

Nor were Mrs. Caraway's opponents unmindful of Long's potential impact. Their campaign advertisements, printed day after day in statewide newspapers, spoke hopefully of an electorate that "cannot be influenced by any sort
of last-minute appeal" or pointed vaguely to the resentment Arkansas voters
should feel at "unwarranted interference by a rank outsider." But, for the
most part, they had no idea how to deal with Long. One of them, former
Governor Charles Brough, tried launching a frontal attack. It was a mistake.
"I hear where one of Mrs. Caraway's opponents is hollering already," Long
derisively replied. "Says I got no business coming up here from Louisiana.
Well, the state lines didn't stop him none when he came from Arkansas to
Louisiana to help impeach me." Brough had done nothing of the sort; but his
angry denials succeeded only in making him look ridiculous, and he quickly
lapsed into silence. In the end, the reaction of Mrs. Caraway's opposition bore
a strange resemblance to the early reactions of Huey's enemies in Louisiana:
confusion and inertia. They were simply no match for the Long steamroller.[47]

Even before the campaign blitz was over, many recognized that the
political outlook had changed. Until Long's intervention, the *New York Times*
noted, "the Senatorial race here had been just another biennial scourge, but
since then Mrs. Caraway was transferred from the list of also-rans to the roster
of candidates entitled to serious consideration." It is unlikely, however, that
anyone (except perhaps Long himself, who rarely underestimated his own
abilities) was prepared for what happened on election day. Only a few weeks
earlier, state political leaders had smugly predicted that Mrs. Caraway would
place dead last in the primary, that she would poll no more than one or two
percent of the vote. On the night of August 9, they looked up and discovered
that she had run away with the election. She had won almost as many votes
as all her opponents combined (47 percent of the total) and had outdistanced
her nearest competitor by better than two to one. There would be no run-off.
Hattie Caraway had clearly won nomination (and in effect, in this one-party
state, election) to a full term in the United States Senate, the first woman in
American history to have done so.[48]

But was the victory properly Hattie Caraway's or was it Huey Long's?
Given the magnitude of her triumph, it seems clear that Mrs. Caraway was
never as weak a candidate as her opponents had supposed; she would undoubtedly have made a strong showing even if Long had not intervened. There can
be little doubt, however, that Long's assistance contributed dramatically to

the victory. It may well have made the difference between a respectable performance and a winning one. For, no matter how the returns are analyzed, they show clearly that Mrs. Caraway did strikingly better in areas in which Long campaigned than in areas in which he did not.[49]

Huey appeared in 31 counties during the Arkansas tour. In those counties, Mrs. Caraway received 52.7 percent of the vote. In the 44 counties in which Long did not appear, she polled 37.4 percent. She received a clear majority in 23 of the counties in which Long campaigned, a plurality in 6 of them; she lost only 2. In the other 44 counties, she received a clear majority in 11, a plurality in 20; and she lost in 13. And if the 75 counties of Arkansas are ranked in order of the size of Mrs. Caraway's percentage of the vote, the top 11 counties on the list, and 22 of the top 29, are ones in which Long campaigned. Of the bottom 20, only 2 are ones in which Huey appeared.[50]

"That Mr. Long was invaluable in his efforts in my behalf is well known," Mrs. Caraway noted demurely as soon as the election returns were in. She was not alone in paying him homage. The Arkansas *Gazette,* which had derided Huey throughout the campaign, conceded at its close that when Mrs. Caraway secured Long's support "she found a champion whom conditions made the man of the hour. He was heard by tens of thousands of people who had known years of depression, unemployment, and low prices of farm products. They wanted a voice to express their feelings and they found that voice in Huey P. Long." From his newfound supporters in Arkansas, Long was receiving congratulatory telegrams as if he himself had been the candidate. "You have won the greatest victory for the people since Andrew Jackson left the White House," cabled a jubilant supporter in Little Rock. "The Kingfish will be president in 1936," exulted another.[51]

Outside Arkansas, some national Democratic leaders recognized what James Farley and Franklin Roosevelt had yet to learn: that Long was rapidly becoming a major national political force. Two days after the primary, John Nance Garner, Speaker of the House of Representatives and Democratic candidate for Vice President, was eating breakfast in the dining room of a New Orleans hotel, where he had stopped en route to New York. He looked up to find Huey Long beaming down at the table. "Hello, Jack," Long bellowed. "Thought you might wish to touch my garment to bring you luck."

"Judging by what you did for Senator Caraway, I think I ought to," Garner replied. He tapped Long's lapel three times.[52]

V

IT WAS A NEW HUEY LONG who returned to Washington after the 1932 elections. He was still strident, still in eager pursuit of publicity, still adept at getting it. But while during his first months in the Senate he had often seemed confused and apathetic, now he exuded deadly purpose. Emboldened by his campaign successes, he was finally ready to take the Senate seriously, and he expected it to take him seriously in return.

Others may have considered the "lame duck" session of Congress that convened in December an unlikely place for significant accomplishments. But Long, using a novel and self-serving interpretation of the election results and citing the worsening economic situation, argued that now was the time for the Senate to carry out the mandate of the electorate. The voters had not merely endorsed Franklin Roosevelt the man, he insisted. Rather, "the President-elect has not only been nominated, has not only been elected, but he has assumed the leadership of this Nation in order that he might carry out the one great necessary decentralization of wealth in America."[53]

Since the voice of the people had been heard, there could be no excuse for delay. On the first day of the new session, Long took the floor to deliver a speech that in its assertiveness and aggressiveness augured much of what the Senate could expect from him in the coming months. He was, he said, willing to work within the Democratic Party "to transform into law the promise that has been made to the people of America." But if Joseph Robinson and the other party leaders opposed this "mandate," some changes would have to be made. Either the Democrats would have to find new leadership or "we on the two sides of this Chamber will have to undertake to secure an organization that will transfer our promises into law. . . . We can not wait any longer."[54]

In the weeks that followed, the members of the Senate finally made the acquaintance of the Huey Long whom Louisianans had known for years. Arrogant, obstreperous, bullying, unbound by the normal rules of decorum, Long ranted and filibustered through one meeting of the Senate after another, attempting to dominate it the way he dominated the state legislature in Louisiana. If in his first months in Congress he had been conspicuous by his absence from the Senate chamber, now he was in place nearly every day. If on the great issues of the previous session Long had remained silent, now he was easily the most outspoken member of the Senate, interjecting himself into every debate and often bringing legislative progress to a virtual halt for days and weeks on end. He was giving notice: if the Congress was not willing to follow his leadership, was not willing to do what he claimed the people had demanded, then he would see that it would have difficulty doing anything at all.

The major economic proposal before the Senate in the first months of 1933 was a banking-reform bill drafted in large part by Carter Glass, the aging and conservative Senator from Virginia, widely considered an authority on banking and finance. Long was impressed neither by Glass nor by the bill. Glass, he implied, was a tool of J. P. Morgan and the Wall Street interests, and the bill—which, among other things, made it easier for the big national banks to open new branches—was a device to rescue the large institutions at the expense of the small. Huey was determined to destroy it. His weapon was an amendment he introduced early in the debate to prohibit any bank from establishing branches outside the "city, town, or village" in which its main office was located. It was a measure in which he appeared genuinely to believe, but it was also a convenient issue around which to build one of the most prolonged and spectacular filibusters the Senate had ever seen.

For nearly three weeks, and at one point for three consecutive days without interruption, Long literally paralyzed the Senate with a series of rambling tirades, some of them passionate and vicious, some cool and witty, but all of them lengthy. Quoting liberally from two Bibles he kept on his desk ("Two Bibles is never too many," he explained), defending the rights of small bankers and businessmen, denouncing the "Morgans, Rockefellers and Baruchs," and calling continually for legislation to redistribute wealth, he delighted the galleries (long lines waited outside every day to hear him) and infuriated his colleagues.[55]

At times, Glass, Robinson, and other opponents managed to frustrate Huey temporarily, but more often than not Long turned their own tactics against them. When Glass objected to Long's routine request that the clerk read a document into the record (the Senate would, Glass said, certainly prefer to hear the "mellifluous voice" of the Senator from Louisiana), Huey simply read the document himself with infuriating slowness, pausing periodically to ask contemptuously, "Am I going too fast?" When the Democratic leadership managed to move debate temporarily to another matter, a bill to provide independence for the Philippines, Long began a filibuster on that issue as well. (He favored immediate independence so as to make Philippine sugar imports subject to protective tariffs, thus helping the Louisiana sugar industry.) When from sheer exhaustion he was unable to hold the floor any longer and his opponents managed to block his request for a recess, he sat down and allowed Elmer Thomas of Oklahoma, another adamant opponent of the bill, to continue the filibuster until Huey was able to return to combat.[56]

"Again," the exasperated Glass exclaimed at the height of the filibuster, "the Senate is confronted with the question of whether or not it shall be permitted to legislate." The spectacle of "The Impotent Senate," as one newspaper editorial phrased it, of a body utterly stalled by a single man, raised cries of anger and disgust both inside and outside the chamber. Joe Robinson stormed about the cloakroom trying to round up enough votes to shut off debate; Carter Glass sat dejectedly at his desk as hope for passage of his beloved banking legislation gradually faded; Millard Tydings of Maryland, in a gesture of splendid rhetorical hypocrisy, threatened to resign from the Senate if something was not done to curb Long; the *New York Times,* in an editorial of unusual passion, asked, "How long will the Senate lie down under his insults? If Senators feel themselves humiliated, how do they suppose the country feels?"[57]

But Long was impervious to criticism. When after three weeks the filibuster drew to a close and a vote on the bill at last seemed near, he rose to explain blithely that

> Twenty-one days . . . have been sufficient so that the men and the women back at the forks of the creek learned enough about this bill . . . that we need have no further worry or concern as to what is going to happen to it at this session of Congress. It is not only as dead as a hammer; it never even had the life a hammer ever had.

In a sense, he was right, for while the Glass bill passed the Senate by a comfortable margin, it arrived in the House of Representatives too late for proper consideration before the session ended; it was buried in committee. A piece of legislation that virtually everyone had assumed would move through Congress with ease had fallen victim, the *Times* lamented, to "a man with a front of brass and lungs of leather."[58]

Long's activities in the Senate may not have won him the respect of his colleagues or the admiration of the press, but they had won him something of far more importance: the fascinated attention of the American public. No longer could he be dismissed as a regional curiosity, another of the clownish demagogues that Southern states sent to Washington periodically to amuse and irritate the Congressional establishment. He was a figure of genuine power, espousing a distinctive philosophy and winning the beginnings of a national following. And no one was more aware of what Huey Long might ultimately become than the man who had just been elected President of the United States.

3

Crisis and Renewal

ARLY IN OCTOBER 1932 a political cartoon appeared in the Republican Washington *Star* deriding the apparent alliance between Huey Long and Franklin Roosevelt. The future President lay propped up in bed beaming proudly at a row of infants lying docilely beside him. The babies bore familiar faces: Cornelius Vanderbilt Whitney, Vincent Astor, Hiram Johnson, George Norris. And at the end of the row, gazing contentedly into space, was the pudgy visage of Huey Long. Roosevelt, admiring them all, was exclaiming triumphantly, "Just look at my little darlings!"[1]

Long and Roosevelt may have looked like the best of friends for a while in 1932, but they themselves knew otherwise. Their relationship was a troubled one from the beginning; and as both men moved further and further into the center of national politics, it did nothing but deteriorate. Each viewed the other with suspicion and some fear. Each knew the other would ultimately be an obstacle to his own goals. Both spoke hopefully at first of friendship and cooperation, but soon the lines of battle were openly drawn.

Even before the election, despite Long's public flattery of Roosevelt and Roosevelt's private cordiality toward Long, tensions were growing. Only a few days after the Democratic convention, when reports began to appear that Roosevelt was conferring with New York financiers, the candidate received a bristling phone call from Louisiana. "God damn it, Frank," shouted the crackling Southern voice. "Don't you know who nominated you? Why do you have Baruch and Young and those Wall Street [sonsofbitches] up there to see you?" Roosevelt replied good-naturedly, but when he hung up, he confided to a visitor that Long was no laughing matter: "He really is one of the two most dangerous men in the country." (The other, he later added, was Douglas MacArthur.) He was still hopeful. "We must tame these fellows and make them useful to us," he noted optimistically. But that Long would not be an easy man to tame was quickly evident when the two men met for the first time several months later.[2]

Early in October, Roosevelt invited Long to join him for lunch at his country home in Hyde Park, New York. It was not an auspicious encounter. Roosevelt displayed no irritation at Huey's outrageous costume (a loud suit, clashing shirt, and pink tie) or at his effort to dominate the conversation during lunch, lecturing the candidate like a schoolboy. Roosevelt's mother, however, was not so tactful. "Who is that *awful* man?" she said in a loud whisper. Everyone pretended not to hear, but Long almost certainly took note. "By God, I feel sorry for him," he later remarked of Roosevelt. "He's got more sonsofbitches in his family than I got in mine." He was not much impressed by the candidate himself either. "I like him," he said condescendingly after this first meeting. "He's not a strong man, but he means well."[3]

A visit to Warm Springs, Georgia, a few weeks after the election only deepened Long's doubts. The conversation was friendly enough, but Huey left puzzled and disturbed by Roosevelt's congenial evasiveness. "When I talk to him, he says 'Fine! Fine! Fine!' " he complained. "But Joe Robinson goes to see him the next day and again he says 'Fine! Fine! Fine!' Maybe he says 'Fine!' to everybody."[4]

When Roosevelt arrived in Washington late in January for meetings with party leaders and members of Congress, he managed to pacify Long briefly. Huey emerged from a meeting in the President-elect's suite at the Mayflower Hotel smiling and content, promising to do whatever Roosevelt asked and praising him as "the same old Frank, . . . all wool and a yard wide." Only days later, however, the cordiality had vanished, as an arrogant and presumptuous message Long sent to Roosevelt suggested. Noting press reports of some disagreement among Roosevelt advisors over a Cabinet appointment, Long wired: "Glad to see you told Farley, Walker and others you wanted none of their advice. I figured all the time you wanted men like me to advise you." Even more ominous was the manner in which Huey chose to convey this "advice." When speculation grew that Roosevelt planned to appoint Carter Glass as Secretary of the Treasury, Long quickly sent out letters to the people on his ever-growing mailing list. He wanted his supporters to write the President-elect and urge him to select Henry B. Steagall, Democratic Congressman from Alabama, chairman of the House Banking and Currency Committee, and a man "who is for all of the people and business, and understands all problems." Roosevelt, apparently, could not be trusted to listen to private advice; he must be subjected to strong public pressure. Already, Huey was dealing with the new President not as an ally with whom one works in concert, but as a potential adversary whom one must threaten and intimidate.[5]

The antagonisms increased with startling rapidity in the first weeks of the new Administration. So desperate had the economic crisis become by the time Roosevelt took office that even the most entrenched conservatives and the most impatient progressives seemed willing at first to follow the new President almost blindly. But not Huey Long. The special session of Congress Roosevelt had called to consider emergency legislation was only a few moments old when Huey seized the floor to stake out his own position on dealing with the crisis.

Long's first complaint was about the bank holiday Roosevelt had proclaimed four days earlier in an effort to halt the alarming wave of bank failures across the nation. The President should have acted to subsidize the banks, not close them, he argued. Roosevelt's first piece of legislation, moreover, had serious deficiencies. The Emergency Banking Act, drafted so quickly that there had not even been time for copies to be printed before the Senate debate, would save the great national banks, Long claimed, but "the little banks in the counties and in the parishes and in the States are most in need of protection." So he offered an amendment "to give the President the right to save the State banks," an amendment that would entitle Roosevelt to declare local banks members of the Federal Reserve System (and thus eligible for increased government assistance) without meeting the stringent capital requirements imposed on larger, national institutions.[6]

The Banking Act was, as Long claimed, an intensely conservative document, drafted in large part by bankers and by conservative holdovers from the Hoover Administration. In an atmosphere that some believed would have enabled Roosevelt to transform the very nature of the banking system, even to nationalize it, he had chosen instead simply to use government funds to stabilize the existing structure. And, as Long claimed, there was little in the bill to help small, local banks, little to guarantee that the crisis would not become a vehicle for the large financial institutions to drive smaller competitors out of business. But while Long, alone among members of the Senate, spoke at great length and with great passion on this question, his colleagues were in no mood to listen. They defeated his amendment by voice vote (Long could not even muster enough support to demand a roll call) and went on to pass the Banking Act unamended that same afternoon.[7]

Long was even more distressed by the second piece of emergency legislation to arrive from the White House: the Government Economy Act, which proposed slashing more than half a billion dollars from the budget largely by cutting veterans' benefits and reducing the salaries of government employees. The bill was the work of bankers and financiers, Long claimed, of "Mr. Morgan" and "Mr. Rockefeller." And it would have "disastrous consequences." If the President was concerned about balancing the budget, then he should support new taxes on private fortunes to raise additional funds, not cut payments to men and women already in need. Administration forces, however, fended off all opposition and won almost immediate passage of one of the most conservative pieces of legislation to move through the Congress in three years. Long was one of only thirteen Senators to vote against it.[8]

As the Roosevelt juggernaut continued to roll through Congress, erecting the basic framework of the early New Deal during the first "Hundred Days" of the Congressional session, the relationship between Long and the Administration worsened. When Congress considered the Agricultural Adjustment Act to provide relief to farmers and stabilize farm prices, Long made vigorous efforts to force through an amendment providing for the remonetization of silver. " 'Expand the currency' was the promise," he charged. "We are not expanding the currency. We are deflating." When Carter Glass began to maneuver through the Senate an only slightly revised version of the banking-reform bill that Long had filibustered to death in January, Huey denounced both Glass for drafting the act and the Administration for supporting it. "We have swallowed enough of this stuff," he explained, referring to the Emergency Banking Act of early March, the evils of which the Glass bill would only compound.

The National Industrial Recovery Act, the keystone of the New Deal program, Long denounced more bitterly than anything else. Although he supported its provisions for public-works expenditures, he lashed out at the system of wage and price codes it established. The codes, he predicted (correctly, as it turned out), would be written largely by the leaders of the industries involved and would become an excuse for price-fixing, for cartelization, for large interests driving small ones out of business. "Every fault of socialism is found in this bill, without one of its virtues," he complained. "Every crime of monarchy is in here, without one of the things that would give it credit."[9]

A number of Roosevelt appointees also came under fire. Treasury Secretary William Woodin he denounced as "mired with the mud of Wall Street and the House of Morgan." Lewis Douglas, the conservative director of the Budget, he called a tool of the financial interests. Hugh Johnson, the first director of the National Recovery Administration, was linked in a "corrupt alliance" with spokesmen for the major banks. Mordecai Ezekiel, Assistant Secretary of Agriculture, was an "enemy" of the farmers. "We got him from the Republicans. He is one of the failures described by our 'new deal.' "[10]

"I want to stay on good terms with the administration," Long insisted in the midst of the Congressional session, "and I am going to do so if it is possible, but I do not have to." Long did make what could be interpreted as efforts to support Roosevelt at certain points during 1933. He backed almost as much of the President's legislation as he opposed: acts establishing the Tennessee Valley Authority and the Civilian Conservation Corps, and other relief measures; repeal of Prohibition; several significant tax and tariff proposals. On some issues over which he and Roosevelt disagreed, Long worked quietly and responsibly to effect workable compromises. He was instrumental in winning adoption of amendments to the administration's banking act to limit branch banking (a provision for which he had fought in vain earlier in the year), to provide federal assistance to state banks (the lack of which had prompted his denunciation of the Emergency Banking Act), and to establish federal insurance of bank deposits. He was not reflexively antagonistic to the President; and he was not, as some argued, an entirely negative force in the Senate.[11]

Yet even at his most supportive moments, Long managed to give the impression of hostility. When he voted to approve the establishment of the Civilian Conservation Corps, he could not resist injecting a swipe at Roosevelt for his earlier transgressions. "There is no harmonizing this bill with the economy bill nor with the administration of the banking bill," he told the Senate. "I am voting for this bill because it is out of harmony with what we have been doing rather than because it is in harmony with what we have been doing." To the surprise of some colleagues, Long voted, finally, in favor of the Senate version of the National Industrial Recovery Act. But again he felt obliged to announce that he was only "half" in favor of the bill; and by the time the conference report on the measure came up, he had changed his mind again and voted against it.[12]

When Congress prepared to adjourn in mid-June, Long rose to address his colleagues. And if demonstration was still needed of how deep his disenchantment with the Administration had become, he gave it now. Noting derisively the feeling of euphoria he sensed among his fellow Democrats, he announced melodramatically: "No; I will not participate in the Democratic victory tonight. I do not care for my share in a victory that means that the poor and the downtrodden, the blind, the helpless, the orphaned, the bleeding, the wounded, the hungry and the distressed, will be the victims."[13]

II

THESE LEGISLATIVE SKIRMISHES WERE, however, peripheral to Long's main battle with the Administration—a battle he waged, characteristically, over an issue of his own devising. It was the issue upon which he had long ago decided to build his national career: the limitation of fortunes and the redistribution of wealth.

The Roosevelt Presidency was barely two weeks old when Long introduced legislation placing strict ceilings on personal incomes, private fortunes, and inheritances. It was an open challenge to the Administration to fulfill what Long insisted had been the major promise of the 1932 Democratic campaign. Yet Long apparently never really expected the President to endorse his proposals, for he moved almost immediately to mobilize public support for them in a way the Administration could not but view as threatening. Five days after Franklin Roosevelt delivered his first "Fireside Chat" over the radio to explain the provisions of the Emergency Banking Act, Long took to the air himself. On free network time provided by the National Broadcasting Company (in accordance, NBC officials claimed, with a long-standing but seldom used policy of allowing access to the air to any member of Congress on request), he delivered the first of what was to become a three-year series of folksy radio addresses designed to move himself to the forefront of the popular consciousness.[14]

Long was no stranger to radio. He had used it effectively in building his popularity in Louisiana, in promoting his cotton-holiday plan in 1931, and in the Caraway campaign of the previous summer. His experience was evident in the skillful and deceptively benign speech he delivered March 17. With liberal use of passages from the Bible and quotations from such popular American heroes as Daniel Webster, William Jennings Bryan, and Theodore Roosevelt, Long made his economic proposals sound simple, logical, and moderate. Even more impressive was his caginess in dealing with Roosevelt. There was no hint in this address of disillusionment with the Administration. On the contrary, he insisted, "our great President . . . has not only kept faith before his nomination, but he kept faith after nomination." In campaign speeches, even in his Inaugural Address, Roosevelt had "declared to help decentralize the wealth of this country." But the new President would need assistance. "He has a hard task ahead," and Huey Long was ready to come to his aid.[15]

To his supporters, Long was presenting himself as a champion of the common man, working selflessly to help a popular President fulfill his campaign promises. To the Administration, however, he was beginning to seem a shrewd and dangerous foe. Long was taking the President's vague commitment to the principle of wealth redistribution and using it to create in the public mind an expectation of specific legislative action. He was maneuvering Roosevelt into an awkward and profitless position.

For a few months, the Administration remained willing to put up with all of this—with the attacks on its legislative proposals, the maligning of New Deal officials, the attempts to appeal over the President's head directly to the public. But by the middle of June, Roosevelt had apparently decided that Long could not be appeased, and he summoned him to the White House for what he told aides would be a "showdown."[16]

The meeting did not have the appearance of a showdown. Long bounded into the President's office dressed in a brilliant white suit and began reminding Roosevelt pointedly of his own great work at the Chicago convention. For a while, he failed to remove his straw hat, except occasionally to tap the President's knee or elbow with it when making a point. James Farley and Marvin McIntyre, also present, were incensed at what they considered a deliberate discourtesy, but Roosevelt remained calm and superficially amiable. By the end of the interview, however, he had made his intentions clear: Huey would no longer be consulted on the distribution of federal patronage in Louisiana.[17]

Long may not have realized fully at first how completely the President had written him off. Although he growled to Farley after the meeting about Roosevelt's evasiveness, he assured reporters cheerily as he left the White House that "The President and I are never going to fall out. I'll be satisfied whichever way matters go." But as the summer wore on and Long watched more and more federal appointments going to his enemies in Louisiana, what little loyalty he may still have felt toward the Administration eroded. In October, he all but formalized the break. First, he directed the Louisiana state government to refuse any federal funds that would be spent under the supervision of his political enemies. Then, when Interior Secretary Harold Ickes began to criticize him for his petulance, Long called a press conference, launched a spirited attack on New Deal officials in Louisiana, and concluded angrily: "While you are at it, pay them my further respects up there in Washington. Tell them they can go to hell."[18]

Why had it happened? And why so quickly? By any normal standards, there seemed to be every reason for both Long and Roosevelt to avoid a public falling out. The President, in the first critical days of an Administration that faced an uncertain future, could hardly have been eager to win the enmity of a powerful and increasingly popular member of his own party. And Long, whose national reputation was still in its earliest stages of development, would seem to have had little to gain from a break with the man who had won the overwhelming confidence of the American people.

For the President, the explanation seems relatively simple. Already, Long was making it clear that he was no friend of the Administration, that he would support it only on his own terms, terms that were unacceptable to Roosevelt. It was becoming apparent, moreover, that Long's attempts to pressure the President into supporting his programs were having some effect upon the public. Members of the White House staff worried when they received letters from people like William Dombrow of Chicago, who wrote of his admiration for the President and added that "Here in Illinois the people would rejoice if they had a leader, such as the Hon. Sen. Huey P. Long. His bill that he recently introduced in Congress on Decentralization of Wealth, is one of the

greatest pieces of legislation that was ever introduced"; and from groups like
an Irish-American political organization, which sent Roosevelt a resolution
praising "Senator Long's zeal for honest execution of the 'New Deal.' " The
President could not afford to let Long continue creating the impression that
his wealth-redistribution proposals were part of the Administration's program. The longer he waited, the costlier the break would be when it inevitably
came. It was better to do it quickly and minimize the damage.[19]

For Long's part, the reasons are more obscure. Perhaps he was, as he
claimed, genuinely disillusioned with Roosevelt. Perhaps he simply over-
estimated the amount of public abuse the President was willing to take. What
seems most likely, however, is that Long quickly realized that Franklin Roosevelt was a more formidable adversary than he had anticipated, and that
anyone with national aspirations of his own would tie himself to the Administration at his peril. "He's so doggone smart," Long remarked in the affected
back-country dialect he sometimes adopted, "that fust thing I know I'll be
working fer him—and I ain't goin' to." Later, he explained further. The only
difference between Hoover and Roosevelt, he claimed, was that Hoover was
a hoot owl while Roosevelt was a scrootch owl. "A hoot owl bangs into the
roost and knocks the hen clean off, and catches her while she's falling. But
a scrootch owl slips into the roost and talks softly to her. And the hen just
falls in love with him, and the first thing you know, *there ain't no hen.*"[20]

III

FRANKLIN ROOSEVELT was taking a calculated gamble when he cast Long
adrift. He was wagering that his own popularity would more than offset
Long's; that without public identification with the New Deal, Huey's national
strength would languish and ultimately die. For a while, it seemed that the
gamble had paid off. During the second half of 1933, it did appear that Long
had entered an irreversible decline—not only in the nation but in his hitherto
unassailable bastion, Louisiana.

Problems beset Long from all sides in that difficult summer and continued through the early months of 1934. From the Roosevelt Administration
came not only the loss of access to patronage. There began, too, a troubling
investigation by the Treasury Department into the income-tax returns of Long
and his political associates. The investigation was not new. The Hoover Administration had ordered it late in 1932, and Treasury officials had already
gathered what they believed was significant evidence by the time Roosevelt
took office the following March. But the new Administration, hoping to keep

the peace with Huey, had ordered the investigation halted. Early in 1934, however, the Treasury Department received orders to reopen the inquiry and "let the chips fall where they may." Not until several years later, well after Long was dead, did the investigation uncover enough evidence to permit major indictments against figures in the Long organization. From the beginning, however, it served as a menacing and embarrassing irritant to Huey, a reminder of the formidable burden he had shouldered in earning the enmity of Franklin Roosevelt.[21]

More immediately disquieting was an investigation, publicly conducted, by a special committee of the Senate into the 1932 Democratic primary in Louisiana. In that contest, Long had supported John Overton, an aristocratic lawyer who had helped him fight impeachment in 1928, against incumbent United States Senator Edwin S. Broussard, whom he described as "one of Wall Street's own." The campaign had been an arduous one, but Overton had won by a comfortable margin. Broussard, however, charged the Long organization with election fraud and demanded that the Senate open hearings, a request that, coming from an incumbent Senator, could not be refused. Although the Senate committee uncovered no startling evidence of illegality and although the full Senate ultimately allowed Overton to take his seat, the investigation was another thorn in Long's side. Embarrassing hearings in New Orleans and Baton Rouge, hostile newspaper coverage throughout the state and the nation, acrimonious exchanges on the floor of the Senate in Washington—all seemed to drag on interminably, a persistent threat to Huey's aspirations.[22]

Long's greatest problem in 1933, however, was one of his own making, a result of the loose and flamboyant life-style he had adopted since his arrival in Washington. During a visit to New York in August, Huey accompanied some friends to a party at a country club in Sands Point, Long Island. He spent several hours getting pleasantly drunk, flirting with pretty women (his wife, as usual, was at home in Louisiana), and bouncing from table to table glad-handing and back-slapping, until finally he disappeared into the men's room.

What happened next has never been entirely clear; but what seems most plausible is that Huey, always impatient, tried to use an occupied urinal by relieving himself between the legs of someone in front of him, succeeding only in soaking the man's trousers. He emerged from the washroom with a bleeding and badly swollen eye. Although Long and his party quickly left the club and drove back to the city, several other guests caught a glimpse of the injured Kingfish; within hours, reports of the incident appeared in the press. For days, even weeks, the stories and editorials continued, presenting one version after another of the fight. Long had never been popular among New York journalists, and they seemed now to vie with one another in ridiculing him. Newspapers and magazines around the country picked up the story off the wires and gave it front-page attention, until soon the incident was as widely known as any in Long's career.[23]

Huey himself tried at first to pretend that nothing of importance had happened, but it was clear that he was angry and embarrassed. Arriving in Milwaukee the day after the incident for a speech to a convention of the Veterans of Foreign Wars, he barked nastily at reporters, ignored questions about the fight, and delivered one of the surliest and most vituperative speeches he had ever made—during the course of which he angrily demanded the ejection of all reporters and photographers. "We've had an exodus of polecats in Louisiana," he told his audience. "But when I picked up your Milwaukee newspapers I knew where all the polecats had gone." Even a day later, arriving home to supposedly friendly ground, Long remained sullen and contentious. Stepping off a train in New Orleans, he surrounded himself immediately with six grim-faced bodyguards who, with fists and elbows flying, hustled him silently past a waiting crowd of reporters. One newsman asked contemptuously as Long whisked by whether it was true that Huey had accepted an offer of $1,000 a night to appear in a Coney Island freak show. Long did not reply.[24]

Soon, however, he developed his own version of the story and began to publicize it with customary vigor. He had, he claimed, walked innocently into the men's room at Sands Point, where a group, estimated variously as four, five, or six men and described as "thugs," "gangsters," and "criminals," seized him and began to pummel him with blows. In one version, he had been struck across the face with a blackjack; in another, he had received a cut while dodging a knife thrust, the knife only grazing his forehead. "I am lucky to have escaped with such trivial injury," he insisted, "and am grateful."[25]

As the publicity surrounding the incident grew, Long apparently reasoned that an even fuller response was necessary. At first, he had attributed the attack vaguely to the dark forces that had threatened him throughout his career. Within a few days, he became more specific. The assailants, he claimed, had been "members of the House of Morgan," Wall Street hit men hired to eliminate the most powerful threat to the financial oligarchy. "The only reason he wasn't killed," one Long-inspired circular maintained, "was because he managed to get away too soon for the men to finish the job."[26]

Few members of the press took these charges very seriously. But Long promoted them assiduously on his own—printing circulars describing the event (of one of them he put out 1,225,000 copies, the largest recorded printing of any circular of his career); recounting and embellishing the episode in public speeches and on the radio; referring to it again and again in his own publications. And among some of his supporters, the story apparently took. For months, newspaper publishers, public officials, and Long himself received letters and telegrams praising him for his courage and denouncing the villains who had attacked him. "When Jesus Christ scourged the money changers from the holy temple," wrote one particularly impassioned Utah man, "he was crucified by those opposed to His formula and program. . . . And when Senator Huey Long of Louisiana launched a campaign to limit the size of fortunes . . . a price was set on his head and thugs were employed by big business to rub him from the national picture." Yet on the whole, as Long himself realized, the Sands Point incident was a significant political liability. As late as 1935, a team of sociologists in Muncie, Indiana, found that, according to one citizen, "People here . . . hold against [Long] that rowdy fistfight down at the Sands Point Casino on Long Island." Coming as it did in the midst of a series of trials, the Sands Point affair seemed to reinforce a growing appearance of trouble and decline.[27]

Even in Louisiana, there were signs that Long's grasp might be weakening. When early in October, only weeks after the Long Island episode, Long began a speaking tour in the state to promote a new tax program, he was greeted by displays of hostility that months before would have seemed almost inconceivable. Crowds many times smaller than anticipated gathered at each stop; instead of the cheering to which Long had become accustomed, he was confronted with booing and heckling, with challenges to talk about the Sands Point affair, and worst of all, at times, with silence. At one rally, members of the audience pelted him with eggs. At another, a group of his opponents stood near the front of the crowd with revolvers bulging conspicuously under their coats, threatening implicitly to fire if Long said anything provocative. He did not. It was a sobering experience, and one to which Long did not respond well. As the hostility grew, he often simply made things worse by launching gratuitous attacks upon Roosevelt, who was highly popular in Louisiana. When hecklers proved particularly infuriating, Long, standing securely behind a wall of bodyguards, hurled out belligerent challenges to "Come down here out of that grandstand" so he could "man-to-man it with you."[28]

The decisive defeat, many of his enemies believed, came in January 1934. Long had thrown the full weight of his organization behind the candidacy of John D. Klorer in the race for Mayor of New Orleans, and Huey himself had spent hour after hour on the radio praising his ticket and deriding his opposition. But the anti-Long candidate of the Old Regulars organization defeated Klorer by an almost overwhelming margin. Long was "on the spot," wrote journalist Hodding Carter at the time of the election. He had gambled by pitting his popularity against Franklin Roosevelt's, and he had lost:

The same small-town day laborers and indigent farmers who built Huey's roads and swelled Huey's majorities are now chopping wood for the N.R.A. and registering for the C.W.A. Though there is an honest effort to keep these organizations non-political, it isn't dishonest to tell the workers that the man Huey is fighting is the man who made their jobs possible.

Hodding Carter was more realistic than many others of Long's enemies, and he realized that, for all the setbacks, Huey "isn't down yet." He "can always make himself heard," Carter grudgingly admitted. For "as long as there are prejudices to appeal to, as long as the voting mass can be swayed by a demagogue preaching discontent and hitting below the belt at the easiest targets, Huey P. Long will be up and about." Long himself, while he would not have shared Carter's venomous characterization of his appeal, also realized that he was far from through. "I have more enemies in the United States than any little man I know of," he boasted defiantly to a Louisiana audience in the midst of his troubles. "I am proud of my enemies." And he would, he promised, beat them yet.[29]

IV

LONG'S VICTORY came more quickly and more decisively than anyone could have anticipated, a result not only of his own political talents but of the incompetence of his opponents. In Louisiana, Huey's enemies sensed at the end of 1933 that the Long regime was ready to topple, that it was time to deliver the final blow. They lacked, however, the means or the will to inflict it. Instead of challenging him within the state, they appealed to outside agencies, pressuring the United States Senate and other federal bodies to investigate the Long organization and, they hoped, expel Huey and his stooge, John Overton, from Congress. Yet when federal officials occasionally succumbed to the pressure and opened hearings, the opposition forces presented such flimsy and inconsequential evidence, and presented it so intemperately and ineptly, that even investigators unsympathetic to Long soon lost patience with them. The investigations collapsed, and the anti-Long leaders suffered damage to their prestige from which they never fully recovered.[30]

In the meantime, Long was moving to shore up his hegemony in Louisiana, and in spectacular fashion. He now completed the structure of power for which he would long be remembered, a structure so vast in its scope that it earned him the almost universally accepted label of "dictator." In a series of special sessions of the Louisiana legislature beginning in the spring of 1934 and continuing until his death fourteen months later, Long rammed through a body of laws that concentrated unprecedented power in his own hands and left his opponents with virtually no institutional support in the state.

Some called it a total destruction of representative government. It was not. Long still required the support of the people, and as 1934 progressed, it became clear that he still had it. Although there had been troubling evidence of public resentment late in 1933, and although the Klorer defeat had been a serious setback, the resentment proved short-lived. The defeat in New Orleans (where Long-endorsed candidates had almost never done well anyway) was, ultimately, an aberration. It was, in fact, the last significant electoral setback Huey was ever to suffer. For nearly two years to come, both in regular state elections and in special referenda to approve Huey's constitutional amendments, the voters of Louisiana affirmed repeatedly their continued faith in the Long organization.

Huey was not abandoning his final accountability to the public, but he was abandoning virtually all accountability to anyone or anything else. More systematically than any politician in American history, Long was destroying the normal functions of basic democratic institutions, turning a government founded on the principle of checks and balances into one directed by a single man. He ran roughshod over the legislature, treating it with such contempt and dominating it with such total mastery that even his most embittered opponents virtually ceased any serious efforts to thwart him. And with this power, he extended his reach to new realms—to hitherto non-political agencies, to county and city governments (especially to such opposition centers as New Orleans, whose municipal officials he effectively emasculated), even to local school boards.

Everywhere that a Long enemy remained, it seemed, a new state regulation appeared to make the enemy powerless or, if he was already powerless, to inflict humiliation and exact revenge. The state capital, a focal point of anti-Long activity, watched helplessly as Huey's organization systematically undermined its autonomy. Soon, Long explained, Baton Rouge would become his "Little District of Columbia." The small city of Alexandria, a center of opposition but hardly a stronghold, woke up one morning to find its mayor and most of its other municipal officials unceremoniously removed from office by act of the legislature, their successors to be appointed by the governor. Even the Standard Oil Company, Long's ancient enemy, was momentarily powerless against his wrath. With hardly a murmur of protest, the obedient legislature shouted through a new tax of five cents on each barrel of oil refined in the state—the same tax for which Long had nearly been driven from office six years earlier. Only by agreeing to purchase more of its crude oil from Louisiana sources was the company able to win a revision of the levy.

Long's enemies, who for years had been almost irrational in their hatred of him, now became virtually apoplectic. Yet there was an air of futility about it all, a sense that in the end Long would prove too strong for any of them. "Others had power in their organization," sighed one Long opponent who finally capitulated, "but he had power in himself. And he brought them all to their knees."[31]

Having secured his position in Louisiana, Long began to repair the damage his setbacks of 1933 had done to his national prestige. He gave up drinking and avoided the racy nightspots at which he had become a fixture in Washington. He started a rigorous diet and shed more than thirty pounds. He even took his wife, with whom he had seldom been seen in recent years, on a belated "honeymoon" to Hot Springs, Arkansas. The time for playing the clown had passed. Long now wanted to appear sober, responsible, and statesmanlike.[32]

More important than these cosmetic moves was a series of practical steps to help him communicate his message directly to the people. In October 1933, after working on it intermittently for a year or more, he published an autobiography, *Every Man a King.* A lively and entertaining if less than fully candid book, it portrayed a sincere and selfless Huey Long whose every thought and effort had been directed toward aiding the common people of America. Reviewers scoffed at it. "There is hardly a law of English usage or a rule of English grammar that its author does not break somewhere," sneered the *New York Times Book Review.* The work made clear, wrote Allan Nevins in the *Saturday Review,* that Long "is unbalanced, vulgar, in many ways ignorant, and quite reckless." But *Every Man a King* was not meant for the East Coast literati. Bound in a striking (some would say garish) gold cover, priced at a profit-denying one dollar a copy, it was intended for men and women not in the habit of reading books. When bookstores managed to sell only about 20,000 copies of the 100,000 Long had had printed, he simply gave the rest of them away.[33]

He also resumed publishing his own newspaper. The *Louisiana Progress,* the propaganda organ he had created to counter the hostility of the established press in his home state, had died quietly in 1932. Now, less than a year later, it reappeared in a new guise—renamed the *American Progress* and aimed at a national, not a regional audience. Like its predecessor, the *American Progress* was an unabashed advocate of the career and the programs of Huey P. Long. It did not, however, devote much space to Long's accomplishments in Louisiana. Instead, it focused on the broader issue of redistribution of wealth. Published weekly for about seven months, monthly thereafter, it had only a small formal subscription list. For the most part, Long mailed it free to whomever he chose—to an audience that averaged 300,000 per issue but that occasionally grew to 1.5 million. It was financed, like everything else Long did, by political contributions from his organization in Louisiana.[34]

By the spring of 1934, Long had established the foundations of a genuinely independent communications network. Just as he had once done in Louisiana, so now in the nation he was ensuring that never again would he have to rely solely upon the establishment press for publicity. His autobiography painted for his followers a picture of his life far more flattering than anything an outsider might publish. His newspaper would supply them with regular accounts of his activities, would interpret his legislative activities in a congenial light, and would explain the virtues of his program. A staff of sixty stenographers, the largest in Congress, would supply the men and women on Long's enormous mailing list with a flood of letters, circulars, and pamphlets proclaiming Huey's message and extolling his triumphs. Most important of all, radio speeches would bring his voice to millions of Americans so that, using his considerable broadcasting skill, he could soothe their fears about him and exhort them to ever greater efforts on his behalf. He used the radio only intermittently in 1933 and 1934, but by early 1935 he had become a frequent speaker on NBC and at times, according to the crude audience estimates of the day, one of the network's biggest attractions.[35]

V

LONG USED HIS NEW TOOLS of publicity to promote a freshly refined set of economic proposals: a plan that took his long-standing commitment to wealth redistribution and translated it into a specific program for reform. Late in 1934, he unveiled what was to be the cornerstone of the rest of his public career: the Share Our Wealth Plan.

The underlying argument for the new proposals was a simple one. The wealth of America, while abundant, was limited, Long said. Each citizen had a basic right to a decent share of what wealth there was. But for too long, a few rich men had been permitted to own so large a proportion of the nation's assets that they had not left enough for all the others. It was, he explained, as if everyone in America had been invited to a great barbecue. "God invited us all to come and eat and drink all we wanted. He smiled on our land and we grew crops of plenty to eat and wear. He showed us in the earth the iron and other things to make everything we wanted. He unfolded to us the secrets of science so that our work might be easy. God called: 'Come to my feast.' " But what had happened? "Rockefeller, Morgan, and their crowd stepped up and took enough for 120,000,000 people and left only enough for 5,000,000 for all the other 125,000,000 to eat. And so many millions must go hungry and without these good things God gave us unless we call on them to put some of it back."[36]

Long did at times explain the problem in more sophisticated terms. He cited figures (usually from such questionable sources as the *Saturday Evening Post* or from obscure government studies made decades before) to show that "2% of the people owned 60% of the wealth," or that "about 85% of the wealth is owned by 5% of the people." The specific numbers, however, were never as important as the broader image: of a problem so obvious that only willful ignorance could obscure it.[37]

The solution, the Share Our Wealth Plan (or, as he often called it, the Long Plan), was as simple as the problem. A new set of harshly confiscatory tax codes would place strict limits on the amount of wealth any one man could own and on the amount he could pass on to his heirs. Each person would be permitted to own capital worth $1 million with impunity. But on every million he owned over that amount he would be required to pay a sharply increasing "capital levy tax." On the second million, the rate would be one percent; on the third, two percent; on the fourth, four percent; on the fifth, eight percent; and so on. Once a personal fortune exceeded $8 million, the tax would become 100 percent. At first, this would permit individuals to retain fortunes of close to $7 million; but since the levy would be reimposed each year, before long "No one would have much more than three to four million dollars to the person."[38]

The proposals for income and inheritance taxes were even simpler. His income-tax plan extended the existing laws "to the point that, once a man makes the net sum of one million dollars in one year, that he gives the balance of what he makes that year to the government." Likewise, the government would confiscate all inheritances of more than one million dollars. The plan would, Huey insisted, "injure no one." It would not abolish millionaires; it might even increase their number ("I'd cut their nails and file their teeth," he admitted with some chagrin, "and let them live"); but his proposals would prevent anyone from accumulating a truly obscene fortune and would make an enormous fund of wealth available to the rest of the people.[39]

That fund would enable the government to enact the second major component of the Share Our Wealth Plan: guaranteed subsistence for everyone in America. Each needy family would receive a basic "household estate" of $5,000, "enough for a home, an automobile, a radio, and the ordinary conveniences." And this would be only a "start." There would be a government guarantee, too, of an adequate annual income for each family, "a minimum of from $2,000 to $2,500 . . . per year," enough, he claimed, to "maintain a family in comfort" once it had acquired the basic necessities that the initial $5,000 allowance would ·allow it to purchase. There were other proposals:

government support for education, old-age pensions, improved benefits to veterans, increased federal assistance to farmers, government-supported public-works projects, limitation of working hours, and more. Some of these provisions survived only briefly as part of the Long program; some of them proved durable. But the limiting of large fortunes and the distribution of the surplus formed its unchanging core.[40]

The Share Our Wealth Plan was politically attractive in many ways. Economically, however, it had serious—indeed, insurmountable—problems. Long failed to provide any clear explanation of the mechanics of redistribution. Not all wealth, of course, was in the form of money. Many, perhaps most of the holdings of the nation's wealthiest men and women were in the form of capital investments—industrial plants, real estate, stocks, bonds, and the like—that could not be easily evaluated, liquidated, or redistributed. Yet Long apparently never gave much thought to such problems. When pressed on the matter, he simply shrugged and admitted that "I am going to have to call in some great minds to help me."[41]

A more fundamental flaw was that the vast surplus wealth Long claimed could finance his program simply did not exist. There were not enough John D. Rockefellers with idle millions lying in bank vaults to satisfy the needs of the nation. One scholarly survey in 1935 suggested that if the government confiscated all wealth owned by those worth $1 million or more (a step even more drastic than Long envisioned) and distributed it among those worth $5,000 or less (precisely what Long proposed), the recipients would receive only a little more than $400 each. According to other estimates (and, given the difficulty in measuring "wealth," such estimates were necessarily crude ones), for every family to receive the minimum $5,000 homestead Long promised would mean that no family could retain more than about $7,000 in wealth. For each family to receive the annual $2,500 income Long promised, no family would be able to keep more than about $3,000 of its earnings a year. Long liked to suggest that effective redistribution was an easy matter, that it involved only skimming the excess from a few large fortunes. "Let no one tell you that it is difficult to redistribute the wealth of this land," he told a national radio audience in 1934. "It is simple." But it was not simple. To effect the sort of reallocation of resources Long promised would have required a process far more drastic and painful than he admitted or realized.[42]

It was hardly surprising, therefore, that Long's critics denounced his program as cynical demagoguery and accused him of pandering openly to ignorance and prejudice in his pursuit of public support. He was, H. L. Mencken once venomously charged (in a description that echoed the views of many), "simply a backwoods demagogue of the oldest and most familiar model—impudent, blackguardly, and infinitely prehensile." Yet to dismiss the

Share Our Wealth Plan as demagoguery is to dismiss it too easily. It was a simplistic program, seriously, perhaps fatally, flawed. It was not, however, an attempt to divert attention away from real problems; it did not focus resentment on irrelevant scapegoats or phony villains. It pointed, instead, to an issue of genuine importance; for the concentration of wealth was, even if not in precisely the form Long described it, a fundamental dilemma of the American economy. Few economists would have disagreed that in referring to the problem Long was, in a crude way, describing one of the basic causes of the Depression: the insufficient distribution of purchasing power among the populace, the inability of the economy to provide markets for the tremendous productivity of American industry and agriculture. For all its faults, the Share Our Wealth Plan was not without elements of economic truth.[43]

VI

WHATEVER THE EVENTS of 1933 had done to Long's political influence, his efforts of 1934 had repaired the damage. He had risen again as a major national figure. He had not, however, merely resurrected his former self. No longer would he define his power in terms of Louisiana politics, the United States Senate, even the Democratic Party. Instead, he would look directly to the nation, moving outside conventional institutional frameworks and establishing himself as an independent political force.

Signs of the change were everywhere apparent, not least in Long's new attitude toward the Senate. Huey continued in 1934 and 1935 to play an active role in Washington, never reverting to the neglect and disinterest that had characterized his first year there. But there was a crucial difference. In 1933, for all his flamboyance and invective, he had involved himself seriously in Senate work, devoting most of his speeches to the business at hand and occasionally making an effective contribution to the legislative process. During his next (and last) two years in Congress, he did neither. Instead, he used the Senate almost exclusively to reach out to the nation, virtually ignoring the legislation it was considering and speaking (interminably) about matters of his own choosing. The filibuster, the device Long had used spectacularly but selectively in the past, now became a routine weapon in his arsenal. Only occasionally, however, as in his successful efforts on behalf of a measure to relieve mortgage-plagued farmers, was his filibustering really intended as an effective lawmaking tool. Instead, he used the filibuster increasingly to launch personal attacks on his opponents.[44]

Long had hardly been a model of restraint even in his first two years in the Senate, but by 1934 he seemed to have rejected all concern for propriety, as a savage attack on Senator Pat Harrison of Mississippi demonstrated. Early in April, during a routine debate on a tax bill, Harrison expressed irritation at Long's obstructive tactics. It was hardly a major provocation, yet Huey responded with ferocious abuse, criticism that questioned not only Harrison's politics but his honor, his loyalty, and his history.

Pat Harrison had entered Mississippi politics years before as an ally and protégé of James Vardaman, the fiery populist-racist orator who had dominated the state for over a decade early in the century. But the relationship soured in 1917 when Vardaman spoke out against American involvement in World War I. Harrison repudiated him, ran for Vardaman's seat in the United States Senate, and won. And sixteen years later he listened in the Senate chamber to Huey Long revive the faded episode, embellish it, and draw a vicious and lurid contrast. Long had spent 1917, he reminded his colleagues, defending his friend S. J. Harper for his unpopular views on the war:

> Now that is my way of standing by my friends. The Senator from Mississippi has another way of standing by his friends. Just the difference between people! One is just as honest as the other. One is, catch your friend in trouble, stab him in the back and drink his blood. The other is stand by your friend and try to heal his wounds.[45]

Language like that, directed at an influential and respected colleague, could only mean that Long was no longer interested in retaining any effectiveness within the Senate. And when, early in 1935, he turned his wrath to new targets, it became clear that he had little interest in maintaining any effectiveness within the Democratic Party either. Early in February, he introduced a resolution calling for an investigation of James A. Farley, Postmaster General, chairman of the Democratic National Committee, and one of Franklin Roosevelt's most trusted subordinates. Farley's administration of both the Post Office Department and the party, Long charged, had been ridden with graft and corruption. He had used his offices to extort campaign contributions from unwilling contributors, to squeeze illegal kickbacks from corporations doing business with the government, and to drive opponents of the Administration out of power. Long had had personal experience with Farley's tactics in Louisiana, he claimed, and he would tolerate them no further. "If I . . . must kneel to such crooks as may be employed by men like Jim Farley, God send me to hell before I bring myself to go through that kind of thing to get patronage."

The Farley controversy raged on for months, with Administration supporters trying tactic after tactic to put Long's charges to rest and Huey frustrating them time and again by introducing new "evidence" or simply filibustering. Not until May, after many hours of Senate debate and many days of extensive newspaper coverage, did Long's resolution finally come to a vote. By a vote of 62 to 20, the Senate refused to authorize an investigation of the Postmaster General. But the episode had served its purpose: to publicize Long and embarrass the Administration.[46]

The Senate had not heard the last of Long. On the contrary, with the Farley controversy behind him, Huey made even more frequent use of the filibuster, speaking endlessly on any proposal the obstruction of which might damage the prestige of the Roosevelt Administration. In mid-June, he held the floor for fifteen and a half hours, reading passages from the Bible and the Constitution and offering recipes for Roquefort salad dressing, in a petty and unsuccessful effort to make NRA employees subject to Senate confirmation. Days later, he tied up consideration of the Social Security Act while trying vainly to force the federal government to assume a greater share of the cost of the new system. And late in August, on the last day of the Congressional session and the last day Huey Long would ever appear in the Senate, he conducted a filibuster against an apparently routine deficiency-appropriations bill. The act did not make sufficient provision for aid to wheat and cotton farmers, he maintained; and although he knew the Senate could not possibly take action on the issue before its midnight adjournment, he announced he would speak until something was done. Ignoring the anguished pleas of colleagues of both parties, he blithely announced, "I have nothing to do. I'm just having a high-heeled good time." When progressive Senators with whom he was usually in general accord attempted to convince him that by killing the bill he would be depriving the government of funds for railroad pensions and other welfare projects, Long simply retorted, "I do not need any advice. . . . All I care is what the boys at the forks of the creek think of me. They would uphold my hands." When the midnight deadline for adjournment arrived, Long was still talking. The deficiency-appropriations bill was dead, and the Senate quietly and sullenly dispersed.[47]

Long's flamboyant and obstructive behavior was one sign of his increasing independence. His Congressional voting record was another. Even during his first two years in Washington, of course, he had shown little inclination to cooperate with the Democratic leadership in the Senate or to bow to the will of the majority. He showed even less in 1934 and 1935. On roll-call votes in 1932 and 1933, Huey voted with the majority only 54 percent of the time, far less than most of his colleagues; over the next two years, that percentage declined further to 51 percent. More dramatic, however, was his deteriorating relationship with the party leadership, and particularly with Joseph Robinson. During 1932 and 1933, Long and the Majority Leader had voted alike 40 percent of the time; during 1934 and 1935, they agreed on only 26 percent of their ballots. Those issues on which they did vote alike, moreover, were usually inconsequential or uncontroversial ones.[48]

It was not surprising, therefore, that Long inspired among many of his Senate colleagues a hatred that far surpassed the normal bounds of political rivalry. Joe Robinson's animosity, born during Huey's first months in the Senate, had only intensified with the passage of years. He derived some measure of satisfaction from seeing his resentment echoed by a growing number of colleagues. "Pat Harrison hated Huey like no one was hated in the Senate in my time," recalled Burton K. Wheeler years later; and after Long's savage attack in 1934, the Mississippi Senator could seldom bring himself even to remain in the chamber when Long was speaking. Carter Glass, as early as 1933, was referring to Long privately as "the creature who seems to have bought and stolen his way into the United States Senate," adding, "He is an unfit associate for any company of gentlemen." As Long's public criticisms of Glass intensified, and as the unfavorable mail they inspired increased ("I have no further confidence in you or anything you stand for," one erstwhile supporter wrote the Virginian. "You had better resign at once"), the Virginian's patience wore thin. After one particularly heated debate, Glass lunged at Long in the cloakroom and would have struck him had not colleagues restrained him. "I couldn't hit you," Long retorted contemptuously. "You are too old a man." Harry Byrd of Virginia asked to be assigned a new seat in the Senate chamber so he would not have to remain next to Huey, "even if I have to sit on the Republican side." Long had, as *New York Times* columnist Arthur Krock observed, become a "pariah." And he was "now almost by himself."[49]

Yet Long did not stand entirely alone in the Senate. There were some Senators who liked and even admired him—Senators from the loose but growing "progressive bloc," men increasingly alienated from both major parties and increasingly disillusioned with Franklin Roosevelt and the New Deal. With Burton K. Wheeler, for example, Long was genuinely friendly. "I liked him," Wheeler recalled in his autobiography. So did other members of his family, as Harold Ickes discovered to his dismay at dinner in the Wheeler home one night. He could hardly suppress his "sense of revulsion" at the glowing accounts of Long's activities he heard from around the table.

George Norris had been one of Long's earliest friends in Congress, and the relationship remained cordial until the end. Norris was reputed to be the only member of the Senate able to "tame" Long, the only one Huey respected enough to defer to. Bob La Follette, Jr., son of the great progressive leader to whom Long was sometimes compared (if only for his skill at filibustering), was on friendly personal terms with Huey, as were such other progressives as Gerald Nye, Henrik Shipstead, Bronson Cutting, Lynn Frazier, and William Borah.[50]

Long was not really an intimate of any of these men. (He had never been a man given to close personal relationships.) Nor was there any firm political alliance among them. Long often disagreed even with the colleagues he admired most, and never did there emerge in the Senate anything resembling the firm progressive coalition Long had once envisioned. There was, nevertheless, evidence, if not of an alliance, at least of a general affinity between Long and the Senate progressives. Just as his Congressional voting record in his last two years displayed a drift away from the Democratic leadership, so it suggested a growing, if still loose accord with his fellow insurgents.

Long had always been more likely to vote with Senate progressives, regardless of their party affiliation, than with his Democratic colleagues. But in 1934 and 1935, as his independence from his own party increased, he voted with Norris, Wheeler, Borah, and senators like them more frequently. He had, for example, voted with William Borah on 58 percent of all roll calls in 1932 and 1933; during the following two years, the two men voted together 74 percent of the time. Gerald Nye and Huey Long had agreed on 66 percent of their votes in 1932 and 1933; after that, they agreed on 80 percent of them. There were less substantial but still significant increases in agreement with other progressives: Lynn Frazier from 68 percent to 77 percent; Robert La Follette from 63 percent to 67 percent; Henrik Shipstead from 71 percent to 79 percent; George Norris from 56 percent to 62 percent. With a few progressives, the rate of agreement remained essentially unchanged; with none did it significantly decline.[51]

It would be easy to exaggerate the importance of such figures. Voting alike on two-thirds or even three-quarters of the roll calls does not a firm alliance make, and it was always clear that Long and the progressives cooperated with one another only when they found it convenient. Yet the voting patterns do indicate that Long was not always the renegade that his detractors (and even he himself at times) portrayed. There were others in the Senate who shared many of his economic commitments, who considered the Roosevelt Administration disappointingly cautious, and who were finding it difficult to work within either major party. If Administration and Senate leaders found Long deeply disturbing, it was no doubt in part because they saw in him only the most extreme and most powerful manifestation of a disenchantment that many others shared.

VII

IT WAS NOT THROUGH THE SENATE, however, that Long intended to chart his political future. If he was to become the power he intended, if he was to make his program for redistribution of wealth the overriding concern of the nation, he would need a vehicle entirely his own. In February 1934, he created one.

Speaking over a national radio hookup for the first time in almost a year, Long announced that he was forming a new political organization: the Share Our Wealth Society, to be composed of a nationwide system of local clubs. Anyone committed to the idea of redistribution of wealth could join. It was time, he argued, "to hit the root with the ax. . . . Enroll with us. Let us make known to the people what we are going to do. . . . Share Our Wealth societies are now being organized, and people have it within their power to relieve themselves from this terrible situation."[52]

The idea for the Share Our Wealth Clubs had apparently occurred to Long spontaneously at three o'clock one morning, and he had excitedly roused Earle Christenberry, his secretary, from bed to work out the details with him. But the concept of creating an independent organization for himself was not a new one. It had its roots in his political career in Louisiana. While he could not hope to re-create on a national scale the iron-clad and pervasive organizational hegemony he had achieved in his own state, he could work to establish a widespread network of supporters with whom he could retain constant communication. And upon them, he hoped, he could build a national following of enough size and power to allow him to achieve his dreams.[53]

How extravagant those dreams were was rapidly becoming clear. It took no great prescience to recognize the thin line dividing the establishment of a national political organization from the establishment of a political party. The formation of the Share Our Wealth Society was the decisive signal that Long was not merely attempting to pressure and cajole the Administration and the Democratic Party, but was planning to supplant it. "It is more and more evident in Washington," wrote Arthur Krock early in 1935, "that many Democrats feel he is getting ready to pounce upon their party and absorb all or a large part of it in 1936."[54]

Such Democrats included officials as powerful as the President himself. Roosevelt was no longer content simply to deny Long patronage and to cut off federal funds in Louisiana. Now that Huey was creating a potentially threatening national organization, the Administration considered more drastic measures. In September 1934, the President went as far as to flirt with the

idea of sending federal troops into Louisiana to "restore Republican government" in the state. Members of the Justice Department and the FBI drew up
elaborate legal and tactical memoranda before Roosevelt finally abandoned
the rash and explosive scheme.[55]

By 1935, the Administration had apparently settled on a different approach. No longer would it attempt simply to pressure or threaten Long; it
would co-opt him. Franklin Roosevelt's widely heralded "turn to the left" in
1935 (a series of ambitious proposals often described as the "Second New
Deal") was the result of many political considerations. There can be little
doubt, however, that Long was one of them. As one "prominent" Democratic
Senator with close ties to the White House disclosed to a reporter early in the
year, "We are obliged to propose and accept many things in the New Deal
that otherwise we would not because we must prevent a union of discontent
around [Long]. The President is the only hope of the conservatives and
liberals; if his program is restricted, the answer may be Huey Long."[56]

One New Deal proposal in particular had the stamp of Long clearly
across its face: Roosevelt's tax message of June 1935. After months of uncertainty, the President had accepted a Treasury Department proposal for
sharply graduated increases in income- and inheritance-tax rates, and he
presented it to Congress as an attempt "to prevent an unjust concentration of
wealth and economic power." Long expressed enthusiastic approval at first,
but he soon made clear that the Administration plan was not nearly drastic
enough to satisfy him. The President's proposal was, he charged (with some
accuracy), little more than a cosmetic move. It would make no fundamental
difference in the distribution of national wealth.[57]

Whether Roosevelt's tax plan and his other new proposals would ultimately have succeeded in undermining Huey's appeal is impossible to determine, for less than three months later Long was dead. At the moment,
however, they had no appreciable effect. Long's national reputation grew at
an astounding rate through the spring and summer of 1935, and the size and
distribution of his Share Our Wealth Clubs grew with it. In the sixth year of
the Depression and the third year of the New Deal, Long seemed to many to
be on the verge of creating a genuine new force in American politics, one
whose ultimate power nobody could yet predict. And there was little doubt
that he intended to use this force to play an instrumental role in the 1936
election. "What is quietly tipped off as being the Huey Long 1936 campaign
badge has made its appearance in Washington," the San Francisco *Examiner*
noted in March 1935. "It is a small gold kingfish, with a crown on its head
and labeled 'Louisiana,' worn in the buttonhole. It is, unlike Huey, exceedingly modest."[58]

Unlike Huey indeed, for, while Long usually insisted that he had as yet made no concrete plans for 1936, every now and then he let evidence of his real ambitions slip out. "I'll tell you here and now," he told reporters one afternoon late in the summer, "that Franklin Roosevelt will not be the next President of the United States. If the Democrats nominate Roosevelt and the Republicans nominate Hoover, Huey Long will be your next President."[59]

4

The Radio Priest

CHARLES COUGHLIN was thirty-four years old, an obscure parish priest in a small suburb of Detroit, when two events persuaded him to request time from a local radio station to broadcast his Sunday sermons. Early in July 1926, a late-night telephone call summoned him to his newly completed church, where he found a blazing cross planted on the lawn—a warning from the local Ku Klux Klan. At about the same time, Coughlin realized that the meager weekly collections from his tiny parish would not be sufficient to meet payments on the diocesan loan that had enabled him to construct the church. The loan obligations were nearly $100 a week; the Sunday collections were averaging less than $50. Disturbed by the anti-Catholic sentiment, concerned about his indebtedness, the young priest looked to the radio as a vehicle for battling both.[1]

A little less than nine years later, in May 1935, Coughlin mounted the podium in a packed convention hall in Cleveland, Ohio, and faced a cheering crowd of more than 25,000 people. For a few moments, he gazed silently at the rapt, excited faces. Then he began to speak. And the voice—a voice intimately familiar to every man and woman in the crowd, a voice resonant with strength and anger and hope and promise—reached out through the enormous hall and gripped every person in it. By the time Coughlin finished, his eyes blazing and his face soaked with sweat, the cheering had built to a roar and the audience was standing, smiling, and finally waving farewell. Coughlin moved slowly from the stage, then, in the next forty-five minutes, repeated parts of his speech three times to groups who had been unable to find seats in the auditorium but had waited patiently for him in smaller rooms in the basement. No one who saw it could forget the impact of this magnetic man in clerical collar. It was impressive evidence of how far Coughlin had traveled from his obscure beginnings of less than a decade before.[2]

Through the first half of the 1930s, with the country struggling to recover from the Great Depression, Coughlin developed and retained a national popularity of bewildering proportions. His radio sermons, once pleasant discourses on the life of Christ and the lessons of the Bible, became after 1930 almost exclusively political in content. Broadcast around the nation on more than thirty stations, they attracted an audience estimated as high as forty million. Coughlin received more mail than anyone else in America—more than any film star or sports hero, more than the President. Dozens of stenographers worked around the clock to deal with it. When he journeyed from Detroit for appearances in other cities, he drew crowds that were the envy of political candidates. In New York, in the fall of 1933, more than 7,000 enthusiastic followers jammed the Hippodrome to hear him speak, while nearly as many stood in the chilly streets outside listening to his voice over loudspeakers. In Cincinnati, Chicago, Boston, Baltimore, and St. Louis, adoring crowds packed stadiums and auditoriums to hear him or lined his route to and from the train stations just to glimpse him passing by.[3]

Yet even as the public appearances increased, it was always his radio voice that entered most frequently and most directly into the lives of his followers. In Brockton, Massachusetts, referees halted schoolboy football games shortly before three o'clock on Sunday afternoons so that parents, coaches, and players could get to a radio in time to hear Father Coughlin. When the sermons were over, the games resumed. In churches around the country, pastors rescheduled Sunday services so they would not conflict with the radio discourses. In urban neighborhoods throughout the East and Midwest—not only Irish communities, but German, Italian, Polish; not only Catholic areas, but Protestant and, for a time, even Jewish—many residents long remembered the familiar experience of walking down streets lined with row houses, triple-deckers, or apartment buildings and hearing out of every window the voice of Father Coughlin blaring from the radio. You could walk for blocks, they recalled, and never miss a word.[4]

Coping soberly and modestly with such unexpected acclaim would have been a difficult task for any man. It was a task too great for Father Coughlin. As the years passed and his popularity grew, a strain of megalomania wore away his self-restraint until finally his excesses destroyed him. But before that happened, Coughlin, like his contemporary Huey Long, played an important role in shaping popular responses to the Depression. In his weekly radio sermons and in his speeches and writings, he created an explanation of the crisis that was in many ways illogical and occasionally dangerously distorted. But it was, nevertheless, a message that reflected some of the oldest and deepest impulses of the American people, a message that raised fundamental questions about the structure of the nation's economic life.

"Perhaps no man has stirred the country and cut as deep between the old order and the new as Father Charles E. Coughlin," the popular *Literary Digest* noted in 1933. Perhaps no man, the magazine might also have noted, would have seemed a less likely candidate for such national prominence a few years before. Coughlin was not only a Catholic priest, presumably removed from the political arena by his vocation, but he claimed as his base only a tiny and struggling parish in a raw industrial suburb. From the beginning, however, Coughlin was a man of unusual abilities and unusual ambitions, a man with a vision of the priesthood that reflected his restless drive for achievement and his obsessive desire for acclaim. It was these traits, exhibited first in his youth, that accounted for most of what was best and what was worst in Father Coughlin's public career.[5]

II

FROM THE MOMENT OF HIS BIRTH, Coughlin was literally surrounded by the institutions of the Catholic Church. On one side of his family's modest house in a working-class neighborhood of Hamilton, Ontario, stood St. Mary's Cathedral, a soaring Gothic structure that dominated the community. On the other side were a convent and a Catholic grade school. Sitting at the dinner table, the family could hear the sound of the cathedral organ clearly through the windows; and they needed only to step out the back door and cross a short lawn to reach the church entrance.[6]

It was less the physical proximity of the church, however, than the religious intensity of his home that had the most profound effect upon Coughlin as a child. His father, Thomas, was a third-generation Irish immigrant whose father and grandfather had been laborers in the American Midwest. Thomas himself had grown up in Indiana and had left there to work as a stoker on Great Lakes steamboats until poor health induced him to seek lighter work. Settling in Hamilton (he had been hospitalized in a Catholic hospital nearby for typhoid fever), he found employment as the sexton of St. Mary's Cathedral; and it was there that he met his future wife.[7]

Amelia Mahoney, too, was of pure Irish descent. She had spent her early years on a farm in Ontario until her struggling parents moved the family to Hamilton to seek work. There she earned a modest income as a seamstress and attended mass daily at St. Mary's, dreaming wistfully for a time of entering a convent and becoming a nun. Although in November 1890 she wed Thomas Coughlin, marriage by no means dampened her religious ardor. As she lay in her home October 25, 1891, giving birth to her first and only son, Charles Edward, she murmured a quiet and revealing prayer: "A girl—for the —convent . . ."; or "a boy—please, God—a priest."[8]

In the years that followed, Charles's mother, the dominant figure in the Coughlin household, continued to transfer her own religious aspirations to her son. She frequently carried the infant with her on daily visits to St. Mary's Cathedral for mass; and as the child grew older, she tried to see that he spent as much time in the company of the priests and nuns of the neighboring buildings as with children of his own age. The birth of a baby girl, christened Agnes, little more than a year after Charles's arrival, seemed to promise the boy some respite from his mother's cloying attention. But when Agnes died at the age of three months, Amelia Coughlin devoted herself even more consumedly to the destiny of her only surviving child.[9]

Coughlin's relationship with his parents, and particularly with his mother, was warm and intimate and remained so until their deaths. Yet there may also have been some ambivalence, some hidden tension. For Amelia Coughlin not only wanted to make her son a priest; she wanted to control even the most mundane details of his life. Incidents like the boy's first day of school almost certainly left their mark. When Charles was about to begin classes at the Catholic school next door, his mother arranged his long hair in curls and dressed him in an immaculate blue-and-white kilt. The result was what to the child must have been a painful rebuke. As he marched nervously to the classroom door, he found his way blocked by one of the priests, who, smiling tauntingly, ordered him home. This was the boys' school, he explained sarcastically. Girls must go elsewhere.

Charles soon persuaded his mother to cut his hair and dress him in conventionally boyish clothes, but the incident was only one of many conflicts between Amelia's pampering and her son's determination to assert his masculinity. If Mrs. Coughlin insisted that he come home immediately after school to practice the piano, Charles could as often as not be found racing through the neighborhood streets, screaming loudly with his friends and soiling his clothes in minor scuffles. If she attempted to interest him in quiet and decorous indoor games, he became ever more attracted to rugged and vigorous sports —baseball, football, rugby.

Growing up as an only child and dealing constantly with his mother's protectiveness may have accounted in part for two important threads of Coughlin's personality. There was the brashness, the assertiveness, the almost boastful manliness, an implicit rebuff, perhaps, to his mother's efforts to pamper and refine him. But there was at the same time an expectation of constant solicitude and approval. Accustomed to being the center of attention and the recipient of acclaim, he grew restless and irritable when he was not. They were expectations that, during his childhood at least, his mother seldom failed to satisfy.[10]

Coughlin resisted his mother in many things, but one pressure he apparently never fought was her effort to tie him to the Catholic Church. Indeed, it may never have occurred to him that there was an alternative, so ubiquitous was the Church in almost every stage of his early life. As a child, he served as an altar boy at St. Mary's Cathedral while attending the parish school next door. When he was twelve, his parents traveled with him on the forty-mile trip to Toronto, where he enrolled in St. Michael's College, a secondary school run by the Basilian Fathers and designed to begin preparing young boys for the clergy. After four successful years of high school (during which his mother visited him every Sunday), he moved unhesitatingly into the St. Michael's undergraduate division—the next step on the road to the priesthood.[11]

Coughlin's college career was a classic campus success story. He earned excellent grades, played starting fullback for the school's championship rugby team, served as president of his senior class. And he developed a reputation at St. Michael's as an unusually talented public speaker, not only because of his successes as a member of the debating team, but because of his impromptu performances in the classroom. Occasionally, when called upon to discuss assignments he had not read, Coughlin simply made a little speech, often leaving his instructors so impressed by his eloquence that they overlooked his lack of preparation. In 1911, he graduated from St. Michael's and, after a three-month trip to Europe during which he apparently resolved any last doubts he may have had about his future, returned to Toronto to enter St. Basil's Seminary, where he began his formal theological training for the priesthood.[12]

Like St. Michael's, St. Basil's was run by the Basilian Fathers; and while the life of a novitiate there was austere and cloistered, the intellectual atmosphere was charged with excitement. More than most other clerical orders, the Basilians were deeply imbued with the emerging spirit of Catholic social activism, a spirit that was helping to transform the traditional role of the clergy.

The Catholic social movement had emerged throughout western Europe late in the nineteenth century when the dislocations of industrialization began to force clerics to re-examine their long-standing aloofness from secular controversies. In the 1880s, there was a timely rebirth of interest in the teachings of St. Thomas Aquinas, and in particular those aspects of Thomistic thought that attempted to balance individual rights with social responsibilities. If there had been any doubt about the importance of these new impulses to the future of the Church, Pope Leo XIII dispelled them in 1891 with an encyclical that became the central document of Catholic social activism: *Rerum Novarum,* or *On the Condition of the Working Class.* It was in many ways an ambiguous document, for Leo's first concern was to counter the growing appeal of socialism in Europe. Yet the Pope openly called for far-reaching reforms in industrial capitalism, not only as a tactic for fighting radicalism but as a prerequisite for a just and moral society. The Catholic clergy, he implied, could play an important role in encouraging such reforms.

The impact of the encyclical upon the most active groups within the clergy was electric, not only in Europe but in North America, where the Church was likewise reconsidering its established role in society. With hundreds of thousands of European Catholic immigrants arriving in American cities each year, with industrial strife and agrarian unrest reaching a fever pitch, with popular reform movements growing in strength, the once small and peripheral North American Catholic Church faced enormous new demands. Cardinal James Gibbons of Baltimore, the most influential Catholic official on the continent during much of this period, helped ease the transition. Although not himself an outspoken social activist, he sternly resisted efforts by more conservative clerics to impose a Church ban on labor-union activity, and he quietly encouraged activist groups within the clergy. Particularly among younger priests, the Church was becoming a vehicle for political and economic as well as religious activity.

As a student of the Basilian Fathers, Coughlin had been exposed to these reform currents since he had entered high school. As a novitiate in the seminary, he was immersed in them. Traditional Catholic doctrine and liturgy received heavy emphasis, but students at St. Basil's took intensive instruction in social theory as well. They studied the *Summa Theologica* and other works of Aquinas; they pored over *Rerum Novarum;* they talked constantly about the clergy's potential for playing active roles in society; and they dreamed of challenges and possibilities little known to earlier generations of priests. To them, as to many others—Catholics and non-Catholics, Canadians and Americans—the idea of "social justice" became in these last years before the First World War a guiding and enduring principle.[13]

One aspect of Thomistic thought resonated particularly clearly with Coughlin and his contemporaries: the concept of the just community. Aquinas recognized the economic rights of the individual; but those rights, he maintained, were qualified by the needs of his neighbors. "Man ought not regard external goods as his own," he argued, "but as common so that, in fact, a person should readily share them when he sees others in need." To Leo XIII and to those Catholics who shared his concerns, the message of such words was clear: social justice required neither rigid collectivism nor laissez-faire individualism; it required, rather, a system of private ownership tempered by recognition of the individual's obligation to his community. No one advocated a literal re-creation of the medieval social arrangements that had shaped Aquinas's own thinking. But many found his vision of organic communities with strong mutual responsibilities powerful and appealing.[14]

Coughlin responded well to the curriculum at St. Basil's; he was an intelligent and articulate student. He responded less well, perhaps, to the austerity of life in the seminary. In the midst of his training, his superiors sent him to Waco, Texas, where he spent a year teaching philosophy and playing baseball at a Basilian college. The reasons for the move are obscure. One biographer suggested that Coughlin needed a change of climate because of poor health, but his health seems not to have interfered with his athletic career. The seminary may have been responding instead to some chafing against its harsh regimen, attempting to allow Coughlin an outlet for his restlessness.

Coughlin returned to Toronto at the end of the year and re-entered happily, apparently, the life of the seminary. By the spring of 1916 (he was now twenty-three years old), he had developed such a reputation for eloquence that St. Basil's allowed him to deliver the Easter Sunday sermon, a rare honor for one not yet ordained. Three months later, on June 29, he took the formal vows of the priesthood; and several days after that he returned home to Hamilton, where he celebrated his first public mass in St. Mary's Cathedral, his proud mother beaming from the front pew.[15]

For the next seven years, Coughlin remained associated with (although not a member of) the Basilian Order as a teacher at Assumption College, a small school just outside Windsor, Ontario, and across the river from Detroit. They were crowded and, in many ways, rewarding years. Coughlin taught English, history, and Greek (a language he was just learning); he coached football and supervised the drama society; he grew popular with his students and his colleagues. But once again there were signs of restlessness. After only a few months at Assumption, Coughlin persuaded his parents to sell their home in Hamilton and move to Windsor, where he could see them more easily and where they could offer him a diversion from the confining life of the college. He volunteered to spend weekends assisting local pastors in Windsor and Detroit with their parish duties. As his reputation for eloquence spread, he eagerly accepted invitations to address the meetings and banquets of neighboring Catholic organizations and even of such secular groups as Rotary Clubs and Chambers of Commerce. The cloistered life of a monastic order, even one as flexible and socially active as the Basilians, apparently was not enough for Coughlin; in 1923, he left the college and the Order to enter the pastoral clergy—to begin work as a parish priest.[16]

Although he may not have realized it at the time, Coughlin was severing his ties not only with the Basilian Order but with Canada as well. Assigned to the Archdiocese of Detroit and to the authority of its new bishop, Michael Gallagher, he began a residence in the United States (of which he was, through his father, already a citizen) that would last the rest of his life. For a little over two years, Coughlin served as an assistant to pastors in large urban churches —first in the fast-growing industrial city of Kalamazoo, Michigan; then in downtown Detroit. But Bishop Gallagher soon realized that Coughlin was too valuable a commodity, too intelligent and organizationally skillful, to be allowed to languish in secondary roles. Michigan was a burgeoning state. The automobile industry and related enterprises were booming with the heady prosperity of the 1920s, and once-quiet rural communities were becoming bustling factory towns. With the economic expansion came population growth as the state attracted thousands of new working men and women—people of German, Irish, Italian, and eastern European stock, many of them Catholics. To serve these new arrivals, the Church needed to expand rapidly; and a priest with Father Coughlin's energy and oratorical talents could help it to do so.[17]

Coughlin's first parish, however, was in the tiny rural village of North Branch, Michigan, a farming town with barely enough Catholics to support its small church. Coughlin quickly displayed his entrepreneurial skills by organizing an elaborate church fair, a successful fund-raising device that enabled him, among other things, to pay for a new garage to house his automobile. After only six months in North Branch, a period his superiors perhaps regarded as an apprenticeship, he received another assignment from Bishop Gallagher. He was to oversee a new parish in a new suburb north of Detroit—in the town of Royal Oak.[18]

III

THERE COULD HARDLY HAVE BEEN a less hospitable setting for an ambitious young priest attempting to establish a new church than Royal Oak, Michigan, in 1926. The town was only twelve miles from downtown Detroit, but until recently it had remained an isolated, largely rural community. Now, with the overflow from Detroit's industrial population pressing steadily outward, Royal Oak was no longer countryside and not yet city, but a sort of intermediate, urbanizing wilderness. Dotted with the cheaply built, shingled homes of newly arriving automobile workers, made even more desolate by large, unkempt vacant lots, it offered a bleak and forbidding landscape. However intimidating its physical attributes, its social climate was even worse; for older residents of the community, fearful of urban, industrial encroachments and hostile to immigrants and Catholics, had gravitated in large numbers to the Ku Klux Klan. Outsiders continued to settle in Royal Oak, but, for the moment at least, the Klan was the dominant force in the community.[19]

Coughlin was aware of the problems he faced, but he also seemed to recognize the potential. Borrowing $79,000 from the Archdiocese of Detroit, he oversaw construction of a new, brown-shingled church at one of the town's principal intersections. A simple and undistinguished structure, it had a seating capacity of 600, remarkably large for a community with only thirty-two Catholic families. Coughlin was looking ahead. When only two weeks after the completion of the building the Klan planted its flaming cross on the front lawn, Coughlin rushed to the scene and helped beat out the fire. For years thereafter, he liked to recall (in a story he no doubt embellished for dramatic effect) standing over the charred embers that night, looking skyward, and vowing that someday he would build on the site a new church, one with "a cross so high . . . that neither man nor beast can burn it down."[20]

A new church would have to wait, however, because for the moment Coughlin did not even have enough money to heat the existing one. Always the entrepreneur, he tried a number of unconventional fund-raising techniques. Instead of installing collection boxes or passing a plate at services, Coughlin placed ushers at the exits to collect offerings as the parishioners left the church, reasoning, perhaps, that contributions would be larger if they had to be placed directly in an outstretched palm than if dropped anonymously in a basket. On one occasion, he asked members of the Detroit Tigers baseball team (of which he was an avid fan) to attend a service and help with the fund-raising. They agreed, and since the New York Yankees were in town, they brought Babe Ruth with them. The church gathered in several thousand dollars that Sunday.

Coughlin even tried to capitalize on his church's name. St. Thérèse, the "Little Flower of Jesus," had been canonized only the year before. A French Carmelite nun who had promised on her deathbed in 1879 to "spend my heaven in doing good on earth" and to "let fall a shower of roses," the new saint was a popular figure among American Catholics; and Coughlin's Shrine of the Little Flower, modest as it was, was the first church in America built in her honor. The pastor missed no opportunity to publicize the connection.[21]

Even these techniques, however, were not enough. The Catholic population of Royal Oak was simply too small to bear the financial burden of the church; and it would probably not grow much larger, Coughlin reasoned, as long as the local Klan remained unanswered. Nor were outsiders likely to travel the extra distance to attend services at the Shrine, particularly since they could look forward only to bumpy dirt roads and swarming mosquitoes for much of the journey. Only unusual inducements, apparently, could attract new parishioners to Royal Oak.

Early in October, only three months after Coughlin's first mass in the Shrine of the Little Flower, he paid a call on Leo Fitzpatrick, manager of radio station WJR and a devout Catholic. Coughlin explained his difficulties and remarked, cryptically, that he wanted to do something to fight bigotry and build up his church. As he had no doubt expected, Fitzpatrick suggested he try preaching over the air. He could have the time free for the first few weeks and would only have to pay the actual transmission costs—$58 per broadcast. If the experiment was successful, they could negotiate further.[22]

Coughlin delivered his first radio sermon October 17, 1926, from a specially installed microphone at his pulpit in Royal Oak. He received five complimentary letters at the church over the next few days, while WJR took in a few more. Still, the response was favorable, and Fitzpatrick and Coughlin decided to continue the broadcasts.[23]

It was not long before both men realized they had hit upon something extraordinary. In the weeks and months following Coughlin's first radio sermon, both the mail and the attendance at the Shrine of the Little Flower increased dramatically. Instead of five letters weekly, Coughlin began receiving dozens, then hundreds, then thousands—not only from Detroit but from throughout Michigan and from neighboring states within the range of WJR's strong signal. And with the letters came money—small contributions primarily, but in large enough numbers to ensure an end to the Shrine's immediate financial worries. Within a year, overflow crowds were jamming Coughlin's services, forcing him to add several extra masses each week. Many of the worshippers were simply visitors, drawn by curiosity about the radio priest. But an increasing number were new Catholic residents of Royal Oak, attracted there by the town's vibrant and prestigious church and settling in such numbers that the Ku Klux Klan could no longer terrorize the community.[24]

If Coughlin was startled by his sudden popularity, he wasted little time in capitalizing upon it. Within months of his first broadcast, he hired several secretaries to help him with his mail and keep track of his finances, the beginnings of a clerical staff that would ultimately number in the dozens. He asked Bishop Gallagher for an assistant priest, a request Gallagher readily granted. And later he announced the creation of his first organization: the Radio League of the Little Flower. The League was, in reality, simply a fund-raising mailing list. It had no formal duties or activities, but it did encourage Coughlin's admirers to contribute generously and regularly.[25]

There is no record of exactly how much money Coughlin was taking in during this period, but it was enough to allow him to do several things. He persuaded his parents to move—to leave Windsor and settle in an eight-room house he found for them in Detroit. (Who paid for it was never clear.) For himself and his assistants, he built a comfortable rectory next to the Shrine. Most important of all to him, he took the first steps toward construction of the magnificent church of which he had dreamed since his first weeks in Royal

Oak. A local architect designed to Coughlin's specifications an enormous octagonal structure, capable of seating 2,600 worshippers and topped by a spectacular granite tower III feet tall. There was not enough money yet to build it all, but construction of the tower began late in 1928. It would serve as a monument to the growing Catholic presence in Royal Oak. And it would contain a private apartment where Coughlin could prepare his radio sermons and from which he could deliver them.[26]

Coughlin's success may have been remarkably sudden, but it was not inexplicable. The crowds who saw him at his altar could offer one explanation: his commanding physical presence. Five feet ten inches tall, with the robust build of the athlete he was, Coughlin exuded vigor and dynamism. He had a firm mouth and jaw, steely eyes that looked piercingly through rimless glasses, and wavy brown hair cut short and combed to the side. At the altar, he could look commanding and serene. Away from it, he appeared, as he had all his life, restless and impatient, chain-smoking cigarettes, seldom able to sit still during a conversation, fond of fast games of handball and brisk walks with his enormous Great Dane, Pal.[27]

Most of Coughlin's admirers, however, could not see him, and it was what they heard that most fully accounted for his success. He had, said writer Wallace Stegner, who listened often, "a voice of such mellow richness, such manly, heart-warming, confidential intimacy, such emotional and ingratiating charm, that anyone tuning past it on the radio dial almost automatically returned to hear it again." It was a deep voice capable of rising to higher pitches when appropriate; and Coughlin retained a trace of an Irish brogue, which he often exaggerated for effect, trilling his r's and changing his inflection to add warmth and color. It was, Stegner believed, "without doubt one of the great speaking voices of the twentieth century. . . . It was a voice made for promises."[28]

It was also a voice that was becoming available to an increasing number of listeners. In 1929, Coughlin added two new stations to his broadcasting "network": WMAQ in Chicago and WLW in Cincinnati. Since WJR could be heard in parts of Cleveland, he was now broadcasting to most of the major cities of the industrial Midwest. His steady mail contributions more than covered the increased costs. (Coughlin always purchased his radio time directly from the stations, rather than allowing broadcasters to market his sermons to sponsors.) Finally, in the summer of 1930, Coughlin traveled to New York, met with officials of the Columbia Broadcasting System, and returned home to announce that he would shortly be broadcasting over the network. Four years earlier, he had felt lucky to speak to two dozen people in his church in Royal Oak. Now, his voice would reach a national audience of up to 40 million people.[29]

IV

COUGHLIN'S RADIO SERMONS during his first three years of broadcasting were generally uncontroversial. He lashed out at the Ku Klux Klan occasionally in the beginning, and later he attacked proponents of birth control. For the most part, however, he kept to religious themes: Biblical parables, Christ's teachings, the meaning of the sacraments, and the like. He directed many of his discourses toward children. But on January 12, 1930, he took to the air with a very different message. No complete transcript of the sermon has survived, but published excerpts reveal that it was a stinging denunciation of communism—the first hint of the political doctrines that would soon come to dominate his rhetoric.[30]

There was no mystery about the reasons for Coughlin's changing emphasis. Even early in 1930, the social effects of the stock-market crash the previous fall and the steadily worsening economy since were becoming evident—in the unemployment rate, the bank closings, and the falling consumer prices. By the end of the year, the signs of Depression were everywhere.

Detroit, a city almost entirely dependent upon the state of the automobile industry, suffered particularly severely. Unemployment had increased sharply late in 1929, as it did late every year when new-car sales began to lag. But while ordinarily the factories could be expected to begin hiring again in the late winter and early spring, in 1930 they did not. The peak employment in the automobile plants in 1929 had been 302,000; in 1930, it was fewer than 230,000; a year later, it was only about 185,000. Over 143,000 workers were unemployed by the middle of 1930, almost 225,000 by the beginning of 1931. Those figures included only the city's permanent residents. Since many transient workers simply left town when their jobs vanished, the real figure was even higher. By April 1930, Detroit had the highest unemployment rate of any major city in the country; and the city's public relief agencies were being taxed beyond their capacity.

"I have never confronted such misery as on the zero day of my arrival in Detroit," wrote the Philadelphia settlement worker Helen Hall, who visited the city in January 1930. She stopped in at the Department of Public Welfare and had to thread her way through throngs of applicants waiting for assistance. "I wanted to look at them and see what type of men and women they really were," she recalled, "but I was ashamed to look." She visited the homes of some of the unemployed and found not only suffering and fear, but shame. "My husband hated to go stand in those lines," said one woman whose family had finally applied for relief, "but I drove him to it. We couldn't see the children starve." It was the desperate hope that was most wrenching—the men who traveled two hours every day from their homes in distant suburbs to stand in line at a downtown employment office, only to find again and again that there were no jobs; the pregnant woman who appeared every morning at the personnel office of a department store pleading for work; the father who spent four months walking the streets of downtown (he could not afford to take a bus or trolley) and getting for his efforts only a brief temporary job shoveling snow. Thousands of Detroit residents were enduring a kind of half-life, unable to comprehend what had happened to them, unwilling to accept that no end was in sight.[31]

Living in a suburb that was filling up with automobile workers, Coughlin could not help but notice the deepening distress. There can be little doubt that his awareness of the crisis was one cause of his turn to politics in his weekly broadcasts. Coughlin himself insisted that he was simply responding to his instinctive sympathy for the poor, that he could not ignore social conditions while he watched the suffering around him. It was a self-serving explanation, certainly; but not an implausible one. Even as a child, Coughlin had warmed to those he perceived as less fortunate, occasionally presenting gifts—and once even his own winter coat—to the poorer children in his school. In Royal Oak, he created a vigorous charitable organization, God's Poor Society, which distributed food and clothing to thousands of needy citizens in the Detroit area. It was financed in large part by the mail contributions from his radio broadcasts. And as the Depression worsened, Coughlin donated large sums of money in the name of the Radio League of the Little Flower to other private relief efforts and national charities.[32]

There were, however, other reasons as well. Coughlin was, he also claimed, responding to the teachings of his faith—and to the wishes of his own bishop. If ever there was an opportunity to act upon the principles of social activism he had absorbed from the Basilians, Coughlin seemed to have it in 1930. He had an effective outlet, a receptive audience, an economic crisis of appalling dimensions. His duty seemed clear. He was to promote the teachings of Leo XIII, publicize the message of *Rerum Novarum,* take his place as one of the new committed priests unafraid to apply the lessons of the Church to the problems of the secular world. And from his first moment in Detroit, Coughlin received encouragement and support from a man he deeply admired: Bishop Michael J. Gallagher. "Next to my own father," he later claimed, "he was the most beloved man in my life." Gallagher had studied in Austria in the 1890s, in the midst of unprecedented Catholic activism in that country; and he had carried away a lasting belief in the responsibility of the Church, and of individual priests, to speak out forcefully about social injustice. He was an old man now, in failing health, and the time had passed when he could play an active public role himself. In Coughlin, he found an eager surrogate. Gallagher's influence upon the priest was significant, perhaps decisive.[33]

Coughlin's sympathy for the poor, his belief in Catholic social theory, his respect for Bishop Gallagher were no doubt genuine; but there was still another reason, equally important, for the changing focus of his broadcasts. Placid religious sermons might have been appropriate for the prosperous and apolitical 1920s, but in the restless atmosphere of the Depression they had begun to seem irrelevant. Coughlin had grown used to popularity, and he looked ahead to even greater triumphs. Speaking directly to the economic and social concerns of a nation in the midst of crisis was, in his view, the only viable tactic for increasing his prominence.

Certainly his first political sermon suggested more concern for attracting attention than for anything else. Speaking on the topic of "The American Family," Coughlin railed against the communist government of the Soviet Union for its assault upon Christianity and its decree that "all children of Russian parentage belonged not to the father and mother who bore them, but to the Soviet under whom they lived." America, he warned, faced a similar fate. The more than two million men and women who had obtained divorces during the last decade, who had "scorned the basic family and national doctrine of Jesus Christ," were evidence of a dangerous tendency toward Bolshevism in the United States.[34]

While his discourses in the weeks that followed continued to dwell upon his abhorrence of communism, socialism, and "kindred fallacious social and economic theories," they also emphasized other concerns: Coughlin's fear that the selfish practices of "predatory capitalism" would drive Americans to embrace these pernicious doctrines. "Have I any suggestions to offer?" he asked in his January 19 sermon entitled "Christ or the Red Fog." "There are plenty of them." Industrialists could take steps to assure steady work and a "just and living wage" to their laborers. They could improve working conditions, and they could contribute "as much money towards providing old age compensation insurance" as they had toward "that figment of fancy," Prohibition. "Let not the workingman be able to say that he is driven into the ranks of socialism by the inordinate and grasping greed of the manufacturer."[35]

By the time he began his second series of political broadcasts in the fall of 1930, Coughlin had turned his attention almost entirely to the domestic conditions that might serve as a breeding ground for communism. "The thoughtful American," he argued, was now convinced that "the most dangerous communist is the wolf in the sheep's clothing of conservatism who is bent upon preserving the policies of greed, of oppression and of Christlessness." While all of his political sermons in the early months of 1930 had dealt prominently, if not exclusively, with the perils of communism, fewer than

one-third of his broadcasts in later months of that year and the beginning of
the next made more than passing mention of the problem; and even in those,
the socialist threat was a distinctly secondary theme.[36]

For the most part, Coughlin talked in general terms. During these first
two years, he generally avoided attacking his villains by name; when he did
single out individuals, it was usually only briefly and halfheartedly. Nor did
he often focus on particular issues. He denounced "greed," "corruption," and,
increasingly, "the concentration of wealth in the hands of a few." He made
reference to the plight of laborers and farmers; he railed vaguely against
internationalism and the League of Nations; he warned against the worship
of "the God of Gold" (meaning money in general, not the gold standard in
particular); and he spoke frequently about the nation's special obligations to
its World War I veterans, even as he questioned the purposes of the war itself.
But he discussed none of these questions at length or in particular detail.[37]

There were exceptions; and one of the most prominent was the issue of
Prohibition. Nearly a third of Coughlin's thirty political sermons between the
fall of 1930 and the spring of 1932 included some extended discussion of
Prohibition; five broadcasts dealt exclusively with the subject. Coughlin as-
saulted this "ignoble experiment" with a ferocity and vindictiveness that
would later become a standard part of his repertoire, but that now stood in
glaring contrast to the usually civil tone of his broadcasts. Prohibitionists were
"fanatics," "scoundrels," and "lying voices." Their efforts had been responsible for gangsterism and lawlessness, for weakening public respect for the
Constitution. Perhaps most importantly, Prohibition had become an agent for
fanning religious hatred—for increasing antagonisms between fundamentalist
Protestants, who had become the most ardent defenders of the experiment,
and Catholics, who had been its most consistent foes.[38]

Coughlin did not begin his career as a social commentator, then, with
well-developed political theories. Nor did he have any concrete ideas about
how to deal with the Depression. Yet compared with the most prominent
competing messages, his was one of understanding and hope. From the
Hoover Administration, struggling Americans heard soothing assurances that
the crisis was merely a temporary downturn, that the economy would soon
return to normal. They heard that the problem was more psychological than
economic, that what was needed was a restoration of business confidence.
They heard reports of dramatic improvement in the economy, reports that
their own experiences belied. And later, as the Depression deepened and such
nostrums became more difficult to defend, they heard that there was little the
government could do domestically to restore prosperity, that the problem was
international and would require an international solution.[39]

From Coughlin, on the other hand, the message, diffuse as it was, was very different. The Depression was not a momentary slump, he told his listeners, but a problem deeply rooted in the economic system. The proper object for concern was not business confidence but human suffering—unemployment, deprivation, dispossession. The solution lay not in some vague notion of international cooperation, a notion he saw as simply an excuse for inaction and as a way to bolster the power of the very financiers and bankers who had caused the problem in the first place. The solution, rather, lay in a concerted effort to redefine the structure and goals of American society at home.

It was not Coughlin's message alone that accounted for his popularity. Other public figures were espousing the same sort of vague radicalism during this period without evoking a comparable response. What made Coughlin different was his medium. Commercial radio was less than six years old when Coughlin began broadcasting in 1926. The first radio network, the National Broadcasting Company, began operations that same year. Coughlin was exploiting a system of communication whose potential conventional politicians had not yet begun to appreciate. And he was exploiting it at a time when the radio was becoming central to the lives of American families. His success, therfore, was in part simply a result of luck. He was a man in the right place at the right time.

It was also a result of his extraordinary skills as a performer. Most important was the warm, inviting sound of his voice, a sound that could make even the tritest statements sound richer and more meaningful than they actually were. And there was, too, his ability to make his sermons accessible, interesting, and provocative to his audience. "I write the discourse," he once explained, "first in my own language, the language of a cleric. Then I rewrite it, using metaphors the public can grasp, toning the phrases down to the language of the man-in-the-street. . . . Radio broadcasting, I have found, must not be high hat. It must be human, intensely human. It must be simple."[40]

Simplicity did not, however, mean uniformity. Coughlin used a wide variety of rhetorical techniques: maudlin sentimentality, anger and invective, sober reasonableness, religious or patriotic fervor. Rarely did successive broadcasts strike precisely the same tone, and in this unpredictability lay much of Coughlin's appeal. He could, for example, reduce some in his audience to tears with an almost bathetic defense of American veterans, whom a leading Prohibitionist had called "perjured scoundrels" for flaunting temperance laws:

And so, buddies, thirteen years have passed [since the Armistice]!
And here I am talking about you as I wander with mistress memory
up and down the aisle of white crosses.

But somehow or other, old Sergeant W., Corporal S.—somehow as I kneel down here beside your graves I know that death has lost both its sting and its victory. I know that no fanaticism can ever defame your names. . . .

Perhaps, old smiling Corporal S., your clean, pure soul is still smiling down at me and upon the hills of North Carolina, smiling from the parapets of heaven as I kneel here beside your grave and kiss the cross and murmur my "Pater Noster." . . . [Y]ou and every other buddy whose cold corpse rests beneath these miles of white crosses—you were heroes and no "perjured scoundrels."[41]

Then, one week later, he could present a sober, straightforward explanation of how "machine competition" had affected the American worker and of how wealth had become concentrated over the past twenty-five years—an explanation filled with "concrete facts," seemingly irrefutable evidence:

According to the *New York Times* of October 1st, 1930, these dividends for the first nine months of 1930 amounted to $3,621,000,000 as compared with $2,395,000,000 during the same nine months of 1929. . . .

In the great year of prosperity, 1929, industries upon which forty per cent of our wage earners depend for a living actually employed 900,000 fewer wage earners than they did in the meager year of 1919 although the business handled was far greater. In manufacturing, our factories fabricated forty-two per cent more products with 546,-000 fewer wage earners, our railroads increased their business by seven per cent with 253,000 fewer employes.

Few listeners could understand or assimilate such detailed information (of which this quotation represents only a small portion); but that Coughlin appeared to have so many facts at his fingertips created an image of erudition and credibility.[42]

In other sermons, he invoked images from the pantheon of American heroes: La Fayette, Webster, Lincoln, Theodore Roosevelt. George Washington, for no readily apparent reason, seemed to be his favorite. "If our American institutions had done nothing else but furnished to the world the character of Washington," he once remarked, "that alone would have entitled them to the respect of mankind." But whatever historical figure he mentioned, the vanished hero was certain to be crying out from his grave about the injustices of modern American society. "What would Lincoln do were he living today?" Coughlin asked in one broadcast. He would use the same courage and love of justice he had used in his fight on behalf of the "enslaved Negro" to do battle against current economic conditions. "Here is the new problem for a new Lincoln to solve. Here is the modern industrial slavery!"[43]

And always Coughlin could invoke the rhetoric of Christianity. Every problem, sooner or later, could be explained as a failure to follow the teachings of Christ. Every example of cruelty and injustice could be traced to ignorance of, or indifference toward Biblical injunctions:

> My friends, Christ and Christianity are the only active, unassailable forces which today have compassion on the multitudes. He, the God of all wealth and power, lies in a manger, cold and impoverished. He knows what it is to suffer from hunger. He slept on hillsides in rain and storm. . . . But through all the vicissitudes of time His teachings still endure, still shine even in the darkness of our nights of sorrow.

Whenever Coughlin's discourses threatened to become controversial or provocative, he emphasized with special force that he was espousing not political but moral and religious doctrines, that he was merely applying the principles of Christianity to the world around him. Who could object to that?[44]

But some people did object—even now, when, in comparison with later speeches, Coughlin's sermons were markedly restrained. Some of the criticisms reflected simple religious bigotry, the same virulent anti-Catholicism that had motivated Coughlin to begin his broadcasts in the first place. A Baptist minister in Washington, D.C., for example, expressed outrage at the "audacity of an eulogy of Lincoln by a Jesuit, after their connection with his assassination." Others were the angry responses of conservatives who interpreted Coughlin's sermons (correctly) as an attack upon them. An Indiana man, incensed at Coughlin's criticisms of President Hoover, charged, "You play to the galleries and the minds of the good honest simple folks. . . . You have not expressed a kindly encouraging word for a living soul engaged in the work of trying to rehabilitate commerce." Still others questioned not the specific content of Coughlin's broadcasts but the propriety of a priest engaging in political controversy. William Cardinal O'Connell, the conservative leader of the Archdiocese of Boston, made this point most bluntly: "The priest has his place, and he had better stay there."[45]

The most serious objection to Coughlin's early sermons, however, came from CBS, the network that was broadcasting them. The radio industry, subject to more government regulation than most private enterprises, was always sensitive to official displeasure. In the early 1930s, with the relationship between government and radio still undefined, fledgling organizations like

CBS were particularly nervous about offending the federal establishment. Coughlin had been injecting politics into his sermons for less than a year when the network apparently decided that he was going too far, and in January of 1931 they quietly but pointedly suggested that he "tone down" his future broadcasts.[46]

Coughlin responded, as he usually did to challenges, with belligerent defiance. Taking to the air at his normal time on January 4, he announced that he would not discuss the topic originally scheduled for the hour, but would talk instead about a more immediate problem: radio censorship. His sermon was an impassioned defense of "free speech" and, by implication, a searing indictment of CBS. Next Sunday, he announced at the conclusion of the hour, he would deliver the discourse originally scheduled for that day, a discussion of the Treaty of Versailles.[47]

He could hardly have scripted a sequence of events more likely to redound to his own benefit. The publicity surrounding the controversy was enormous. CBS, flooded with letters from Coughlin's followers protesting the interference, was suddenly on the defensive, explaining weakly that it had no intention of "censoring" Coughlin, that his future on the network was purely "up to him." In Royal Oak, Coughlin spent the week sending out letters and talking to reporters, building up interest in what he liked to call "the unpreachable sermon" he would deliver the following Sunday. The January 11 discourse, entitled "Prosperity," was indeed his most provocative to date, tracing the events leading up to the Peace of Versailles and blaming on that "evil" document many of the nation's present financial woes. But it was hardly the inflammatory statement that the publicity had suggested. The result, nevertheless, was virtually the same as if it had been; Coughlin was now more widely known and, among those galvanized by the controversy, more intensely admired than ever before.[48]

For CBS, the affair was a considerable embarrassment. But more important to the network was that Coughlin continued to deliver what broadcasting (and government) officials considered "inflammatory" sermons. When his contract expired in April of 1931, CBS refused to renew it, deceiving no one with its explanation that the decision had nothing to do with Coughlin himself, but simply reflected a new network "policy" against selling air time to religious groups. The National Broadcasting Company was similarly evasive but equally adamant. It could offer no broadcasting time to Coughlin.[49]

By now, however, corporate approval meant little to him. His reputation was secure, his popularity undeniable. With little difficulty, he organized his own network. Beginning again with WJR in Detroit, the Radio League of the Little Flower arranged individual contracts with eleven private stations in the East and Midwest. By the middle of 1932, there were more than twenty; and by the end of 1934, Coughlin could be heard on over thirty stations, a network that excluded few areas of the nation. Occasional conflicts with individual stations erupted, but Coughlin could simply threaten to take his business to a competitor. In the end, few owners were willing to risk losing so popular a program.[50]

In the absence of public-opinion polls or reliable audience measurements, it was impossible to gauge with any precision either the composition or the size of Coughlin's following. The priest himself claimed that his listeners were a varied group, that as many were Protestant as Catholic, that some were Jewish. There is no evidence to suggest that he was wrong, and, given the relatively ecumenical tone of his early broadcasts, such a response would hardly be surprising. There was, however, considerable evidence, if imprecise, that Coughlin's audience was large and growing. Contributions from listeners were making even the burden of buying national radio time seem light. As if to provide tangible evidence of his strength, Father Coughlin gave a picnic for children on the grounds of his church in the spring of 1931; nearly 20,000 people showed up. Newspapers around the country ran stories each Monday about the radio sermon of the day before, and national magazines carried feature articles about the phenomenal success of the "Radio Priest." At the White House, Herbert Hoover was receiving letters from Coughlin followers, enclosing printed copies of radio sermons and warning the President to follow the priest's advice or, as one said, "lose the vote of myself, my wife and all others I can turn against the administration policies as they exist today."[51]

This last response and others like it were beginning late in 1931 and early in 1932 to concern some political figures and intrigue others. Until now, Coughlin had remained aloof from partisan politics, had restricted his sermons to broad issues and moral generalities. But were he to attempt to exercise more direct public influence, were he to involve himself overtly in governmental affairs and in political campaigns, there was no way to predict how powerful he might become. Coughlin was perhaps more aware of the possibilities than anyone else; and during this period, even while his broadcasts remained relatively vague and muted, he was begininning to consider ways to move more directly and forcefully into the national political arena.

V

DURING EACH WEEK of the broadcasting season, which normally ran from October to early April, Coughlin would retire to his study on Friday night or Saturday morning to prepare his sermon. Normally, he had by then sketched out his ideas and discussed them with Bishop Gallagher, but it was during the weekend that he did the real work. Closeted in his office alone, he would write and rewrite, read the sermon to himself, and consult his extensive library of reference works, magazine articles, and newspaper clippings. An assistant would bring meals in on a tray and leave quietly, or Coughlin might prepare a light supper for himself in a small kitchen adjacent to his study. On Sunday morning, he would emerge, often having had little or no sleep, and spend the morning celebrating mass and attending to normal parish duties. Finally, at 3:00 P.M., Coughlin would sit down at his microphone, listen to a bit of organ music and some singing from a male choir, and announce the beginning of the "Golden Hour of the Little Flower."[52]

It was hard work, and, perhaps more importantly to Coughlin, it was lonely work. In the early years, moreover, it was not tempered by many personal contacts during the rest of the week. Father Coughlin, the man who spoke to millions, the man who communicated by mail with more people than anyone else in America, lived a rather solitary life. He saw his parishioners, of course, his colleagues at the Shrine, and his parents. He spoke frequently with Leo Fitzpatrick of WJR, who had become a close friend, and with Bishop Gallagher, who continued to support and encourage him. But otherwise his personal network was small. For Coughlin, a man whose self-image required constant attention and approval, such a situation was not likely to remain tolerable for long. Early in 1930, therefore, he began to expand his world.

Coughlin's first political public appearance was a direct result of the virulently anti-communist tone of his early sermons. Hamilton Fish, Jr., scion of a great New York political family, conservative Republican Congressman, and relentless crusader against communism, was in Detroit in July 1930 for two days of Congressional hearings on the subject of domestic subversion. He asked Coughlin to appear as a witness. It was a heady honor for a priest who had only months earlier made his first tentative steps into public affairs, and Coughlin determined to make the most of it. Although in his radio sermons he had so far avoided personal attacks, he calmly sat down in the committee's hearing room, folded his arms, and announced that "The greatest force in the movement to internationalize [i.e., communize] labor throughout the world is Henry Ford." Through ignorance, rigidity, and greed, he explained, Ford and industrialists like him were responsible for conditions that were driving workers toward socialism. Fish, who had expected something quite different from his witness, interrupted him repeatedly, attempting to soften the denunciations and turn the testimony back to the communists themselves; but Coughlin's message came through. It was one of his first public statements to receive wide press attention in Detroit and elsewhere; and although not until considerably later did Coughlin bring a similarly inflammatory tone to his radio sermons, his experience at the hearing—the crowds jostling to see him, the flashbulbs popping, the august committee members listening respectfully to his remarks—was one he was not likely to forget.[53]

At the same time, Coughlin was cultivating political friendships closer to home, most notably with Detroit's new Democratic mayor, Frank Murphy. Coughlin had been friendly with Murphy and his Irish-Catholic family almost since the priest's arrival in Detroit in 1923. The two men had communicated only socially during the late twenties, when Murphy was a Recorder's Court judge and Coughlin a purely religious figure, but they developed a more intense and more political relationship as their public careers expanded in the early thirties. Coughlin encouraged Murphy's political ambitions and privately supported his successful mayoralty campaign in 1930 (in a special election resulting from the recall of the inept incumbent, Charles Bowles). He lauded Murphy's record during his first year in office and supported him again when he ran for a full term late in 1932. Murphy, in return, became a member of the Radio League of the Little Flower, flattered Coughlin constantly by asking for advice, and invited him frequently to his home. In 1933, when Coughlin traveled to Washington for the inauguration of Franklin Roosevelt, he stayed with the Murphy family in their suite at the Mayflower Hotel. Later, when Murphy was serving as Governor General of the Philippines, Coughlin was a consistent and voluble correspondent.[54]

Coughlin was also beginning to seek out ideological advice, and for this he looked beyond Detroit. Sometime late in 1931 or early in 1932, during a visit to New York, he became acquainted with two disenchanted Eastern financiers who were to become significant forces in his intellectual development. Robert M. Harriss was an influential member of the New York Cotton Exchange as well as the owner of vast tracts of farmland in the South. Concerned about plummeting farm prices and the scarcity of liquid currency, he began in the early years of the Depression seriously to question the nation's financial system. His friend George LeBlanc was equally troubled. Once a prominent international gold-trader and banker, LeBlanc, too, was harshly critical of the international banking practices of which he had been a part. By late 1932, Harriss and LeBlanc were in frequent contact with Coughlin, writing him often and even traveling occasionally to Detroit for long conversations about economic issues.[55]

Less clear was Coughlin's relationship with Pennsylvania Congressman Louis McFadden. A voluble and erratic figure, McFadden was one of the Congress's severest critics of the Versailles Treaty, a persistent advocate of monetary reform, and, increasingly in the early thirties, an outspoken anti-Semite. Whether Coughlin and McFadden were "close friends," as some

observers have suggested, and whether McFadden was influential in Coughlin's later turn to anti-Semitism, as others have claimed, is difficult to determine. But the two men did maintain some communication. It was, for
example, information supplied to Coughlin by McFadden that formed the
basis for the controversial "Prosperity" sermon about the Versailles Treaty in
January 1931.[56]

By the spring of 1931, Coughlin was ready to leap even more directly into
public controversy. On April 27, he stood before a crowd of 2,000 at the
annual communion breakfast of the New York Fire Department's Holy Name
Society and delivered a resounding defense of the embattled Mayor of New
York, Jimmy Walker. How Coughlin reached the dais, whether at the invitation of the Society, at the urging of Walker, or on his own initiative, is not
clear. But it is not difficult to speculate upon his reasons for wanting to
appear.[57]

Jimmy Walker had been Mayor of New York since 1926, a representative
of the now-fading Tammany Hall, a protégé, originally, of former Governor
Al Smith. He was a man of enormous charm, an impeccable dresser, an
eloquent speaker, a popular figure in New York's nightspots. He was also a
generally unsuccessful mayor. Incompetent as an administrator, he was unable or unwilling to keep graft and corruption even within the rather generous
limits usually tolerated in New York. He seemed always to be vacationing in
Florida or California, remaining visible to his constituents through newspaper
pictures showing him basking on beaches or beside pools surrounded by pretty
young women. Yet Walker remained, like Frank Murphy in Detroit, a popular hero to his city's Irish Catholics; and when reformers began in 1931 a series
of investigations of his administration that threatened to drive him from office,
the New York Irish rose to his defense, perceiving in the public attacks the
same kind of religious and ethnic bigotry they had resisted for decades.
Walker himself added to the hysteria surrounding the controversy by charging
that a "communist plot" to destroy him was afoot.[58]

For Coughlin, probably unaware that the evidence against Walker was
so overwhelming that he would survive in office hardly another year, the
situation must have seemed enormously inviting. An Irish-Catholic mayor,
the champion of the immigrant and the workingman, was battling the aristocratic defenders of the old order. Walker's self-righteous critics, Coughlin
seemed to be reasoning, were the same men whose blindness and cupidity were
preparing the way for socialism or communism. It would not be surprising if
the communists themselves, realizing that Walker's popularity among the
common people threatened their own plans, were secretly encouraging the
attacks upon the Mayor. In his speech in New York, Coughlin portrayed
Walker as a beleaguered innocent, a man whose only crime was that he was

popular and that he was an Irish Catholic. He had make mistakes, to be sure. "The Chief Executive of your city never was an angel," Coughlin admitted. But he was, when all was said and done, a good and decent man who deserved public support. The speech concluded with an appropriately dramatic flourish. As Coughlin finished his remarks, a commotion began in the rear of the hall, and Jimmy Walker himself strode into the room. While 2,000 Catholic firemen rose to cheer him, the Mayor walked to the dais, warmly embraced Coughlin, and whispered a quiet "Thanks." "Don't mention it," Coughlin replied.[59]

Coughlin should have been thanking Walker; for, while the speech ultimately did the New York Mayor little good, the publicity surrounding it (it was reported widely in the local press and carried live over two New York radio stations) moved Coughlin more directly into the center of the city's, and to some extent the nation's, political consciousness. New Yorkers who would soon repudiate or forget Jimmy Walker—he resigned in disgrace in September 1932—would long retain memories of Father Coughlin, the disinterested observer who had risen to his defense.[60]

Six months later, another impressive crowd gathered to hear Coughlin, this time in Royal Oak at the base of the recently completed Charity Crucifixion Tower, where dedication ceremonies were in progress for the first stage of the new Shrine of the Little Flower The six-story granite structure was elaborately decorated—topped with an enormous sculpture of Christ on the Cross, surrounded by carvings of archangels, seraphim, and saints, adorned with a prominent balcony from which speakers could address crowds in the large plaza below. At night, the tower was to be illuminated with floodlights so it would be visible from miles away. And in the glare of the lights could be seen a particularly prominent figure: a representation of the Archangel Michael, the Biblical warrior and conqueror of Satan, whose carved features clearly resembled those of Bishop Michael Gallagher.[61]

That the occasion was as political as it was religious in nature was apparent from a glance at the program. There was a full complement of Church officials, including Joseph Schrembs, Bishop of the Diocese of Cleveland, who praised Coughlin as a leader not only of religious but of secular thought. There was a speech by Bishop Gallagher, broadcast by radio from his home, where he was confined because of illness. There were clergymen and lay officials from the Royal Oak parish, beaming with pride in their new church and in their famous priest, who had built it. There were also Frank Murphy, Democratic Mayor of Detroit, William Brucker, Republican Governor of Michigan, and numerous other members of the city and state governments and of leading political organizations.[62]

Coughlin may not have expected or wanted this kind of prominence when he began his radio broadcasts in 1926. He may have been as surprised and as disconcerted as many of his colleagues in the Church by the sensation he was creating in Detroit and beyond. But, having tasted the limelight, he was not about to give it up. Whether because he believed his message was indispensable to the American people, or because the acclaim he was receiving was indispensable to him, Coughlin was looking ahead to an even deeper involvement in the political life of the nation.

5

"Roosevelt or Ruin"

NOT UNTIL 1932 did Coughlin finally meet Franklin Roosevelt, the man with whom, for better or worse, his public career was to become inextricably entwined. But the future President had been aware of Coughlin's possible usefulness for some time. In the spring of 1931, he had received a letter from a relative in Detroit who described not only Coughlin's political strength but his interest in the Roosevelt campaign. "He would like to tender his services," the message stated, and the candidate should take the offer seriously. For Coughlin "has a following just about equal to that of Mr. Ghandi [sic]. . . . He would be difficult to handle and might be full of dynamite, but I think you had better prepare to say 'yes' or 'no.' "[1]

For nearly a year, Roosevelt said nothing. Finally, after Frank Murphy interceded early in 1932, he and Coughlin met for a conference in Roosevelt's town house in New York. No record of the meeting survives; but by the time it was over, Coughlin had apparently resolved whatever doubts he might still have harbored and had enthusiastically committed himself to the Roosevelt drive for the Presidency.[2]

Why he did so was difficult to determine. By 1932, aglow with the successes of his early excursions into politics, Coughlin was eager for an even larger role in public life and was casting about for an appropriate vehicle. It was clear that that vehicle would not be Herbert Hoover, whose economic policies Coughlin had long ago rejected as hopelessly outmoded. But why Franklin Roosevelt? Most American Catholics in the early thirties still looked to Al Smith for political leadership; and Coughlin's own relations with Smith, although they were later to sour, were warm and cordial. Coughlin may have been impressed by Roosevelt's relatively progressive record in New York. He may have been converted by Frank Murphy, an early Roosevelt enthusiast. He may have reasoned that Roosevelt was a strong candidate for nomination and election while Smith was not.[3]

Or he may simply have succumbed to Franklin Roosevelt's famous charm, for he was always susceptible to flattery, and the future President was always quick to dispense it. Once Roosevelt had decided that Coughlin would be useful to his political strategy—a strategy centered on an effort to bridge the gulf between the Democratic Party's rural Protestant and urban Catholic wings—he showered the priest with attention and compliments and soon won him over completely. When, for example, Coughlin wrote him a few months after their first meeting to ask his help on behalf of the embattled Jimmy Walker, Roosevelt responded with the evasiveness for which he would later become famous. But he was careful to include lavish thanks for Coughlin's interest and to add his hope "that I shall have the privilege of seeing you again."[4]

Coughlin's enthusiasm for Roosevelt only increased as the campaign progressed. He could not, he informed the candidate after the Democratic National Convention, openly endorse him (even though he had attended the convention and worked quietly for Roosevelt's nomination). As a priest, he must maintain a technical neutrality. He could, however, give valuable public support to Roosevelt's political views. ("Already I have twenty-six of the most powerful stations grouped in our network," he reminded the candidate.) While he never mentioned Roosevelt by name in his broadcasts during the 1932 campaign, the ferocity of his attacks upon Hoover left little doubt where his sympathies lay. When Roosevelt won a resounding victory in November, faring particularly well in urban Catholic districts where Coughlin considered his influence strongest, the priest interpreted the results as evidence of his own contribution to the Democratic cause. When the President-elect invited him to Washington for the inauguration the following March, Coughlin assumed that Roosevelt had reached a similar conclusion.[5]

With the new Administration safely installed in office, Coughlin no longer felt any inhibitions about making his loyalties public and explicit. Throughout most of 1933, his radio sermons were so lavish in praise of the President as to be almost embarrassing. Sprinkling his speeches with slogans such as "Roosevelt or Ruin!" or "The New Deal is Christ's Deal!," he showered tributes not only upon Administration actions that were clearly compatible with his own proposals, but upon those that seemed directly contradictory to them. The man who had been urging payment of the soldiers' bonus for more than two years happily endorsed Roosevelt's Economy Act, which reduced government payments to veterans. It was, he explained, simply a long-overdue effort to cut government waste and purge Washington of "racketeers."[6]

There seemed at times to be no limit to his enthusiasm for the new President. Opponents of the Administration were "crack-brained publicity seekers" spewing "damnable lies." "I have listened to that tommy-rot," he snapped, "and I am just about surfeited with it." Members of the President's circle became selfless heroes simply as a result of their allegiance to Roosevelt. "How inspiring it was to find Vice-President Garner and his wife working at their desks through long, tedious hours as if they were the humblest clerks in Washington," he gushed in a particularly rapturous moment. "How impressive the dynamic activity of James Farley! How inspiring to sense the atmosphere of humility, of determination and of sterling honesty which was manifest in every member of the Government from the head of the Cabinet down to the lowliest officer!"[7]

He was equally fulsome in his private communications with the White House. Hardly a major speech or legislative action passed in 1933 without inspiring a Coughlin letter, telegram, or telephone call offering warm words of approval. "I want you to convey to the President for me my most sincere congratulations," he wrote a White House assistant after one Roosevelt speech. "He is magnificent." To the President himself, after an economic address, he wired that "All America rejoices in . . . your speech last night." And after Roosevelt's first Fireside Chat, Coughlin conveyed what must have been the highest praise he could envision: "As far as radio is concerned he is a natural born artist."[8]

For a time, members of the Administration did not know quite what to make of their new ally. They were grateful for his support, but they were vaguely uneasy about him nevertheless. Roosevelt himself, reportedly, was suspicious of Coughlin from the first day they met. Just as he did Huey Long, he considered Coughlin an unpredictable and potentially dangerous figure, a "demagogue" who should be tolerated and hopefully "tamed" but never trusted. And while the President considered Long vaguely engaging, he harbored a genuine dislike of Coughlin, whose arrogance and presumptuousness he tolerated only with difficulty.[9]

Other members of the Administration soon developed a similar distaste, for Coughlin rapidly became something of a pest. In his communications with the White House, he expressed not only rapturous enthusiasm but, increasingly, an irritating assumption of intimacy. In letters to the President's secretary, Marvin McIntyre (who served as the White House intermediary with the priest and whom Coughlin chummily addressed as "Mac"), he referred to Roosevelt familiarly as "the Boss," shared little jokes and anecdotes, and talked bluntly about internal White House matters as if he were himself a member of the Administration. He made frequent trips to Washington for no apparent reason other than that they gave him a pretext for "stopping by" at the White House. He telephoned McIntyre and other Administration officials frequently with unsolicited advice and offers of unwanted assistance.[10]

Still, Coughlin was too influential a figure to be antagonized lightly, and Roosevelt and his staff were willing to put up with a great deal. They were unfailingly polite (Roosevelt almost always instructed his assistants to respond to the priest with a "nice letter"). Even when deflecting a Coughlin request, as they often had to do, they took care to disguise the rejection. To one breezy announcement that Coughlin planned to "drop in" on the President, McIntyre responded by explaining that Roosevelt's schedule was full. But he added soothingly that he would gladly relay to the President "anything you want me to take up with him"; and he sent Coughlin an address where he could be reached while Roosevelt was vacationing in Hyde Park.[11]

Administration leaders could not, however, long ignore the growing ideological differences between Coughlin and the Administration, differences that emerged in part from a gradual transformation of the "Golden Hour of the Little Flower." By late 1932, Coughlin was no longer restricting himself to vague expressions of populist and progressive themes. He was arguing now for specific economic reforms, reforms that the new Administration would find at first troubling and ultimately entirely unacceptable.

II

THE PRESCRIPTION for the economy Coughlin offered beginning in 1932 had many facets, and even its most important components seemed at times to change almost weekly. At its core, however, the message was clear and relatively consistent: the problem of the Depression was a problem of money and banking; only by reforming the currency and restructuring the nation's financial institutions could the government hope to restore prosperity.

Many factors had conspired to create the Great Depression, Coughlin explained, but one loomed larger than all the others: a "cursed famine of currency money which blights our progress and which multiplies starvation," a famine sustained by greedy bankers and financiers who had subverted the economic system to their own ignoble ends. Yet, while the problem was obvious, the solution had remained elusive. "Any proposal to destroy this famine of money," he complained, "is called radical and unsound. Any attempt to restore the purchasing power of the dollar to what it was is considered inflationary." Only by rejecting such fallacies, he insisted, only by removing control of the financial system from the hands of self-interested "plutocrats," only by pumping more and cheaper currency into the economy could there be any hope for recovery.[12]

At first, Coughlin's public statements extended little beyond these basic premises. By the beginning of 1933, however, he had become more specific.

Denouncing America's rigid adherence to the gold standard ("Wedded to the false philosophy that gold is the value and not the measure; that it is the master and not the servant . . . we have been overwhelmed by catastrophe"), he urged immediate revaluation—a doubling of the price of gold per ounce from the present level of $20.67 to $41.34. The government would thus be able to issue twice as much currency on the basis of its existing gold supply. Revaluation would encourage, indeed, almost force the wealthy to put their "hoarded dollars" back into circulation; it would enable debtors to bear mortgages and other loans more easily; it would promote peace by making America's allies better able to repay their wartime debts; and, most important of all, it would stimulate the economy sufficiently to restore jobs and create prosperity for all. Coughlin stopped short of claiming that gold revaluation would alone solve the nation's economic problems, but he implied strongly that little more would be necessary. For nearly a year, he dwelt upon the issue incessantly.[13]

By late 1933, however, he realized that he needed a new approach. For Franklin Roosevelt, in one of the first acts of his Presidency, had done very much as Coughlin had suggested and announced that the United States was unilaterally abandoning the traditional gold standard as the basis for its currency. Six months later, the Administration declared an even bolder monetary strategy. The government would buy gold in an effort to drive up its price and increase the number of dollars in circulation. Coughlin lauded both developments as examples of "inspired leadership"; but it was quickly apparent that, whatever palliative effects revaluation might have, it was not going to end the Depression by itself.[14]

Faced with this discomforting realization, Coughlin turned to a second monetary proposal: the remonetization of silver. It was far from a new idea, and Coughlin's was far from the only voice to promote it. Silver-backed currency had been the constant demand of agrarian dissidents, Western miners, and many others for nearly sixty years; and the issue had gathered new momentum almost as soon as the Depression had begun. Even in 1933, when Roosevelt seemed on so many issues to have almost unlimited latitude to behave as he liked, pressure from silverites in Congress grew so strong that the new Administration ultimately had to bow to it. The President did not, at heart, believe in bi-metallism. ("Bryan killed the remonetization of silver in 1896," he once said privately to an argumentative Senator.) But he agreed nevertheless to legislation that would permit, although not require, him to begin issuing currency on the basis of silver.[15]

Coughlin urged the Administration to do more. By the end of 1933, silver remonetization had taken the place that gold revaluation had once occupied in his radio sermons. Week after week, Coughlin recounted the "fraudulent" process by which the dollar had been divorced from silver after the Civil War and the "wholesome, honest" impact a restoration of the metal would have. He urged a "new American dollar, which contains approximately 25 cents in gold and 75 cents in silver," a ratio that assigned to silver a value far below its "real" worth but still significantly above its present "artificial" level. The results he claimed could be expected from silver remonetization resembled those he had once claimed could be expected from a revaluation of gold: an end to "foreclosures and bankruptcies," a stabilization of the banking system, the elimination of "so-called panics," and the emergence of a "sound and adequate currency" that would "bring to a speedy end the continuance of unemployment."[16]

Like gold revaluation, silver did not long remain the central tenet of Coughlin's philosophy. By 1934, for reasons he never explained, he had moved on to other concerns. Beginning in November of that year, most of his radio discourses and other public statements centered on a set of "Sixteen Principles of Social Justice," which were, he claimed, the basis of his public philosophy.* These principles said nothing about specific schemes for inflation—nothing about gold revaluation, nothing about silver. Instead of measures to change the *composition* of the currency, they urged reforms that would shift *control* of it from private bankers to the federal government. "I believe in the abolition of the privately owned Federal Reserve Banking system," read the sixth of Coughlin's Credo-like sixteen points, "and in the establishment of a Government-owned Central Bank." Stated the seventh: "I believe in rescuing from the hands of private owners the right to coin and regulate the value of money, which right must be restored to Congress where it belongs."[17]

In his sermons, he expanded on these skeletal proposals. Early in 1935, he proposed legislation to create a "Bank of the United States of America," an institution that would replace the hopelessly banker-dominated Federal Reserve System with a true "financial democracy." The new bank would be controlled not by governors appointed from the financial world, as the Federal Reserve was, but by popularly elected representatives, one from each state. It would be authorized to issue currency, "which shall be full legal tender at face value," and it would be mandated to retire within a year all outstanding paper money issued by other institutions. Ultimately, the notes of the Bank of the United States would be the nation's only legal currency.[18]

Implicit in all this was an assumption that the new bank would expand the currency supply; indeed, Coughlin's proposed legislation made passing mention of the bank's right to "purchase or sell gold, silver, foreign exchange instrumentalities, or the obligations of foreign governments . . . to regulate the value of money of the United States and of foreign nations." But the specific

*See Appendix III.

The Long family at home in New Orleans. From left to right: Palmer, Rose McConnell, Huey, Russell, Rose. *(Wide World Photos)*

Long speaks in Magnolia, Arkansas, during the 1932 campaign for Hattie Caraway. *(United Press International Photo)*

Long and John Overton during Senate hearing on charges of fraud in Overton's election to Congress. *(United Press International Photo)*

With cheerleaders at L.S.U. *(Louisiana State Museum)*

National Guardsmen surround Long during tense 1934 Louisiana election. *(Wide World Photos)*

Senators Joseph T. Robinson and Hattie Caraway of Arkansas. *(Arkansas History Commission)*

Coughlin listens, hat in hand, as Bishop Michael J. Gallagher of Detroit (seated) talks with reporters. *(United Press International Photo)*

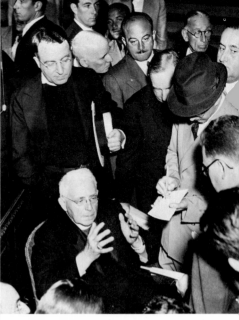

Left: Coughlin speaks from stone pulpit of the new Shrine of the Little Flower on the occasion of the dedication of the Shrine's tower in 1931. *(Wide World Photos) Below:* The Shrine as it appeared shortly after its completion in 1936. *(United Press International Photo)*

Above: Governor Eugene Talmadge of Georgia wearing his celebrated red galluses. *(Wide World Photos) Left:* Senator Theodore Bilbo of Mississippi. *(United Press International Photo) Below:* Dr. Francis Townsend addresses a meeting of a chapter of his Old Age Revolving Pension organization. *(Wide World Photos)*

Above left: Long watches a session of the Louisiana House of Representatives from the speaker's rostrum with Speaker Allen Ellender on September 9, 1935. Fifteen minutes later, he would be fatally wounded in a nearby corridor. *(Wide World Photos)*

Below left: Long's coffin being carried out of the Louisiana State House in Baton Rouge to the public funeral on the front lawn.

Coughlin visits the White House for the last time, January 1936. *(United Press International Photo)*

The Union Party triumvirate after Coughlin's controversial speech to the 1936 convention of the Townsend organization. From left to right: Townsend, Gerald L. K. Smith, and Coughlin, who moments before had shed his coat and clerical collar in the midst of his heated speech. *(United Press International Photo)*

Representative William Lemke speaking during the Union Party
Presidential campaign in 1936. *(Wide World Photos)*

Senator Robert M. La Follette, Jr.
("Young Bob"), of Wisconsin.
(Culver Pictures)

course the government would follow to inflate the currency was now less important than that the government seize full control of the financial system. "Need I explain the chief error of capitalism any further?" he cried in mock desperation during one sermon. "Need I ask you if you favor the principle . . . of permitting bankers to manufacture their own money, to expand and contract currency at will . . .?"[19]

From gold revaluation to remonetization of silver to nationalization of the banking-and-currency system—Coughlin moved with so few apparent qualms from one proposal to another that it seems surprising at first that anyone could keep track of where he stood. Yet while Coughlin's contemporaries often found his shifting positions on other matters confusing, seldom did they make much mention of the changes in his economic programs. One reason, undoubtedly, was that the proposals were to some extent cumulative. Coughlin may have shifted his emphasis, but he never repudiated his earlier demands as he moved on to others. At times, he argued that they were all of a piece. In one sermon, for example, he listed what he said were the "rungs" in "the ladder which leads to the plane of prosperity." The first rung was gold revaluation; the second, remonetization of silver; and the third, the establishment of a government bank "which will issue currency and credit."[20]

Above all, however, Coughlin's audience could remain untroubled by his frequently changing positions because beneath each of his proposals lay two common assumptions: that money was artificially scarce, and that bankers and financiers were the chief obstacles to constructive change. Inflate the currency and wrest control of the monetary system from the "plutocrats," he was saying, and a reinvigorated economy would inevitably emerge, an economy more efficient in the production of wealth and more just in its distribution. The details of Coughlin's economic program accounted for his popularity far less than these unchanging principles.[21]

Like Huey Long, Coughlin became, as he promoted these proposals and attacked those who opposed them, a target of denunciation from critics who believed his plans to be economically unfeasible and socially disruptive. His economic positions were, charged the *Nation* in 1934, "based upon the theory that the imbecility of the plain people is usually greatly underestimated. . . . He illustrates perfectly the way of the demagogue." And, like Long, Coughlin in some respects deserved the label. There was in his prescriptions for recovery an alluring and deceptive simplicity, an implication that a few painless alterations in the banking-and-currency system would restore prosperity. More complicated problems of distribution and investment received no attention. What was left was, in large part, a simplistic promise of quick and easy wealth.[22]

Yet, just as Long's Share Our Wealth Plan cannot be dismissed as mean-

ingless nonsense, so Coughlin's monetary proposals were something more
than mere demagoguery. He exaggerated when he claimed that monetary
problems were alone responsible for the Depression, that "Wall Street" and
the "international bankers" had singlehandedly precipitated the crisis. But in
directing attention to the scarcity of currency in the 1930s, and in attacking
the blindness and intransigence of the financial establishment, he was focusing
on real and serious problems. There can be little doubt that the inflationary
policies he proposed, whatever their flaws, were generally more appropriate
for the money-starved 1930s than the hard-currency orthodoxies he was challenging.[23]

Franklin Roosevelt, however, was never willing to move nearly as far
along the road to inflation as Coughlin hoped and expected. The President
realized from the beginning that Coughlin's demands were in many ways
incompatible with his own policies. Yet for many months Coughlin himself
seemed oblivious to the growing gulf. He wrote occasionally to protest specific
Administration actions or to warn of new problems that required attention (as
he did in July, several months after Roosevelt repudiated the gold standard,
to suggest that "there has been but a psychological revaluation. . . . there must
be an issue of federal greenbacks"). Most of his public and private statements,
however, bespoke continued confidence in the President's intentions. Indeed,
although Roosevelt never gave him any reason to believe that he was planning
major inflationary steps, time and again Coughlin insisted in his radio sermons
that the Administration was preparing to do exactly that. Seizing upon vague
Presidential platitudes (like Roosevelt's statement in his Inaugural Address
that "there must be provision for an adequate but sound money"), he assured
his audience that "you can expect very prompt action . . . the President is
about to remonetize silver." It sounded as though he were making an official
announcement.[24]

Such statements were both troubling and embarrassing to the Administration. Coughlin's assumption that he was, in effect, a member of the White
House staff may have seemed preposterous to the staff itself; but to much of
the public it was eminently believable. Letters to the President alternately
praised and denounced him for relying upon Coughlin's advice. Some people
appeared to assume that the priest was actually an official in the Treasury
Department. Most disturbing of all, a number of Roosevelt supporters were
coming to believe Coughlin's assurances that major inflationary policies were
just around the corner. Expectations were being raised that the President was
unwilling or unable to fulfill.[25]

Nothing, however, so troubled members of the Administration in its first
months as Coughlin's intervention in a major banking controversy in Detroit
just after the inauguration. It was an episode that earned Coughlin national

publicity and became an important steppingstone in his public career. But it also exposed him to the White House as an untrustworthy, even devious ally.

III

IT BEGAN with one of the characteristic events of the first months of 1933: a bank failure. Shortly before Roosevelt took office, the Union Guardian Trust Company, one of Detroit's leading banks, closed its doors—only one such incident in an epidemic that was sweeping the state and the nation in that troubled winter and that threatened to destroy the financial structure of the entire country. In Detroit, there was reason for particular alarm. The closely interlocking organization of the city's banking community made it possible, even likely, that the Union Guardian failure would result in the collapse of other banks throughout the city.

The arcane structure of the Detroit banking system in 1933 is worth examining—not only because it was the basis for Coughlin's controversial statements at the time but because it illustrates the sort of irresponsible financial arrangements of the twenties and early thirties that won for bankers the hostility of so many Americans. Most of the city's banks, although nominally independent of one another, were in reality components of either of two great holding companies—one controlled primarily by the Ford family, the other, larger one by a consortium of twelve influential businessmen. With stock ownership distributed exceedingly narrowly and with a few men serving as directors of many different banks, financial abuses had become almost irresistibly easy. During the heyday of the great bull market, bank directors had borrowed liberally from their own banks (often without sufficient collateral) to finance their indulgence in the stock-buying mania of the day. After the 1929 crash, they had found themselves unable to continue payments on the loans. Virtually all Detroit's major banks had begun the Depression, therefore, with a severe shortage of capital.[26]

The problem was compounded by the behavior of the two holding companies in the three years that followed. Concerned primarily with keeping themselves afloat, the companies drained their individual units even further, using the already strained assets of the banks to pay generous dividends to the directors of the larger trusts. The First National Bank of Detroit, for example, had paid its stockholders a total of about $975,000 annually in dividends throughout most of the 1920s while it was still operating independently of the holding companies. In 1929, it fell under the control of the Detroit Bankers Company, the larger of the two great combinations; its stock, therefore, fell into the hands of the holding company's small directorship. Over the next three years, even while the bank's assets were shrinking as a result of the Depression, the dividends it paid its stockholders were soaring: to more than $1.1 million in 1930, to an astounding $4.65 million in 1931, and down to a still remarkable $2.8 million in 1932. By then, according to a later report by a national bank examiner, "the First National Bank of Detroit was not rotten —it was putrid."[27]

The collapse of the Union Guardian, therefore, frightened no one more than the directors of the rest of Detroit's banks, for they knew how inadequate the resources of their institutions were to meet a sudden large demand for cash from depositors. They responded in several ways. They succeeded first in persuading Governor William Comstock to call a statewide bank holiday beginning February 14, a holiday that continued into March when it merged with the nationwide banking moratorium that Franklin Roosevelt proclaimed during his first day in office. Granted time to resolve their difficulties, the bankers turned next to the Reconstruction Finance Corporation, pleading desperately for loans sufficient to prop up their sagging institutions. It was here that both the Roosevelt Administration and Coughlin intervened.[28]

The RFC, reluctant to approve loans to institutions so shaky, had taken no action by the time Roosevelt took office. A few weeks later, the new Treasury Department came up with an alternative plan. Instead of bailing out the existing banks, the government would insist upon a thorough reorganization of them, including a merger of the city's two largest institutions into a new Detroit National Bank. In the debate that followed, Coughlin, unsurprisingly, sided immediately with the Administration. He telephoned Marvin McIntyre in the midst of the crisis to warn of efforts by local businessmen to sabotage the President's plan; and he offered his own services in building public support for the reorganization proposal. McIntyre was evasive, but he suggested a call to Treasury Secretary William Woodin. No record survives of Coughlin's conversation with Woodin the same day, but the Secretary evidently gave him some encouragement, even if unwittingly. For that same night Coughlin made a special broadcast over WJR—a defense of the Administration's proposals that was in itself relatively mild. He made overt and repeated references to his connections in Washington ("Secretary Woodin . . . asked me to take the air . . . ," "Secretary Woodin asks me to tell this audience . . . ," etc.), portraying himself unmistakably as a spokesman for the Administration. The claims were clearly presumptuous, but Coughlin's relatively restrained discussion of the banking reorganization plan offended few and raised little comment.[29]

That, perhaps, was the trouble; for Coughlin undoubtedly envisioned attracting more attention than calm stories on page nine of the morning newspapers. In his next regular Sunday broadcast, therefore, he launched an attack on the Detroit banking community as savage as his praise of the government's merger plan had been warm. By the time of Roosevelt's inauguration, he charged, "modern banking had degenerated into a crap game where the dice were often loaded; a crap game played by the unscrupulous experts with other people's money." At the national level, it was "the Morgans, the Kuhn-Loebs, the gamblers of Wall St. . . . well assisted by the Mitchells and the Harrimans and their lieutenants in crime" who were responsible for the degeneration. But citizens of Detroit did not have to look to New York for villains; they had an ample supply immediately before them. The city's own bankers had misappropriated funds, had lied to the public about their reserve supplies (the First National Bank, for example, "was 12½ per cent liquid when depositors were being told it was 80 per cent liquid"), and had falsified their records. Singled out for special criticism was E. D. Stair, president of the larger of the holding companies and, not coincidentally, publisher of the Detroit *Free Press,* a newspaper hostile both to Coughlin and to the Administration reorganization scheme. Through it all, Coughlin wrapped himself in the mantle of the New Deal, referring repeatedly to Woodin and to other White House contacts.[30]

The response was fast and furious. For the next few weeks, Coughlin found himself at the center of a controversy so heated that many city officials feared violence might erupt. (Not without reason, it turned out, for early in the morning of April 1 a small bomb exploded in the basement of Coughlin's house; no one was injured.) Splashed across the front pages of Stair's *Free Press* every morning for days were responses to Coughlin's criticisms ("Cold Facts Refute Every Charge," stated one headline) and accusations against the priest. Coughlin himself had gambled irresponsibly in the stock market, the paper claimed, jeopardizing the funds collected from his trusting parishioners and radio audience. He had cheated on his tax returns (a charge that a federal investigation showed to be groundless). Above all, he had engaged in vicious and slanderous demagoguery. "While others of the world sought to awaken in the hearts of all mankind the peace and understanding of God," the *Free Press* noted sanctimoniously, "Father Coughlin, in a disjointed harangue that at times became hysterical, poured forth venom and vituperation." Even some of Coughlin's staunchest allies were stunned by his outbursts. Bishop Gallagher, in the closest thing to a rebuke he had ever issued to his celebrated priest, called the charges against Stair "unthinkable" and the radio address "tremendously ill-advised."[31]

Coughlin was not, however, without supporters. Mayor Frank Murphy had been lambasting Detroit's bankers for weeks before Coughlin took to the air, even going so far as to fire one member of his administration simply because he had once been a bank officer. "The banking business used to be an honorable profession," he explained, "but it has now become the curse of the country. I do not propose to allow bankers to sink my ship." While he made no public statements about Coughlin's charges, it was clear where his sympathies lay. More important, Coughlin had struck a responsive chord with much of the public. Letters to the White House during the controversy praised the priest for his "honesty," "courage," and eloquence. He was "one of the great orators of our time," wrote one admirer. "It seems that he is part of the New Deal," added another, "and let's pray that no money powers can snuff out his voice."[32]

No one was more aware of the simultaneous hatred and adoration Coughlin was arousing than the members of the new Administration in Washington. Without warning, they found themselves squarely in the middle of the controversy—praised by some and damned by others for allowing Coughlin to speak for the White House. Angered by the priest's claims to be representing the Administration ("Confidentially, I think the Reverend Father took considerable liberties with the facts," Marvin McIntyre complained in a memorandum to Presidential advisor Louis Howe, "and most certainly misquoted me"), they were at the same time unwilling to repudiate him publicly. There was a brief debate within the White House over "whether we should just pass this up or take some action." In the end the decision was to remain quiet and hope the storm would pass.[33]

By mid-April, it seemed that it had. The Detroit banks were finally reorganized and reopened, ending an almost two-month-old holiday and allowing the city's economic life to return to something approaching normal. Coughlin, after a few final blasts, had turned his attention to other issues. The *Free Press,* eager to direct attention away from its publisher's finances, dropped the matter from its pages. But the controversy had sowed seeds that would result in further trouble. Coughlin's accusations had helped launch a federal investigation of the Detroit banking system, and by the middle of August, a special grand jury had convened in the city to hear testimony. One of its first witnesses was Father Coughlin.

For three days, in a courtroom packed with spectators, reporters, and photographers and in an atmosphere that resembled a circus more than a judicial hearing, Coughlin renewed his attacks on Stair, repeated his charges against the now defunct Union Guardian and First National banks, and showered praise upon "a Protestant President who has more courage than 90 per cent of the Catholic priests in the country." It was the kind of scene he relished: government officials listening respectfully to his "expert" testimony, crowds jostling to see him, spectators murmuring in appreciation as he clenched his fists or pounded the table to emphasize points, newspapers throughout the country giving prominent coverage day after day to his testimony. When accusations against the local banking community threatened to become dull, he added new targets: Al Smith (who had criticized his tactics), the Bank of England, and Herbert Hoover (sending the former President and his friends into a sputtering but private rage). By the time it was over, Coughlin had survived new and bitter denunciations by Stair and his newspaper to emerge as a figure of greater public renown than ever before. And the White House was once more in the midst of a troubling dilemma. Not only was Coughlin acting presumptuously again, speaking for the Administration without authorization, but he was generating an enthusiastic public response that reminded the President and his colleagues of how costly a public repudiation of him could be.[34]

IV

IT WOULD BE an exaggeration to say, as some observers did in 1934 and 1935, that Father Coughlin was the second most important political figure in the United States. But his remarkable popularity during the first three years of the Roosevelt Administration often appeared to cry out for hyperbole. Coughlin's influence, it seemed, was spreading everywhere.

There is no way accurately to measure how many people were listening to his radio sermons by the middle 1930s. Even his most inveterate foes, however, had to admit that his audience was vast and widespread—at least ten million on an average Sunday, most radio experts estimated, perhaps many more than that. It was, some said, the largest regular radio audience in the world.

His voice did not reach everywhere. He had outlets in some of the border states (Maryland, Kentucky, Missouri), but none in the South, where a Catholic priest with an Irish brogue would probably have found scant sympathy. His broadcasts almost never crossed the Rocky Mountains at first; conservative station-owners on the West Coast apparently resisted him until finally he penetrated the region late in 1935. But by 1934, the Coughlin network of nearly thirty stations covered virtually every major population center in the East and Midwest. And there he was, according to *Fortune* magazine, "just about the biggest thing that ever happened to radio."[35]

The staggering flow of mail he inspired was one indication of his impact. By 1934, he was receiving more than 10,000 letters every day (65 per cent of them, he claimed, from non-Catholics), and after some broadcasts his weekly total surpassed a million. His clerical staff at times numbered more than a hundred; and although his expenses were steadily mounting, so was his income. A virtual flood of cash and postal money orders poured out of the letters opened in the basement of the Shrine of the Little Flower. One morning in 1934, Coughlin walked into his local bank to deposit $22,000—in one-dollar bills. Every week, he could be seen staggering into the local post office lugging a canvas sack heavy with postal money orders to be cashed. During a month early in 1935, the Royal Oak postmaster paid out almost $55,000 on such orders.[36]

There were other, more public signs of his popularity. When New York station WOR asked its audience in February 1934 who, other than the President, was "the most useful citizen of the United States politically in 1933," almost 55 percent of the responses named Coughlin. NRA director Hugh Johnson was a distant second. When WCAU in Philadelphia asked its listeners to choose between the "Golden Hour of the Little Flower" and the New York Philharmonic on Sunday afternoons, 112,000 letters supported Coughlin, 7,000 the Philharmonic. The first edition of Coughlin's complete radio discourses, published late in 1933, quickly sold nearly a million copies. At about the same time, Coughlin received offers of $7,500 a week from a food company that wanted to sponsor his sermons and of $500,000 from a Hollywood studio that wanted to produce a film entitled "The Fighting Priest," with Coughlin playing himself. He refused them both.[37]

That this popularity had major political implications was obvious. When in a broadcast late in 1933, for example, he casually suggested that his listeners write Franklin Roosevelt to express their gratitude for his inspired leadership, the White House mail room was inundated with hundreds of rapturous letters, so many that the normally swift replies were delayed up to several weeks. When Coughlin traveled to New York in November 1933 to address a rally at the Hippodrome, called to support "President Roosevelt's Sound Money Policy," lines began to form at eight o'clock in the morning before the evening meeting. By the time the doors opened, an estimated 20,000 people, three times the capacity of the hall, were blocking traffic, fighting police, and trampling one another in desperate efforts to get inside. It was "astonishing," one reporter noted, to remember that the next Presidential election was still three years off, for the meeting "had the fury and the fire of last-minute campaign rallies." Even more striking was the reaction of Coughlin's audience to his blistering attack upon Al Smith, who had become a loud and conservative critic of the New Deal in recent months. After Coughlin had lambasted him for several minutes, every reference to the once beloved Governor drew hisses and jeers. "The controversy between Father Coughlin and Al Smith is the gossip of the hour in New York," an astonished Broadway producer and political activist wrote the White House after the incident. "Al was booed Monday nite, at the Hippodrome, for the first time in his life in New York."[38]

The network of political contacts that Coughlin had begun to assemble as early as 1931 now grew rapidly. In Congress, he found new allies in both houses among members of the so-called "Progressive bloc"—advocates of forceful economic reforms and immediate inflation, mostly from the West and Midwest. He maintained a friendly correspondence with Senator Elmer Thomas of Oklahoma, who would eventually become the most loyal and fervent of his illustrious supporters. Burton K. Wheeler of Montana, one of the Senate's most vocal proponents of silver remonetization, conferred with Coughlin in Washington on inflation in 1933 and found him "very well informed." George W. Norris of Nebraska, Gerald Nye of North Dakota, William Borah of Idaho—all took steps to identify themselves both publicly and privately with Father Coughlin. Bronson Cutting of New Mexico arranged a dinner in the spring of 1934 for "35 or 40 Senators and Congressmen" to discuss New Deal economic policies. Almost as a matter of course, he included Coughlin among the guests. And when, in June of 1933, Franklin Roosevelt was assembling a delegation to attend a major economic conference in London, ten Senators (including Huey Long) and seventy-five Congressmen (largely from the Midwest, but also from as far west as California and as far south as Texas) signed a petition urging the President to appoint Coughlin as an advisor to the group. "We believe that his presence at the Conference would instill confidence in the hearts of the average citizen of our country," they explained. (The White House made no response, just as it did not respond the following year to entreaties from private citizens and a few public officials urging the President to appoint Coughlin Secretary of the Treasury.)[39]

It was not only in Washington that Coughlin attracted attention and admiration from politicians. Officials in state and city governments were likewise eager for association with the priest, as a 1935 Coughlin visit to Boston illustrated. He had been vacationing in the Berkshires in western Massachusetts when, early in August, he paid a surprise visit to Governor James Michael Curley at the statehouse on Beacon Hill. "I couldn't dream of being so disrespectful to Governor Jim as to be right in his State without going to see him," Coughlin explained. He and the Governor were "close personal friends."

Curley was ecstatic. Calling reporters into his office, he passed out cigars and beamed proudly for photographers as he presented Coughlin with a Massachusetts state flag. ("I will cherish this flag," Coughlin responded solemnly. "I will not put it in my home, but in the church where it belongs.") A few moments later, the Governor walked arm in arm with the priest to the chamber of the House of Representatives, where, to thunderous applause, Coughlin was introduced by Speaker Leverett Saltonstall and made a brief address. By the time he had finished and had begun making his way across the building to the Senate chamber, word of his presence had spread across

Beacon Hill. "To say that the popular radio priest . . . created a furor would be putting it mildly," the Boston *Globe* reported. "The business of the State stopped" as clerks, secretaries, and "the usual throng of . . . hangers-on" poured into the corridors, buzzing and shrieking and jostling to see him. The House called a recess while its members rushed to the Senate chamber for the second speech; well before Coughlin arrived, both the floor and the usually sparsely populated galleries were filled to overflowing. Again, members of the legislature stood and cheered as Coughlin spoke to them briefly about "the dangers threatening the world today such as Nazism [and] Communism." When he left the city late the same evening, the presses of the Boston newspapers were already turning out the next morning's editions with stories and pictures of Coughlin's visit emblazoned across the front pages.[40]

There were obvious political reasons for elected officials, particularly those in Irish-Catholic Boston, to want to bask in Coughlin's public glow; but even some figures not immediately dependent upon the approval of the voters were paying him respect. The League for Independent Political Action, an organization composed largely of intellectuals (John Dewey was its chairman) dedicated to exploring alternatives to traditional reform, invited Coughlin to participate in a summer institute it was sponsoring in 1933. Henry Wallace, Roosevelt's Secretary of Agriculture, worked with Coughlin for a time to try to influence Administration monetary policies and once urged a constituent inquiring about currency questions to send away for copies of Coughlin's sermons. Raymond Moley, one of the President's original "brain trusters," published a Coughlin article on inflation in early 1934 in a magazine he edited. William Aberhart, the radical Premier of the Canadian province of Alberta, traveled to Detroit in 1935 to discuss the program of his own Social Credit Party with Coughlin. He was, he explained, seeking "the most expert advice on the continent."[41]

As might be expected from a man who once boasted that he had taught the President everything he knew about economics, Coughlin reveled in the attention he was receiving and missed few opportunities to publicize (and exaggerate) his relationships with the mighty. Journalists calling on him at the Shrine of the Little Flower were treated to a frenetic, almost dazzling display of Coughlin's importance. A *New York Times* reporter, for example, visited Royal Oak in the fall of 1933 and was stunned by the pace of Coughlin's world:

> One sees him standing with a foot on the running board of a dust-covered automobile with a Maryland license plate advising a worried family not to "give up your home." An anxious cleric calls from the porch that "the Governor of Pennsylvania is on the phone." A secretary waits patiently in the front study to remind him that "you

are due in Washington for that conference with So-and-So." A long distance call from Minnesota has to do with the very unchurchly subject of the "plowing in" of pigs. "That's no way to raise prices," says Father Coughlin. "Just hang on for another week. I'm going to Washington. Everything will be all right."

His guests could be forgiven for wondering how much was reality and how much performance. Another visitor wrote later of attending one of Coughlin's Tuesday-evening "Forums" at the Shrine—public meetings at which Coughlin responded to written questions from his audience. A crowd of nearly 1,000 packed the tiny church; and after ushers had taken a collection ("Your donation makes broadcasting possible," read a sign over the door), Coughlin appeared, acting conspicuously harried and referring distractedly to the calls he was receiving from Senators, Congressmen, and governors. Visitors to Coughlin in his office would occasionally see a secretary burst officiously into the room to announce that some important public official was on the telephone. More often than not, Coughlin would wave the message aside, remarking casually that he would return the call when he had time. Public adoration had, it seemed, become an intoxicating brew.[42]

6

Searching for Power

COUGHLIN UNDOUBTEDLY REALIZED that he owed much of his new popularity to his prominent identification with Franklin Roosevelt and the New Deal. Yet such was his thirst for power and acclaim that when, early in 1934, he finally recognized that he was not to play the major role in the Administration he had envisioned, he began to explore the possibilities of charting an independent course. His break with Franklin Roosevelt was not sudden; indeed, not until 1936 would it become complete. But the days of his rapturous and unwavering support of the New Deal came to an end in the spring of 1934.

No single factor or incident soured the relationship. Coughlin's excesses of 1933 had, perhaps, begun the process, eroding what little confidence members of the Administration may once have had in him and producing an attitude from the White House that Coughlin recognized as increasingly hostile. He was particularly upset by Roosevelt's refusal to endorse or even acknowledge his defense of the President's monetary policies at the New York Hippodrome in November. Coughlin had telephoned the White House shortly before the meeting to inform McIntyre that he was "going the limit" for the President and would appreciate some informal sign of approval. There was no response. "I was never stupid," he recalled years later of the last months of 1933. "I realized the President now considered me burdensome." Yet for a while he remained confident that the men around Roosevelt had misled the President, and that Coughlin could still "win him back over to my side."[1]

At the same time, however, he was growing impatient with New Deal monetary policies. It was clear by 1934 that the President was not going to remonetize silver, as Coughlin was urging, and the confident public predictions to the contrary were ringing more and more hollow. Yet Coughlin might have been willing to swallow even this disappointment, at least for a time, had it not been for the crude tactics of the Treasury Department, which began trying to discredit members of the "silver bloc" in the spring of 1934. Late in April, Treasury Secretary Henry Morgenthau (who had succeeded Woodin) authorized the release of a list of major speculators in silver. On it was the name of Amy Collins—personal secretary to Father Coughlin. She was, the report indicated, the holder of contracts for 500,000 ounces of silver, purchased for $20,000 on behalf of the Radio League of the Little Flower. No one believed her when she explained that she had made the investment on her own initiative, that Coughlin had known nothing about it.[2]

There was, of course, nothing illegal or even necessarily unethical about investing in silver futures. Yet Coughlin's critics could now accuse him of advocating silver remonetization for the sake of personal profit. It was an embarrassing incident, one that provided the foundation for years of characterizations of Coughlin as a financial charlatan and a fraud, and one for which he never fully forgave Roosevelt. Publicly, he lashed out only at Morgenthau and some of the President's "assistants." Privately, however, he blamed Roosevelt himself. "We were supposed to be partners," he remarked acidly many years later. "He said he would rely on me. That I would be an important adviser. But he was a liar. He never took my advice. He just used me and when he was through with me he double-crossed me on that silver business." His pride wounded, Coughlin was developing a personal bitterness toward Franklin Roosevelt that would last for over three decades.[3]

Disenchantment with the New Deal now crept into Coughlin's public statements, inaugurating a period of marked ambivalence toward the Administration that continued for more than two years. Never entirely certain that his popularity could survive an open break with the President, still hopeful that Roosevelt would turn to him again for advice, Coughlin alternated erratically and often confusingly between enthusiastic support and open hostility. But the trend was unmistakable. Slowly, tentatively, he was putting distance between himself and the White House.[4]

Even before the appearance of the Morgenthau list, Coughlin had expressed reservations about the course of the New Deal. In January, in an open letter to a supporter in the House of Representatives, Coughlin urged the Congress to "take the initiative" away from the President and launch a recovery program of its own. Roosevelt's monopoly of power was, he warned, beginning to resemble a dictatorship; it was time for members of Congress to become "imbued with the idea of your personally rectifying our rotten financial system instead of becoming a group of acquiescing sycophants." On March 4, the anniversary of Roosevelt's inauguration, Coughlin reviewed the first year of the New Deal and could muster only enough enthusiasm to call it "more or less successful." He openly criticized the administration of the National Recovery Administration and charged that the Home Owners' Loan

Act, an effort to prevent foreclosures on mortgages, "has not functioned at all." One year ago, he added, "we were an optimistic people"; now, "something like consternation is beginning to be felt as the clouds of suspicion are darkening our hope."[5]

His drift away from the President accelerated in the months following his dispute with the Treasury Department. There were new criticisms of New Deal actions, but the most noticeable change was perhaps an even more ominous one: he ceased for a time to speak about the Administration much at all. While his sermons through much of 1933 had often been little more than admiring catalogues of Roosevelt initiatives, his 1934 discourses concentrated instead on Coughlin's own monetary programs, on his harsh denunciation of bankers, on his impatience with "modern capitalism," and on his vision of a reformed system that would eliminate the cruelest abuses of the present one. He did not have to speak about Roosevelt directly, for implicit in all this was Coughlin's rejection of some of the major premises of the Administration.[6]

By the end of the year, he was once again talking openly about the New Deal, and he was now making his reservations explicit. "The Democratic party," he said threateningly in November, "is merely on trial. Two years hence it will leave the courtroom of public opinion vindicated and with a new lease on life, or will be condemned to political death if it fails to answer the simple question of why there is want in the midst of plenty." And later in the same sermon: "Our Government still upholds one of the worst evils of decadent capitalism, namely, that production must be only at a profit for the owners, for the capitalist, and not for the laborer." When he spoke now about specific New Deal programs, he was more likely to mention those he detested —the crop and livestock destruction of the AAA, the cartelization that had resulted from the NRA, the restrained monetary policies that failed to offer sufficient inflation—than those he had once publicly admired. And when he insisted on his loyalty to the President, he measured his words carefully. "More than ever," he said in one of the first broadcasts of his fall 1934 season, "I am in favor of *a* New Deal."[7]

Both Coughlin's own supporters and the Administration itself, however, made it difficult for him to move quickly toward an open break. Every time he criticized the President even indirectly, he received anguished and occasionally angry responses from members of his audience imploring him to reconsider. Every time he thought the President had written him off for good, a tantalizing bit of flattery or conciliation would emerge from the White House. When Coughlin cautiously asked Marvin McIntyre for help in the fall of 1934 in securing an appointment as a naval chaplain for one of his friends, the President himself wrote the Navy Department to expedite the matter.

Several weeks later, Roosevelt received Coughlin at the White House and listened patiently for over an hour as the priest explained a proposal for allotting federal jobs to college graduates. (The President agreed to "study" the plan, but took no action on it.) And when relations became particularly strained, the President would send a friendly emissary like Frank Murphy or Joseph P. Kennedy to intercede with Coughlin and persuade him to return to the fold. He nearly always did—briefly.[8]

What made Coughlin's public statements seem particularly vacillating during this period were his painful efforts to repudiate many of the major initiatives of the New Deal without denouncing the President himself. It was an impossible task, but one Coughlin approached with alacrity. When he resumed his sermons in the fall of 1934 after his usual summer hiatus, he was once again outspoken in support of the President, yet once again ambivalent about some of the central policies of the New Deal. "It is not fair," he insisted, "for our citizens to suspect even momentarily the motives of our President. He is endeavoring to bring about a union of forces, a union of efforts." In the same sermon, however, he referred obliquely to the government as the "slave" of the "unbridled ambition" of "modern capitalism." It was a continual balancing act: at one moment, a denunciation of New Deal policies; at the next, an insistent reminder of Coughlin's continued loyalty to Roosevelt. The harsher the attack, it sometimes seemed, the more enthusiastic the ensuing praise.[9]

Despite the occasional gestures of conciliation, Franklin Roosevelt had by mid-1934 already decided privately to break with Coughlin. Thus, at the same time that some members of the White House staff were treading carefully to avoid antagonizing Coughlin, others were working quietly to undermine and perhaps to destroy him. James Farley initiated a study of the Coughlin radio network, complete with research into the finances and political connections of station owners. If the situation deteriorated too far, he may have reasoned, the Administration could use its considerable power over the broadcasting industry to force Coughlin off the air. Another government investigation examined Coughlin's finances, attempting to assess the extent and source of his wealth. The Immigration and Naturalization Service, apparently at the request of Louis Howe, undertook a study of Coughlin's citizenship status to determine whether he was living in the country legally. (They concluded that he was.) And at the top of a memorandum explaining one such inquiry was a cryptic but significant handwritten note: "Mac—This will help in your talk with Father Burke. FDR." Cautiously but deliberately, the Administration was trying to put pressure on Coughlin through the one institution capable of stopping him entirely—the Catholic Church.[10]

II

THE STORY of Coughlin's relations with his own Church during the 1930s is a confused and murky one. A controversial figure from the moment his radio sermons began, he attracted both praise and criticism from American Catholic officials until the end of his public career. Yet, despite the often outraged attacks by eminent cardinals, despite occasional indications of displeasure from the Vatican, despite Franklin Roosevelt's cautious efforts to mobilize Catholic leaders against Coughlin, the Church appeared for nearly a decade to have virtually no control over its most famous and outspoken priest.

The reason was simple: Bishop Michael J. Gallagher of Detroit. No matter how harshly Catholics elsewhere denounced Coughlin, as long as he retained the support of his own bishop, the only official outside the Vatican with any statutory control over his activities, he could operate with impunity. And Gallagher continued not only to defend but to encourage his priest even as Coughlin's sermons became harsher and more inflammatory.[11]

Coughlin's standing within the Church was important to him, both personally and politically. There is no reason to doubt his repeated claims that nothing, not even the loss of his political career, could make him abandon the priesthood. "A Catholic priest who is not a Catholic priest is a washout," he said in 1935. "I am a priest and I hope to die as one." Indeed, when in 1942 he finally did receive orders from his ecclesiastical superiors to cease his public activities, he unhappily but obediently complied. Equally important to him, perhaps, was that the priesthood—its mystique, its prestige, its image of integrity, respectability, and compassion—may have been his most valuable political asset. Time and again, Coughlin's supporters referred to his clerical status as evidence of his credibility and his selflessness. Time and again, political figures who might otherwise have openly attacked him restrained themselves for fear of appearing irreverent. The approval of his own bishop, essential as it was, was not all Coughlin needed to be concerned about. It was important, too, that he retain a reasonable standing within the Church at large, that he keep the respect and admiration of leading Catholics throughout the nation. Yet, just as he seemed unable to maintain cordial relations with the President despite the importance of such relations to his popularity, so he was increasingly incapable of, and apparently increasingly uninterested in, mollifying his critics within the Church. For the controversy that he created among Catholic leaders as early as 1931 grew steadily each year thereafter.[12]

Attacks came from many quarters: from Boston's William Cardinal O'Connell, who was opposed in principle to political activities among the clergy; from New York's William Cardinal Hayes, who resented Coughlin's 1932 appearance in Manhattan to defend that embarrassingly prominent Catholic Jimmy Walker; from clergy and laymen throughout the Church who were offended by Coughlin's harsh attacks upon Al Smith in the fall of 1933. For a time, however, Coughlin's defenders within the Church far outnumbered his detractors. Among liberals, he seemed at first to be the most eloquent and powerful spokesman for the newly revived spirit of Catholic social activism.[13]

The Catholic social-justice movement, which had displayed great strength in the early years of the century, had shown signs of ebbing during the 1920s. The Depression infused it with new life; and the appearance in 1931 of an important papal encyclical inspired even greater interest in social reform. Pius XI's *Quadragesimo Anno (After Forty Years),* like Leo XIII's influential *Rerum Novarum* of 1891, which it was intended to commemorate, called upon Catholics to re-examine the teachings of St. Thomas Aquinas and to oppose the unjust economic conditions that had created the present crisis. It is the "function of government," Pius urged, "to adjust ownership to meet the needs of the public good." Where government had a special obligation was in the case of excess wealth and power, for "a man's superfluous income is not left entirely to his own discretion."[14]

Coughlin seized upon the encyclical almost at once as justification for his own public role, and he referred to it constantly, both in his sermons and in private communications. In March 1934, he sent copies both to Marvin McIntyre (whom he urged to "Take time off—if necessary go and sit on the toilet while you read the enclosed book") and to Franklin Roosevelt (to whom he wrote somewhat more respectfully that "I hope the contents of this book will help to guide you during these troublesome days"). But Coughlin was not alone in his enthusiasm. Liberal Catholics throughout the nation interpreted the encyclical as a mandate for involvement with social problems, and they quickly moved to the fore in many areas of the Church. Taking control of existing publications or establishing new ones, they made Catholic periodicals into forceful advocates of reform. *America,* long one of the most conservative of Catholic magazines, began in 1932 to support the concept of labor unions and call for expanded government control of the economy. "Suppression of the corporation or business by the state is not merely permissible," claimed a 1932 editorial, "but the state's duty." A year later, it spoke even more strongly: "Capitalism as we have known it in this country has ever been a stupid and malicious giant." *Commonweal,* too, was expressing reservations about capitalism and echoing Pius XI's cry for reform: "the system is vicious, both ethically and ontologically. . . . capitalism degrades men to mere economic factors of cost, to be bargained for at lowest possible market prices."

Others—the radical *Catholic Worker* and the Catholic Trade Unionists' *Michigan Labor Leader*—were even more outspoken.[15]

Catholic organizations, too, began to shed the apolitical demeanor they had adopted in the 1920s and work actively for social change. The National Catholic Welfare Conference, for example, was openly critical of Herbert Hoover in 1931 and consistently urged the government to become more responsive to the needs of the unemployed. A year later, the Catholic Alumni Federation called for a reconstruction of the capitalist order. The Catholic Central Verein likewise advocated major reforms.[16]

Most important, perhaps, individual priests were becoming influential spokesmen for social justice. While none ever rivaled Coughlin in popularity or influence, several had significant impact. Father James R. Cox of Pittsburgh, for example, began in the early 1930s to broadcast political sermons over a local radio station, and he soon developed a large and impassioned following among his city's jobless. In January 1932, he addressed a shivering crowd of 60,000 in Pitt Stadium, denounced the government and the banks for their indifference and inaction, and then led a motley army of some 12,000 protesters to Washington, where he was received at the White House by an uncomfortable President Hoover.[17]

By the middle of 1933, the diffuse reform efforts of liberal Catholics had begun to congeal, and the Church's social activists became among the loudest and most enthusiastic supporters of Franklin Roosevelt and the New Deal. Virtually every major Catholic publication and organization went on record in support of the new President. Church officials, from Cardinal Mundelein in Chicago and Cardinal O'Connell in Boston to obscure parish priests throughout the nation, praised the Administration's efforts. "All Catholics who desire to give practical effect to the principles of social justice laid down by Pope Pius XI," wrote *Commonweal*, "will see that . . . Roosevelt's opportunity to lead . . . is likewise the Catholic opportunity to make the teachings of Christ apply to the benefit of all."[18]

To some such Catholics, Father Coughlin appeared for a while not only a welcome and compatible ally but the Church's brightest hope. Although organizational pronouncements and Catholic publications could influence clergy and lay officials, only Coughlin, it seemed, had ready access to the Catholic masses. The man most aware of Coughlin's potential importance was Father John A. Ryan, a professor of theology at Catholic University in Washington. A leader of the National Catholic Welfare Conference, an outspoken admirer of Pius XI's teachings, and a harsh critic of traditional capitalism, he had long been one of the most prominent and influential of the Catholic liberals. It was his influence, perhaps more than anyone else's, that persuaded Church intellectuals to support Roosevelt. And he attempted simultaneously to convince his colleagues of the importance of Coughlin's work as well. Coughlin was "on the side of the angels," he claimed after the 1933 Al Smith imbroglio, and was performing an essential and difficult task:

> . . . he is stirring up the animals, and that has got to be done by some one. The masses are sluggish-minded and have not shown any faint signs of rebellion until recently. The recovery program opposed by the moneyed interests cannot be carried through on an intellectual plane alone. The masses must be enlisted to fight for it before you can put it over. Father Coughlin is arranging that kind of thing to a considerable extent, and in doing so is a useful citizen.[19]

It was, however, conditional praise. Catholic intellectuals such as Ryan were willing to defend Coughlin, even to praise him, as long as his message remained compatible with their own. But they never considered him an intellectual equal. He was performing a useful service by bringing the messages of the encyclicals to the masses, but that did not make him a serious social theorist or a real leader among Catholic liberals. Thus, in 1934, when Coughlin began to repudiate Franklin Roosevelt, whom Ryan and most other Catholic liberals continued strongly to support, his standing among them started to erode.

Open criticism of Coughlin was slow to emerge, but by early 1935 the warm references to him by other Church activists, the indications that they considered him a welcome ally, had all but ceased. *Commonweal,* for example, commented less and less frequently on Coughlin's activities throughout 1934; and in the spring of 1935, it remarked that he was "following up the work begun through his radio addresses with extraordinary personal success, but with extremely dubious results." John Ryan, beginning along the road that would by 1936 take him to an ugly, open confrontation with Coughlin, issued intermittent rebuttals in 1935 to Coughlin's attacks upon the Roosevelt Administration.[20]

Occasionally, evidence of lingering collegiality would surface briefly. Increasingly, however, its character suggested less admiration for Coughlin than a general defensiveness among Catholics against attacks from outsiders, a lingering sensitivity to the anti-Catholic prejudice that had afflicted the Church in the 1920s. When, for example, the interdenominational *Christian Century* published a savage attack upon Coughlin by David Carl Colony, an Episcopal minister, the magazine was flooded with letters from Catholics protesting what they saw as the religious bigotry of the polemic. A letter from John Ryan called the article "extremely interesting," but concluded that "it includes a considerable amount of exaggeration, some pretty faulty logic, and a small bit of anti-Catholic bias."[21]

Yet even this limited camaraderie was becoming rare, partly because of Coughlin's own provocative belligerence. When he learned late in 1934 that Cardinal O'Connell of Boston had once again publicly criticized him, he replied with what even the most progressive of his Catholic colleagues considered unwarranted and unseemly harshness:

> For forty years William Cardinal O'Connell has been more notorious for his silence on social justice than for any contribution which he may have given either in practice or in doctrine toward the decentralization of wealth and toward the elimination of those glaring injustices which permitted the plutocrats of this nation to wax fat at the expense of the poor.

Besides, Coughlin somewhat gracelessly added, O'Connell "has no authority to speak for the Catholic Church in America." He had jurisdiction only inside his own diocese. The remark was not, perhaps, directed only at O'Connell. Coughlin seemed also to be writing off many of his other colleagues in the Church, reminding them that he did not need their support and was not subject to their authority.[22]

What, then, of those who did have authority over Coughlin? The question arose with growing frequency as he turned more forcefully against Franklin Roosevelt. Neither the White House officials seeking leverage with Coughlin nor the members of the Church growing impatient with him could find a clear answer. Bishop Gallagher, certainly, could not be expected to curb his devoted priest. In the spring of 1935, he went out of his way to announce his full support for the Coughlin broadcasts: "I pronounce Father Coughlin sound in doctrine, able in his application and interpretation. Freely I give him my imprimatur on his written word and freely I give him my approval on the spoken word. May both be circulated without objection throughout the land."[23]

Critics of Coughlin continued to hope that, if Gallagher would not discipline him, the Vatican might. But from Rome came only confused and conflicting signals. On the one hand, there were recurrent rumors that Coughlin was soon to be removed from Gallagher's jurisdiction, even reassigned to the Vatican itself. On the other, there were reports that he retained the confidence of the Pope himself (who was a longtime personal friend of Bishop Gallagher). One journalist recounted a conversation that supposedly occurred in Washington in 1935 between an American Church official critical of Coughlin and a highly placed papal delegate. "But my dear sir," the delegate told the American, "what the Holy Father teaches, Father Coughlin preaches!" Occasionally, there were veiled criticisms of Coughlin's most inflammatory statements in the Vatican newspaper, *Osservatore Romano;* even more occasionally, Gallagher himself, perhaps on orders from Rome, would direct Coughlin to retract some particularly troublesome comment. But until the fall of 1936, when Papal Secretary of State Eugenio Cardinal Pacelli (later Pope Pius XII) visited the United States and reportedly ordered Coughlin to moderate his public statements, there was virtually nothing to suggest how the Vatican viewed the priest's political activities.[24]

Under such circumstances, Coughlin was willing to weather the increasing hostility of other Catholic leaders in America. Although their criticisms did his public image no good, the alternative—moderating his positions to regain their approval—was unacceptable. As long as he retained the tacit approval of the Vatican and the open support of his own bishop, he reasoned, he could afford to ignore the attitudes of other members of his Church. About the long-range consequences of this growing gulf, he was, for the present, unconcerned.[25]

III

ON NOVEMBER 11, 1934, in the first sermon of a new broadcasting season, Father Coughlin announced what he claimed was a new departure both for his own public career and for the political life of the country. He had, he said, been spending many hours recently, "far into the night," reading the thousands of letters he received from his far-flung radio audience. "In them, I possess the greatest human document written within our times." And from them he had drawn a new challenge, "a challenge for me to organize these men and women of all classes . . . for obtaining, for securing and for protecting the principles of social justice." Accordingly, he was calling upon his many listeners "to organize for action . . . to organize for social united action which will be founded on God-given social truths." Their vehicle would be a new nationwide association, the National Union for Social Justice.[26]

The National Union would ultimately become something very close to a third party, supporting candidates and attempting to influence elections. But Coughlin's original conception of it was quite different. It was not to be a partisan organization "any more than the United States Steel Trust or the United States Chamber of Commerce or the American Bankers' Association . . . constitute a political party." It was, rather, to be "an articulate, organized lobby of the people to bring united pressure upon the representatives at Washington for the purpose of securing the passage of those laws which we want passed." It would be "reckoned with by every Senator, by every Congressman and by every President," but it would not nominate or elect Senators, Congressmen, or Presidents of its own.[27]

Coughlin was hoping that the existence of a vast new pressure group under his control could do for him what his speeches and lobbying efforts alone could not: restore him to what he believed was his rightful position as an important policy-making influence in Washington. Members of Congress and officials of the executive departments would look upon him with renewed respect if he could give them concrete evidence of his enormous following; even the President, who Coughlin still believed had been turned against him by advisors, would once again show him the deference he deserved. He was charting an independent course as never before, but the independence he was seeking was still sharply circumscribed. He did not as yet seek to overthrow the existing power structure or to replace the present government leaders with men of his own choosing. He wanted simply to return himself to the inner sanctums of federal power, to convince the politicians in Washington, and particularly the President, that he could not safely be ignored.

It was this unlikely strategy—the organizing of opposition to public officials to win their respect and trust—that best explains what was otherwise a series of inconsistencies in Coughlin's 1935 public statements even more baffling than those of the previous year. His attitude toward the President seemed more than ever to swerve almost crazily from enmity to support, one week prodding the Administration with reminders of Coughlin's demands and his strength, the next week enticing it with evidence of his continued willingness to cooperate. The pattern continued for months: a combination of carrot and stick that would, Coughlin believed, ultimately bring Roosevelt back to his side.[28]

The plan could work only if the National Union displayed sufficient strength to convince officials in Washington of its importance. Coughlin was careful to lay the groundwork before he made the first test: exhorting his followers every week to write him of their intention to join (there were no other formal membership requirements), sending out hundreds of thousands of reprints of the "Sixteen Principles" that formed the ideological core of the movement. By the end of January 1935, less than three months after his original announcement, he decided he was ready; and he launched his organization into its first major confrontation with the Administration.

The issue was a natural one for Coughlin: the President's effort to win Senate ratification of a treaty providing for American membership in the World Court. Not since Woodrow Wilson's ignominious failure to win approval of the Versailles Treaty sixteen years before had any President dared urge American membership in a major international organization. Even Franklin Roosevelt, who had served in the Wilson Administration and had as the 1920 Democratic Vice Presidential candidate campaigned vigorously for membership in the League of Nations, had been until now relatively silent about whatever internationalist sentiments he may have harbored. But by 1935, concerned about instability in Europe and Asia, he had decided that the country was ready for a tentative step back into international politics. Membership on the World Court, a judicial body of limited authority set up by the League of Nations, would mean little in a practical sense. It would, however, be an important symbolic gesture, an indication that the United States was beginning to accept some international responsibilities. Winning ratification by the Senate would be difficult, the President knew, but he felt certain that he could muster the required two-thirds majority.[29]

So did most members of the Senate as debate on the treaty drew to a close on Friday afternoon, January 25, 1935. But with the necessary votes apparently in the Administration's pocket, Majority Leader Joseph Robinson, a supporter of the treaty, made a fatal mistake. Instead of calling for a vote on Friday, he agreed to an adjournment for the weekend. The matter would be decided the following Tuesday, when the Senate reconvened.[30]

Had the vote been taken on the 25th, Coughlin would have remained at best a minor figure in the World Court controversy. His opposition to the treaty was obvious to anyone familiar with his public statements, for he had been attacking "internationalism"—an insidious disease that he equated with communism on the one hand and the international banking community on the other—ever since he had begun broadcasting. He had, however, made only passing criticisms of the treaty itself (perhaps because he had been unaware of the imminence of ratification). But on Sunday, January 27, only two days before the final vote and with the issue apparently already resolved, Coughlin jumped headlong into the battle.[31]

In a sermon entitled "The Menace of the World Court," he tore savagely into the treaty, arguing that the Senate was about "to hand over our national sovereignty to the World Court" and thus drag the United States into the sordid affairs and bloody wars of Europe. Instead of rescuing the country "from the hands of the international bankers," the Administration was "ready to join hands with the Rothchilds [sic] and Lazerre [sic] Freres, with the Warburgs and Morgans and Kuhn Loebs to keep the world safe for the inevitable slaughter." He was not, he claimed, alone in his opposition. The spirits of Washington and Jefferson, with their policy of "no foreign entanglements," were behind him. So was most of the "press of the civilized world"; and to prove his point, he quoted exhaustively from editorials denouncing the treaty. But all of this would not be enough unless the citizens of America made their voices heard. "Today," he commanded members of the National Union for Social Justice, "tomorrow may be too late—today, whether you can afford it or not, send your Senators telegrams telling them to vote 'no' on our entrance into the World Court."[32]

The response was astounding. Within hours of the broadcast, Western Union reported that its telegraph lines into Washington were jammed with messages and that even more were expected later in the evening when the rates went down. It had become impossible to keep track of the numbers. By Monday morning, the desk of nearly every Senator was groaning with telegrams, tens of thousands of them in all. And the sentiments they expressed were nearly unanimous: reject the treaty. A message to Senator George Norris from one of his constituents in Nebraska was typical:

> You could use your influence. Lets keep out of the World Court. We have had enough of Europe.
>
> I am not a Catholic, but this man Father Coughlin expresses my mind exactly. I think he is right on the issues he has been lecturing on. . . .
>
> If they vote in favor of the World Court and it becomes a law, I predict President Roosevelt and most of the Democratic Party will be defeated at the next election.

By Tuesday morning, the tide had turned. After a brief and rather desultory debate, the Senators cast their votes: 52 for ratification, 36 against, 7 absent. The treaty was lost—short of the necessary two-thirds majority by the surprisingly large margin of seven votes.[33]

"I regard this as a decisive defeat of the Administration," Harold Ickes confided to his diary. It was, indeed, a major embarrassment for the President, who had staked more than the usual amount of personal prestige on the outcome. It was also, Roosevelt believed, an ominous setback to hopes for peace, and he reacted, therefore, with particular bitterness. "As to the thirty-six Senators who placed themselves on record against the principle of a World Court," he wrote to Robinson on January 30, "I am inclined to think that if they ever get to heaven they will be doing a great deal of apologizing for a very long time—that is if God is against war—and I think He is."[34]

It was impossible to determine how much of the outcome was a result of Coughlin's intervention. Few observers agreed with Walter Lippmann that the treaty had been doomed to fail from the beginning, but it was clear that public opinion had been overwhelmingly opposed to membership in the Court even before Coughlin's sermon. Other opponents of ratification speaking out at about the same time may, therefore, have been equally influential. Huey Long, for one, had made a series of impassioned and, in the opinion of some observers, effective attacks on the Senate floor. William Randolph Hearst had mobilized his powerful newspaper chain against the treaty, using the sensationalist scare techniques that had made him for almost forty years one of the nation's most successful purveyors of hysteria. (There was some speculation that Coughlin, an admirer and personal friend of the publisher, had made his own attack on the treaty at the urging of Hearst.)[35]

But in the eyes of most observers, Coughlin had played the central role in the episode. "The deluge of letters, telegrams, resolutions of legislatures, and the radio talks of people like Coughlin turned the trick against us," Roosevelt confided to Elihu Root. The Coughlin broadcast alone, wrote Senator Tom Connally, had robbed the Administration of enough votes to defeat the treaty. Intensive propaganda that "originated with Father Coughlin" had been the crucial element in the defeat, the *New York Times* reported matter-of-factly after the vote. "The voice of the priest, as he preached his first sermons, was heard only by the twenty-six families of his congregation," the paper added. "Last week that same voice was one of the mighty of the land."[36]

Coughlin, of course, was jubilant. "Our thanks are due to Almighty God in that America retains her sovereignty," he said as soon as he heard the result. "Congratulations to the aroused people of the United States who, by more than 200,000 telegrams containing at least 1,000,000 names, demanded that the principles established by Washington and Jefferson shall keep us clear from foreign entanglements and European hatreds." As gratifying as the defeat of the treaty was the evidence the incident gave both to him and to the nation of the size of his following and of his ability to lead it. He seemed to be emphasizing the point in his next sermon when he told his supporters: "Your excursion into the affairs of the World Court politics has demonstrated to you a newer concept of democracy whereby you need not be satisfied with the mere casting of a vote to select a representative. Through the medium of the radio and the telegram you possess the power . . . to direct your representatives on individual matters of legislation."[37]

Surely now, with Coughlin's influence over Congress so clearly demonstrated, public officials in Washington would welcome him into their midst. Surely now, the President himself would once again listen to his advice. One week after the World Court affair, launching into his harshest and most sustained attacks on the Administration to date, he announced confidently that "Our next goal is to clean out the international bankers." Denouncing the President's banking proposals, he proposed major banking and currency-reform legislation of his own. The parish priest from Royal Oak,

Michigan, was, he believed, about to become a major power within the federal government.[38]

IV

BUT THE CONFIDENT PREDICTIONS were premature. The months following the World Court battle brought only defeats and disappointments, and by midsummer the bright promise of January had faded. President and Congress resisted Coughlin's influence, and only fitfully now could he feel any real hope of a reconciliation with the White House or of a continuing influence on Capitol Hill.

Throughout most of February and March of 1935, Coughlin concentrated singlemindedly on promoting a single measure: his legislation to restructure the Federal Reserve System and impose full government control over the nation's banking system. Obliging allies in Congress introduced the Banking and Monetary Control Act of 1935, as Coughlin titled it; and for weeks, he attempted to mobilize on behalf of his new proposals the sort of pressure he had generated against the World Court. The bill was, he claimed, a "drastic" measure, one that would finally restore to the people their right to control their own wealth. "I ask you," he said, "if we will not reform our ranks and move forward to recapture that heart of our Constitution which is so imperiled? Today each member of the National Union is, as it were . . . another captain in our army."[39]

This time, however, the army proved less effective. The banking bill was in trouble from the moment it was introduced; even some of Coughlin's most stalwart admirers in Congress were reluctant to support it. Elmer Thomas, long his most loyal ally in the Senate, openly repudiated the plan, supporting instead a much milder Administration proposal for reform of the Federal Reserve. For months, Coughlin exhorted his followers to work for passage of the bill and railed against the Administration for opposing it and for introducing a plainly inadequate substitute. All the while, however, his legislation languished in Congress, attracting little attention or enthusiasm in either house.[40]

In May, Coughlin attempted to put the strength of his new organization behind another cause: the revival of the Patman Bonus Bill. Despite the setbacks in 1932, demands for immediate payment of the soldiers' bonus had never died. In 1935, although Roosevelt continued to oppose it, proponents had grown strong enough to force the issue again. Despite the threat of a Presidential veto, the new Patman Bill moved quickly through both houses of Congress and late in May arrived on Roosevelt's desk.

Coughlin had played some part in winning passage of the measure. He had supported it in his sermons and had sparked a new (if less decisive) flood of telegrams to members of Congress on its behalf. Few would have argued, however, that his support had been a crucial factor in the outcome. Where his influence would be most important was either in persuading the President to sign the bill or in pressuring the Congress to override a veto. He failed at both. While Roosevelt was still deliberating, Coughlin openly appealed to him, "in the name of the greatest lobby the people ever established," to cast aside his objections and approve the measure. The President was unimpressed, and in an unprecedented gesture, he appeared in person before a joint session of Congress to read a stirring veto message. Coughlin next attempted to turn the tide with a new wave of telegrams to Capitol Hill, but again the effort was in vain. The Senate sustained the veto, and the Patman Bill was dead. Coughlin had been powerless to save it.[41]

Indeed, after the triumph in the World Court battle, 1935 provided Coughlin with one legislative defeat after another. He called for new legislation to nationalize gold; Congress did not respond. He supported measures for greatly increased agricultural relief; nothing happened. He proposed a new Constitutional amendment to expand the meaning of the interstate-commerce clause; no one in Washington ever even discussed it. By June, Coughlin's influence in the capital had palpably deteriorated; and by July, the Administration was ready to inflict what it hoped would be the final blows.[42]

Late in the month, the President's supporters in Congress, with almost no advance warning, hustled Coughlin's long-dormant banking bill onto the floor of the Senate for consideration. It was devastatingly defeated, as the President had known it would be. "It was a deliberate attempt to humiliate Father Coughlin, and to show how little power he had left," commented T.R.B. in the *New Republic;* and it had worked. A few weeks later, there was another blow. Roosevelt reached an agreement with bonus advocates in Congress by which he would allow consideration of the Patman Act again in January 1936 in exchange for their support of his pending tax proposals. He was, in other words, removing from open debate one of the last issues on which Coughlin retained any influence—the final step, it seemed, in the long process "of letting the air out of Father Coughlin."[43]

Only months earlier, Washington observers remarked, more than a half-dozen Senators and some fifty Representatives had been Coughlin's "bond-slaves," making regular pilgrimages to Royal Oak, soliciting his advice, valuing his approval. Now, his support in Congress had dwindled to nearly nothing. He had been outmaneuvered by a President whose power and political skill he had underestimated. As if to acknowledge his dashed hopes,

Coughlin suddenly and unexpectedly closed down the Washington office of
the National Union for Social Justice in July 1935 and ordered his personal
lobbyist home.[44]

 V

YET IF COUGHLIN'S INFLUENCE in Washington had dwindled, in the nation
at large it remained strong. Roosevelt's tactical triumphs did not so much
weaken Coughlin as change the direction of his efforts. Aware that he could
no longer hope to play an important role within the government, Coughlin
began to consider how he might operate effectively outside it.

As a leading figure in the Detroit community, Coughlin could scarcely
avoid contact with the labor movement and the automobile industry. In a
general way, he had been a spokesman for Michigan auto workers for years
—advocating better working conditions, calling for improved wages and
hours, and speaking vaguely of the responsibilities of management for the
welfare of laborers. Not until 1935, however, did he begin to play a direct role
in the union activities that had by then been embroiling the industry for
several years. As if to compensate for his setbacks in Washington, he thrust
himself into the center of controversy, determined to make himself a major
figure within the labor movement in a single stroke.

His vehicle was the Automotive Industrial Workers Association, a new
and fragile organization that drew its support largely from employees of the
Chrysler Corporation's Dodge division. Founded late in 1934, the AIWA
remained the following summer a small organization competing indirectly
with the much larger United Auto Workers. Yet with the future of the
automotive labor movement still in doubt, it seemed possible that any of the
several competing unions could still establish primacy within the industry;
and to the leaders of the AIWA, Father Coughlin appeared to be a valuable
potential ally. Sometime in July, union president Richard Frankensteen and
several other officers visited Coughlin to ask his support. To their delight, he
not only gave it, but offered to participate actively in their recruiting efforts.[45]

For the next several months, Coughlin's hand seemed to be everywhere
in the organization. He addressed a union crowd of 10,000 at the Michigan
State Fair Coliseum in July and made it clear that he expected to play a leading
role in their efforts. "Father Coughlin seemed to feel that this was his organization," Richard Frankensteen recalled. "He started to say, 'Your dues are
this—we will have another meeting.' " He outlined for his enthusiastic audience not only the union's platform (a demand for a guaranteed annual wage
of $2,150) but its internal structure. Weeks later, he spoke at another AIWA

rally in Detroit's Belle Isle Park, attracting what union officials described as a "fantastic crowd" and helping to enlist countless new members. "It was really the biggest labor gathering, I believe," Frankensteen claimed, "that had ever been established in Detroit or its environs."[46]

By the fall of 1935, Coughlin had identified himself with the AIWA so closely that among auto workers it was widely known as "Coughlin's union." While some AIWA officials later claimed that Coughlin had never had any real power within the union hierarchy, there was abundant evidence to the contrary. News letters of the organization made frequent admiring references to him; officers visited him at his home in Royal Oak almost weekly; the first "yearbook" of the AIWA bore a large portrait of Coughlin on the front page and carried a pointed inscription: "To our advisor and supporter Father Charles E. Coughlin, the friend and educator of the masses, we dedicate this book." Coughlin was at the very center of the organization; and, for a while, union leaders were delighted. "Well, of course, we were tickled pink," Frankensteen admitted, "because on the strength of his name and his program at the time, we organized a lot of people."[47]

The union activities were only one aspect of a new Coughlin strategy. Haltingly but determinedly, he was moving toward a genuine political independence. Workers should not put their faith in either political party, Coughlin warned the AIWA, because "the only time they are friends of labor is just before election time." It was a message he was conveying to others of his followers as well.[48]

Coughlin had always claimed that the National Union for Social Justice was "above politics and politicians." It was "seeking to establish no so-called third party, but crossing the centre aisle which divides each house of Congress." By mid-1935, however, there were indications that he was harboring other ideas. To a writer for *Collier's* magazine, he predicted in May that the two existing major parties would not survive for much more than another decade. A month later, he was claiming that "a new, or third party, is inevitable." Although he continued to deny that he himself had any plans either to create or to join one, the implications of his statements were clear.[49]

As the summer of 1935 progressed, he obfuscated further. In August, asked whether he would play a direct role in the coming Presidential campaign, he replied coyly that he would have something to say about his plans in November. Two months later, the *New York Times* reported that Coughlin had decided to abandon his National Union and return to the New Deal fold in 1936. Coughlin quickly telephoned the paper to deny the story. "I am neither supporting President Roosevelt nor opposing him," he insisted. At the same time, he noted pointedly that "the National Union is determined to increase its membership this coming broadcast year," and he announced that he had secured new radio outlets in California, Washington, Oregon, Colorado, and Utah. A few weeks later, he opened his new series of radio sermons with the statement that "the slogan 'Roosevelt or ruin' must be altered to read 'Roosevelt and ruin.' "[50]

Coughlin's drift away from the existing party structure was slow, but its general direction was clear to anyone who cared to look. His breach with the Administration and his lust for power and influence were pushing him inexorably toward open insurgency. "It must be remembered," he remarked in June 1935, "that although the principles of a party may be wonderful, the party is no better than its leaders." As the year progressed, it was increasingly apparent that he considered the most promising leader to be Charles Edward Coughlin.[51]

7

The Dissident Ideology

THE SUDDEN RISE of Long and Coughlin to national prominence raised many questions among their contemporaries, but none so frequent or compelling as a simple one: why? Why did so many Americans find these two men appealing? What did their political power represent? Certain answers were obvious. Long and Coughlin were flamboyant, charismatic personalities who seemed to invite notice whatever they were doing. They exercised rare skill and imagination in using the media—and particularly the radio—to make themselves known. They were, in short, hard to ignore. And their style and visibility were prerequisites to their power.

But style and visibility alone were not enough. Many public figures manage to draw attention to themselves. Only a few move from there to the creation of powerful, sustained national movements. Personality, eloquence, media skills: all were for Long and Coughlin only the most obvious sources of a popularity that rested ultimately on a far deeper and broader set of concerns—on the evocation of a distinctive ideology.[1]

The ideological content of the Long and Coughlin messages was often muddled and simplistic, at times nearly incoherent. Neither man was a careful or sophisticated thinker, and neither had much patience with complexities or ambiguities. Perhaps it should not have been surprising that, of all aspects of their movements, it was ideology that received the least serious attention from their critics. To their supporters, however, Long and Coughlin offered a message of real meaning. They provided, first, an affirmation of threatened values and institutions, and a vision of a properly structured society in which those values and institutions could thrive. They suggested, second, an explanation of the obstacles to this vision, a set of villains and scapegoats upon whom it was possible to blame contemporary problems. And they offered, finally, a prescription for reform, resting upon a carefully restricted expansion of the role of government. Some observers dismissed it all as meaningless and, as

such, ominous: a demagogic attempt to delude the public with empty, impractical promises. They were not entirely incorrect. But the Long and Coughlin
ideologies were not simply creations of the moment, designed to exploit current concerns. They rested on some of the oldest and deepest impulses in
American political life.

II

THE MOST TROUBLING FEATURE of modern industrial society, Long and
Coughlin maintained, was the steady erosion of the individual's ability to
control his own destiny. Large, faceless institutions; wealthy, insulated men;
vast networks of national and international influence: all were exercising
power and controlling wealth that more properly belonged in the hands of
ordinary citizens. These same forces had created the economic crisis of the
1930s and threatened, if left unchecked, to perpetuate it. Out of such concerns
emerged the central element of the messages of both men: an affirmation of
the ideal of community. Power, they argued, should not reside in distant,
obscure places; the individual should not have to live in a world in which he
could not govern or even know the forces determining his destiny. Instead,
the nation should aspire to a set of political and economic arrangements in
which authority rested securely in the community, where it could be observed
and, in some measure, controlled by its citizens. Concentrated wealth and
concentrated power had damaged the nation's social fabric; a system of decentralized power, limited ownership, and small-scale capitalism could restore it.

Neither Long nor Coughlin offered any precise definition of what a
proper community should look like: how large it should be, how it should be
structured. That was not the point. A community, they suggested, was less
a particular place than a network of associations, a set of economic and social
relationships in which the individual played a meaningful role and in which
each citizen maintained control of his own livelihood and destiny. Such a
community could exist in a small town, in an agricultural region, within a
large city. What was important was that its essential institutions remain small
and accessible enough to prevent abuses of power and excessive accumulations
of wealth.[2]

The community ideal had, to be sure, certain collective implications. Not
only did Long and Coughlin explicitly denounce untrammeled self-interest—
what Coughlin called the "outworn and impractical" doctrines of " 'free
competition,' and 'rugged individualism' and 'laissez-faire.' " They asked, as
well, for a redefinition of the concept of property ownership. No individual,
they argued, should be allowed to accumulate so much wealth that his owner-

ship of it became injurious to the rest of the community; nor should he be permitted to use his wealth in ways that were harmful to his neighbors. The rights of ownership were not absolute. "We can allow our people to accumulate and grow prosperous," Long said in 1934. But "beyond that point where the accumulation of [property] becomes a menace to our society and the well-being of others no one should be permitted to go." Coughlin was even clearer. "Private ownership of private fortunes does not argue their unrestrained, uncurtailed and unlimited private use," he said in one of his first political sermons. "To put it in a way so that the humblest in this audience can understand," he later explained, "by the fact that I own an automobile, it does not argue that I may drive it on the wrong side of the street or park the car on your front lawn."[3]

But if the vision smacked of collectivism, it was a collectivism of a decidedly unradical kind. Though Long and Coughlin denounced the tyrannical excesses of modern capitalism, they remained committed to a determinedly capitalist, middle-class vision. What, after all, was Long promising to those who supported his Share Our Wealth Plan but a guarantee to every family of "a home and the comforts of a home, including such conveniences as automobile and radio," all "free of debt"? As if material acquisitions were a part of Catholic religious dogma, Coughlin told his radio audience that "The Church is anxious for the workingman and the farmer to own his own home." "To multiply private ownership and not impede it," he explained, was a "sensible, socially just and American" approach to economic problems.[4]

Essential to the survival of the community, therefore, was an economy of small-scale, local enterprise. How important such an economy was to Long and Coughlin was apparent in the frequency with which both men lamented its disappearance. One by one, they complained, the autonomous local institutions that sustained a meaningful community life were vanishing in the face of distant, impersonal forces. Small farmers, for example, had been transformed, as Coughlin put it, "from a happy, prosperous army of God-fearing men" to pitiful figures who must "throw themselves at the feet of the Government and beg for relief." Local financial institutions—what Long described as "the little banks in the counties and the parishes" and what Coughlin termed the "small bankers outside the great ring of Wall Street"—were in dire peril.[5] So were the "small industrialists," who had, Coughlin claimed, "been bought out or . . . destroyed by questionable competition." Similarly troubling was the erosion of the local press. Coughlin spoke darkly of "the mounting tide of direct bank ownership of the nation's daily newspapers," while Long's *American Progress* charged that the "money powers" had come to "control the editorial policy of almost every publication in the United States." They were "only allowed to give us such information as the big fellows want us to have." The implications of this change were particularly ominous: without an independent press, freedom itself was in jeopardy. "The small rural newspapers," one Long supporter argued, "have the greatest opportunity today that they have ever had."[6]

Nothing, however, more clearly symbolized the decline of meaningful community life than the plight of the local merchant. No institution had been more central to the community than the small, independently owned store; and none created greater anxiety when it began to flounder and disappear. It was a problem that concerned residents of rural and urban areas alike. In agricultural communities, the small merchant had traditionally been more than a supplier of goods. He had served, too, as a crucial instrument of credit, a banker, a purchaser of farm produce; his store had been a gathering place, at times a community's only social center. In larger towns and cities, neighborhood shops often catered to the tastes of particular racial or ethnic groups, to members of certain occupations, to residents of homogeneous urban enclaves. They reinforced a sense of community within the impersonal urban world. The arrival of the chain store, the mail-order house, and the other institutions of modern merchandising were, therefore, a source of particular alarm, one that Long, Coughlin, and their supporters cited repeatedly. "Where is the corner groceryman?" Long cried in a Senate speech. "He is gone or going. . . . [The] little independent businesses operated by middle class people . . . have been fading out . . . as the concentration of wealth grows like a snowball."[7]

Such complaints found a ready audience, unsurprisingly, among local merchants, who formed an important part of the constituencies of both men. Faced with competition from regional or national corporations, which benefited from vastly larger capital bases and could profit from economies of scale, the local shopkeeper often felt virtually helpless. "The chain stores have complicated things," admitted an independent merchant in North Carolina in the late 1930s, speaking with a dispassionate honesty that others did not always display. "Their specialization in cheap, flashy merchandise, attractively displayed and carrying easy-to-read price tags gets the business. . . . They usually have more attractive stores, know how to dress their windows, make shopping so easy." More common were the harsher complaints of shop owners who spoke not of the attractions of the new merchandising, but of the burden it forced them to bear. "Over half the trade is going to organized greed and its chain store and mail order corporations," a disgruntled Michigan merchant wrote Coughlin. "All of the profit on this vast amount of trade leaves the state." Another shop owner exhorted Long: "Go after chain stores with all your power, and every small merchant . . . will jump to your band."[8]

But the disappearance of the local shopkeeper was dispiriting to other members of the community besides the merchant himself. It created a sense of something lost, a feeling of disconnection from the central institutions of local economic life. At its worst, it could mean the loss of crucial services— of, for example, an informal credit mechanism for those who could not qualify for the more rigid requirements of institutionalized credit. A woman in Muncie, Indiana, facing the unemployment of her husband in the mid-1920s, expressed a fear that many more Americans would confront several years later. "Now they have a new man at the grocery," she worried, "and we're afraid he won't allow us to charge things as long." A Long admirer, writing to the *American Progress* in the summer of 1933, expressed similar concerns:

> The forgotten merchant is one who has the forgotten man on his books and has not asked the government for an appropriation to take care of the millions of dollars in lost credits. The forgotten merchant is responsible for keeping the forgotten man with food, drugs and clothing, etc. thereby keeping many people well and happy through this past period of chiseling and starvation wages. The powerful groups responsible for chiseling and starvation wages have contributed nothing towards the upkeep of the forgotten man. By slicker methods they are already crowding the forgotten merchant. . . .

That it was most often stores offering essential goods—food, clothing, medicine—that appeared to be losing business to the chains only intensified the sense that something important was disappearing from the network of mutual supports that gave meaning to the idea of community.[9]

It was not just the loss of services, however, that made the passing of the local merchant disturbing. It was the disappearance, as well, of a form of interaction. Men and women in the 1930s spoke wistfully of such trivial but valued features of local retailing as the neighborhood grocer who "advertised" by "giving the children a bag of candy or cookies when they pay the monthly bill," or the dry-goods merchant who visited his customers at their workplaces, displaying samples, taking orders, and giving them "each a pair of shoelaces." "We independents have to depend much on personal relationships and know our customers," a small Southern merchant noted. "Once we forget a man's name or neglect to inquire about the health of his family, the condition of his crops, or about his hobby, we are in a way to lose his business." A comfortable neighborly relationship between merchant and customer seemed to be vanishing with the rise of standardized, impersonal retail establishments.[10]

The invasion of the chain store could produce a more specific economic anxiety as well: the narrowing of opportunities for social mobility. In a society that placed a high value on ownership, on "bossing oneself," one of the most accessible routes to self-employment had traditionally been retail trade. The concentration of ownership of stores in a few large corporations meant a significant decline in opportunities for aspiring merchants; it "increased this helpless commitment of a growing share of the population," Robert and Helen Lynd noted in 1937, "to the state of working for others with a diminished chance to 'get ahead.' "[11]

When Long and Coughlin railed against the decline of the local merchant, therefore, they were doing more than appealing to a particular interest group. They were expressing a concern with which even the least politically sensitive American could identify; they were describing a visible threat to the survival of a meaningful local existence, a danger to what one supporter of Father Coughlin called "the foundation so welded together by the independent merchants, forming the foundations of boroughs and towns, and cities." They were evoking, in short, the most compelling symbol of the debilitation of the community.[12]

III

GENERAL CONCERNS about the erosion of community life and the concentration of wealth and power in distant places did not alone, however, constitute a political ideology. Only by fusing such images with specific explanations of the problem could Long and Coughlin hope to translate the vague anxieties of their audiences into active political commitments. To accomplish that, they offered—with great vigor and relish—a cast of clearly identifiable villains. There was nothing surprising about whom and what they chose. If centralized wealth and power were the problems, then it was those in possession of that wealth and power who were to blame.

Their messages were not identical. They did not, for example, always attack the same people. Coughlin, for the most part, directed his hostility toward the bankers and financiers whom he believed to be in control of the monetary system, men such as J. P. Morgan, Andrew Mellon, Bernard Baruch, Eugene Meyer, Ogden Mills. Long denounced them too, but, far more often than Coughlin, he added to his litany men identified less with finance than simply with great wealth: John D. Rockefeller (who was perhaps his most frequent target), the du Ponts, the Vanderbilts, the Astors.

They differed, too, in the style and tone of their attacks. Coughlin's descriptions of his enemies tended to remain fuzzy and abstract, more ominous, perhaps, for their lack of personal detail. He ridiculed his targets for their arrogance. "The divine intelligence of the international bankers," he proclaimed scornfully, "has found its deserved place with the theory of the divine right of kings. Both are putrid corpses." He denounced their deviousness and malignity. "Like grinning devils," he cried, "there stand at the gates of this Eden of plenty the protectors of privately manufactured money." But even when he mentioned villains by name, he seldom discussed personalities.[13]

Long, by contrast, reveled in vivid personal abuse. At times savagely, at times almost whimsically, he assailed his targets not just for their power, but for their personal habits, their appearances, and their life-styles. They were, as he described them, fat, slothful, profligate, at times even ridiculous men, "pigs swilling in the trough of luxury," who were too concerned with their own "ease and comfort" to take notice of the plights of others. Cartoons in the *American Progress* time and again presented graphic illustrations of this image. Florid men with puffy cheeks, heavy eyelids, and enormous bellies served as visual symbols of excess. Dressed in flamboyant vested suits (usually with gold watch chains and diamond tie pins), they sat smugly counting their money and chuckling over their nefarious victories.[14]

When J. P. Morgan traveled to Europe for the hunting season, Long's newspaper ran a biting front-page account of "poor Mr. Morgan . . . hard at work over in Scotland" ruthlessly shooting down "little birds." When Huey sought to illustrate how even the wealthy could live comfortably within the limits envisioned by his wealth redistribution plan, he presented a preposterous "annual budget" for a family of four to prove that survival was possible on an income below one million dollars a year. Among the "essential" items it listed were "1 new suit a day at $100," "new set of jewelry per season at $10,000," "upkeep of doggy . . . $17,405," and "1 suit of B.V.D.'s a day at $10."[15]

Ridiculing the profligacy of the rich was also the favorite rhetorical technique of Long's sycophantic assistant Gerald L. K. Smith, as he journeyed through the rural South recruiting members for the Share Our Wealth Clubs. "All of you that ain't got four suits of clothes raise your hands," he liked to shout to his audiences with evangelistic fervor. Hundreds of arms of farmers and small-town merchants would shoot into the air.

"I thought so—I thought so, brethren. Now all of you that ain't got *three* suits of clothes, raise your hands." Again, virtually everyone in the audience would oblige.

"Just like I knew, brethren. Oh, blessed are the poor. But what a row to have to hoe. Now all of you that ain't got two suits of clothes, raise your hands." And for the third time, the crowd would become a sea of upstretched arms.

"Not even *two* suits of clothes," Smith would wail. "Oh, my brethren, J. P. Morgan has two suits of clothes. He has a hundred times two suits of

clothes. And that ain't all. Now all of you that ain't got *one* suit of clothes
—not one single suit of clothes that the pants match the coat—raise your
hands."[16]

The contrast was unmistakable. Coughlin evoked an image of cunning,
manipulative, miserly men working carefully and artfully to maintain their
power. Long and Smith spoke of bloated and sybaritic plutocrats wallowing
in sensual luxury. The one picture was of pinched, haughty, cold-blooded
schemers, an Irish-Catholic image of puritanical Protestants or Jews. The
other was of self-indulgent hedonists, a vaguely fundamentalist view of the
sinful excesses of modern urban life.

Whatever their differences, however, Long and Coughlin shared a central
concern. These "plutocrats" were dangerous chiefly for the remoteness and
inaccessibility of their power. Local problems were not usually the fault of
local people or institutions, they were suggesting; the blame more properly lay
with what Long described as the "distant power centers," or what Coughlin
termed "the hidden forces which have conspired against the common people
of the world." Oppressed factory workers, for example, were engaged in a
struggle not with their immediate superiors, the local factory owners and
managers; their real enemies were the remote financial moguls who were
exploiting workers and managers alike. "Your actual boss, Mr. Laboring
Man, is not too much to blame," Coughlin advised workers in his audience.
"If you must strike, strike in an intelligent manner not by laying down your
tools but by raising your voices against a financial system that keeps you today
and will keep you tomorrow in breadless bondage." From Long came a similar
message. "Neither the owners of the factories nor the men who work in them
are responsible for this trouble which impends in your home city," he told
laborers in Akron, Ohio. The real enemies were the wealthy tyrants of Wall
Street, before whom, as an *American Progress* reader complained, "the small
manufacturer is suffering both depression and suppression."[17]

The problem did not, however, stop at Wall Street. As if to give even
more forceful expression to their warnings about distant, inaccessible forces,
Long and Coughlin emphasized, too, a dangerous link between the American
financial establishment and the larger and stronger international banking
community. The flow of power from local organizations to national institutions in New York was only the first step. From these Eastern establishments,
power flowed on to London, Paris, and other European capitals, where it was
exercised with even greater callousness.

The influence of the international bankers, like the influence of their
American counterparts, stretched far back into the nineteenth century, as
Coughlin in particular often explained. As early as 1816, he claimed, the
"international Rothschilds" had been subtly directing the monetary policies

of Great Britain; and by the 1860s, the Bank of England had become a mere tool of the great banking families of Europe. At the same time, these plutocrats had begun to extend their control to America. Their influence had been responsible for the tragic deflation of the currency after the Civil War. ("It will not do to allow the greenback, as it is called, to circulate as money," explained a circular Coughlin claimed they had distributed at the time, "as we cannot control that.") And the same international bankers had helped suppress every effort to reform the currency system for decades thereafter.[18]

Far more important than these nineteenth-century conspiracies, however, were more recent events: above all, the First World War. This European financial struggle, into which the United States had been led by deception and subterfuge, was the crowning triumph of the international bankers. Someone with a "malignant mind," Coughlin claimed, had created the myth that Germany had provoked the conflict. In fact, the villains were England and the international financiers who ruled it. As "German thrift and industry . . . began slowly but surely to threaten England's leadership in the commercial world," he argued, the British responded by forming dangerous alliances, accumulating armaments, and instigating what was, in effect, a "great contest for commercial supremacy." Worse, the international bankers supporting England had finally succeeded in dragging America into the war, persuading "an easily deceived people to take up arms for the defense of international investments." American financiers, munitions makers, and other opportunists had been their willing allies. "We made a mistake in getting into Europe's tangle in 1917," Long proclaimed on the floor of the Senate. The only beneficiaries had been the English and the bankers profiting from interest on war debts.[19]

The widely publicized Congressional investigations instigated by Senator Gerald Nye, which exposed a purported link between the American decision to enter the war and the lobbying of the munitions industry, seemed to confirm what Long and Coughlin were saying. A New York woman wailed in 1935: "I lost three cousins in the last European war and as you must know, we are still paying for that war. Father Coughlin and the Nye investigations have opened our moronic eyes." Even veterans, many of whom had once believed the idealistic explanations of the war, now harbored deep resentment. "Wall Street and the Dollar dynasty knew it was a sham," a Long supporter who had served in 1918 claimed,

> that in fact we were fighting to make the world safe for despots and
> dictators. . . . This despotism, degradation, debt, desolation and
> despair that covers the world is the climax and final result of a base
> conspiracy formed in the Bank of England . . . whose merciless greed

has provoked wars all over the world converting the butchery of those wars into unmeasured billions of money for themselves.[20]

The world of international politics and finance was a corrupt and murky one. Powerful international bankers and industrialists, menacing institutions such as the Bank of England, the governments of Great Britain and other European powers, the American plutocrats allied with these forces—all combined to create a seething cauldron of financial intrigue and oppression. It was a cauldron that Americans must avoid at all costs. Long and Coughlin were predictably adamant in denouncing efforts to involve the United States abroad, insisting that only insulation from the financial tyranny of Europe would permit meaningful economic reform. By the 1930s, the battered Treaty of Versailles and the struggling League of Nations were virtually moot as issues in American politics, but both men continued to denounce them nevertheless. "The most loathsome after-birth of the World War," Coughlin called the League in one sermon. Long argued "that the Rockefeller fortune has been the one great bulwark that has kept the fires lighted for the League of Nations in America." Whenever the prospect of new international involvements reared its head, a new round of denunciations was sure to follow. "Get out of Europe! Get out of the Orient!" Long demanded in a 1934 speech. "Less care for internationalism and more concern for national prosperity," was Coughlin's frequent refrain.[21]

It was hardly surprising, therefore, that the 1935 controversy over American entry into the World Court, in which both Long and Coughlin played prominent roles, crystallized in the minds of many of their followers a host of resentments—against the war, against international bankers, against the British, against Wall Street, against the whole process by which power was flowing into distant and malevolent institutions. "America is being betrayed by the Administration," one angry Long supporter charged during the World Court debate, "and promoted by the evil influence of the Proenglish. The American people don't want any entanglement with Europe. If we could drop all exports to and imports from Europe we would soon climb out of the Depression."[22]

As the World Court controversy suggested, there was another disturbing aspect to the problem of centralized power. American government itself, Long and Coughlin charged, was becoming subservient to the great financial interests. The problem was not a new one. Ever since Alexander Hamilton, they argued, selfish plutocrats had battled the defenders of the people for control of political institutions. At times, they had succeeded—in 1873, for example, when they pressured Congress to agree to "the illegal outlawing of silver," as Coughlin put it; or in 1896, when they had combined to defeat William

Jennings Bryan. Even greater blows had occurred in more recent years. In 1913, Woodrow Wilson had steered the Federal Reserve Banking Act to passage; few institutions more clearly symbolized unwanted concentration of power than the Federal Reserve Board the act had created. It was, Coughlin claimed, "the Temple of the moneychangers . . . the Temple which ruins the lives of millions who came as devotees to worship at its altar but remained its slaves in the courtyard of its misery." Most cruelly of all, the Great Depression, a result of centralized wealth and power, was spawning government policies that served to reinforce them. Herbert Hoover had been a willing tool of the plutocrats throughout his Administration, Long and Coughlin charged, establishing as his principal agent for recovery the Reconstruction Finance Corporation, through which the government loaned money not to the common citizens who needed it but to the great financial and industrial interests whose only concern was the preservation of their own hegemony.[23]

Nor had the financial parasites loosened their grip in the first years of the Roosevelt Administration. Whatever Long and Coughlin thought of the President himself, they were not pleased with some of the men he had invited to participate in his Administration. Roosevelt had not been in office a month before Long began charging on the floor of the Senate that the Treasury Department had fallen under the control of "members of the Morgan House." Coughlin, similarly, denounced Secretary of the Treasury William Woodin as "the beneficiary of the Morgan blood money." Particularly offensive to Long and Coughlin was the apparent influence of financier Bernard Baruch—"the heeled henchman of Wall Street," Long called him; "fullback Barney," Coughlin described him, "whose agile legs had sidestepped the conventions of democracy from the days of Harding to those of Hoover." The new Administration had pledged itself to protect the influence of the common man; but the "gamblers of Wall Street aided by our great banks," a Virginia man wrote the *American Progress* early in 1934, were still "trying to enmesh our government." As a Coughlin supporter from Chicago warned Harold Ickes in 1933: "THE MONEY CHANGERS ARE STILL ON THE JOB, FIGHTING WITH THE IMMENSE POWER THEY STILL WIELD IN EVERY AVENUE OF LIFE. These forces of darkness are using every subtle influence to undermine . . . President Roosevelt."[24]

IV

GOVERNMENT WAS NOT ONLY part of the problem, however; it was central to the solution. Only government was powerful enough to provide the needed counterforce to the "financial plutocracy." Only government could protect the community and the individual against the menacing institutions of the modern economy.

Yet those committed to a decentralization of wealth and power were no more eager to see the state encroach upon their lives than they were to accept the influence of the great private interests. The picture Long and Coughlin presented of an active, responsible government was, therefore, carefully drawn to eliminate such concerns. Public institutions could, they claimed, be both forceful and unobtrusive; they could protect the individual and the community from the threatening financial powers without becoming intrusive powers themselves.

This idea of government power as both expansive and strictly limited found its clearest expression in the economic proposals of both Long and Coughlin—simple, self-sustaining reforms that would, they insisted, require no large bureaucratic structures. Long's Share Our Wealth Plan called for a clean, clear set of tax codes that would alone destroy concentrated wealth and erect no menacing power center in its place. Coughlin, similarly, based his hopes for change on what he considered simple, unobtrusive monetary reforms. Government would change the composition of the currency and the structure of the banking system. It would then permit the natural workings of the economy to produce and maintain a proper distribution of power, so that the wealth of America, as he often said, would "flow freely into every home." Each plan, in other words, envisioned a substantial increase in the power of government. But it was to be a largely negative, almost passive power. Government was to protect the individual, enhance the vitality of the community. It was not to become an intrusive behemoth.[25]

Indeed, both men were outspoken in denouncing the expansion of federal power that they detected during the first years of the Depression. Coughlin decried "the harrowing growth of bureaucracy for the maintenance of which . . . the national liberty has been jeopardized." The "age-old curse" of such growth, he warned, was "the tendency of bureaucracy to become a law unto itself. The very nature of its development makes inroads upon the rights and liberties of citizens; its ultimate goal is inevitably some type of tyranny." Long, similarly, argued that the proliferation of government agencies and commissions was "contrary to the American system," was "tangling up the people's business to where they did not know how to handle it."[26]

Such concerns were crucial in shaping the apparently conflicting attitudes of Long and Coughlin toward Franklin Roosevelt and his New Deal. Both men attacked Roosevelt constantly for not doing enough: for not acting to curb the power of the rich, for not reconstituting the currency, for not redistributing wealth. But they denounced him equally vigorously for doing too much: for creating programs of overbearing intrusiveness, for constructing a ponderous bureaucracy to meddle in what were properly local and individual matters. The National Recovery Administration, for example, had failed to act forcefully enough to curb corporate abuses, had become a tool of the moneyed interests. But perhaps even more disturbing, Long and Coughlin agreed, was the very concept of the NRA and other New Deal programs, which gave to the government dangerously excessive powers. The NRA, Long charged, was a plan "to regiment business and labor much more than anyone did in Germany and Italy. . . . The Farleys and Johnsons combed the land with agents, inspectors, supervisors, detectives, secretaries, assistants, etc., all armed with the power to arrest and send to jail whomever they found out not living up to some rule in one of these 900 catalogues." Coughlin found similarly disturbing the activities of the Public Works Administration, whose authority to acquire property and employ workers, he claimed, suggested "a radical leaning toward international socialism or sovietism."[27]

Even when other criticisms of the New Deal evoked only a lukewarm public response, attacks upon its intrusiveness produced passionate agreement. "N.R.A. and A.A.A. are tyranny," a Long supporter complained to Harold Ickes. "I have lost my status as a free man. I must obey laws not made by any representative of mine." A Pennsylvania man, a self-proclaimed "conservative," reminded the President in a letter, "At least Huey Long and Father Coughlin are not advocates of the Government going into business in competition with its citizens." A disgruntled Mississippi reader of the *American Progress* moaned, "Now hasn't our new DICTATOR President, Mr. Roosevelt, kind of messed things up . . . in putting in effect all the wide Mussolini powers the congress gave him?" (Long's reputation as "dictator" of his home state made such statements seem sharply incongruous. But the contradictions appeared not to bother him and seemed to be lost on most of his supporters.)[28]

It was not only individuals who were threatened by the expanding federal presence, but state and local governments. The rapid growth of the national bureaucracy imperiled the very basis of the Constitutional system. "A definite plan is afoot," the *American Progress* warned, "to end the sovereign powers of the states and to destroy the republic and substitute a social democracy." Coughlin spoke approvingly of "a very deep and growing feeling which is gaining headway constantly that the States should not be interfered with by the Federal Government in working out their own social welfare and educational programs." Roosevelt, a Coughlin supporter in Chicago charged, "radically is changing our form of government, usurping Federal power and obliterating state boundaries." Warned an *American Progress* reader, "A blueprint for the new form of government abolishing States Rights has been drawn up and published by Henry A. Wallace."[29]

The imagery of these concerns was striking. The government bureaucracy was ominous because of its "craftiness," its cunning and "deceit." It was jeopardizing the citizen's "status as a free man." It was threatening to produce "tyranny," "slavery," "dictatorship." It was, in short, behaving exactly like the great private financial interests that oppressed the common man. An overbearing government, no less than a tyrannical plutocracy, endangered the individual and the community. Only by carefully defining and limiting the role of the state in any program of reform could the nation escape replacing one oppressive centralizing force with another.

V

ONE REASON for the appeal of the messages of Long and Coughlin was that they described an objective reality. The concentration of wealth and power they decried was real, part of a larger process of national consolidation that was affecting all of American life. The United States in the 1930s was in the late stages of a great transformation already many decades old: a change from a largely rural, provincial, fragmented society to a highly urban, industrial one linked together by a network of large national institutions. The cultural effects of the transformation were everywhere apparent. Revolutions in transportation and communication—most recently and most notably the automobile and the radio—had brought even the most provincial Americans into contact with national events, personalities, and fashions. Elements of a new mass culture, based largely on urban, middle-class values, intruded into virtually every home. And to many the experience was threatening and unsettling. The social turmoil of the 1920s—the resurgence of the Ku Klux Klan, the bitter controversies over Prohibition fundamentalism—was clear evidence of how deeply many Americans resented the intrusion of new, modern values and institutions into their lives.[30]

The arrival of the Great Depression added new dimensions to these anxieties. It forced Americans to take note of the fundamental changes that had been occurring not only in their culture, but in the structure of their economy as well. Ever since the emergence of the great railroad companies in the mid-nineteenth century and the growth of large industrial combinations a few decades later, economic power had been moving steadily from relatively small, local institutions to large, national, highly bureaucratized corporations. It had become increasingly difficult for individuals and communities to retain control of their own destinies in the face of the new power centers.[31]

Yet while the economic transformation had been in progress for decades, opposition to it had been sporadic and often weak until the economic crisis of the 1930s made it a visible and powerful issue. Before the Depression, many of the economic changes had occurred almost unnoticed—small, incremental alterations in surroundings to which most people could easily and unthinkingly adjust. In the absence of a sudden, cataclysmic jolt, few had connected this halting evolution with any broader sense of process or structure. The Great Depression provided that jolt. Men and women who had scarcely noticed the small, scattered economic changes in their communities now began to recognize them and to associate them with a larger shift in the locus of economic power. And they began to connect that shift with their own distress. In expressing anxiety about excessive centralization, therefore, Americans were for the most part responding entirely rationally to a real economic problem.[32]

When they responded to Long and Coughlin, however, they were responding not only to a realistic description of economic conditions, but to a distortion of those conditions. For the way in which both men framed their denunciations helped to obscure important elements of the problem, deflecting the resentments of their followers away from what should have been important concerns. The specific villains—the individual men and institutions—to whom Long and Coughlin directed attention were not, certainly, irrelevant to the problem of economic concentration. Neither, however, were they the whole of it. They served, rather, as symbols of larger concerns that were more difficult and painful to express. It was not simply the power of particular men and institutions that was at issue; it was the power of historical forces so complex that no one could easily describe them. It was, ultimately, modernization itself—and the idea that human progress rested on continuing economic growth and organization—that Long and Coughlin were indirectly challenging.

It is hardly surprising that neither man was willing to admit, perhaps even to himself, that fundamental reality. To accept that the problem was not an identifiable person or institution but a vast, abstract process would have been to admit that there were no easily discernible explanations or solutions. It would have been to accept that diffuse, incomprehensible forces were governing society. It would have been to invite a sense of futility and hopelessness. Far less frightening, and far more effective politically, was the narrower, more specific explanation that Long and Coughlin offered.

Emphasizing individual villains and institutions rather than the general process of economic consolidation also helped Long and Coughlin avoid other contradictions in their argument. As much as they might decry excessive concentrations of wealth and power, they were never willing fully to repudiate the changes that had caused them. On the contrary, both men took great pains time and again to assure their publics that, in general, they approved of economic modernization. "There will be progress," Coughlin insisted. "More advances in production and in science are in store for us." Those who wished otherwise, he made clear, lacked foresight and wisdom. "It is only an untrained and cowardly mind which will disparage our high-powered tools, our better arrangement of materials, our more efficient management." The only way to prevent such advances would be to "make it a crime for a man to think." Long, similarly, spoke glowingly of the benefits of material progress, promising that under his economic plan "the most modern and efficient machinery would be encouraged, so that as much would be produced as possible so as to satisfy all demands of the people." In their own minds, there was nothing incompatible about denouncing concentrations of wealth and power on the one hand and coveting the fruits of material progress on the other. It was possible, they were suggesting, to have a modern industrial economy that was also decentralized. Yet there were moments when the conviction seemed to falter, when they confronted the uncomfortable implications of their own arguments and retreated quickly. For almost every time either man moved beyond his analysis of particular villains and immediate problems into a discussion of broader economic forces, he encountered troubling contradictions.[33]

Coughlin, for example, spoke frequently in the early years of his public career about the price of technological progress: the displacement of workers, the encouragement of large-scale enterprise at the expense of smaller establishments, the dehumanization of work. "The machine is becoming the laborer," he lamented. "And the laborer is becoming the wet nurse of the machine with the duty to turn a switch there, to release a lever here." Yet such concerns did not long survive as part of his rhetoric. What, after all, was the alternative? Coughlin was unwilling to contemplate halting or even significantly decelerating technological progress; and he was unable to articulate any other solution to the perplexing problem he had raised. Perhaps recognizing the contradiction, he dropped the issue.

Long confronted similar difficulties every time he tried to explain how surplus wealth, once confiscated, was to be distributed to the people who needed it. What was to happen to the great corporations that he so frequently denounced? At times, he implied that they might have to be dissolved. More often, however, he seemed to have accepted that they—and even the capitalists who ran them—would survive intact; that only stock ownership would be reallocated. How such arrangements would effectively limit the concentrated power of corporate bureaucracies he was unable fully to explain. Perhaps that was why he avoided discussing such matters through most of his lifetime.[34]

Long and Coughlin were not alone in attempting to reconcile conflicting attitudes. Members of their audience almost certainly harbored similarly ambiguous feelings. The men and women who lamented the passing of the local merchant were often the same people who took their business to the newer, flashier chain stores when these became available. "Every day we see cars full of people passing us by to go to Norfolk or Richmond to buy," a small-town Southern storekeeper noted in the late 1930s. "Often as not they could do as well at home, but they enjoy the excitement of travel and the contacts with the larger city life." The people who chafed at the intrusion of alien cultural values into their communities were often the same ones who gathered regularly before their radios, the most powerful vehicles for the transmission of those values. Indeed, it was the radio, the greatest of all centralizing forces, that made it possible for Long and Coughlin to disseminate their appeals for decentralization. That both men resisted exploring the full implications of their attacks upon concentrated wealth and power, therefore, was because those implications raised conflicts and contradictions that they were willing or unable to resolve.[35]

VI

THE EMPHASIS upon individual scapegoats instead of the general process of centralization was only one of the ways that Long and Coughlin distorted and narrowed their picture of the economic crisis. They avoided a whole range of other, equally fundamental issues by focusing on the conflict between localism and centralism at all. The sense of powerlessness that afflicted so many victims of the Depression was not alone the result of external threats to the community. It was often a result of social and economic relationships within a community, relationships that had more to do with questions of class and social status than with questions of scale and location of power. The followers of Long and Coughlin might rail against the great bankers of Wall Street and London; but local bankers also were foreclosing on mortgages and restricting credit. They might lash out against the chain stores that were destroying the local merchant; but small shopkeepers too often denied credit to needy customers. (In many communities, in fact, the arrival of the chain store, far from eliminating credit, made it available for the first time.) There was, in short, an element of romanticization in the veneration of community institutions that Long and Coughlin encouraged. The country store with a monopoly in its market, the small-town bank owned by a local patriarch: these and similar establishments could be at least as harsh and exploitive as larger, centralized institutions. By evoking the image of the distant power center as the major source of distress, Long and Coughlin were not just giving voice to a real concern about centralization. They were also absorbing and deflecting concerns about more immediate and tangible sources of exploitation and powerlessness.[36]

That their emphasis upon centralization was in conflict with some of the daily realities of economic distress was clear in their own personal experiences. Long had risen to political prominence in Louisiana not by attacking Wall Street, but by raising class-based objections to the exploitation of the poor by local elites. His first professional triumph was a lawsuit against the tiny Winnfield bank owned by members of his own family. And for the rest of his career, his success in Louisiana reflected at least as much a concern about local differentiations in class and status as about the flow of power to distant places. His stature in the state, after all, relied upon a remarkable concentration of authority in the government in Baton Rouge at the expense of local communities. It was only in his rhetoric that the issue of centralization became his almost exclusive concern.

Coughlin, too, experienced conflicts between the ideology he was transmitting and the realities he was confronting. One of his first major political escapades, for example, was his involvement in the Detroit banking crisis of early 1933. The problem there had little to do with the obscure financial forces that he most often decried. It was, rather, a matter of fecklessness and corruption by a local consortium of bankers and financiers. In this case, the image of distant power centers faded before an example of purely local exploitation.[37]

Long and Coughlin were, in short, speaking to men and women troubled not just by the abstract problem of centralized power, but by the immediate crises of loss of livelihood, of assets, of savings, of social status. Several explanations of their plight were available to such people. One was a radical critique of capitalism, blaming their problems on the class structure, requiring them to confront the realities of visible, daily exploitation. Another was the message that Long and Coughlin offered, attributing the crisis to the concentration of wealth and power in distant places and muting concern about local inequalities and injustices. Some Americans were willing to accept the radical explanation of their difficulties; but a far greater number found it unconvincing and, perhaps more to the point, frightening. To them, the Long and Coughlin messages, by evoking comfortable and traditional images and by avoiding the troubling implications of radical reform, could become appealing alternatives.

VII

THE FAILURE of more radical political movements to take root in the 1930s reflected, in part, the absence of a serious radical tradition in American political culture. The rhetoric of class conflict echoed only weakly among men and women steeped in the dominant themes of their nation's history; and leaders relying upon that rhetoric faced grave, perhaps insuperable difficulties in attempting to create political coalitions. The Long and Coughlin movements, by contrast, flourished precisely because they evoked so clearly one of the oldest and most powerful of American political traditions.

Opposition to centralized authority and demands for the wide dispersion of power had formed the core of American social and political protest, the nation's constricted version of a radical tradition, for more than a century. The American Revolution had reflected a profound fear of distant, inaccessible power; and American politics through the first half of the nineteenth century had been permeated with the ideology of republicanism, which rested upon a vision of virtuous and independent citizens living in a nation of general economic equality and broadly distributed authority. The defense of the yeoman farmer, the sturdy freeholder, and the society of small, independent communities of which they were a part underlay two of the dominant political visions of the early nineteenth century: first, Jeffersonian and then, in somewhat different form, Jacksonian democracy. A fear of concentrated, hidden power had fueled several less central but still powerful movements of the "age of reform" in the 1830s and 1840s: anti-Masonry with its exaggerated warnings of an aristocratic conspiracy against the liberties of the common man; and anti-Catholicism, with its dire portrayal of the secret machinations of the "Papist" clergy. And similar concerns had helped shape one of the most profound political developments of the 1850s: the growth of the free-labor ideology that became the philosophical core of the new Republican Party. The "slave-power conspiracy" against which so many Northerners warned in the last years before the Civil War appeared to them as more than a threat to the liberty of the black man; it seemed also to be a danger to the freedom of the independent freeholder. The aristocratic concentrations of wealth and power that the slave system encouraged, the early Republicans warned, would ultimately erode the liberty and equality of all citizens.[38]

It was but a small leap from opposing the excessive wealth and power of the old aristocracies to opposing the even more excessive wealth and power of new ones. Although the arrival of large-scale industrialization after the Civil War worked in many ways to transform and erode the tradition of republicanism, in other ways it helped it to survive. The Greenbackers, the Grangers, the Knights of Labor, and other dissident groups of the post-bellum era perpetuated if not the specific issues, at least the spirit and rhetoric of earlier, anti-aristocratic movements. But the phenomenon that most clearly illustrated how powerful the opposition to excessive centralization remained was the rise in the 1880s and 1890s of American populism. The populists took many of the general themes of earlier political traditions and shaped them into an elaborate explanation of the inequities of a modern industrial economy.

And they left a vivid legacy from which later protest movements, including those of Huey Long and Father Coughlin, could draw.

The extent to which Long and Coughlin themselves viewed populism as the source of their own ideology is obscure. Neither man ever openly acknowledged the connection; and except for rare, passing references to William Jennings Bryan and to the free-silver movement, neither even mentioned populism. When Long talked about the origins of his ideas, which he did only rarely, he described a broad and diffuse group of sources: the Bible (particularly the Hebraic codes), the law (especially the Napoleonic system of Louisiana), unspecified readings in "history" and "economics." The almost chaotic construction of some of his major speeches—endless strings of quotations culled from an eclectic array of authorities—suggested that he was willing to borrow explicitly from almost any source—except from populism. Coughlin was far more forthcoming in attributing his ideas to specific influences. It was the social teachings of the Catholic Church, he proudly and openly acknowledged, that formed the core of his political thought, and in particular the papal encyclicals of Leo XIII and Pius XI. There were American leaders as well whom he claimed to admire and from whom he insisted he had learned: Washington, Jefferson, Lincoln—the standard pantheon of heroes. Nowhere, however, did he pay tribute to any political figure associated with populism.[39]

Neither man, however, could have remained immune to the influence of populism. The Catholic social activism from which Coughlin so openly drew may have had few direct connections with American traditions; but it owed much to late-nineteenth-century political movements in Europe that had reflected some of the same concerns and made use of many of the same themes as agrarian protest in the United States. And while Coughlin had spent his youth in eastern Canada and most of his adult life in urban, industrial areas where populism had never much penetrated, he almost certainly came into contact with the potent tradition of Irish-American dissent. Like the Catholic reform movement, Irish radicalism had arisen in response to the monopolistic, centralizing features of the new industrial economy. It had been closely tied for a time to the Greenback Party, a precursor of the populist movement. While Irish groups had not become directly involved in the People's Party, they had absorbed much of its rhetoric and had helped in the twentieth century to perpetuate some of its concerns about currency and finance. Coughlin may well have felt few direct ties to the populists, but there was a strong indirect link.[40]

Long, on the other hand, almost certainly recognized the connection. He had spent his youth in the town that had been the center of populist agitation in Louisiana. He had come of age surrounded by men, including members of his own family, whose political views had been shaped by the struggles of the 1890s. He had associated himself openly with older politicians, such as S. J. Harper, who drew explicitly from the populist legacy in defining agrarian socialism. Long's failure to acknowledge his debt to populism was, one suspects, not simply inadvertent. It may well have been a calculated effort to obscure his uncomfortable proximity to a failed and, in the eyes of many, discredited movement.[41]

Whatever Long's or Coughlin's personal feelings about populism, however, there can be little doubt that their messages resonated clearly with its legacy. They did not precisely re-create populist ideology, which was, in any case, diffuse and diverse enough to resist exact duplication. But the links with populism were often so obvious that only a willful refusal can account for their failure to acknowledge them. Most clearly evident were the similarities in rhetoric and imagery. When Long and Coughlin depicted their foes as scheming financiers or sybaritic plutocrats, they evoked images with deep roots in the populist past. For example, the famous free silver tract *Coin's Financial School,* one of the most widely read books of the 1890s, decried the power of the "English Octopus" which had absorbed so much of the world's wealth; and it linked that nation's financial power to the machinations of the Rothschilds. Coughlin presented the same scenario, even if in slightly less lurid terms. Ignatius Donnelly, one of the most prominent of populist spokesmen, wrote in 1890 of the "destructive power of the ignorant and brutal Plutocracy. . . . they blindly and imperiously insist on their own destruction; they strike at the very hands that would save them. . . . [They] batten down the hatches over the starving crew . . . and then riot in drunken debauchery on the deck." Hardly an issue of Long's *American Progress* failed to contain virtually identical language.[42]

And nothing more clearly augured the dissident messages of the 1930s than a passage from the preface to the 1892 platform of the People's Party:

> The fruits of the toil of millions are boldly stolen to build up colossal fortunes for a few, unprecedented in the history of mankind; and the possessors of these in turn, despise the Republic and endanger liberty.

Or the statement of a populist leader to an 1895 meeting of a Farmers' Alliance:

> There is wealth enough and to spare, but it goes to the pampered few. Let us not forget that the millions of toilers are in more pressing need of remedy that shall prevent the unjust concentration of wealth,

than they are for one which can only insure increased production of wealth.[43]

There were similarities, too, between the specific solutions that Long and Coughlin offered and the political proposals of the populists. There was a noticeable connection between the financial demands of the People's Party and Father Coughlin's call for greenbacks, remonetization of silver, and a frontal assault upon the powerful banks. And while Long's wealth-redistribution plan had no precise counterpart in the 1890s, his emphasis upon breaking up great fortunes and destroying monopoly as a prerequisite to general prosperity did. Both men resembled the populists, too, in their insistence that the federal government must play an important, if limited role in the regeneration of the economy. Gabriel Weltstein, the visionary hero of Ignatius Donnelly's 1889 novel *Caesar's Column,* suggested the populist expectations of the state. "Government," he said; "government—national, state and municipal—is the key to the future of the human race." Long and Coughlin were saying much the same thing forty years later.[44]

Even the differences between the messages of Long, a Southerner, and Coughlin, a resident of the Midwest, were reminiscent of the different populist movements of the two regions. Southern populism was always somewhat broader in focus and more radical in outlook than its Midwestern counterpart. Southerners emphasized such issues as ownership of land and wealth, the destruction of monopoly, and the redistribution of resources more insistently than Westerners, who were likelier to focus instead on money, banks, and currency. When the issue of free silver began to spread through the populist movement, gaining such force that it gradually extinguished many more fundamental demands, it emerged first in the Midwest. The Southern populists resisted this narrowing of their focus for several years after the Westerners had capitulated. By the same token, Long was always far more likely than Coughlin to attack directly the maldistribution of wealth and to call for a frontal assault upon great fortunes. Coughlin's message tended to emphasize the somewhat less direct remedies of currency manipulation and banking reform.[45]

Most of all, the concern of the Long and Coughlin movements with the idea of community—with protecting the integrity of local institutions, with restoring to the individual the control of his life and livelihood—revived the central, animating spirit of populism. Populist rhetoric echoed constantly with images of community and localism—of a society in which power and wealth were widely and democratically dispersed. Populist organizations—alliances, sub-alliances, marketing cooperatives, and others—were not simply political or economic units; they were agents for the regeneration of the community, and they placed a high value on neighborliness and local social dynamics.[46]

By connecting their messages so clearly with the residual appeal of the populist tradition, Long and Coughlin were providing one of the essential qualities of any effective political ideology: familiarity. Mass audiences are not easily swayed by entirely new ideas; they respond best to themes of which they are already at least partially aware. Whether Americans of the 1930s fully realized it or not, they were gravitating to the Long and Coughlin movements not only because those movements seemed to explain present conditions, but because they evoked older political impulses as well, themes so deeply imbedded in the political culture that they remained capable, generation after generation, of producing a powerful response.[47]

VIII

POLITICAL IDEAS ARE NOT, however, immutable entities to be passed intact from one era to the next. The legacy of populism may have endured in the 1930s in the messages of Long and Coughlin, but it had also been transformed —reshaped by forty years of changes in the social and economic context in which political beliefs must live. When Long and Coughlin evoked themes and images from the past, therefore, they illustrated not only the survival but the debilitation of the populist tradition.

The populist movement had itself suffered from important limits to its own vision. Committed at heart to capitalist, bourgeois values, populists shied away from genuinely radical challenges to their economic system and remained vulnerable to co-optation by the culture of the increasingly powerful corporate economy. In its most advanced form, however, populism had been far more willing than its later counterparts to explore the radical implications of its own message; and it had offered a far more expansive and practical vision of reform. While dissidents of the 1890s decried the trend toward centralization of wealth and power no less stridently than those of the 1930s, they did not obscure the reality of local exploitation. Long, Coughlin, and their followers seldom lashed out against the most immediate and visible manifestations of class inequality; the populists did so repeatedly. Instead of the consistent romanticization of local bankers and shopkeepers, populist rhetoric contained harsh denunciations of the community "furnishing merchant," to whom thousands of farmers remained tied by a harsh and rigid system of credit, and of independent banks that were responsible for foreclosing on mortgages and confiscating land. The populists might charge that these local malefactors were allied with larger, more distant forces such as the railroads and other trusts, but they recognized as well the enemy in their midst. "The furnishing

man was the boss, pure and simple," complained an Alabama woman recall-
ing the populist era; "his word was law." He was, she claimed in the clear
language of class discontent, "The Man." A South Carolina populist conveyed
the same message in even starker terms: "All of us hated bankers and we hated
merchants. We hated them because they robbed us."[48]

More importantly, when the populists denounced the specter of centralization, they accompanied those denunciations with a vision of how a decentralized economy could work and of how individual citizens could participate
in its construction. Theirs was not only a movement of angry rhetoric; it was
an attempt at direct political and economic action at the community level, an
experiment in local education and self-help. The Farmers' Alliances that
formed the core of the People's Party not only helped spread an ideology; they
encouraged an active process of community institution-building. From them
emerged marketing cooperatives, community cotton gins and flour mills,
cooperative stores, and credit unions. They helped to spawn direct economic
measures such as boycotts against offending companies, agitation for state and
local legislation to prohibit fencing and land engrossment, and even such
seemingly mundane activities as cooperation in rounding up stray livestock.
Whatever the limitations of or distortions in the rhetoric of the populists, they
were for a time engaged in an active effort to construct an alternative to the
emerging, centralized, corporate economy.[49]

Long and Coughlin, by contrast, adopted the rhetoric of populist localism, but little of its substance. Nowhere in their messages was there any vision
of the active building of local economic institutions; nowhere did they suggest
that an individual or a community could counter the strength of the modern
consolidated economy through independent, local efforts. What was most
conspicuously absent from the Long and Coughlin movements, in short, and
what differentiated them most clearly from their populist forebears, was a
genuine belief in possibilities. Neither the leaders nor the followers would
admit it, even to themselves, but there was in their vision a thinly veiled sense
of resignation, an unspoken belief that it was by the 1930s already too late for
a fundamental restructuring of American society. This implicit acceptance of
defeat was visible, above all, in the nature of the reforms that Long and
Coughlin proposed, reforms that relied upon a single agent: the federal government. It was no longer possible, they were tacitly admitting, for individuals
or communities to do anything meaningful on their own to regain control of
their economic future. The only remaining antidote to centralized power was
the greatest of all institutions of centralized power.

Both Long and Coughlin insisted that a forceful and effective federal
government did not need to be an intrusive one; that there was no necessary
contradiction in relying upon a national force to protect local autonomy. Their

own awkward explanations of their proposals, however, suggested on occasion that they themselves were not convinced. Long, who assiduously avoided giving details of his plans to redistribute wealth during his lifetime, sketched his vision of a reformed federal government in the "Utopian" novel published after his death: *My First Days in the White House.* In it, he proposed the creation of a "Federal Share Our Wealth Corporation," a vast holding company that would "operate as a steward and trustee for the American people in the redistribution of wealth." The new "corporation" would seize all the excess wealth and property confiscated under Long's confiscatory tax plan; but rather than redistribute such assets directly to the people, it would distribute its own stock. A single federal institution—a new bureaucracy of wealth and power so vast as to reduce all previous power centers to insignificance— was to be the vital agent for the restoration of a decentralized economy. The paradox is so striking that it was perhaps no accident that the proposal never appeared while Long lived.[50]

Coughlin, similarly, campaigned ardently for a major financial reform that would, he claimed, destroy the menacing power of the great private banks. To replace them, he called for a new banking system in which power would reside in a single federal agency. The menacing institutions of Wall Street would become, instead, benign arms of the national government. What would happen in the process to the independent local banks he claimed to defend he did not explain. Perhaps he envisioned them remaining outside the new system. Or perhaps he, like Long, sensed the contradictions in his proposal and simply shied away from them. Both men were unable in the end to imagine an efficient, productive economy in which large, national institutions did not play a central role.[51]

It was not difficult to detect what had produced this enfeeblement of the populist vision in the forty years since the collapse of the People's Party. In the 1890s, many Americans had still believed that it was not too late to change the course of their society and economy; by the 1930s, such faith was far more difficult to maintain. The agrarian economy, which throughout American history had embodied the virtues of individualism, independence, and localism, had experienced a fundamental transformation. Not only were rural Americans now a minority of the population, as the 1920 Census disclosed; they were also fewer in absolute numbers, millions having fled the land for the more promising world of the city. And those who remained were increasingly benumbed by the spreading blight of tenantry. By 1930, nearly half of all farms in both the South and the Midwest were operated by non-owners; concentration of landholdings had proceeded so far that effective action against it now seemed far less possible.[52]

Within the industrial economy, similarly, chances for fundamental changes seemed to be rapidly diminishing. The modern corporate system based on large-scale bureaucracies had been in its first uncertain stages in the 1890s. Now it was so entrenched that even the Great Depression did little to challenge it. The nation's financial structure, precarious though it remained, had nevertheless moved so far in the direction of centralized control by large institutions that few realistic alternatives presented themselves. A standardized national culture, only barely visible outside the major cities forty years before, was now penetrating even the most remote rural areas. The whole process of centralization and consolidation—social, economic, and cultural—had by the 1930s moved so far that it was scarcely possible to believe that it could be reversed save through a major economic revolution. Unwilling to contemplate that, Long and Coughlin relied upon paradoxical proposals of reform through a drastic expansion of federal power. In doing so, they were in effect conceding that their hopes for a decentralized economy were all but dead.

It would be a mistake, however, to exaggerate the limits of the vision of Long and Coughlin and neglect its elements of boldness. Faced with an economic dilemma of bewildering proportions, they might have relied, like other leaders, upon far more simplistic and distorted explanations. They might have focused their wrath upon Jews (as Coughlin ultimately did in the last stages of his career), upon communists (whom both denounced, but upon whom neither dwelled), upon blacks, immigrants, intellectuals, or other seemingly alien groups. They might have emphasized, as many unhappy Americans did in the 1920s and as many more would do in later years, irreligion, immorality, and other cultural phenomena. They did not. They spoke instead about economic issues of genuine importance; they denounced men and institutions who bore no little responsibility for the problems of the era; and they offered solutions that, whatever their many failings, represented rational, concrete approaches to knotty, problems. Indeed, the Long and Coughlin movements may well have been the last effective expressions of the themes of populism in basic economic terms.

For all that, however, the movements were failures, not only as quests for political power but as efforts to articulate a consistent, persuasive, and enduring vision of reform. They were doomed, ultimately, by their own timidity; and perhaps, too, by their growing irrelevance in a modern, consolidated nation in which basic choices had long since been made.

8

Organizing

BY THE SPRING OF 1935, the public careers of both Long and Coughlin had moved into their penultimate phase. The initial task of proposing economic programs, offering broader public messages, and gaining national reputations was complete. The prospects for a working relationship with Franklin Roosevelt had been destroyed. Both men now moved toward establishing themselves as independent political forces. They would operate outside the two-party system. They would work to increase their public exposure and expand their constituencies. They would attempt to influence the 1936 Presidential election.

Thus it was that Long and Coughlin turned with renewed vigor to their national organizations. Both men had announced the formation of the groups some months before (Long in February and Coughlin in November of 1934). But only in the first months of 1935 did they began recruiting in earnest. They envisioned organizations broad in scope, immense in size, muscular in political influence. In order to achieve these goals, they embarked upon campaigns of frenzied activity.

Long, whose life was frenzied whatever he was doing, now worked strenuously to increase the number and visibility of his Share Our Wealth Clubs. His most important step was the decision to expand his use of radio. He had made broadcasts over a national network only twice in 1933 and once the following year. In the first three months of 1935, he doubled his previous total, speaking over NBC six times; and while his pace slowed somewhat through the spring and the summer, he continued to make use of the network frequently thereafter. No one doubted his effectiveness. He was, one of his Louisiana opponents noted in despair, "the best radio speaker" in America, "better even than President Roosevelt." After an average broadcast, Long would receive up to 60,000 letters through the network and more than that through his own Senate office.[1]

Long rapidly increased his personal appearances as well in the first months of 1935. Early in February, he traveled to Atlanta, where the Georgia House of Representatives, after acrimonious debate, had invited him to speak. Crowds followed him wherever he went—from the train station to his hotel (where he lunched with Governor Eugene Talmadge) and finally to the state capitol, where he delivered a fiery speech to a packed and cheering House chamber. (For weeks thereafter, the question of whether or not to invite Long to speak embroiled the legislatures of half a dozen states, most of which ultimately decided against it.) A month after Atlanta, he was in Philadelphia, where a crowd of over 16,000 packed the city's Convention Hall to hear him denounce Franklin Roosevelt and describe his own wealth-sharing proposals. The speech was relatively tame, but the audience was enthusiastic neverthe- less. The hall was almost as packed at the end as at the beginning of the hour-and-a-half-long address, surprising observers who knew Philadelphia as a city where, as one policeman noted at the time, crowds would leave the World Series early to beat the traffic. "There are 250,000 Long votes in Philadelphia," ex-Mayor Harry Mackey remarked.[2]

From Pennsylvania, he moved on to South Carolina. He had been invited to speak at the state university in Columbia; but when faculty opposition threatened to interfere with the plans, he secured permission to move to the grounds of the statehouse, where a crowd of over 5,000 gathered on short notice to see him. Governor Olin Johnston, who had done his best to discour- age Long's visit, took one look at the size of the audience and decided to sit prominently on the capitol steps during the speech. The Mayor of Columbia introduced Huey enthusiastically as a man whose "theories are deeper set on the minds of the people of this country than many think." Long was so pleased at his reception that he decided to remain in South Carolina for several more days and travel to other areas of the state. By the time he left, he claimed, he had recruited 200,000 new members for the Share Our Wealth Society.[3]

Things did not always go so well. In April, he traveled to Des Moines, Iowa, to address the national convention of an insurgent farm organization; and while the farmers greeted him warmly, other Iowans did not. Making a surprise appearance at the Drake Relays, a major regional track meet then in progress, he was roundly booed by sports fans impatient with the interruption. In June, he made plans for his first excursion into New England, accepting an invitation from local Share Our Wealth organizers to appear in Stamford, Connecticut. The proposal received a notably unsympathetic response from the Democratic mayor, a Roosevelt ally, who refused Long permission to speak in the city park (it was needed for a baseball game, he claimed). Long supporters failed to generate enough popular pressure to force officials to reconsider, and Huey finally canceled the visit.[4]

But such experiences were the exception rather than the rule. Long usually had little difficulty arranging for local visits, whether elected officials wanted him or not. And almost always he found a large and enthusiastic audience waiting for him when he arrived. As the summer progressed, he began casting an even wider net, accepting invitations to speak in such places as Pittsburgh, Oklahoma City, and Nashville, and sketching out plans for a major tour of the Far West in the fall.[5]

Long's travels were the most spectacular elements of the Share Our Wealth Society's organizational strategy. The bulk of the field work, however, fell not upon Long but upon his remarkable deputy Gerald L. K. Smith. Smith had a seamy political career of his own after Huey's death (he lived until 1976), the excesses of which have tended to obscure or distort his role in the Long movement. But except for Huey himself, no one was more effective in 1934 and 1935 in the work of spreading the Share Our Wealth gospel and organizing local chapters of the Society.

Smith was born in Wisconsin in 1898 (five years after Long), descended from three generations of ministers of the Disciples of Christ; and at a young age, he decided to continue the family tradition. Ordained in 1916, he devoted the next twelve years to parish work in Indiana, where he was successful, popular, and apparently happy. Had it not been for his wife's poor health, which finally dictated a change to warmer climes, he might have remained in the Midwest for life; but in 1928, he made a fateful move to Shreveport, Louisiana.[6]

For a time, he was as successful there as he had been in Indiana, attracting new members to his church, extracting generous contributions from local businessmen, even starting a series of popular radio broadcasts over several stations in Louisiana and neighboring states. Before long, however, his dynamism began to create more problems than it solved. His Shreveport parishioners grew irritated as he expanded his activities outside the church and spent more and more time traveling. Particularly troubling to conservatives, who formed the bulk of his congregation, were the minister's political views. They could tolerate attacks on abstract evils such as poor working conditions and exploitation of laborers; but when Smith criticized local utility companies, accused Shreveport businessmen of corruption, and even helped to organize unions, their patience grew strained.[7]

The final straw was Smith's increasingly public connection with Huey Long. He had been an admirer of Long almost from the moment he arrived in Louisiana, and a personal association began when he took it upon himself to intercede with the Governor for legislation to protect homeowners from mortgage foreclosures. After that, the relationship flowered. When Long entered the Senate, Smith made periodic trips to Washington to consult with and "advise" his mentor. Whenever Huey returned to Louisiana, Smith was almost always at his side. Once in 1933, a photograph of the minister turned up in Shreveport newspapers showing him leaving a New Orleans hotel with Long and identifying him as one of Huey's bodyguards. Smith sued the paper, but his denials failed to mollify his angry parishioners. The following February, after months of unchurchlike wrangling, he bitterly resigned. And almost immediately he became in name what he had long been in fact: a member of Huey Long's political staff.[8]

Smith's relationship with Long was a curious, even a disturbing one. His devotion to Huey was so total, so slavish as to seem at times almost unbalanced. Although in later years Smith would become something of a tyrant and megalomaniac in his own right, in Long's presence he was a deferential, almost simpering sycophant. One Long associate later claimed that he had on occasion walked into the Senator's bedroom at night and found Smith asleep on the floor near the bed—"just so that he could be close to Huey." (Smith denied it.) Others recalled him taking cast-off suits and ties from Long and proudly, boastfully wearing them.[9]

In 1935, the liberal *New Republic* decided to publish a debate on the dangers and merits of Huey Long. Hodding Carter, one of Long's most implacable enemies in the Southern press, composed a hostile article, and Gerald Smith wrote the reply. In the simple, determined rhetoric of a zealot, he lavished adulation on Long, praising not only his statesmanship and his political skills but his wit ("He is Louisiana's greatest humorist"), his literary skill ("He is the greatest headline writer I have ever seen"), and his temperance ("He abstains from alcohol. He uses no tobacco"). "Huey Long is a superman," Smith continued. "I actually believe that he can do as much in one day as any ten men I know." More than that, he was a saint. "He keeps all of his campaign promises. We, who follow him, adore him and consider ourselves flattered when he asks our help. He never lies to us. He never uses the fall-guy method of protecting himself. He takes the blame for our mistakes." Perhaps the most troubling aspect of this excessive and embarrassing tribute was its apparent sincerity.[10]

Long no doubt found such adulation flattering for a time, but it also made him nervous. He realized that Smith was an unstable man, and ultimately he decided he was a dangerous one as well. By 1935, he had developed an actual aversion to him, ordering his bodyguards to keep Smith away from him, to seat him in a back car in motorcades so that Long would not have to see him. "He's needling me," he once complained to an assistant. "You see that brown tie, suit—he got them from me—he wants to be like me." Shortly before Huey died, associates recalled, he decided that Smith would eventually have to go.[11]

Yet Smith's extraordinary skills were as obvious to Long as his weaknesses. He was a remarkably charismatic man, "one of the most magnetic and ingratiating personalities ever encountered by this writer," wrote a St. Louis reporter in 1935. Tall, muscular, well proportioned, with clear blue eyes and wavy brown hair, he attracted notice by his handsome appearance alone. His musical voice and his finely polished diction increased his appeal. Not even Long himself could stir up a crowd as skillfully as Smith, could awaken farmers, storekeepers, factory workers so effectively to their wants and their resentments. Combining populist rhetoric with Christian evangelism, he electrified audiences wherever he went, driving them to a fever pitch of excitement, then closing with an impassioned prayer:

> Lift us out of this wretchedness, O Lord, out of this poverty, lift us who stand here in slavery tonight. Rally us under this young man who came out of the woods of north Louisiana, who leads us like a Moses out of the land of bondage into the land of milk and honey where every man is a king but no man wears a crown. Amen.

He was, wrote an amused but impressed H. L Mencken, "the gustiest and goriest, loudest and lustiest, the deadliest and damndest orator ever heard on this or any other earth . . . , the champion boob-bumper of all epochs."[12]

Through the last months of 1934 and the winter and spring of 1935, Smith used his talents tirelessly in travel throughout the South, stirring up controversy and winning recruits for the Share Our Wealth Clubs wherever he went. Borrowing Long's sound trucks, he drove from county to county in rural Georgia and South Carolina, stopping in town squares and speaking to whoever happened to be in the vicinity. In Atlanta, Augusta, Columbia, and Baltimore, he hired hotel ballrooms for meetings of local Share Our Wealth enthusiasts. At every stop, he handed out membership applications to members of the audience and collected them before he left; and by the end of March, when he claimed to have visited twenty-three states, he announced that his proselytizing was bringing in 20,000 new recruits a day, that the Share Our Wealth Society had passed the five-million mark in membership and was growing steadily. No one could either verify or dispute his claims, but few could disagree with his statement that "The popular appeal of our movement can't be discounted whether its philosophy is accepted or not."[13]

To Long, the popular appeal of the movement was the most important thing. From the start, he envisioned the Share Our Wealth Society as a vehicle for his own political advancement. In public, he remained somewhat coy about his objectives, claiming at first that the Share Our Wealth Clubs were simply to be a cluster of pressure groups that would work on behalf of legislation to redistribute wealth. But no one who knew Long really believed that. By March of 1935, in the aftermath of the Hugh Johnson controversy, he was hinting that the Society would support political candidates. And during one of his frequent visits to New York, he remarked casually to one member of the constant stream of reporters flowing through his hotel suite that "there positively will be a 'share-the-wealth' ticket in the field in the 1936 campaign. No doubt about that." Still, he refused to speculate about what his own role would be; and although his increasing political travels suggested otherwise, he generally denied that he would become a Presidential candidate himself.[14]

Privately, however, he was making plans to play an important and, he hoped, a decisive role in the coming national election. He was quietly studying the possibility of buying a radio station in New Orleans, putting it under the control of LSU (and thus of himself), and giving it the most powerful signal of any station in the country—one that would enable him to beam his message across the entire Deep South almost at will. He was discussing proposals for developing an organized national following among students. He was, according to some reports, communicating secretly with conservative Republican businessmen who wanted to help finance his efforts in the hope that he would undermine Franklin Roosevelt's chances for re-election. And he was hinting broadly to some of his Senate colleagues that he planned to participate in many of the Democratic Presidential primaries the following spring, either as a candidate himself or as the principal supporter of a candidate of his choosing.[15]

Finally, in mid-August, during another visit to New York, Long spoke openly about his plans. His first choice for the Presidency, he claimed, was Republican William Borah, "the greatest lawyer since Daniel Webster." (Long knew perfectly well that Borah would never receive the nomination of his party.) He would also be willing to support George Norris, Gerald Nye, or Lynn Frazier, should one of them receive the Republican nomination. Among Democrats, he favored Burton K. Wheeler, Elmer Thomas, and several other unlikely progressives. He was not, however, optimistic about the chances of either party choosing a suitable candidate; and if the race became a repeat of 1932—pitting Franklin Roosevelt against Herbert Hoover—Long himself would almost certainly run. "The people ought to have some choice between high cockalorum and low cockahiram," he explained. "All you would get for voting for Roosevelt or Hoover would be a ticket to hell. . . . They are the twin bed mates of disaster."[16]

Long probably still did not know precisely what he would do in 1936, but he knew he would do something. He discussed different possible scenarios with his advisors and with friendly reporters almost until the day he died. He knew, or at least suspected, that he had little chance of winning the Presidency in 1936. His hope, apparently, was to play the role of a spoiler, dividing the Democratic Party and drawing enough votes away from Roosevelt to ensure the election of a Republican. Roosevelt was adept at "whispering words of hope to the country to put people to sleep so they won't know what's killing them." A conservative Republican would not be able to do even that. By 1940, he reasoned, the nation's plight would have become so desperate that voters would at last be ready for Huey Long. He could afford to wait. In 1940, he would be only forty-six years old.[17]

II

COUGHLIN HAD ENVISIONED his National Union for Social Justice as "an articulate, organized lobby of the people" when he formed it in the fall of 1934. By the following April, however, with his influence in Washington rapidly ebbing, it was becoming clear that it was neither articulate nor organized enough. And so, although he had done little at first to promote the new organization, he now decided upon a far more active approach.[18]

In mid-April, Coughlin announced plans for what he described as a major speaking tour, during which he would address mass meetings in cities throughout the Northeast and Midwest. He hoped to enroll ten million new voters in the National Union before the 1936 elections; to organize them by Congressional districts; and to mobilize them in support of candidates for the House and the Senate (he said nothing about the Presidency) who endorsed Coughlin's social and economic principles. The focus was shifting from legislative politics, from attempting to influence the deliberations of Congress, to electoral politics, to attempting to affect results at the polls.[19]

The tour began, appropriately, in Detroit, where Coughlin addressed an enthusiastic crowd of some 17,000 people at the Olympia Auditorium. The speakers' platform was crowded with dignitaries: Senators Elmer Thomas and Gerald Nye; Congressmen from Massachusetts, Ohio, Wisconsin, North Dakota; the secretary of the National Farmers' Union; and Coughlin's parents. They looked down on an audience composed, according to one newspaper, "largely of men and women who appeared to have come from the more humble walks of life." Communists and socialists passed out hostile leaflets at the doors, but inside all was adoration and excitement as Coughlin took the stage (following a warm introduction by a local rabbi) and sketched out his plans for the National Union. He would not himself be involved in running the organization, he implausibly insisted. Instead, there would be a nine-man board of trustees who would oversee the Union until a convention could be held (perhaps two years in the future), at which point members could elect their own officers. In the meantime, Coughlin supporters should concentrate on garnering new support for the Sixteen Principles of Social Justice and on recruiting new members in every Congressional district. Most in the audience cheered his every word; some observers, however, remained skeptical. "Such a session is not apt to produce real organization or cohesion," the Detroit *Free Press* sourly observed. But "as a clearing house for ideas," the paper conceded, "the meeting doubtless had its value."[20]

Two weeks later, Coughlin was in Cleveland, addressing an even larger audience, perhaps 30,000 people, in the enormous Public Hall. This time, there were not even any opponents outside the building; the police had charged a communist picket line in front and dispersed it before the meeting began. For more than an hour, Coughlin spoke with a passion unusual even for him, buoyed evidently by the enthusiasm of the crowd. His criticisms of President Roosevelt, more vehement than his usual complaints in his radio sermons, fueled press speculation about an open rift between the two men. His attack upon Ohio Senator Robert J. Bulkley, an opponent of the soldiers' bonus, gave clear evidence of the direction he hoped the National Union would take. "If the senior senator from Ohio does not see fit to alter his judgment," Coughlin warned, "then his career ends tonight. . . . [Elected officials] who are so drunk with the wine of aristocracy as to oppose the expressed will of their constituents . . . must be removed from the halls of Congress." It was a triumphant evening, and Coughlin left Cleveland elated.[21]

But his most stunning triumph was still to come. For fifty years, Madison Square Garden in New York had been the mecca of political candidates, the scene of some of the most fevered and dramatic American rallies, the site of the culmination of innumerable campaigns. William Jennings Bryan had chosen it to launch his Presidential drive in the East in 1896. Franklin Roosevelt had closed his campaign there in 1932. Now, Father Coughlin was coming for the first time (he had spoken in New York in 1933, but at the Hippodrome), and the mere fact that he was appearing at the Garden heightened interest in his visit. This, the location seemed to say, was to be no ordinary meeting.

And indeed it was not. There were 18,000 seats in Madison Square Garden. Hours before the rally was to begin, it was obvious that they would not be nearly enough. Coughlin had refused to allow any radio broadcast of his speech, fearful of reducing the size of his audience; and by early evening, according to police estimates, some 30,000 people were thronging streets in every direction, waiting patiently to purchase tickets. It was a quiet, well-behaved crowd, "plain men and women," wrote reporter Hamilton Basso, "workers clean and shaven and wearing their best clothes, little business men and shopkeepers." There were, he noted, an Irish mechanic from Brooklyn with a group of friends, also workmen; a female stenographer in neat office clothes; a businessman in suit and tie, carrying a pair of binoculars; a simply dressed mother escorting her teen-age son. The group was a diverse one, but almost all were people of modest means. The forty- and fifty-cent seats in the Garden sold out almost immediately, but the higher-priced tickets moved sluggishly until organizers slashed prices from two dollars to a dollar and less. It was a sober crowd, but not a passive one; it represented, some believed, a level of political activism new to Depression America. As Basso observed, "You realized, lost among them, that this would have been impossible ten years ago . . . the American people roused from their lethargy and taking an active vital interest in the politics of their country."[22]

Even the concessionaires suggested the political activism of the crowd. In the lobby, souvenir salesmen offered buttons welcoming Coughlin to New York, photographs of the priest, and printed copies of his sermons. Newsboys did a thriving business selling copies of Huey Long's *American Progress.* Yet all was not politics. There was entertainment as well. In the auditorium, a brass band blared out festive music and lavish bunting created swatches of bright color. Many in the audience sang and clapped during the long wait before the speeches began.

Finally, Coughlin walked slowly onto the stage, surrounded by brightly uniformed VFW members carrying American flags. For several minutes, he simply stood at the podium, smiling faintly, waving modestly, and enjoying the adulation of the crowd—a deafening ovation, one that resembled nothing so much as the reaction of a political convention to the appearance of its Presidential candidate. From the balcony came showers of confetti, made from torn programs. On the floor, a man leaped onto his seat and brandished a placard reading "The Modern Patrick Henry." Other signs read "President Coughlin" or "Our Next President." Time and again, when the cheering seemed about to die, some particularly vocal fan would raise his voice and start it all again. The audience, a New York *Herald Tribune* reporter wrote, "almost went mad" for a time, until finally there was enough quiet for Coughlin to begin.[23]

The speech was not notably different from many Coughlin had given before. He lashed out at international bankers, newspapers, England, World War I, and other members of his litany of villains. He criticized New Deal policies. He denounced what he described as "plutocratic capitalism" and proclaimed that if it continued to stand in the way of social justice, it "must be constitutionally voted out of existence." Above all, he urged everyone— "the laborer, the farmer, the small business man, and all others"—to join the National Union.

What made the speech a remarkable event was not its content but the reaction of the audience. "Not Bryan with his 'Cross of Gold' speech," wrote a clearly dazzled reporter, "nor the first Roosevelt with his 'malefactors of great wealth,' nor the second with his 'New Deal,' ever had a crowd more completely in the hollow of his hand than Father Coughlin did last night." The event invited comparison with great moments in the history of Madison Square Garden. "Battles of the century have been held over and over again in the Garden," observed another reporter, "but it is doubtful if that great auditorium ever housed so wild and fanatically enthusiastic a gathering as the cohorts who attended Father Coughlin's Battle of the Millennium."[24]

Flushed with satisfaction, Coughlin returned to Detroit. He could be forgiven for believing that his efforts had at last breathed life into the National Union for Social Justice. Most others who had seen his rallies believed the same thing. In fact, however, Coughlin's speaking tour had established no solid institutional footing for the organization. It had created great excitement and had undoubtedly won new supporters to Coughlin's cause, but it had failed in its primary objective.

Some of the reasons were obvious. The lavish "swing around the circle" through the East and Midwest that he had originally announced never materialized. The Detroit, Cleveland, and New York speeches were all he made. Nor did he accompany his public statements with any private organizational efforts. When he visited these cities, he had no meetings with local organizers, made no attempt to set up local units of the National Union. He did have several assistants, but none of them performed anything like the function of Gerald L. K. Smith in the Long organization, traveling to promising localities to fan enthusiasm for the National Union. When, at a New York press conference before his Garden speech, someone asked him about the local representatives of the organization, Coughlin replied bluntly, "I am the Union for Social Justice. There are no representatives here."[25]

Equally important, perhaps, was Coughlin's failure to capitalize upon the momentum his speaking tour had generated. His New York rally had come very near the end of his broadcasting season, and for much of the next few months he did what few serious politicians riding the crest of a wave would have considered: he went on vacation. Through most of the summer, while Huey Long was making news every day from Washington, while Franklin Roosevelt was slowly regaining the political initiative with new legislative proposals, Coughlin was silent, resting quietly at a resort in the Berkshires and allowing crucial months to pass without giving his undeniable popularity any solid organizational base.[26]

Above all, however, Coughlin's problems stemmed from his continuing uncertainty about where he stood and where he wanted to go. Although it was during this period that he at last recognized that Franklin Roosevelt was through with him, he still had difficulty making a formal, public break with the Administration. In an interview in New York, he called Roosevelt's programs "splendid . . . the most wonderful ever enunciated by the leader of any nation." All he wanted, he claimed, was for the President to deliver what he had promised. At times, he hinted broadly about supporting a third-party Presidential candidate in 1936 (always insisting that he himself would never be such a candidate). At other moments, he stoutly denied any third-party plans. "I foresee none," he said shortly before his trip to Cleveland. "I have given the matter no thought at all." Without knowing precisely what the National Union was supposed to do, whom it was supposed to support or oppose, it was difficult for Coughlin to invest it with any real organizational strength.[27]

Despite all the problems, however, Coughlin's call for the formation of the National Union was widely heard. It came, after all, from the man with the largest regular radio audience in the world. And if what emerged was not a model of organizational efficiency, it was at least large and growing. There were already, Coughlin claimed, 8.5 million members in April, as he began his speaking tour. There would, he expected, be many more by the time of the 1936 elections. Like Huey Long, Coughlin stood at the head of a huge, if uncertainly defined constituency; and everyone involved in American politics in 1935 had reason to wonder exactly what both these movements had become.[28]

III

THOSE WHO HOPED FOR or feared a potent third-party challenge to the President in 1936 saw much in the Long and Coughlin organizations to support their visions. In the spring of 1935, both the Share Our Wealth Clubs and the National Union for Social Justice appeared to be vibrant, growing movements with almost limitless political potential. Yet those who looked more closely often reached a different conclusion: despite the impressive façades, both movements were less than they seemed. Large they undoubtedly were; but they were far from the kind of coherent, centralized organizations that could easily be transformed into an effective third party. Instead, they were highly diverse, loosely structured, and greatly decentralized: clusters of local interest groups more concerned with local problems and local rivalries than with national goals.

That should not, perhaps, have been surprising to leaders who had built their popular appeal largely by appealing to a sense of embattled localism. Long and Coughlin were apparently unprepared, nevertheless, for the heterogeneity of the movements they led. Long, in particular, found the structure and behavior of his Share Our Wealth Clubs so diverse and localistic that at times he seemed not to know what to make of them. In the beginning, he had outlined a relatively uniform, coherent, and disciplined structure for the clubs established in his name. Local units were, the official manuals and directives ordered, to hold regular meetings, elect officers, form committees, solicit members, and promote the creation of additional clubs elsewhere; they were to discuss Long's wealth-redistribution proposals; and they were to coordinate their activities closely with the national headquarters. "We're going to organize the United States," Long once boasted. "There won't be a town or a community that hasn't one of these clubs."[29]

But Long was soon forced to concede that the organization was far more loosely structured than he had planned. Occasional remarks that were perhaps more revealing than intended suggested that the national headquarters not only did not control what its local leaders were doing; often it did not even know who its local leaders were. Gerald L. K. Smith, for example, made a recruiting trip to Baltimore in 1935. When asked whether he planned meetings with local Share Our Wealth organizers, he answered that, no, he had only come to get a "general impression" of the movement in Maryland. The leaders, he lamely explained, were "more or less in secret." On another such trip, this time to Georgia, he spoke more freely about the individual autonomy of the clubs. "We are like a comb of honey," he told reporters in Augusta. "If you push a nail in it, you lose only the contents of a single cell. But if you push a nail in a pail of milk, it all leaks out. The honeybee is smarter than the cow." Statements like these suggest that Smith's much vaunted "organizing campaigns" in the South and elsewhere were really something quite different. Neither he nor Long did any real substantive work at the grass-roots level to create local units. They simply appeared in what they considered promising communities, attempted to generate publicity, and hoped that Share Our Wealth Clubs would spring forth spontaneously once they had left.[30]

Spring forth they did, but in forms that might often have surprised Long and Smith. In some places, apparently, Share Our Wealth membership involved no club at all; there was some truth to Raymond Gram Swing's observation in 1935 that "The 'Share Our Wealth' organization is first of all a glorified mailing list." In most communities, however, the clubs did become more than mailing lists. They were genuine organizations, with officers, meetings, local activities, occasionally even clubhouses. But beyond that, they had little in common with one another, and little in common with Long's vision of what they should become.[31]

Louisiana, predictably, had more units than any other state, and the Louisiana clubs were the most tightly organized, the most carefully controlled from above, the most responsive to Long's own wishes. Even there, however,

Share Our Wealth activity was far more local than national in focus. Clubs emerged virtually everywhere in the state, but usually not with any great spontaneity. They were, rather, new manifestations of the power of Long's Louisiana organization, and they worked far more assiduously to promote Huey's political aims within the state than to advance his visions of national reform. Meetings were often indistinguishable from ordinary campaign rallies; organizers attracted crowds by promising barbecue, beer, watermelon, and free parking. And at election time, the clubs became effective arms of Long's state campaign efforts, mobilized to help local candidates and to get voters to the polls.[32]

Elsewhere in the South, the local orientation of Share Our Wealth Clubs was even clearer, and the detachment from Long's own purposes occasionally almost complete. Most clubs expressed at least a nominal loyalty to Huey Long and his programs, but their primary attachments were to the institutions and established hierarchies of their own towns. Local Share Our Wealth leaders were not rebellious outsiders challenging an established power structure. They were men and women closely tied to the fabric of the community, and they presided over organizations almost indistinguishable from other local institutions.

In the small towns and rural hamlets where the Share Our Wealth Clubs seemed to grow most rapidly, it was often the local school or church that formed the focus of community life. Share Our Wealth Clubs, therefore, frequently emerged directly out of these existing social centers. In a remote village of Arkansas, for example, a Share Our Wealth Club worked closely with local education officials and held its meetings in the grammar school. The principal and superintendent treated the organization much as they would have treated a chapter of the PTA, perhaps because members of the club included many of the "leading citizens" of the community, men and women involved in other, school-related activities. Similarly, ministers in small communities throughout the South were often involved with the formation of Share Our Wealth units. The president of the club in Fort Myers, Florida, was W. H. Edwards, the Baptist preacher. In a tiny hamlet near Richton, Mississippi, an aging minister, whose stature in the community was such that the local church bore his name, presided over a Share Our Wealth meeting from his altar.[33]

It is difficult to determine precisely what these local clubs actually did. Many seem merely to have assembled occasionally for informal meetings. A Sarasota, Florida, unit more closely resembled a bridge club than a political organization, its members gathering from time to time in private homes to sip tea and listen to Long's addresses over the radio. Others, however, apparently took Long's injunctions to publicize his program and recruit new members seriously. In Jacksonville, Florida, Long supporters took out newspaper advertisements with messages like "Senator Huey P. Long wants every man and woman in Jax to hear him speak at 11:30 tonight over NBC." The Publicity Committee of the Bainbridge, Georgia, Share Our Wealth Club sent out a barrage of postcards to generate interest in Long's broadcasts. (One card found its way into the hands of the Governor of Florida, who forwarded it to Jim Farley. "The significant thing to me," he noted, was that it gave evidence that "somebody is doing some real organizing himself.") In Riviera, Texas, Long supporters took over the local community hall on the evening of one of Huey's speeches, set up a radio, and advertised a "big meeting . . . so that everyone can hear him."[34]

Elsewhere, Share Our Wealth meetings lacked even these tenuous connections with Long's own goals. Often they served as occasions for the discussion of purely local concerns. A meeting in Picayune, Mississippi, in 1935 illustrated how quickly such meetings could stray from their ostensible purpose. A local attorney who had reserved the Picayune City Hall for the occasion had been scheduled to address the gathering, but at the last moment he was unable to attend. In his place, unexpectedly, a member of the audience simply rose from his seat and, according to a reporter covering the meeting, "surprized [sic] his hearers with his oratory and logic." He spoke briefly about the Long Plan, explaining that Share Our Wealth members "were merely petitioning for their rights and freedom, and did not expect to attain their objective by violence and bloodshed." But talk soon turned to other matters: to falling crop prices, to problems of agricultural marketing, to local utility rates. By evening's end, the tone of the meeting was hardly distinguishable from an open session of a town council.[35]

IV

IN LARGER TOWNS AND CITIES, particularly outside the South, it was often more difficult for a Share Our Wealth Club to reflect the general concerns of the entire community. There the organizations tended to become the vehicles of particular local-interest groups, entrepreneurs, or political figures.

In some locations, the clubs became so entwined with the interests of local veterans (who admired Long for his stand on behalf of immediate payment of the bonus) that they became little more than extensions of existing veterans' organizations. A unit in Hoboken, New Jersey, for example, operated directly out of the headquarters of the Disabled Veterans of the World War; its officers were active in both organizations. In suburban Philadelphia, two veterans publicized a Share Our Wealth Club by distributing flyers praising Long's vote on the bonus bill, but saying nothing about wealth redistribution.[36]

Other Long admirers regarded the Share Our Wealth movement not only as a useful forum for promoting ideas, but as a good place to make money. In their communities, the clubs came to resemble small businesses, with local entrepreneurs using them to market books, pamphlets, newspapers, and other merchandise likely to appeal to Long supporters. Undoubtedly, some such organizers were genuinely loyal to Huey, but decided simply that there was no reason not to combine good works with personal profit. Edgar Norton, a "charter member" of the Springfield, Ohio, club, boasted years later that he had secured "the local agency in selling [Long's] paper and they sold like hot cakes on the streets of this city." But he added, apparently sincerely, that "In my opinion Huey Long was the greatest figure in American history."[37]

Others were more blatantly opportunistic, as the case of Arthur E. Mullen suggests. A former aviator, salesman, and radio announcer, Mullen began in 1934 to organize the Share Our Wealth movement in St. Louis. By the spring of 1935, he had achieved remarkable success. He had opened a regional headquarters in a downtown office building, recruited a staff, and established local clubs throughout the city, the leaders of which reported directly to him. "We want to go Tom Pendergast [the legendary Democratic boss of Kansas City] one better," he explained to a reporter, "and put a man and woman in each half block. It is time to get ready now for 1936—we're going to put a State and local ticket in the field, from Governor to constable." An effective speaker, Mullen attended dozens of organizational meetings in the city, explained the details of Long's Share Our Wealth Plan, and generated increasing enthusiasm among his audiences.

Skillful, zealous, energetic, Mullen seemed to be an ideal organizer. Gradually, however, other, more troubling characteristics began to appear. He boasted constantly about his personal friendship with Long, although there is no evidence that the two men had ever even met. He was, in addition, something of a tyrant, determined to dominate every phase of the St. Louis Share Our Wealth movement, unwilling to tolerate even modest autonomy among other local organizers. His appearances at club meetings were intended not only to generate enthusiasm but to remind members that he was the "organization manager," the man in control. Complaints came to Long's Washington office that Mullen was obstructing the efforts of Share Our Wealth organizers in the city who were not working through him. Earle Christenberry finally sent him a formal rebuke, chastising him for assuming too much authority and reminding him that no one needed his permission to establish a club.[38]

What finally made Mullen's activities intolerable to the national headquarters was his effort to use the clubs to turn a profit for himself. From Washington, he received a shipment of 400 copies of *Every Man a King,* with instructions to distribute them free of charge to Share Our Wealth members. Instead, he sold them. Long made it clear in the literature he mailed to local organizers that Share Our Wealth Clubs were not to be fund-raising agencies. Nevertheless, Mullen sent members into the streets to collect funds for the local organization. (One of his greatest problems, ironically, was preventing impostors from soliciting in his name.) The national headquarters sent literature and other paraphernalia to local units, but it did not provide money for expenses (one of the reasons, undoubtedly, that many clubs were so modest in size). Mullen, however, wrote Long's office constantly requesting support, claiming that he needed funds for rent on his office and for a private telephone.

Long was usually willing to tolerate any number of excesses on his behalf, but Mullen became too much even for him. The Washington office openly rebuked his tactics, refused to advance him any funds ("I don't know where you think we are getting the money," Christenberry wrote sharply), and, whether intentionally or not, succeeded in getting the controversy into the St. Louis newspapers. As quickly as he had emerged, Mullen faded away— closing his office, dispersing his staff, and disappearing from view. He was, he claimed shortly before the end, "as enthusiastic as ever," but there was little he could do, for there was "not a dime to carry on." Yet, as intolerable as Mullen's presence had been to Long's national headquarters, his absence may have been even more disturbing. So closely tied had the St. Louis Share Our Wealth Clubs become to Mullen that, once he left, pro-Long activities in the city seemed virtually to cease. If Long had been gambling that the national loyalties of his supporters in St. Louis exceeded their local ties, he clearly had lost the wager.[39]

The Share Our Wealth Society was, above all, a political organization, and it was local politics that most often intruded into the clubs to divert them from their purported goals. In Louisiana, Long himself used the clubs as arms of his immediate electoral efforts. It should not have been surprising, therefore, that local political figures in other states and communities would try to do the same thing. These were, for the most part, marginal politicians—men who had been on the fringes of public life, who had never enjoyed electoral success, but who now, in the turbulent atmosphere of the Depression, saw a chance to improve their lots. Association with Long seemed at times to help, although it seldom helped enough to be decisive. A candidate for Mayor of Denver, for example, transformed his campaign structure into a Share Our Wealth Club and invited Long to Colorado to campaign for him. Huey never came. And while the publicity the invitation generated may have been its own reward, better-known and better-established candidates prevailed.[40]

California provided the best example of the incursion of local politics into the Share Our Wealth Clubs. Dissident politics there had by 1935 reached an intensity unmatched by any other state. The previous fall, the novelist Upton Sinclair had nearly captured the governorship on a vaguely socialist platform he entitled "End Poverty in California." Within months of his defeat, the powerful insurgent movement he had created was in confused disarray, and new dissident leaders began trying to move into the vacuum. Among the most conspicuous was Robert Noble. An erstwhile lieutenant of Sinclair, at times a supporter of some of the many Utopian schemes gaining currency in the state, Noble had decided by early 1935 that his own political ambitions dictated charting an independent course. He had broken privately with Sinclair even before the 1934 election; shortly thereafter, he openly repudiated him.

An accomplished radio speaker, Noble began a series of broadcasts in Los Angeles—for a time, speaking as often as twice a day—and used them to attack the EPIC movement, the flailing Utopian Society, and other local rivals for the large dissident constituency in the area. He founded a newspaper whose title seemed to change almost weekly but whose purpose never varied from what one of its early names—*Noble News*—suggested. And little by little, he introduced complimentary references to Huey Long into his speeches and his publications. By April, he was talking and writing about almost nothing else.[41]

What followed was an ugly and prolonged battle between Robert Noble and his former allies in the EPIC movement. Almost daily, accusations of treachery and ignorance flew back and forth—Noble's publications attacking Sinclair as an opportunist and a hypocrite, Sinclair and his followers denouncing Noble as a "potential MURDERER," a "betrayer," a "racketeer," and a maniac. Factions within the crumbling EPIC movement shifted between the two camps, with an increasing number, apparently, gravitating toward Noble and, as a result, toward Long. "As Huey Long Share-the-Wealth groups are coming together with a high degree of spontaneity all over the city and its suburbs," one reporter noted, "other organizations which have been figuring in the news are being eclipsed. . . . One group leader claims that his entire EPIC organization of 14,000 has gone over en masse to Huey Long." Robert Noble, he added, was the central figure in the phenomenon.[42]

Noble was, in fact, far more central than he was willing to admit. While he spoke constantly about his allegiance to Long, gave the organizations he founded the name Share Our Wealth Clubs, and even renamed his newspaper for a time *Share the Wealth,* the real beneficiary of this activity was intended to be not Huey Long, but Robert Noble. This was evident from his publicity tactics—in which his own name, on newspapers, leaflets, and handbills, received at least equal billing with Long's. It was evident in the numerous rallies he organized on Long's behalf in Los Angeles, rallies that occasionally drew up to 2,000 people and were always planned to make Noble's speech the prime attraction.[43]

But it was evident, above all, in the substance of what Noble was saying. He was not, except in a vague and indirect way, espousing Huey Long's economic philosophy or promoting his wealth-sharing plan. He was, rather, using Long's name to support his own position within the factional struggle of California dissidents. Virtually never did he spell out the details of the Long wealth redistribution plan in his speeches or writings; he referred instead to Huey's belief that "Every man should share and share alike in the wealth he produces," a phrase that seemed more appropriate as a description of EPIC's "production-for-use" philosophy than of the Share Our Wealth program. Noble's most frequent public statements were to decry Sinclair's apparent retreat from the EPIC program and to suggest that Long was his appropriate heir.[44]

Noble also attempted to identify himself prominently with the California Technocrats. Originally a movement among intellectuals at Columbia University in the early 1930s, Technocracy had begun as a plan for restructuring the mechanisms of production and distribution along scientific lines to promote efficiency, prosperity, and economic justice. By 1935, it was in decline as a serious intellectual movement; but in California it survived in a popular form as another EPIC offshoot, espousing many of the same vaguely socialistic reforms that Sinclair had advocated in 1934. To attract the support of the Technocrats, Noble began portraying both Long and himself as true champions of Technocracy; and he recruited prominent members of the movement to write columns for his newspaper and to speak at his rallies. That Long himself had never shown any sign of interest in (or even knowledge of) Technocracy was of little importance. In California, as elsewhere, it was the imperatives of local politics, not the needs of national leadership, that determined the shape of the Long organization.[45]

V

AT FIRST GLANCE, Coughlin, like Long, seemed in 1935 to have created a vibrant national political organization. The evidence was difficult to ignore: the barrage of telegrams from National Union members during the World Court fight; the enormous crowds at Coughlin's public appearances; the impressively financed operations in Royal Oak. "Figures show," an Iowa enthusiast wrote in April, "that the National Union for Social Justice is being popularly acclaimed and acknowledged by every state in the union."[46]

The reality, however, was quite different. Huey Long's Share Our Wealth Society may have been in many ways an enigma; but the National Union for Social Justice, for the first year of its existence at least, was largely a myth. Being a member of the National Union initially meant little more than being a member of Coughlin's radio audience. Late in 1935, Coughlin finally did begin to impose a formal structure on the organization—establishing local chapters, creating a pyramidal hierarchy. But the effort did little to enhance the National Union's power. On the contrary, Coughlin faced a strong and continuing tension between his own desire for consolidation and central control of the organization and the attempts of local units to behave autonomously. The more he tried to suppress local diversity, the more his constituency seemed to drift away. In both phases of National Union organization, in other words, its members, like members of the Share Our Wealth Clubs, responded at best uncertainly and at worst with hostility to Coughlin's efforts to provide central leadership. It was little wonder that years later Coughlin himself admitted that the Union was "more notorious for its *lack* of organization than for its organization."[47]

In large part, the fault was Coughlin's own. The crucial months for the National Union were those of late 1934 and early 1935. Through most of those months, Coughlin not only made no efforts to spawn formal organizations at the local level; he expressly forbade them. His radio discourses never referred to official structural arrangements; and when he received inquiries from potential local leaders, he sent them unambiguous instructions. "There are no local offices," he bluntly explained; "no one is authorized to hold meetings or establish any sort of local units for the National Union. . . . Absolutely no one is authorized to accept contributions." In June, he modified his instructions to local leaders slightly, announcing his "desire that neighborhood meetings be held in your homes for the purpose of . . . evangelizing your non-member neighbors with our proposals." But he cautioned that "no newspaper publicity of any type whatsoever is to be encouraged or permitted" and reaffirmed that "We are working on the principle that officers are not required."[48]

For the most part, Coughlin got what he wanted in this first stage of the National Union—an organization that consisted primarily of names on a mailing list. But despite Coughlin's injunctions to the contrary, there were occasional signs of organizational activity at the local level—activity suggesting that the National Union possessed the same diversity, the same divided loyalties, and the same focus on local concerns that the Share Our Wealth Clubs displayed.

At times, of course, local activity took forms that Coughlin undoubtedly found gratifying. In Dayton, Kentucky, Coughlin organizers gathered 775 names on a petition and sent it to their Congressman, asking him to forward it to the White House. "We are helping Father Coughlin by urging all voters to write directly to him, and unite with his National Union," they claimed. "In addition, we have set out to get A GREAT BODY OF ALL THE VOTERS in our community, to enter into this SOLEMN PACT—pledging themselves to vote AGAINST any candidate of any party who has a record of opposition to the proposals of the NATIONAL UNION FOR SOCIAL JUSTICE." Robert T. Malone, a building contractor and political activist in Lincoln, Nebraska, organized a small group of Coughlin supporters to write letters and editorials on behalf of the National Union and send them to local newspapers for publication. ("Our newspapers here are very reactionary," he explained to Coughlin, "as is the community.") The National Union was, wrote one friend of Malone to an Omaha newspaper, "serving a good purpose in counteracting the propaganda from the right which never ceases to say, 'Come on and play ball with special privilege, it's the only "practical" thing to do.' "[49]

Other varieties of local activity were more disturbing. Like Long, Coughlin attracted his share of crackpots and rogues, whose efforts on his behalf were at times embarrassing. But even where National Union leaders behaved honestly and rationally, they often displayed more interest in the specific concerns of their own communities than they did in Coughlin's broader principles. In New Rochelle, New York, for example, a group of National Union members led by a local priest appeared at a meeting of the Board of Supervisors to demand a reduction in utility rates. They were, the priest claimed, representatives of "Charlie Coughlin," and they were there on his behalf to undertake "a courageous mission—to fight the power monopoly." When pressed, he admitted that Coughlin had not asked them to appear at the meeting, that National Union headquarters in Royal Oak had not even been informed of their plan. But as a member of the organization, he insisted, he represented Coughlin "ipso facto."[50]

Occasionally, local politics intruded into the National Union so prominently that Coughlin himself became a decidedly secondary figure. The 1935 municipal elections in Cincinnati were a case in point. Early in the year, Dr. Herbert S. Bigelow, a liberal Protestant clergymen, had established himself as the leading Coughlin supporter in the city. His credentials were impressive. As pastor of the well-known People's Church, a congregation composed largely of dissidents (some said "radicals") from other parishes throughout the city, he had for over thirty years maintained one of Cincinnati's few forums for open discussion of controversial issues. During the Red Scare following World War I, he had dared to host Norman Thomas and other political insurgents when almost no one else would have them.

But he had also been a political activist in his own right. In 1912, he had served as president of the Ohio constitutional convention and had helped introduce progressive principles into the structure of state government. Five years later, he had been an outspoken critic of American involvement in World War I, an unpopular stand that resulted in his being dragged from his home one night, carried to a deserted hillside, and savagely beaten by a group of men who claimed to be acting in "the name of the women and children of Belgium." And in 1924, he had translated his long-standing abhorrence of machine government in Cincinnati into enthusiastic support for a reformist city charter (drafted by a member of his own congregation).[51]

By 1935, he had turned his energies, in part, in other directions, attacking the bankers and "moneyed interests" and chiding the Roosevelt Administration for not doing enough to limit their power. He had created his own political organization, the People's Power League; he had begun publishing a weekly newspaper, the *People's Voice;* and he had become an increasingly vocal supporter of Father Coughlin. In many ways, his organization operated as a local branch of the National Union for Social Justice. One of the first issues of the *People's Voice* devoted its entire front page to Coughlin and the Union ("This brave priest is the mightiest force in America," it claimed). When Coughlin took to the air to warn that he was dangerously short of funds, Bigelow wrote a vigorous appeal to his readers for help:

This is alarming news. Father Coughlin may be forced off the air. Not by the bankers. But by the very people who hang on his words. . . . It must not be that we who love this priest, who wait from Sunday to Sunday to drink in his words, and who look to him as to no other, as our champion, it must not be that we shall fail him or let him lack for funds.

By early February, he claimed, his People's Power League had processed over 25,000 applications for membership in the National Union for Social Justice.[52]

But Bigelow's attachment to Coughlin was not entirely unselfish. He was in 1935 engaged in political struggles of his own, and his identification with the National Union became a springboard for personal success. Ever since Cincinnati had approved its new city charter in 1924, municipal elections had been a contest between Republicans, who represented the old machine forces in the city, and Charterites, the reformers who had won the initial battle for a restructuring of the city government. For ten years, the Charterites had been victorious, achieving a majority of the seats on the city council and controlling the appointment of the all-important city manager. Through much of those same ten years, however, Herbert Bigelow had been impatient with the charter administrations, insisting that speedier and more sweeping reforms were necessary. With the onset of the Depression, his demands took on renewed urgency; and in 1935, he announced his candidacy for election to the city council as an independent.

In the course of his campaign, Bigelow missed no opportunity to publicize his connection with the National Union for Social Justice. He incorporated Coughlin's Sixteen Principles into his platform (even though most of them were basically irrelevant to the needs of city government). He continued to lavish praise upon the priest in his newspaper. He distributed copies of a personal letter from Coughlin wishing him luck at the polls (a vague message that Coughlin no doubt considered a routine courtesy but that Bigelow used as evidence of an intimate friendship between the two men). On election day, Bigelow roared to a totally unexpected victory, the first independent to win a council seat since adoption of the charter. In a field of thirty-three candidates, only the city's popular mayor polled more votes; and Bigelow was now the crucial swing vote on the nine-member council, whose other eight seats were evenly divided between Republicans and Charterites.

Bigelow's prominent identification with Coughlin may not have been the only factor in his victory, but it was certainly important. The overwhelming support he, a Protestant minister, received in Catholic wards was one indication. The comments of politicians and journalists after the election were another. Wrote one reporter: "Father Coughlin has thus become a major factor in Cincinnati's government by his part in destroying the charter's majority of a decade's standing." Yet Coughlin himself had had little to do with it, and he would have even less to do with Bigelow's performance on the council in the future. His name, his reputation, and his organization had been used to promote a local political cause of which he apparently had little knowledge and in which he had no particular interest.[53]

VI

COUGHLIN HAD AVOIDED imposing a formal structure upon the National Union in part to keep local interests and loyalties from intruding into his movement. They intruded despite him. And when, in December 1935, eager to expand his political reach, he finally moved to create a genuine organizational apparatus for the Union, the problems intensified.

The restructuring of the National Union would, Coughlin insisted, be ambitious and complete. The leadership would recruit "20,000 selected workers" to begin the work of purging the Congress of "rubber-stamp" members and replacing them with advocates of genuine reform. No longer would the Union be an informal mailing list. Coughlin supporters should now establish official organizations in every Congressional district, elect officers, recruit members, and raise funds. Each local unit was to support candidates without regard to party affiliation; the only criterion would be their willingness to endorse the principles of social justice. And each unit was to remain in constant contact, through an elaborate hierarchical structure of command, with the national headquarters in Royal Oak. No one was to engage in any activities not sanctioned by Coughlin himself.[54]

How difficult it would be to enforce this central control became evident within months. By early 1936, the pages of Coughlin's new weekly newspaper, *Social Justice,* were filled with evidence—in the form of letters from National Union members and of complaints by Coughlin himself—of problems. Local organizers wrote constantly to bemoan the lack of discipline and commitment. "Our lagging members sit down and take it easy," a Detroit National Union operative complained, "while the officers must trudge wearily to their homes after them." The president of an Ohio local noted, "It is very peculiar how many people will laud Father Coughlin to the skies . . . and will not go two blocks away to attend their unit meetings . . . and are extremely loath to be placed on committee work that involves a little time or effort." Other organizers pointed similarly to "idlers," "laggards," and "absentees" in their local units. "It is becoming increasingly apparent," *Social Justice* warned, "that many of the local units are carrying along on the financial support of only about 20% of the members."[55]

Even more disturbing to Coughlin was the evidence that very often those members who were taking the organization seriously were not paying much attention to his own wishes and directives. "From every congressional district," *Social Justice* reported with dismay,

> reports are coming to our central office to the effect that local politicians, together with certain local political machines, are beginning to infiltrate the National Union. . . . Local unit meetings are called for the purpose of studying the principles of social justice. As worthy as any other cause may be, no other subject should be introduced at these gatherings.

The response to such warnings was not encouraging, and expressions of alarm by Coughlin and his associates continued. "In our midst," Coughlin warned in an April sermon, "we will not tolerate any local unit president or elected officer who is not willing to endorse the candidate whom we endorse." A few weeks later, he threatened to "expel individuals or remove them from office" if any attempted to "pervert the minds of those who have joined our organization." "If necessary," he warned, "I shall 'dictate' to preserve democracy." On other occasions, he complained that local officers were not submitting to

Royal Oak a report of each meeting and, more importantly, an account of "every penny of revenue which is received. . . . More than six thousand local units have yet to hand in their first secretary's and treasurer's reports."[56]

Despite these strident warnings, there was apparently little Coughlin could do to prevent local concerns from intruding into his organization. He tried, for example, to ban all social activities from National Union meetings, denouncing them as irrelevant to the organization's basic concerns. Public protest against the order (and defiance of it) were so intense that he was forced to retreat. "Small affairs, such as bunco and card parties, may be held in the homes of members," he finally conceded. He attempted to prevent local politicians such as Herbert S. Bigelow in Cincinnati from "infiltrating" the National Union. In March, *Social Justice* denied flatly that Bigelow was in any way a spokesman for the Coughlin organization. Yet, less than a month later, the National Union in Cincinnati endorsed Bigelow's candidacy for Congress.

"An idle organization whose units are loosely knit toegther," *Social Justice* continued to insist, "will not only fail to function efficiently but will be the cause of disorder and disaster to itself and to other citizens with whom it comes in contact." The National Union for Social Justice had become precisely such a loosely organized, locally oriented organization. And Coughlin was powerless to change it.[57]

VII

WHY DID THE SHARE OUR WEALTH CLUBS and the National Union fall so far short of becoming the organizations their leaders had envisioned? There were several obvious explanations. One was the nature of the ideology to which Long and Coughlin supporters were responding, an ideology that stressed the importance of the local community and denounced the idea of centralized control of its institutions. A related factor was the traditional nature of American politics. Long and Coughlin were discovering, as innumerable public leaders had discovered before them and as others would discover later, that the focus of the nation's political behavior remained primarily a local one. To the extent that they had succeeded in mobilizing popular support, it had not been by turning the gaze of their followers away from community concerns and toward collective national goals. It had been by providing labels, symbols, and images around which local groups could gather while still retaining a measure of autonomy. Long and Coughlin themselves were important parts of such local activities, but within limits: distant figures, offering little more than vague (and adaptable) ideological umbrellas under which members could express their own grievances and concerns.

But there was also a failure of leadership, the dimensions of which are apparent from a comparison of the efforts of Long and Coughlin with those of the populists of the 1890s. The Farmers' Alliances, and the People's Party that emerged from them, were, like the Long and Coughlin movements, insurgent organizations emerging outside, and in competition with, the major parties. The populists, however, never relied on the appeal of a single leader or group of leaders for their organizational strength. The Alliances produced thousands of lecturers and organizers, who traveled from community to community generating support for the movement and educating farmers in its ideas and proposals. Independent local efforts on behalf of the movement and the party, far from being affronts to a central leadership, were its backbone. Long and Coughlin, by contrast, relied almost entirely on their own personal efforts to attract support and build organizational strength. Coughlin had no local organizers; Long had only Gerald L. K. Smith. Neither encouraged their followers to undertake active political efforts of their own. There was, in short, nothing for members of either organization to do, if they obeyed their leaders, besides write letters to the President and listen to the radio.[58]

Yet it was the radio itself that was, in the end, the most important influence upon the character of the Long and Coughlin organizations. It gave both leaders direct, immediate access to millions of men and women; it produced a special bond of intimacy and friendship between the speaker and his audience. But that same ease of access had destructive effects upon the movements Long and Coughlin were creating, producing among their followers a sense of detachment from the organizational process.

Insurgents in the 1890s, without access to instruments of mass communications, had no choice but to engage in elaborate grass-roots proselytizing. A dissident leader in the 1930s could reach a larger audience in a single radio broadcast than an orator could have addressed in a lifetime forty years before. There was, it seemed, no pressing need for elaborate local efforts. The message could be transmitted without them. Yet it was just such local organizational activity that worked most effectively to give ordinary men and women a strong sense of connection with dissident politics. By making the relatively passive process of listening to the radio the dominant activity of their followers, Long and Coughlin ensured that their movements would never become what the populist movement had once been: a constant, visible presence in the lives of communities. The two leaders remained, rather, the diffused voices of a new and non-involving medium.[59]

9

Followers

WHEN WILLIAM C. SCHIMPF, a struggling real estate broker in Germantown, Pennsylvania, began in 1934 to work publicly on behalf of Father Coughlin and the National Union for Social Justice, he was taking another hopeful step on what had been a long and troubled road. What led him to Coughlin and what he ultimately did on Coughlin's behalf suggest much about the larger outlines of Depression protest.

Born in 1895, the son of a grocer who owned his own small business, Schimpf had as a child watched his father lose his store and take a job as a machinist in a nearby steel company. The family income, though steady, was small; and at age eleven, the boy began supplementing it by working afternoons and evenings as a pin-setter in the bowling alleys of a nearby cricket club. He made seven dollars a week. Graduating from grammar school in 1911, he enrolled in a "manual training" high school, studied for two years, and quit to take a position in the real-estate department of a local bank.

Schimpf was not, however, content with his eight-dollar-a-week job as an office drone. For two years, he attended night courses at the Drexel Institute in nearby Philadelphia, studying real-estate law and finance. The experience enabled him to land a new position in a real-estate firm at a salary nearly twice what he had been making as a clerk. He was moving up in the world, and over the next few years, he handled a series of successful transactions that earned him what he considered a "small fortune." In the midst of his success, he left Germantown to serve in the Army during World War I. When he returned two years later, he simply picked up where he had left off. "They were happy days," he later recalled. "There were times when six or seven sales were made in one day." Feeling confident and secure, he married, bought a house, and settled contentedly into the life of a prosperous local businessman. His success, he believed, "was assured—with a good income and a home with low carrying charges, what more could be desired?" By the late 1920s, he had established his own company—William C. Schimpf, Inc.— and had expanded into insurance, appraising, and estate management.

But the Depression hit him hard. Business tailed off, at first slowly, then more rapidly. More and more often, he found himself saddled with bad debts. His father, now seventy years old, lost his job after thirty years with the steel company and added a new financial burden. "I am in a business that requires me to visit the middle class and the class below them," he wrote Franklin Roosevelt in 1933 (in what was probably a roundabout reference to Schimpf himself). "I enter their homes and find real distress and heartaches." The comfortable middle-class life-style and the community status for which he had worked so long and of which he had become intensely proud was ebbing away. His business was failing; his home was threatened; banks and government agencies refused him loans; and the specter of genuine indigence loomed menacingly on the horizon.[1]

It was Franklin Roosevelt who became the first beacon of hope on what was an otherwise bleak horizon. "Keep up the good work," Schimpf wrote him late in 1933. "[The people] are for you and trust in you as a last resort and as a sinking swimmer grasps for a life-preserver." A year later, there were reservations. He still supported the President, he insisted, but he feared that Roosevelt had not been "firm enough," had not succeeded in "drowning out opposition to things that are for the good of the majority." It was at this point that Coughlin (who was by now saying much the same thing about the President) entered Schimpf's life. With several neighbors, Schimpf decided in the summer of 1934 to form what he called a "new political party." Its purpose: "to watch either of the present major parties as to legislation offered and passed, etc." Its name: Coughlin's Party. There is no evidence that Schimpf's organization ever attained a size to justify the label "party," or that Coughlin had authorized the use of his name. (Indeed, Coughlin publicly disassociated himself from it shortly after reports of its creation appeared in the press, and Schimpf reluctantly proposed a new title: the Melting Pot, a name whose significance he did not explain.) But of his allegiance to Father Coughlin there can be little doubt, for no sooner did Coughlin announce the formation of his National Union for Social Justice than Schimpf enlisted in the cause.[2]

At the same time, a note of desperation was creeping into Schimpf's impassioned letters to Roosevelt, and it was evident that he was slowly losing his grip. In March of 1935, disaster struck. Schimpf was arrested and charged with larceny. He had collected $275 in rents from a building he managed and, instead of turning the money over to the owner, pocketed it. When pressed for an explanation, he plaintively and pathetically explained that he had "invested" the funds in the National Union for Social Justice and had lost them all. "I expected to get my money back through the sale of handbills expounding Father Coughlin's principles," he explained, "but they did not sell. . . . I had the name of the Father Coughlin party pre-empted and became treasurer." (When the story appeared in the press, Coughlin wrote Schimpf to say he regretted that his name had been used.)

William Schimpf—a man with conventional middle-class aspirations and a modest but treasured financial stake in his community, a man who had watched his world crumble slowly about him—had turned in anger, frustration, and hope to the words of Father Coughlin. Fearful and resentful of the menacing outside forces that were eroding his position in the community (the banks foreclosing on mortgages and refusing him loans, the government bureaucrats raising taxes and ignoring his plight), he had lashed out in a way that expressed both a modest radicalism and a conservative regard for traditional local values. "As Abraham Lincoln once said," he wrote, "let this be a government 'Of the people, by the people and for the people. . . .' What is taking place in my personal opinion is just that. Governments the World over are being taken over by the people and each and everyones right to 'Live and let live.'" Or, as he lamented on another occasion, "I had position and influence in my town. What has happened to me will happen to others until we local business men receive some protection."[3]

II

WHAT HAPPENED TO SCHIMPF DID, of course, happen to others. And while his story (with its sad denouement) is hardly typical of the experiences of Long and Coughlin supporters, it is indicative of the particular experiences that many of them seem to have shared. Observers in the 1930s might refer to the Long and Coughlin constituencies as "faceless legions" about whom "even the most basic characteristics are unknown." But enough people like William Schimpf left evidence of their circumstances to suggest that both movements drew their greatest strength from similar groups: men and women clinging precariously to hard-won middle-class life-styles; people with valued but imperiled stakes in their local communities.[4]

One such follower of Huey Long was A. L. Boley, a resident of Claremont, California. Early in his career, Boley had been a public-works inspector in the Puget Sound Navy Yard near Seattle, Washington, a secure and relatively lucrative government job that carried with it a measure of responsibility and modest status. He had married, fathered two children, bought a house in the Seattle area, and settled into a comfortable middle-class existence.

Boley's problems began not with the Depression, but earlier—with the First World War. In 1917, he resigned his civilian job to accept a commission as Lieutenant of Engineers in the Army. When he received his discharge two years later, he was a broken man. The nature of his medical problems— whether they were the result of a combat injury, of illness, of psychological strain—is unclear. But the Veterans' Administration declared them "service related," and Boley began in 1920 to receive a pension that, when combined with the modest income he received from intermittent jobs and his wife's earnings as a schoolteacher, allowed him to preserve at least a semblance of his former life-style. He kept possession of his Washington house (although by 1933 he was living in California); he managed to maintain an adequate, if not lavish standard of living for his family; he accumulated a modest savings and an equity in his Washington property "as a partial guarantee of security against the approaching infirmities of old age." Suddenly, in 1933, everything fell apart.[5]

Boley had been forced to make sacrifices during the first years of the Depression, as his occasional earnings became less frequent. But it was the passage in March 1933 of the Economy Act, the early New Deal measure that, among other things, substantially reduced government benefits for veterans, that finally shattered Boley's fragile economic security. "My wife and myself," he complained to Franklin Roosevelt, "will lose every dollar we possess because we cannot possibly protect our equity in property which we are paying for due to the sudden lopping off of this income which we had every reason to believe would be permanent." He was, he claimed, like "the many thousands of men whose families stand to lose the very roof from over their heads and who deserve this consideration in terms of their status as dependable citizens in their home communities."

To Boley, as to countless other veterans, Huey Long became a voice of hope and promise. His outspoken opposition to the Economy Act, his frequent defense of the rights of veterans, and his denunciations of concentrated wealth and financial privilege struck a responsive chord in Boley's anguished mind. When Senators from Washington state and California failed to solve his dilemma, Boley began writing instead to Long, asking for advice and expressing "my ever growing regard for your stand on matters concerning the common people as a whole, and the disabled exservice men in particular."[6]

Few supporters of either Long or Coughlin left equally full accounts of their circumstances and experiences; many, however, provided evidence of the essentially middle-class nature of both movements. Their names appear repeatedly in the scanty records that survive. James Zuccarelli, a pharmacy owner in Belleville, New Jersey—a Coughlin admirer. Paul Black, a teacher at an engineering school in Illinois—a Long supporter. Thomas Alessi, a lawyer in Buffalo, New York (conducting his profession "through my home") —a faithful member of Coughlin's radio audience. Even W. E. Warren, presi-

dent of a struggling bank in a small town in Montana—who wrote Franklin
Roosevelt that "Huey Long is the man we thought you were when we voted
for you" (a letter that so alarmed Louis Howe that he forwarded it, from his
deathbed, to the President for special consideration). These and others—
realtors, barbers, department-store saleswomen, grocers, bank clerks, chiro-
practors, professionals of modest means—seemed to find in the messages of
Long and Coughlin plausible explanations for their plight. It was little wonder, then, that observers attempting to diagnose the nature of the two movements and expecting to find in their ranks only the destitute, the indigent, and
the ignorant, often expressed surprise when they discovered, as the *New
Republic* noted in 1935, that Long and Coughlin seemed to be rallying the
"lower middle class," "small business men and professionals," in a "militant
and honorable protest."[7]

The term "middle class" is a vague one, to be sure; and if the conventional, popular image of the American bourgeoisie were to be the standard,
few Long and Coughlin supporters would qualify. They were not usually men
and women who lived in neat suburban bungalows or who worked at comfortable, white-collar jobs. More often they lived precariously and somewhat
shabbily. Their membership in the middle class was less a result of their level
of material comfort than of a certain social outlook. They were, they believed,
people who had risen above the lowest levels of society, who had acquired a
stake, however modest, in their community, who were protecting hard-won
badges of status and carefully guarded, if modest, financial achievements.
Others may have suffered more in absolute terms from the 1930s economy, but
those on the fringes of the middle class confronted an especially agonizing
form of loss. Having gained a foothold in the world of bourgeois respectability,
they stood in danger of being plunged back into what they viewed as an abyss
of powerlessness and dependence. It was that fear that made the middle class,
even more than those who were truly rootless and indigent, a politically
volatile group.

III

IT WAS A SIMILARLY BOURGEOIS OUTLOOK that drew to the Long and
Coughlin movements many farmers and workers. Among them, as among
others, Long and Coughlin tended to attract people who had achieved some
level of success, who had acquired stakes in their communities that they were
eager to protect or regain.

Long's own rural background and his reliance upon agrarian support in
the first stages of his public career made natural his popularity among farmers.

That popularity increased as his movement grew. Greatest in the Southern states, it extended to other areas as well. Farmers in Iowa gave him an enthusiastic reception during his 1935 visit there. A small farmers' weekly in Oklahoma, the Stroud *Democrat,* noted happily that "No man in the past quarter century has been as potent a factor in our national political life as Long." A Congresswoman from an Arizona farm district praised Huey in 1934 for his "friendship and kind help" on farm issues in Washington.[8]

Coughlin, whose background was as urban as Long's was rural and whose position as a priest was not likely to enhance his appeal to predominantly Protestant farmers, managed nevertheless to attract significant support in rural areas. Both his populist imagery and his inflationary monetary proposals resounded clearly with many unhappy agrarians; and while his popularity among them may not have been as great as Long's, it was enough to attract notice. A group of Iowa farmers, for example, told a reporter in 1935 that they not only admired Coughlin, but preferred him to Long. "I'm afraid of Huey Long," one man commented. "He's a radical. Father Coughlin's got the right idea." In another area of Iowa, a local farm organization passed a resolution praising Coughlin for "his tremendous and marvelous influence" and sent it to the President. A Midwestern farm journal lauded Coughlin in an editorial as "a great speaker and thinker"; and an Oklahoma landowner wrote Senator Elmer Thomas to ask "if it would be all right with you" for him to "correspond with Father Coughlin on my farm proposition."[9]

No one was more firmly wedded to the ideals of property ownership and local autonomy than the small farmer; and the appeal of Long and Coughlin to such men and women fit comfortably into a tradition of agrarian dissidence that combined strident attacks upon distant financial powers with rejection of radically collective solutions. Among industrial laborers, however, the popularity of these movements cannot be so easily explained. The populists had conspicuously failed to attract substantial working-class support, despite their concerted efforts to do so. Long and Coughlin, whose attempts to woo labor were only marginally more strenuous at best, succeeded far better. That they did suggested much about the difference between populist insurgency and Depression dissidence. Unlike agrarian activists of the 1890s, Long and Coughlin had not emerged from an elaborate grass-roots organization closely tied to agricultural communities; nor had they developed economic programs based upon concrete proposals to assist farmers. Their movements were far looser in organization and vaguer in ideology—a condition that may have given them the problem of fuzziness, but also provided the advantage of adaptability.

Their appeal was, however, specific enough to limit their support to a particular segment of the working class: skilled and relatively conservative laborers and the entrenched craft unions that represented them; those who had acquired at least modest social and economic status and who felt uncomfortable with the idea of allying with their less privileged colleagues. In Coughlin's case, this tendency was particularly striking because it stood in sharp contrast to some of his own public statements. An avowed defender of the right to organize, he often criticized the conservative, craft-oriented American Federation of Labor for its cautiousness, its elitism, even for its infiltration by "racketeers" and "gangsters." He called, instead, for a new approach to labor organization, one that would take the needs of unskilled assembly-line workers more fully into account, one that would unite laborers on the basis of an entire industry rather than a particular craft.[10]

Yet Coughlin's militancy, his commitment to the concept of industrial unionism, was more apparent than real. In practice, he advocated a moderation more characteristic of the AFL craft unions than of the emerging industrial organizations he claimed to support. In Detroit, for example, he spoke boldly about the need for automotive workers to organize along industry-wide lines. Yet he associated himself with the most cautious and moderate of the many competing organizations, one that earned the contempt of some auto workers as a "company union." It did not deserve the label; but neither was the Automotive Industrial Workers Association at the center of the labor militancy that would ultimately produce the United Auto Workers.[11]

Within the union, moreover, Coughlin was a frustratingly conservative voice. Even in his most impassioned speeches to AIWA rallies, he felt obliged to remind his audiences that "I do not come before you to wave the red flag. . . . I still believe in the doctrine of private initiative." And when in the fall of 1935 the union called its first major strike—against the Motor Products Corporation—Coughlin refused to support the effort, even after four people died in violent confrontations with strikebreakers and company police. "Father Coughlin just let us down cold," Richard Frankensteen recalled. "He did not do a thing for us."[12]

"That was the end of Father Coughlin in labor circles," one union leader later claimed. It was not. It was simply a sign of how artificial his support of labor militancy had always been and how rapidly his working-class support was narrowing to those with relatively limited aims. Despite his denunciations of the AFL, Coughlin was by 1935 moving toward a far cozier relationship with its established hierarchy than with the dissidents who would later form the Congress of Industrial Organizations. AFL President William Green took note of the "wide interest taken by a large number of the members of the Federation in Father Coughlin" and suggested sending an unofficial delegate to the National Union for Social Justice rally in Detroit in April 1935. Frank

Duffy, secretary of the Carpenters' Union, reported substantial support for Coughlin within his organization. The head of the Chicago Federation of Labor let the city's parks commissioner deny his organization a permit for its annual Labor Day celebration in Soldiers' Field rather than promise not to invite Coughlin to speak. And James L. Ryan, president of the New York branch of a skilled metalworkers' union, wrote in 1933: "Father Coughlin is a messenger of God, donated to the American people for the purpose of rectifying the outrageous mistakes that have been made in the past." There was little evidence of such support from the newer, more radical labor organizations; and it was hardly surprising, therefore, that when the great schism in the AFL occurred in 1937, Coughlin harshly repudiated the CIO as dangerously communistic.[13]

This association with the more conservative, skilled, and elitist elements of the labor movement may help to explain Coughlin's strong appeal among older immigrant groups—the Germans and Irish in particular. Better established, more thoroughly assimilated than some of their eastern and southern European counterparts, members of these national groups were likelier to hold skilled jobs, to belong to craft unions, and to view themselves as part of the "labor aristocracy." It was perhaps this sense of relative status, as much as a clear religious or ethnic identification, that made the Coughlin message appealing to them. The priest's popularity among Poles in Detroit suggests as much; what evidence there is indicates that he appealed almost entirely to second- and third-generation Poles who had, like the Irish and Germans, secured relatively skilled and lucrative positions. He produced little enthusiasm among less successful Polish Catholic workers. Coughlin even attracted significant support from Protestants of Anglo-Saxon stock (many of them emigrants from Appalachia) who had obtained relatively prestigious jobs within the auto industry.[14]

Long's involvement with the labor movement was neither as direct nor as intense as Coughlin's, and his opinions about unionization are more difficult to gauge. He insisted that he was a friend of the workingman. "I've always been 100 per cent for labor," he liked to boast, "and labor's always been 100 per cent for me." But beyond that, he was frustratingly and perhaps purposely vague. "Huey would have fitted the labor movement into the picture one way or the other," one of his associates later insisted; but by the time of Long's death in 1935, he had made no basic decisions about how he would do so.[15]

Nevertheless, even without a direct, orchestrated appeal, Long attracted substantial labor support; and it was support that displayed many of the same characteristics as Coughlin's. There was occasional evidence of approval from the emerging industrial unions and the more militant leaders within the movement. For the most part, however, the interest came from the more traditional unions and the more conservative workers. The Oklahoma City Trades and Labor Council invited Huey to a Labor Day celebration over the outraged objections of dissident members, who called him a "notorious scab." The monthly publication of the Order of Railroad Telegraphers noted in 1935 that "Huey Long has reached a pinnacle no one has attained heretofore." And a Chattanooga chapter of the Brotherhood of Railroad Trainmen voted to endorse the Share Our Wealth Plan. National leaders of the AFL remained generally silent about Long (despite open endorsements from some state organizations in the South). But reprints of speeches and articles by William Green appeared regularly in the *American Progress.* If Green did not sanction the practice, neither did he denounce it.[16]

The laborers Long and Coughlin attracted did not suffer more from the Depression than other workers. In many ways they suffered less. What set them apart from many of their colleagues was that they usually had more to protect: a hard-won status as part of the working-class elite, a vaguely middle-class life-style, often a modest investment in a home. And while the evidence is limited, there is reason to suspect another important distinction: that laborers who supported Long and Coughlin tended to work in surroundings more reminiscent of middle-class occupations than other workers. Both men had followers among workers in large factories. Coughlin's most celebrated connection with labor, after all, was with an automobile workers union. But on the whole, they seemed to generate more support among those who worked relatively autonomously outside the factory environment: on construction sites, in small shops, or on independent jobs. Carpenters, electricians, plumbers, postal workers, bricklayers, railroad workers: all had substantial representation in the Long and Coughlin movements. Such men and women were members of the working class by any reasonable definition; yet by operating outside the regimented, hierarchical environments of mass-production industries, they maintained at least an illusion of independence.[17]

To many Long and Coughlin followers, therefore, the idea of industrial unionism was simply irrelevant. It was also unappealing. The prospect of uniting in common cause with laborers of fewer skills, lower pay, less social status—workers whom they had perhaps come to view with condescension or contempt—seemed a denial of the social gains they had so painfully won. And in that, they shared much with the other members of the Long and Coughlin constituencies: the local merchants, the small businessmen, the modest professionals, the family farmers.

Supporters of both movements were not usually indigent. Neither were they rootless. They were people with something to lose. They were, therefore, people particularly susceptible to the messages Long and Coughlin transmitted: the defense of local institutions, the excoriation of distant power centers. Such men and women sensed, if only vaguely, that the networks of local associations which gave their lives meaning were threatened by the emergence of a modern, integrated economy. And they looked for ways to defend not only their wealth, their status, and their influence, but the community institutions in whose terms they measured their success. Followers of Long and Coughlin differed greatly from one another in their occupations, their regions, their religious or ethnic backgrounds. What they shared was an imperiled membership in a world of modest middle-class accomplishment.

IV

WHAT INTERESTED MOST OBSERVERS IN 1935, however, was less the social characteristics of the Long and Coughlin constituencies than the simpler question of their size and distribution. Few public figures believed that either movement had as large a following as Long and Coughlin claimed. Nevertheless, they were concerned. A Democratic Party official in Ohio warned the White House early in the year that Coughlin's popularity now threatened every Democrat in the state. *Time* magazine reported with some alarm that Long had been one of the top five vote-getters in balloting for "Man-of-the-Year" for 1934. "It looks to me," a Kansas publisher wrote Franklin Roosevelt in March 1935, "as if this fellow [Long] is going to be a real menace to the United States and especially to the Democratic Party."[18]

There was little definitive evidence of the size of either movement, but some striking conclusions about the popularity of Long and Coughlin were possible. There were, for example, abundant indications of organizational activity on behalf of the Share Our Wealth Clubs and the National Union for Social Justice in almost every area of the nation.

The Long organization seemed to be expanding the more rapidly of the two in 1935. Most numerous in the South, the Share Our Wealth Clubs were springing up in other regions of the country as well. In the Northeast, clubs were proliferating in Pennsylvania, where the conservative Philadelphia *Evening Bulletin* noted with alarm that "There is no question that [Long] has, already, a substantial following in this state among people who have little or nothing." In New York, Share Our Wealth enthusiasts were publicizing new units in the Bronx and in Riverhead, on the eastern end of Long Island. Clubs were emerging in New Jersey, where a twenty-one-year-old college student, sitting in his living room surrounded by books and pamphlets on the Long

Plan, told reporters, "I can see no reason why we shouldn't have 50,000 members in Newark and an equal number in the rest of New Jersey"; and where Long himself was running full-page advertisements in local newspapers urging the "PEOPLE OF AMERICA" to "get together at once and organize a Share Our Wealth Society." From Connecticut (the only New England state, apparently, with any significant Share Our Wealth activity) came reports of clubs in Stamford, Hartford, and other towns. "We believe we have enough courage and backbone to force our ideas across to the people, and are organizing our society," one Connecticut loyalist wrote *American Progress.* [19]

Interest in the Share Our Wealth Society was growing more slowly in the Midwest than in most other regions, but Long was establishing a significant foothold there nevertheless. An attorney warned James Farley early in 1935 that "a great body of citizens are forming a Long for President club here in Kansas City," a message Farley immediately relayed to the President and to New Deal allies in Missouri. In Indiana, a lawyer defending Standard Oil in a court suit asked prospective jurors whether they were members of the Share Our Wealth Society before he would accept them. In Chippewa, Wisconsin, the Chippewa Baking Company took out an advertisement in the local paper in which it heralded not only the "Aroma of Butter-Krust and Sally Ann Bread" but the virtues of the Share Our Wealth movement. "Senator Huey Long may sound like a fool," the bakery noted (in a caption beneath a photograph of Long), "but, after all, he may be telling the truth." Long himself had spent little time in the Middle West, but, as a St. Louis man warned an official in the Commerce Department in Washington, he was "a factor to reckon with and he is gaining ground every day." His opponents in the region agreed. The publisher of the Des Moines *Register* observed in a letter to Herbert Hoover that "Long is developing a more dangerously large following than most people realize."[20]

Perhaps most striking was the extent to which active Share Our Wealth Clubs were emerging in the Far West, a region Long had never visited and to which he had devoted little attention. Frank Joesten, a one-time Farley lieutenant in Utah, for example, recounted a meeting he had attended early in 1935 of the Reform Taxpayers League, a statewide organization that had developed such strength that its proposals were gliding through the legislature almost without opposition. The main speaker for the evening began with a complimentary reference to Roosevelt, evoking modest applause. Then he remarked that Huey Long had already imposed in Louisiana the reforms the League was urging in Utah. As Joesten wrote Farley:

> Jim, I never saw a crowd turn loose like that, not for a long time,
> they just about lifted the roof and amongst them were several that

had referred to Long not more than a year ago as a d--n fool and a "nut," also in the crowd I recognized a lot of local democrat politicians some political appointees on the various F.E.R.A., H.O.L.C., and other Government organizations too numerous to mention, and they were applauding with the rest.[21]

There were similar reports from other Western states. "There will be," wrote the Arizona *Republic* in 1935, "a surprisingly large vote cast for Long [in 1936] because of his 'Share the Wealth' program. . . . The campaign in Arizona is said to be in flourishing condition." In Spokane, Washington, a Share Our Wealth organizer claimed 8,000 members in local clubs, a claim with which owners of KHQ, the local NBC affiliate, were likely to agree. When the station declined to air one of Long's radio addresses, it received a barrage of letters and telephone calls in protest and watched in horror as Long supporters began organizing a boycott of the station's advertisers to force a change in programming policy. Long's next broadcast returned to KHQ. In Portland, where one major newspaper was observing that "There can be no doubt that Long has a heavy following [in the state], not only of radio listeners but of partisans," a cancellation of a Long radio address produced a similarly angry reaction. "Can the NBC stations afford to disappoint some 30,000 or 40,000 Share Our Wealth society members," wrote one unhappy listener, "by excluding Senator Long's address to the nation? Something seems to tell me that this time KGW will broadcast Senator Long's speech."[22]

Of all the Western states, California proved the most fertile ground for the growth of Long organizations, as the fevered activity on his behalf by men such as Robert Noble suggested. Long's office in Washington received reports almost daily of new clubs springing up in the state. The *American Progress* was being ordered in lots of a thousand by some of the larger news dealers in Los Angeles. There was talk that the California legislature planned to invite Long to address it. Knowledgeable observers spoke with something approaching amazement of Long's growing popularity. "He has passed from the clown to the menace," warned the San Francisco *Chronicle*. "If this movement solidifies," a Los Angeles reporter noted, "politicians are beginning to wonder whether the advent of a third party might not result in the defeat of the Democrats next year." William Jennings Bryan, Jr., state chairman of the Roosevelt-Democratic organization, wrote to James Farley, "I have been astounded to learn the extent of the organizational work being carried on by the Huey Long forces in California. It has gained such momentum that I feel it is another serious factor in the California situation, which was already complicated enough."[23]

Letters to the *American Progress* likewise suggested an increasing geographic diversity for the Share Our Wealth movement. In 1933 and 1934, before the clubs had begun to take shape in any substantial numbers, mail to the newspaper (if letters published by the editors were any indication) came overwhelmingly from the South: 47 percent in 1933, 57 percent in 1934. Almost half of those were from Louisiana alone. The remaining mail was distributed relatively evenly among other regions. In 1935, however, with Long's organizational efforts at full strength, the picture was considerably different. Only 33 percent of the letters to the editor were from Southern states (only 11 percent from Louisiana), while all other regions were now well represented. Twenty-one percent of the mail came from the Northeast, 24 percent from the Midwest, 22 percent from the Western states. Louisiana and the South remained Long's strongest regions, and his support in other regions was somewhat disproportionately concentrated in a few states (Illinois and Minnesota in the Midwest, California in the Pacific region). But the letters clearly suggested that the Share Our Wealth Clubs were now a national phenomenon.[24]

The National Union for Social Justice was less successful in penetrating all regions of the country. By 1935, Coughlin had made few organizational inroads into the South and had won little support in the West. That was hardly surprising. A Catholic priest could hope for little political success in the South, and Coughlin never even tried to establish himself there. In the West, where his prospects might have been brighter, he had only recently succeeded in finding outlets for his sermons and was receiving little or no attention as yet from the local press. In the rest of the country, however, Coughlin's organizational support, like Long's, was proliferating rapidly. The National Union had a powerful foothold in New England. James Michael Curley once claimed that Boston was the "strongest Coughlin city in America"; and in Springfield, Massachusetts, a newspaper poll in 1935 disclosed that National Union membership was increasing dramatically, that "upon Father Coughlin rather than President Roosevelt the hard hit depression victim now pins his hope of financial rehabilitation." There were large Coughlin organizations in Connecticut and Rhode Island as well.

The huge crowds that greeted Coughlin when he spoke in New York were not composed simply of the curious; he claimed, and the *New York Times* agreed, that the National Union had by the end of 1935 attracted more members in that state than in any other. New Jersey, Pennsylvania, and Maryland (where Baltimore newspapers received a daily flow of letters to the editor praising Coughlin as "a man of courage" and one who "acts for the good of the people") also produced sizable memberships. It had been in the Midwest that Coughlin had first attained prominence, and the National Union attracted a particularly large following there. Coughlin's home state of Michigan was always a stronghold, but it may have been second to Ohio (where he had wide popularity in Cleveland and Cincinnati) as the leading National Union bastion of the region. Minnesota, Wisconsin, Illinois, Iowa, and Missouri all contributed significant memberships.[25]

Social Justice, the newspaper of the National Union, began publication only in March of 1936, so it offered a far less useful gauge of the organization's spreading influence than Long's *American Progress.* Nevertheless, letters to the editor during the paper's first four months of publication displayed a wide distribution of support. Four states—New York, Ohio, Illinois, and Pennsylvania—accounted for a disproportionate number of letters: 16, 13, 12, and 11 percent respectively. The remainder, however, were scattered relatively evenly among a large group of states. Just under half the letters came from residents of seventeen Northeastern and Midwestern states, each of which accounted for only between one and seven percent of the total. Coughlin's organization may have been far more limited by region than Long's, but it was gaining wide support throughout the two most populous areas of the country.[26]

V

ORGANIZATIONAL ACTIVITY ALONE, however, was not a sufficient indicator of the popularity of Long and Coughlin. Both men had supporters who, for various reasons, had not become active members of a Share Our Wealth Club or the National Union. Most observers could only guess at how many such followers there were, but one political organization tried to do more. In the spring of 1935, the Democratic National Committee commissioned a secret public-opinion poll to assess the threat that Huey Long might pose to the President's hopes for re-election the following year. The results were ominous. And that the survey unexpectedly gave sketchy evidence of the range of Coughlin's influence as well only deepened the discomfort of party leaders.

The survey was the work of Emil Hurja, a pioneer in the use of modern polling techniques; and it was one of the first such efforts to use scientific principles in the selection of its sample. Approximately 31,000 voters, chosen to reflect both regional and economic diversity, received ballots in the mail on which they were asked to choose among Franklin Roosevelt, an unnamed Republican candidate, and Huey Long in a hypothetical Presidential contest. Roosevelt led by a decisive margin—54 percent of the total vote, as opposed to only 30 percent for the Republican. But nearly 11 percent of those sampled expressed a preference for Long, which meant, James Farley believed, that

Long might receive as many as six million votes. "It was easy to conceive a situation," he wrote later, "whereby Long . . . might have the balance of power in the 1936 election."[27]*

Most striking, perhaps, was how evenly distributed Long's support was. He was strongest, predictably, in the South, where he received 14.5 percent of the ballots. But he did nearly as well in other regions: 13.6 percent from the Rocky Mountain states, 12.5 from the Great Lakes region, 12.1 from the Pacific Coast. Only in New England (8 percent) and the mid-Atlantic states (7.8) was there any significant relative weakness. The poll suggested, too, that Long was as strong in urban areas as he was outside them. Hurja compiled returns from thirteen major cities; and while occasionally Long did somewhat better in a particular metropolis than he did in the state as a whole (13 percent of the vote in Boston, for example, as opposed to 9.6 percent for all of Massachusetts), there was on average almost no variation at all. In the five mid-Atlantic cities examined, Long received 7.1 percent of the ballots; in the region as a whole, he received 7.8 percent. In five cities of the Great Lakes states, Long received 12.7 percent of the responses, while in the entire region he compiled 12.5 percent. In short, the Hurja poll strongly suggested that Long was neither a regional nor a rural figure; his support was distributed throughout the nation and relatively evenly between country and city.

There was, however, a significant variation in the response Long received from different economic groups. In thirty-two states, Hurja divided his sample into two categories: those who were receiving some form of government relief and those who were not. Long did strikingly better among the first group than among the second. From relief recipients, he polled 16.7 percent of the ballots; from the others, he attracted only 7.8 percent. There was no indication of how Hurja identified relief recipients or of whether they made up a proportion of his total sample comparable to their proportion of the population as a whole. But there could be little doubt that Long's appeal was greatest among the economically troubled. In certain areas, it was remarkably strong. In Louisiana, 49 percent of the relief recipients supported Long for President (to only 47 percent for Roosevelt), in Arkansas 38 percent, in Washington state 32 percent, and in Utah 23. (This preponderance of relief recipients was not incompatible with the picture of the Long constituency as predominantly middle class in occupation or outlook. Middle-class men and women in decline were among the largest groups benefiting from New Deal relief programs.)

Coughlin's name did not appear on Hurja's ballot. He had, moreover, never given any indication that he was eyeing the Presidency, and even his

---

*See Appendix II for a description and detailed breakdown of the Hurja poll.

most fervent admirers seldom considered a Catholic priest as a potential candidate. So the poll would have been unlikely to reflect his real popularity even if he had been listed. There were, however, so many write-in votes for Coughlin that his became the only additional name for which Hurja tabulated returns. His total showing was almost negligible: 280 ballots out of almost 31,000, or slightly fewer than one percent. But if the response said little about how many followers Coughlin had attracted, it did suggest several things about the distribution of his support.

Coughlin did not receive a single write-in vote from the entire South, nor from the Rocky Mountain states. From the Pacific Coast, he received only six votes, or .2 percent of the regional total, and from the border states only fourteen, or .5 percent. He was strongest where he had always been most visible: in New England, where he received 2.2 percent of the ballots; in his own Great Lakes region, where he polled 1.4 percent; and in the mid-Atlantic states, where his total was 1.3 percent. If this fragmentary evidence suggests anything, therefore, it is that Coughlin had by the spring of 1935 been far less successful than Long in reaching out to all areas of the nation, but that his popular support, as the distribution of the National Union likewise suggested, was spread relatively evenly among the populous states of the East and Midwest. It was also notable that Coughlin seemed strongest in the areas where Long was weakest—in New England and in the mid-Atlantic states. It was possible to conclude from the poll, therefore, that Long and Coughlin were, between them, mobilizing support throughout the nation, that each was compensating in some regions for the weakness of the other.[28]

VI

IT WAS THAT POSSIBILITY—that Long and Coughlin would not only continue to gain support, but that their movements would begin to complement each other and to merge—that politicians like Franklin Roosevelt and James Farley found particularly alarming. Separately, Long and Coughlin were formidable foes; together, many feared, they might mobilize a popular following of truly remarkable proportions.

At first glance, Long and Coughlin seemed so different from each other that a meaningful political relationship between them was difficult to envision. Long was a Protestant, a rural Southerner, a man who reveled in a coarse, anti-establishment public demeanor. Coughlin, a Catholic priest from a northern industrial city, strove constantly for intellectual and political respectability. The two men differed in important ways as well in their explanations of the Depression and their prescriptions for its cure. The connection between

Long and Coughlin, however, did not take the form of a personal relationship or an active political alliance; it manifested itself instead in a natural and increasing association of the two men in the public mind, an association that was by 1935 drawing their two movements together in countless ways. It was a development that neither man attempted to discourage, even though privately each viewed the other guardedly and with some contempt.

Long and Coughlin were not friends. Indeed, their personal association was so limited as to be almost nonexistent. Only one meeting between them can be documented with any certainty: a three-hour conversation in Long's hotel suite in Washington in 1935, a meeting precipitated by neither Long nor Coughlin, but by Senator Burton K. Wheeler, a friend of both. The conversation was said to have been cordial, each man expressing gratitude for the other's role in defeating the World Court treaty. But it was far from the beginning of a meaningful political understanding. There may have been other meetings (Long referred casually to one in a Senate speech several months later), but there is little reason to believe that the encounters were frequent or intimate. In an unguarded moment, after a tiring train trip to Chicago, Long gave reporters what may have been his frankest evaluation of the relationship: "Father Coughlin writes to me once in a while when he wants to know about some things, and my secretary supplies him with information. I write to him, too."[29]*

Even had they never met, they could scarcely have avoided forming opinions about each other. But when they attempted to express them, the distance between them often became uncomfortably clear. "Father Coughlin has his own road. So have I," Long told reporters in Philadelphia in March of 1935. "I am not lined up with him. It happens that we have agreed with each other on most things until now, but this will not necessarily be so in the future." And to a reporter for the *Nation,* he revealed what was perhaps his strongest feeling about Coughlin: uneasy jealousy. "Coughlin is just a political Kate Smith on the air," said the man who considered himself the nation's leading radio orator. "They'll get tired of him."[30]

Coughlin seemed, if anything, even less kindly disposed toward Long than Long was toward him. When he discovered, for example, that Long planned to attend a mass meeting in Iowa organized by farm leader Milo Reno, he quietly canceled his own plans to speak there and announced that no representative of his organization would appear. When a reporter for *Collier's* asked him once whether Long was someone he would trust to enact his principles of social justice, Coughlin dismissed the idea out of hand. "No, no," he replied. "Let's not talk idly."[31]

*No correspondence between Long and Coughlin survives.

An actual working alliance between Long and Coughlin was never very likely. Neither man was willing to consider sharing the authority and adulation that he was enjoying as leader of his own movement; neither was willing to contemplate the possibility of being overshadowed by the other. Yet neither was willing to go too far toward a public rift. Each recognized that it was in his own political interest to encourage public assumptions of accord. Each cast covetous eyes upon the constituents of the other and happily dangled before them the bait of a possible alliance. Coughlin, for example, responded with calculated coyness to speculation in 1935 that his National Union for Social Justice would soon merge with Long's Share Our Wealth Clubs. He knew the speculation was unfounded; but, unwilling to deny it, he said only that he planned to leave direction of the organization to its elected officers; the decision would not be his. On another occasion, he told the audience at one of his weekly "forums" in Royal Oak that Long was "a much maligned man." "Don't believe all you hear against him. . . . I want to say now that Huey Long is an honest-to-God devotee of social justice."[32]

Long waxed even more enthusiastic about Coughlin. "We are good friends," he lied to a correspondent for *America,* the Catholic journal. "He almost always has a visit with me" when the two were in Washington. When the same correspondent asked him to list his disagreements with Coughlin, Long was unable to think of any. "Well, there isn't much difference," he claimed. "I don't disagree with Father Coughlin very often. . . . I would almost say that we are working for practically the same principles." In another interview several weeks later, he went even further: "I think Father Coughlin has a good platform and I'm 100 per cent for him and everything he says."[33]

Both Long and Coughlin seemed to go out of their ways at times to emphasize the similarities between their economic programs. Long never agreed with Coughlin that currency reform alone would remedy the nation's problems. "Unless we get down to the basic and fundamental situation [wealth redistribution]," he once insisted, "free silver is not going to cure it, inflation of the currency is not going to cure it." But he supported most of Coughlin's monetary schemes nonetheless—denouncing rigid adherence to the gold standard, supporting a return to silver-backed currency ("We are practically the only country in the world to-day that has not remonetized silver," he complained), and ultimately calling for nationalization of the banking-and-currency system.[34]

Long was undoubtedly sincere about most of these positions; they were not, after all, incompatible with his own program, and they fit comfortably into the populist traditions he was so skillfully evoking. But there was almost certainly an element of calculation involved as well, an effort to make himself appealing to the admirers of his greatest rival for the dissident constituency.

Why else would he propose as one of the first events of his mythical Presidency, as recounted in *My First Days in the White House,* his drafting of a special message to Congress urging immediate enactment of the "Coughlin Banking Reform Act"?[35]

Coughlin, for his part, always refused to endorse Long's Share Our Wealth Plan, and he was said by associates to have considered the scheme unworkable. Nevertheless, he did give signs, particularly after 1933, of trying to associate himself with the wealth-redistribution issue in a more direct and intimate way than he had in the past. He began, for example, to stress the role of taxation in attacking economic inequality, and he gave increasingly explicit attention to the perils of concentrated wealth. "I believe in the broadening of the base of taxation," read the thirteenth of his Sixteen Principles of Social Justice. "The time has come," he noted in a radio sermon late in 1934, "when, if these Congressmen refuse to legislate against the concentration of wealth . . . then we are perfectly justified in accusing them of playing politics with misery." And in May 1935, in perhaps the most important speech of his career, he told the crowd jammed into New York's Madison Square Garden that "the social problem of paramount importance . . . is concerned with the distribution of our national wealth."[36]

Long and Coughlin were not only moving tentatively toward closer agreement on their central economic proposals. They were also—perhaps by coincidence, perhaps by design, or more likely by some of each—taking similar positions on many secondary issues. Both strongly supported immediate payment of the soldiers' bonus and sharply criticized Roosevelt's veto of the Patman Bill, which mandated that payment. Both endorsed limitation of working hours and changes in the length of the work week. Both called for government limitations on agricultural production and support of farm prices, and both harshly denounced the destruction of surplus crops and livestock under the Agricultural Adjustment Administration. Both expressed support for the concept of government pensions for the elderly, even if without much enthusiasm. And both enthusiastically endorsed massive federal spending for public works. Long, of course, was simply extending to the national level a commitment to such programs he had begun in Louisiana; but Coughlin, who was new to the issue, nevertheless came up with a public-works scheme of such vast dimensions (construction of 18,000 miles of federal highways, reclamation of 60 million acres of farmland, enlistment of "an army of idle workmen, armed with dynamite" to demolish existing slums and build 900,000 new homes) that he put even Huey's plans to shame.[37]

VII

THERE WERE, however, stronger reasons for interaction between the two movements than the calculated efforts of either leader to encourage it. Far more important was the general ideological affinity between their two messages. Supporters overlooked differences between the Long and Coughlin economic programs not just because Long and Coughlin themselves attempted at times to de-emphasize those differences, but because the specifics of the programs simply did not seem to matter very much. Letters to both men are replete with examples of this ideological flexibility. Long supporters wrote frequently of their enthusiasm for greenbacks, for elimination of private banks, and for other issues more clearly associated with Coughlin; while the priest received regular indications from his followers of their support for confiscatory taxation and federal guarantees of a subsistence income for every citizen, proposals that closely resembled Long's. And both men received countless letters advocating schemes that neither had ever proposed: an end to all federal taxes, federal licensing of all large corporations, an obscure plan for government "industrial certificates" to provide a capital pool for loans to speed recovery, and others.[38]

Such men and women were not consciously disagreeing with Long and Coughlin. They were, however, exposing a vital characteristic of both movements. The specific proposals that Long and Coughlin advocated were only one element, and by no means the most vital element, of their appeal. More important was the broader set of symbols, images, and values they had invoked, the diffuse ideology they had presented. At that level, the similarities between what Long and Coughlin were saying were often so striking that an interaction between their movements as each continued to grow was not only possible but virtually inevitable.

By the spring of 1935, a strong impression was growing in the public mind that the two movements were indeed becoming one. Hugh Johnson's March speech attacking both men as a common menace was the most visible expression of this new assumption, but it was far from the only one. Much of the press began to talk about Long and Coughlin in the same breath, as if neither could be understood without the other. "You are bound to compare Father Coughlin with Huey Long," wrote Walter Davenport in *Collier's.* Columnist David Lawrence spoke knowingly of the gossip in Washington that "both Father Coughlin and Huey Long were making serious inroads into the administration's strength." *Newsweek* confidently recounted Coughlin's role in persuading Long "to stop boozing so he could think more clearly" and Long's announcement that Coughlin "approved his 'share the wealth' and 'every man a king' platform." The *Times* of London gloomily predicted that the American people would soon turn to Long and Coughlin if Franklin Roosevelt's stalemate with Congress continued.[39]

More to the point, followers of Long and Coughlin were themselves making the connection. There was growing evidence in 1935 that in many places the two groups of supporters were beginning to merge, viewing the two men as part of the same movement. "It is too bad that there are not more men in our country like Long and Coughlin," a Connecticut man wrote the Hartford *Courant,* in a reflection of the increasingly natural association of the two names in the public mind. "I am just home from a trip out over parts of this state," a Wisconsin man wrote Harold Ickes in April 1935, "and I was surprised to find life-long Democrats and Republicans saying bluntly, We are all done with both of the old parties, and we are for Senator Huey Long, and for Father Charles E. Coughlin's National Union for Social Justice." And a New Jersey man, incensed at commentator H. V. Kaltenborn's attack on Long and Coughlin, fired off an angry letter. "I guess you are one of those big shots that have nothing coming from the government," he said. "We need about 10 more just like Father Coughlin and Huey Long."[40]

Evidence of organizational connections between local Share Our Wealth Clubs and units of the National Union for Social Justice is somewhat sketchier. There is nothing to indicate any formal mergers of the two groups (both were so loosely structured that such an arrangement would have been difficult in any case). But there was occasional cooperation. In Chicago, for example, a local Share Our Wealth Club joined with representatives of the National Union in an effort to win city permission for Coughlin to speak at Soldiers' Field, noting that the club's members, "as citizens," wished to take a stand alongside Father Coughlin. In Springfield, Massachusetts, a longtime Coughlin stronghold, a journalist noted in the spring of 1935 that "interest in Huey Long's 'Share the Wealth' program has perked up considerably during the last few weeks" among National Union members. A small political organization in Cincinnati that was closely linked to Father Coughlin began, shortly after the World Court fight (itself an important event in linking the two men in the public mind), to publish accounts of Long's activities. One reader wrote the editor in delight that he was "highly pleased indeed to note the featuring of Father Coughlin and his wonderful work for humanity as well as the splendid space you have allotted to Senator Huey P. Long."[41]

It was not, then, a cheerful prospect that Democratic politicians regarded in the spring of 1935. Just when the Roosevelt Administration seemed finally to have succeeded in routing the conservative opposition, a new and apparently more menacing threat was emerging. As the publisher of the St. Louis *Star-Times* wrote Franklin Roosevelt early in the year: "A power has arisen in this country greater than that of government itself. The new power, unless checked, will itself become government." The phrasing may have been melodramatic, but the sentiment was genuine enough. Even so knowledgeable a politician as Richard Roper, executive secretary of the Democratic National Committee, was saying much the same thing: "Powerful minorities opposed to our program are becoming better organized every day. Many keen observers believe that these minorities can be far more effective in undermining the New Deal than a strong partisan organization." Long and Coughlin may not yet have decided precisely how to intrude themselves into the 1936 campaign; they certainly had not yet decided how to deal with each other. But their stars were rising quickly.[42]

10

Uneasy Alliances

Long and Coughlin had reasons for optimism beyond their own undoubted strength. When they surveyed the political landscape in 1935, they could see a spreading pattern of popular dissidence that was extending to every area of the country. Were these many protest movements to unite into a single force, they might be capable of toppling the entire structure of traditional party politics. And no two men were better poised to become the leaders of this new force than Long and Coughlin, whose movements had alone transcended the bounds of a particular region or interest group.

Yet there was also reason for concern about the spreading insurgency, for other popular leaders were not only potential allies, but possible rivals. As much as Long and Coughlin might welcome the support of other movements, they also feared that such movements would ultimately sap their own strength. And so it was undoubtedly with ambivalence that they watched in 1935 as their constituencies began to overlap and on occasions to merge with those of other dissident spokesmen. They could never be fully certain whether they stood to gain or to lose from the process.

To Long, the possible benefits and the potential costs of this interaction were nowhere more evident than in his native region. Even before he became a figure of importance in the nation at large, he was a powerful figure throughout the South; and he intruded constantly into the efforts of other insurgent leaders to mobilize popular discontent. He posed a particularly puzzling dilemma to Eugene Talmadge of Georgia.

Talmadge had entered politics in 1926 as the anti-machine candidate for state Agriculture Commissioner projecting the image of a stormy agrarian populist. Campaigning almost exclusively in rural areas (he once boasted that he had never spoken in a county that had a streetcar), he spouted anti-establishment rhetoric, denounced banks, railroads, and monopolies, and delighted his supporters by wearing bright red galluses, which he snapped against his chest as if to flaunt his distaste for elegant city slickers.

Talmadge's public life was seldom without controversy, but it enjoyed a steady upward trajectory: victory in the Agriculture Commission race in 1926, re-election in 1928 and 1930, successful campaigns in 1932 and 1934 for the governorship. Yet while Talmadge owed his ascent to the disgruntled Georgia farmers who looked upon him as their spokesman, in office he did little to translate his incendiary rhetoric into action. There were a few highly publicized gestures. As governor, he once dismissed the entire Public Service Commission and appointed new members, who promptly reduced railroad and utility rates. He lowered state licensing fees and fought for property-tax reductions. But more characteristic of his administration was its relentless and indiscriminate budget-cutting, its massive reductions in state services, its militant opposition to all unions, and its cozy if quiet relationship with the Georgia business community. Above all, Talmadge was notable for hostility to Franklin Roosevelt and all his works, denouncing the New Deal as a "combination of wet nursin', frenzied finance, downright Communism an' plain damfoolishness." And on this issue he developed a highly publicized connection with Huey Long.[1]

It was a relationship with which Talmadge never felt entirely comfortable. As a result, his public statements about Huey often differed markedly from one day to the next. At times, he went out of his way to publicize his abhorrence of Long's economic "radicalism." "His ideas of government and mine are as far apart as the north pole from the south pole," he told reporters in April 1935. "His doctrine of 'share-the-wealth' is out Rooseveluing Roosevelt."

Yet Talmadge recognized that he and Long shared a concern for defending states and localities from external incursions, and that Long had a powerful appeal for members of his own constituency in Georgia. He was careful, therefore, to mute even his most strident criticisms. "Personally, I like Senator Long," he said in the same April interview. "I think that Senator Long has probably waked up the American public more than anyone else by making them think of what is going on at present in Washington." Earlier the same year, he had invited Long to address the state legislature about his agricultural and economic schemes; he even swore in Huey's bodyguards as Georgia fish-and-game wardens to exempt them from a law forbidding them to enter the state with firearms.[2]

Long, for his part, held Talmadge and his Georgia organization in palpable contempt. He confided to one Atlanta reporter, "That Talmadge ain't got the brains to suit his ambition." To other members of the press covering his visit to the state, he dismissed the Talmadge organization with savage brusqueness: "It's a goddamn bush league outfit." But, like Talmadge, he avoided a total repudiation, and on most public occasions he kept his personal views to himself. Arriving in Atlanta in February for his speech to the legislature, he donned a pair of red suspenders (borrowed from the Governor's son Herman) and told a friendly crowd, "Everybody in Georgia ought to be wearing these. Governor Talmadge is the best chief executive in the United States. . . . I'm going to make Governor Talmadge the secretary of agriculture."[3]

Rumors about an impending political alliance between the two men abounded in the spring of 1935. Drew Pearson reported that Long planned to challenge Roosevelt in the 1936 Georgia Democratic primary and that he already had a pledge of support from Talmadge. Others predicted that Talmadge's growing public animus toward the Roosevelt Administration would soon lead to a third-party alliance with Long's Share Our Wealth movement. Neither man did anything to confirm such rumors, but each was careful to remain at least slightly ambiguous in his denials. Long could not ignore Talmadge's popularity among the plain people of Georgia, and Talmadge could not help but notice the tumultuous reception Long received from those same people as he traveled through Georgia early in 1935. It was a strange alliance (if alliance it could be called), one mandated less by the two leaders' personal or ideological affinity than by the perplexing and inchoate nature of the popular dissident sentiment upon which both relied.[4]

In Mississippi, where Long had always been influential, his impact upon local insurgency was even clearer. It was most visible in his troubled relationship with Theodore Bilbo, a leader of dissident sentiment even if he was for the most part an ideologically conventional politician. A native of the bayou section of southern Mississippi, a region as empty of cotton and blacks and large plantations as Huey Long's Winn Parish in Louisiana, Bilbo entered politics in 1901, served several terms in the state legislature as a disciple of the popular racist-populist James K. Vardaman, and, despite a series of accusations of bribery and corruption (several of them apparently well documented), won election to the governorship in 1915. He was a surprisingly progressive governor, reforming the tax codes to shift some of the burden to corporations and public utilities, providing state aid to education, and extending governmental regulatory powers in numerous areas. Barred by law from succeeding himself, he left the statehouse, but not the public limelight, in 1918; and after several unsuccessful campaigns, he returned to the governorship in 1927.

Once again, Bilbo advocated a progressive program—"books and bricks," he called it. But by now his political style, more than the substance of his program, was his chief distinction. A short and by no means handsome man, he possessed nevertheless a magnetic personality (particularly appealing, apparently, to women—his romantic liaisons were legion and fabled) and a gift for rabble-rousing rhetoric matched by no other politician in the state. Stripped to his shirtsleeves, wearing a flaming red necktie with a diamond stickpin, he campaigned with a contagious passion, whipping crowds into frenzied excitement with his denunciations of "Wall Streeters," entrenched political interest groups, corporate monopolies, and the establishment press —much as Huey Long was doing at about the same time in Louisiana.

Unlike Long, however, he had little success in dealing with the conservative legislature, whose members openly loathed him (a "slick little bastard," one particularly prominent Mississippi conservative labeled him, expressing a not uncommon sentiment). His legislative efforts almost completely frustrated, his term in office spent largely in petty and fruitless wrangling, he left the governorship in 1932 a seemingly discredited man. His humiliation was compounded when, desperately in need of money, he took a menial job in Franklin Roosevelt's agriculture department. His responsibilities consisted largely of compiling a collection of newspaper references to the Agricultural Adjustment Administration—in short, keeping a scrapbook—and his opponents in Mississippi wasted no time labeling him the "pastemaster general."

Once again, however, Bilbo rose from the political dead—this time to enter the race for a United States Senate seat in 1934. Although he was already giving evidence of the virulent racism that would later dominate his rhetoric, he continued for the most part to voice the same anti-establishment, vaguely populist philosophy that had excited his followers in the past. This time, however, he had to confront a new complication—the spreading influence of Huey Long.[5]

Bilbo's dilemma was particularly acute because his animosity toward Long was both long-standing and deeply felt. He had resented Huey's incursions into Mississippi politics in the past. He had been embarrassed in 1932 when his estranged wife, having heard about the Caraway campaign in Arkansas, reportedly asked Long for help in a Congressional contest she wanted to enter against her husband. (Long refused, and neither Bilbo nor his wife ultimately ran.) And he had begun his campaign in 1934 with a denunciation of Long ("Within five or eight years he will end in one of three places, or all three; in an asylum, in the penitentiary, or in hell") and with a promise to counter his power in Washington ("I will raise more hell than Huey Long ever thought of raising, but I'll do it in my own way"). Yet even before the campaign got under way, Bilbo was becoming aware of forces that would require a major shift in strategy. For Long's influence in Mississippi was visibly growing, and growing fastest among the same men and women upon whom Bilbo would have to depend for support. Bilbo could attack Huey only at great peril.[6]

The evidence came in many forms. Frequent letters from Mississippi voters urged Bilbo not only to endorse Long's program, but to embrace his organization. "There have already been two or three 'Share the Wealth' clubs organized in this county," a lawyer from Starkville wrote, "and the movement is gaining ground." Wrote a Bay St. Louis woman, "If you are really firm in your conviction for the Redistribution of wealth then I believe you will believe [sic] in the 'Share Our Wealth Societies.' " And another Bilbo supporter wrote ominously: "I suggest you and Long be as friendly as possible."[7]

Among Bilbo's campaign workers and among local political leaders allied with his cause, there was growing concern that Long might openly intervene in the contest. But even without Huey's direct interference, they warned, a public break with him could be fatal. "In his speech here last night," a supporter in Laurel wrote Bilbo's secretary:

the Governor [Bilbo] made some reference to Huey P. Long. I have been advised since he made his speech that there are quite a number of "Share Your Wealth" clubs in Jones County and I think it would be best for the governor to leave out of his speech any reference to Huey P. Long . . . as it might cause him to lose some votes because Huey P. Long's paper, I understand, has a good circulation in the State of Mississippi, and there are quite a number of people who are sold on Long.

"The Commercial Appeal to-day carries a feature story about 'the day when Bilbo and Long clash,' " another ally wrote the candidate. "Don't let it happen. . . . [Long] still gains in his hold on people."[8]

The advice evidently was not lost on Bilbo, for very early in the campaign he began not only to mute his criticisms of Long but to adopt many of the very tactics and positions that had contributed to Huey's popularity in the state. His campaign platform, which he issued in mid-May after much delay, included a wealth-redistribution plank whose debt to Long was embarrassingly obvious. In a speech at the closing rally of his primary campaign, he informed his audience that "In the scheme of this government it was intended that every man should be a king and every woman a queen." He even considered commissioning a sound truck for use in his campaign travels. Several Louisianans, reading about all this, wrote a Bilbo aide to ask when the candidate was speaking in western Mississippi. "Frank and I wanted to get up a little crowd from here and go over to hear him speak, and to let some of these fellows compare him with Huey P."[9]

Bilbo won his Senate seat by a decisive margin, but not even the security of a six-year term of office emboldened him to speak out against Long. Newspapers and politicians, both in Mississippi and in Washington, reminded him constantly of his earlier pledges, but during his first year in office he was uncharacteristically silent. What he did say, moreover, seemed designed to portray him more as a friend of Long than a foe. "I intend raising hell with the money lords," he said in an interview shortly after the primary, "the privileged few, the men who hold 90 per cent of the wealth of the nation." In a more exuberant moment at about the same time, he exclaimed: "Bilbo, Long, and Roosevelt, that isn't a bad line-up, now is it?" Otherwise, he said virtually nothing about Huey; he even contrived to be absent from the Senate during the most heated clashes between Long and Joe Robinson, fearing, perhaps, that he might otherwise be forced to join the battle. A Washington friend captured the irony of the situation, perhaps unintentionally, when he wrote Bilbo that "you have shown that you are the Kingfish of the State of Mississippi."[10]

Not until late in the summer of 1935 did Bilbo make more than the faintest gestures of opposition to Huey. He cabled colleagues in the Senate urging passage of a pending farm-relief measure. "It is absolutely necessary . . . to successfully rout Huey Long in the South," he told them. "And besides," he added almost as an afterthought, "our people need it." He was careful to keep the messages from the press. Yet he attracted scarcely more attention when he spoke publicly about Long, so feeble were his criticisms. Huey had better "stay out of Mississippi," he warned after reports had circulated for months that Long would campaign in the state against Pat Harrison. When asked what would happen if Huey did not heed the warning, Bilbo had nothing to say (although his reticence did not stop him from cabling the President to boast that "The first treatment to that madman Huey Long . . . was administered yesterday. . . . several more doses will be administered in due and ancient form"). Only when Long was safely dead several months later did Bilbo muster the courage to express openly the real depth of his distaste for him.[11]

Bilbo's timidity was understandable. Every time he opened a letter or picked up a newspaper from Mississippi, it seemed, he read more accounts of Long's growing power. Long, however, had reasons for restraint as well. He was not averse to intervening in Mississippi politics as a rule. He had shown that in 1931, when he had meddled in a gubernatorial contest, and in 1934, when he intervened once again on behalf of a candidate for governor. He was openly threatening to enter Mississippi to campaign against Pat Harrison in 1936. But against Theodore Bilbo, whom he disliked at least as much as Bilbo disliked him, he said nothing. It was to the voters of Mississippi, not to each other, that both Long and Bilbo were looking—voters of whose loyalties neither man could be entirely certain, voters who seemed content to support both leaders without giving themselves fully to either.[12]

II

NEITHER TALMADGE NOR BILBO ever had any significant following outside his own state, and neither had any real hope of developing national political influence. Talmadge, it was true, made noises late in 1935 about starting a national "Grass Roots" party to compete with the Democrats and Republicans. But it was difficult to take him seriously, and nothing much ever came of it. Bilbo was more than content with the prestige (and the salary) of a United States Senate seat, and he remained there, embroiled in scandal, until his death in 1947.[13]

There were, however, other dissident leaders with more serious pretensions to national influence, men who had bases in particular states but who were by 1935 reaching beyond them for support. For them, a relationship with Long and Coughlin was of vital importance. In any contest for national power, almost all insurgent leaders were beginning to realize, Long and Coughlin would be either valuable allies or dangerous foes.

It was in California, where dissident groups seemed to be springing up more rapidly and in greater numbers than anywhere else, that the most truly national of these movements began. Its unprepossessing leader was a tall, gaunt, white-haired physician, Francis E. Townsend. Born in 1867 on a small farm in Illinois, Townsend spent his youth in a variety of rugged occupations before entering medical school at the age of thirty. For seventeen years, beginning in 1903, he ran a modest practice in the Black Hills of South Dakota. But in 1920, concerned about his health, he moved with his family to the warmer climes of southern California. (The change evidently agreed with him; he lived until 1960.) He ultimately settled in Long Beach, where he passed more than a decade in pleasant anonymity, practicing medicine, speculating in real estate, and, later, working for the local health department—until the Great Depression suddenly called him to his unexpected destiny.[14]

Townsend was, he later claimed, standing in his bathroom shaving one morning late in 1933 when he glanced out the window to see three old women rummaging through the garbage cans in his alley for food. "A torrent of invectives tore out of me," he recalled, "the big blast of all the bitterness that had been building in me for years." His wife came running. " 'Doctor! Doctor!' She's always called me doctor, ' . . . Oh, you mustn't shout like that. All the neighbors will hear you!' "

"I want all the neighbors to hear me," Townsend shouted in reply. "I want God Almighty to hear me! I'm going to shout until the whole country hears!" And thus was born, so legend has it, the Townsend Old Age Revolving Pension Plan.[15]

The story has an apocryphal ring, but there was nothing mythical about the plan itself or about the astounding response it evoked. Beginning with a letter to the Long Beach *Press-Telegram* in September 1933, Townsend devoted his life to promoting what he claimed was a solution both to the problems of the elderly and the crisis of the Depression. The federal government, he proposed, should provide everyone over sixty with a pension of $150 a month (the figure soon jumped to $200), "on condition that they spend the money as they get it." The result would be to pump new money into the economy, open up jobs for younger people, and ultimately put an end to the blight of hard times. A nationwide transactions tax (a tax on all sales, wholesale and retail) would finance the system.[16]

Townsend was not the first to suggest such a plan. Bruce Barton, the well-known author and advertising man, had proposed a vaguely similar scheme (although largely in jest) in 1931; and a Seattle dentist, Stuart McCord, had begun advocating a system much like Townsend's at about the same time. But if the idea was not entirely new, Townsend's success in publicizing it was. The movement began quietly enough: a few elderly volunteers circulating a petition around Long Beach to obtain endorsements for the pension plan. But Townsend, impressed by the initial response, soon started casting about for a "super-salesman," as he put it, to help spread the enthusiasm further.[17]

He settled on an associate from his real-estate ventures: Robert E. Clements, a thirty-nine-year-old Texan whose high-powered hucksterism was a useful complement to Townsend's ideological fervor. Together, they incorporated Old Age Revolving Pensions, Ltd., as a non-profit organization on New Year's Day 1934, opened a one-room office, and mailed literature to almost everyone they could think of. Within weeks, they were being flooded with inquiries. Physicians and ministers in southern California added their prestige to the movement. Local Townsend Clubs emerged throughout the state. A startling amount of money poured into the central office in Long Beach. By January of 1935, the movement had spread beyond California—into the Midwest and the Northeast; paid membership in Townsend Clubs was approaching one-half million. The organization had moved to larger quarters in Los Angeles, recruited a staff of nearly a hundred, opened an office in Washington, and begun publishing a newspaper—the *Townsend National Weekly.*[18]

With the intensity of an evangelist, Townsend (known reverently within the organization as "the Founder") now mobilized his followers for an assault on the United States Congress. Senators and Representatives soon were receiving torrents of letters, telegrams, and petitions urging enactment of the pension plan. (In San Diego, California, where one-sixth of the city's residents were dues-paying members of Townsend Clubs, 105,000 men and women out of a population of 180,000 signed an appeal to their Congressman on behalf of the scheme.) John S. McGroarty, an otherwise conservative California Representative who owed his election in 1934 to the support of local Townsend Clubs, introduced a pension bill in the House early in 1935. But despite the intense public pressure, the measure was doomed from the start. The Roosevelt Administration strongly opposed it, and even the most progressive legislators considered the plan an impossibly expensive and unworkable delusion. Townsend forces could not muster even enough support to win a roll-call vote (although nearly 200 Representatives, fearful of the political repercussions of opposition, contrived to be absent from the floor when the issue came up).[19]

The Townsend Plan was dead as a serious legislative possibility; indeed, in that sense, it had never really lived. And the movement was not without other problems. Robert Clements, who referred to the organization frankly and cynically as "the racket," angered many Townsendites with his open concern about keeping the operation lucrative. (He himself turned a tidy personal profit from the movement.) Local Townsend Clubs often bridled at the attempts of the national office to impose a rigid hierarchical structure upon the organization ("There are always hell-rumblings in a Townsend organization at all times, I guess," the Founder once said resignedly). President Roosevelt's support for the 1935 Social Security Act, which was at least in part a response to pressures from Townsendites, drew off some important support. And Dr. Townsend himself was unable to answer the growing and persuasive criticism of his plan as naïve and impractical. "When forced to deal with the fundamental problems," the writer E. B. White once noted, "he quietly came apart, like an inexpensive toy."[20]

But, despite everything, the Townsend Clubs survived and prospered, developing into a large and vibrant national movement, infiltrating the fabric of insurgent politics in nearly every region of the country, and encouraging the hopes of those who believed a major new force was establishing itself in American public life. Tom Amlie, the radical Congressman from Wisconsin, summarized the attitude of many dissident leaders toward the Townsend movement in 1935. "As I see it," he wrote, "this is all indicative of a very healthy ferment."[21]

Although the Townsend movement was more particular in its demands and more narrowly defined in its constituency than many major dissident movements, it became increasingly intertwined with other insurgent uprisings. In particular, it found it necessary to deal with the influence of Long and Coughlin. Like others, Dr. Townsend did so warily, fearful that too close an association with them would erode the integrity of his own movement (and vitiate the strength of his own position). But, as elsewhere, the choice was not entirely his to make. For, with or without Townsend's approval, the large groups of elderly citizens drawn to his cause were beginning to interact and, in many cases, to merge with the Long and Coughlin constituencies.

Townsend himself refused publicly to consider the idea of cooperation, much less alliance, with either Long or Coughlin, despite press speculation that a union of the movements was imminent. "The gates are open for anyone to join us," he insisted in April 1935, "but we are affiliating with no other movements." The *Townsend Weekly,* in an editorial several weeks later, observed that "The consensus of opinion among the Townsend Clubs thus far seems to be strongly against the formation of a third party." About Coughlin and Long in particular, the organization seemed at times to go to great pains to express a studied indifference. "We don't know anything about it," the paper editorialized in the midst of the Hugh Johnson controversy. "All we know is that we're gonna have the Townsend Plan and recovery."[22]

But the aloofness was in part disingenuous. Townsend in fact knew a great deal about both Long and Coughlin, and he was more interested than he was willing publicly to admit in what they knew and thought of him. Early in 1935, he had an assistant write Father Coughlin to request an interview. Townsend was, his aide insisted, willing to travel to Detroit if necessary to attempt to enlist Coughlin's assistance. (The meeting finally took place—in Royal Oak—in November.) "Huey Long is also getting interested in us," a Townsend official noted with pleasure, but, uncertain how to deal with him, the organization was careful to "handle him with kid gloves."[23]

Townsend began as well to make subtle public gestures of conciliation toward Long and Coughlin—in the hope of attracting new followers from their ranks, and to keep his own supporters from deserting to them. Editorials in his newspaper began on occasion to praise the Long and Coughlin programs. "The vast majority of the American public agree with Huey," said one, "that incomes should be limited. No other leader but Huey is advocating these reforms. . . . The same way with Father Coughlin. His fundamental plea is 'to drive the money changers out of the temple.' Isn't he right about it?" There was prominent coverage of Long's and Coughlin's speeches and activities, occasionally approving, more often neutral, but seldom openly hostile. And on rare occasions, there were even implicit suggestions that all three leaders were really part of the same movement, as in the April 1935 editorial that denounced the "plutagogues" who issue the "curiously pusillanimous cry" labeling "Huey Long, Father Coughlin and Dr. Townsend as 'demagogues.' "[24]

If Townsendites could detect grudging approval of Long and Coughlin from their own leaders, they could find even more persuasive evidence elsewhere of the links among the movements. Both major wire services reported in 1935 that Townsend was quietly working with Long to "mass America's millions" behind their joint ideas. Hugh Johnson, who seemed never to learn from his mistakes, gave a second, highly publicized speech in New York late in March in which he lumped the Long and Townsend plans together as dangerous Utopian folly. And Long and Coughlin themselves gave additional encouragement: Long by boasting constantly that it had been "my pleasure and privilege to introduce last year the first old age pension bill ever offered in the United States Congress"; Coughlin by remaining evasive on the pension issue and allowing the public to speculate that he had assured Dr. Townsend of his support.[25]

The result was a largely spontaneous interaction among the three movements. "Both Long and Townsend admit that their strength overlaps," a United Press reporter observed early in 1935. "Hundreds, perhaps thousands, of persons in California belong to both the Townsend club and the Share-the-Wealth club." A small local paper in upstate New York carried an editorial proposing a national ticket with Long as the Presidential candidate, Townsend as Vice President, and Father Coughlin as "Treasurer." In North Platte, Nebraska, a Townsend club began writing Long's office in Washington, asking for assistance. And in Texas, Townsendites wrote a local newspaper asking "How about a Huey Long for President Club for El Paso?"[26]

Even those who denounced the Townsend Plan most harshly were never entirely sure what to make of the kindly physician who led the movement. His rhetoric lacked the stridency and vitriol that made Long, Coughlin, and others so unappealing to their critics. His followers—thousands, perhaps millions of elderly men and women whose misery could not be denied—evoked sympathy far more readily than contempt. But the movement was troubling nevertheless. To those who feared an insurgent threat to the American political system, it was additional evidence of the depth and extent of dissident sentiment. "The danger is not Dr. Townsend, who in himself is as harmless as a dove," observed Raymond Gram Swing. The real danger was that other "demagogic movements" would make inroads on his supporters. "He is sure to offer a temptation to the radical aspirants to dictatorship, who will see a chance to pick up the Townsend following at a cheap price." It was clear to whom he was referring.[27]

III

"THE MIDDLE AND WESTERN STATES are crawling with radical farm leaders," wrote columnist Jay Franklin Carter in 1935, "whose individual influence may be small and localized but whose aggregate power to make or break

Administrations would be great, if they are ever brought together in a national campaign." Whether such leaders could reach accord was no clearer in the Middle West than it was anywhere else. But it was evident that by 1935 the farm belt had produced, as it had been doing for decades past, a wide array of insurgent movements, some of which had achieved a dominance in state or local politics matched in few areas of the country. What happened in such states as Minnesota and Wisconsin would go far toward determining what would happen to the phenomenon of dissident politics nationally.[28]

Minnesota politics was for a time early in the 1930s the almost exclusive preserve of the Farmer-Labor Party and its dynamic young leader, Floyd B. Olson. The organization was not born of the Depression. It had emerged in the early twenties, out of farmers' disillusionment with the conservatism of the two major parties. It was not until 1930, however, when Olson became the first Farmer-Labor candidate to win election as governor, that the party truly came of age.

Olson was thirty-nine years old in 1930, the son of Scandinavian immigrants, the product of a rugged youth spent working in shipyards, on railroads, and in mines. A lawyer, he had served for ten years as county attorney in Minneapolis and had run once, unsuccessfully, for governor in 1924. His political views had been relatively moderate early in his career, but by the time he took office, he had emerged as an unabashed spokesman for the left. "I am not a liberal," he once firmly declared. "I am what I want to be—I am a radical." As such, he advocated forceful economic reforms: public appropriation of idle factories for operation by the unemployed (a variation of Upton Sinclair's "production-for-use" scheme in California), state ownership of utilities and some basic industries, a moratorium on mortgage foreclosures, exemption of low-income families from property taxation, a government-owned central bank. When angry farmers staged a tumultuous strike in 1932, Olson quickly voiced his support. When strikebreakers threatened violence to Minnesota truckers during a 1934 walkout, Olson declared martial law. He spoke warmly of Franklin Roosevelt, but by 1934 he was vehement in his warnings that the New Deal would have to move much faster if it hoped to avoid a national third-party challenge in 1936 or 1940.[29]

The concrete progressive achievements of the Olson administration (which lasted until the Governor's tragic death from cancer in 1936) were not inconsiderable: the establishment of "co-operative" business enterprises in a variety of fields, new environmental legislation, increased public regulation of utilities. But they were hardly the drastic reformulation of society of which he so often spoke. Olson's radicalism was, in the end, more evident in his words than in his deeds. When his party, in his absence, adopted a platform in 1934 declaring that "capitalism has failed" and calling for "a system where all . . . machinery of production, transportation and communication shall be owned by the government," Olson at first endorsed it but then began subtly to disassociate himself from it by "interpreting" the platform in far more moderate terms than its framers had intended. "Changes so far reaching come slowly," he explained. "I believe in evolution." But it was this very cautiousness, and the national respectability it earned him, that helped make Olson an admired, even a lionized figure among dissident leaders throughout the Midwest. He would, most believed, figure prominently in any national movement.[30]

Wisconsin had a tradition of political insurgency that stretched back to the beginning of the century. For twenty-five years, the dominant figure in the state had been Robert M. La Follette, Governor, United States Senator, leader of the progressive wing of the state Republican Party, a candidate for President in 1912 and again (as head of the national Progressive Party) in 1924. He died in 1925, but he left behind two sons dedicated to continuing his work. Robert, Jr. ("Young Bob," as he was known in Wisconsin), succeeded his father in the Senate, where he worked quietly and patiently to keep alive the spirit of the now institutionally defunct Progressive Party. Five years later, his younger brother, Phil, won election to the governorship as a Republican.[31]

By 1932, however, the Republican Party in Wisconsin, in decline because of the popularity of Franklin Roosevelt and seriously divided, was becoming an inhospitable home for both La Follettes. Phil failed in his attempt to win renomination for the governorship; family supporters fared equally poorly in other races; and there was good reason to fear that Bob would do no better in 1934 when he would face re-election to the Senate. The only way to keep the progressive tradition alive in Wisconsin, La Follette supporters began to argue, was to establish a new party. And while the brothers were reluctant at first, ultimately they had no alternative. In May 1934, they founded the Progressive Party.

In name, the new organization was simply a resurrection of the national party "Old Bob" had led ten years before. In reality, however, it operated only in Wisconsin. In the elections that fall, Phil ran as the party's candidate for governor, Bob for Senator, and a host of their allies for other state and federal offices. Their victory was almost complete. The La Follettes themselves were swept decisively back into office. Progressive candidates captured the office of Secretary of State, seven of ten Congressional seats, a plurality in the state House of Representatives, and a near plurality in the Senate. Phil and Bob La Follette had emerged as two of the most successful insurgent leaders in the nation.[32]

They were not at all alike. Phil was flashy, gregarious, a fine orator with a quick, probing mind. Bob was a study in understatement, slow, cautious, some thought plodding, with an unremarkable public presence. (Their father had always believed Phil to be the more gifted and had apparently chosen him as his successor in the Senate; but when he died in 1925, Phil was two years too young, and Bob, barely thirty, took the seat.) Yet together the two La Follettes were a powerful force. In Washington, "Young Bob" became perhaps the most highly respected member of the "progressive bloc" in the Senate, supporting the New Deal more often than not, but maintaining an unmistakable independence. In Wisconsin, meanwhile, "Governor Phil" secured a series of economic reforms—mortgage relief, public-works projects, a progressive income tax, banking reform, property-tax reductions, and a crude form of unemployment insurance—that made the state seem once again a "laboratory" of progressivism.[33]

As leaders of a third party in their own state, it was natural that they would attract the attention of those who hoped for a new party in the nation at large. At times, they appeared to encourage hopes that they might join such a movement. The family newspaper in 1935 seemed to signal a retreat from what had until then been a consistent approval of the Roosevelt Administration. Comments on the President's performance were now decidedly mixed. In the Senate, Bob expressed occasional dissatisfaction with the pace of the New Deal. And Phil, who had, to Roosevelt's distinct displeasure, refused eight different offers of federal jobs during his two years out of office, remained conspicuously aloof from the national Administration. Neither was ready to break openly with Roosevelt, but neither was so closely allied with him to make a schism unthinkable.[34]

The successes of the Midwestern insurgents were heartening to a group of Eastern intellectuals eager to advance the work of radical reform. Since 1929, some of America's most fertile minds (John Dewey, Lewis Mumford, Archibald MacLeish, among others) had been working through the League for Independent Political Action to promote alternatives to a capitalist economic system they considered obsolete and cruel. Attracted in certain respects to Marxism, they nevertheless rejected communist dogma, espousing instead a pragmatic socialism more suited, they believed, to the realities of American society. In the early 1930s, they sought to fuse their ideological fervor with the popular enthusiasm that the Minnesota and Wisconsin dissidents were creating.

The League had always considered the creation of a new political party as one of its ultimate purposes, but not until the fall of 1933 did it take the first substantive steps to attain the goal. At a meeting in Chicago in September, League members and supporters created the Farmer-Labor Political Federation, a semi-autonomous unit within the LIPA intended to form the nucleus of a third national party. Almost immediately, the new Federation set out to

forge alliances with the leading Midwestern insurgents. It lent crucial assistance to the La Follettes in 1934 when they were working to establish the
Progressive Party. And it made even stronger overtures to Floyd Olson:
inviting him to submit regular editorials to *Common Sense,* the LIPA newspaper (Olson agreed, but only when one of the editors agreed to write the
editorials for him); directing Howard Y. Williams, an LIPA stalwart in Minnesota, to assist in the work of the Farmer-Labor Party (Williams was in large
part responsible for the party's radical 1934 platform); and making no secret
of the organization's hope that Olson would emerge as the leader of a national
crusade.[35]

The third-party efforts stalled, however, in the spring and summer of
1935. Leaders of the Farmer-Labor Political Federation called a meeting in
Chicago that July to discuss still another "political federation." But although
delegates gathered, passed motions, and created a new organization—the
American Commonwealth Political Federation—the convention was most
notable for the absence of the most important potential participants. The La
Follettes never even acknowledged the meeting. Olson sent a perfunctorily
courteous message of regret. Federation leaders claimed not to be discouraged,
but it was clear that they were growing concerned about the future. For not
only were the Midwestern insurgents apparently balking at the prospect of an
active political union, but there were signs as well that their movements were
moving into an uncomfortable association with those of Huey Long and
Father Coughlin.[36]

IV

OF THE COUNTLESS DISSIDENT GROUPS in the nation, few would seem less
likely to have any connection with Long and Coughlin than these Midwestern
insurgents and their Eastern admirers. Leaders of the LIPA, the Farmer-
Labor Party, the Progressive Party—all maintained carefully guarded images
of sophistication and intellectual respectability. They were, they liked to
believe, "radicals." Long and Coughlin, by contrast, were something quite
different. "Irresponsible demagogues," the fiery Wisconsin Congressman Tom
Amlie called them. Howard Williams warned of their "Fascist tendencies."
The *Progressive,* the organ of the La Follettes, denounced Long as a "demagog
who likes to present an easy formula to cure all social ills." Alfred Bingham,
the aristocratic editor of *Common Sense,* claimed that what Long and Coughlin were creating showed signs of "becoming a Hitler movement."

Nor, the Midwesterners claimed, did they appeal to the same people as
Long and Coughlin. The "radicals" attracted, they liked to believe, "thinking

people"; Long and Coughlin, by contrast, appealed to a "blind following"—
what Amlie called "masses grasping at the straws that every demagog holds
out." "Our people," he insisted, "have absolutely nothing in common" with
such movements.[37]

Amlie, however, was wrong. Despite the ideological differences between
the vaguely socialist messages of the Midwestern dissidents and the more
muted programs of Long and Coughlin, substantial common ground remained. All spoke forcefully about the problem of "excessively concentrated
wealth"; all railed against Wall Street and the "money changers"; all denounced "internationalism"; all, in short, appealed similarly to those who
were suffering not only from economic privations but from the sense of help-
lessness in the face of distant, centralized power. Their support, as a result,
came from many of the same people. Whether the Midwestern insurgents
liked it or not, those whose loyalties they hoped to enlist were giving unmistakable evidence of interest in Long and Coughlin.

The editorial pages of the *Progressive,* for example, carried letters almost
every week from readers expressing support for Long and Coughlin—com-
plaining when the paper had made unfavorable mention of either man, almost
cooing with pleasure when it praised them. "When you printed the [hostile]
article on Sen. Huey Long," wrote one unhappy reader, "you injured the cause
of the common people." Said another, displaying a curious reversal of priori-
ties, "My admiration for the La Follettes is as great as for Long." A Progressive Club in Kenosha, Wisconsin, announced proudly that not only was it
prepared to support Bob La Follette on a national ticket, but "we are also in
with and backing Father Coughlin." And in Minnesota, Farmer-Laborites
were writing party leaders to suggest that "you get on the right side of Father
Coughlin, Huey Long."[38]

It was the leaders of the Farmer-Labor Political Federation, however,
who received the most voluminous evidence of how difficult it would be, as
a Michigan organizer put it, to "wean" the Long and Coughlin followings
"away from their wet nurses"; of how hard it would be, in fact, to prevent
the FLPF supporters from gravitating to the Long and Coughlin banners. As
the 1935 Chicago convention approached, pleas from Federation supporters
throughout the Midwest and beyond began pouring in, pleas to include Long
and Coughlin somehow in the planning for a new party. "I have talked to
different ones of our friends," an Iowa attorney wrote Howard Williams in
a typical letter, "and invariably they feel that every progressive leader should
be invited." Included in that number, he made clear, were Long, Coughlin,
and Townsend. Williams himself wrote dejectedly to Amlie that only with
great difficulty had he restrained Federation leaders in Iowa from passing a
motion to include Long and Coughlin in the Chicago conference. Word soon

arrived that members in Idaho had actually approved a resolution "that Senator Long, Father Coughlin and all the rest should be invited." And from Ohio came word that "the sentiment [among FLPF supporters] is at the boiling point for a new party with a Coughlin, Long–Alfred Lawson combination platform."[39]

A Lewiston, Montana, supporter of the Federation gave a particularly vivid example of how the dissident constituencies were beginning to overlap. He enclosed with his letter an elaborate diagram placing the major political movements in appropriate categories. There were the communists, whom he listed as "left wing" revolutionaries; there was the New Deal, described as "wasted energy"; there was the right wing, whose goal was "fascism." And there was a final cluster of movements grouped under one heading. Among them were the Farmer-Laborites, the Farm Holiday Association, the Townsend Clubs, and the adherents of Long and Coughlin. All were united behind one basic goal: "SHARE OUR WEALTH." "What difference does it make which one of the programs we rally around," he asked, "when it is apparent that any number of them will bring us to the same objective and same goal?"[40]

The message of such statements was not lost on the leaders of the Midwestern insurgent organizations. As a result, some began to swallow their distaste for Long and Coughlin and search for avenues of accommodation. In Wisconsin, the La Follettes tempered the criticisms that had been appearing in the *Progressive,* first by inserting prominent (and generally neutral) coverage of the activities of the two men and soon by including limited but unmistakable praise. "The Progressive may not agree with every conclusion reached by Father Coughlin and Senator Long," said one editorial. "When they contend, however, as they have, that the tremendous wealth of this country should be more equitably shared for a more abundant life for the masses of people, we agree heartily with them." In Minnesota, Floyd Olson was giving rise to speculation about his relations with Long and Coughlin by accepting an invitation to appear jointly with them at a meeting of insurgent farmers in Des Moines (although he ultimately canceled the plans). "It is most disheartening," Alfred Bingham complained at the time, "when the best available leaders we have, like Olson, have neither the guts nor intelligence to take the leadership themselves, but instead allow themselves to be drawn into the wake of men like Long."[41]

Yet it was to Bingham himself, and to his allies in the Farmer-Labor Political Federation, that Long and Coughlin were of the most pressing concern. "The issue which at this time overshadows all others," Bingham admitted in 1935, "is whether the whole movement we have been encouraging and fostering and pinning our hopes on is going to fall into the hands of Long and Coughlin. At the moment I am very pessimistic." Unless the Federation moved quickly, warned Paul Douglas, an influential member of the LIPA, "I believe we will find Huey Long and Coughlin rushing into the vacuum."[42]

There was no easy solution to the dilemma. Even Tom Amlie was forced ultimately to admit that the new party could not hope to succeed without appealing to those who followed other insurgents, that "the people who today are following Coughlin, Long, etc., are our friends. . . . We can not afford to estrange them in any way." But while some, like Williams, tried to cast things in an optimistic light, arguing that Long and Coughlin were "winnowing the chaff and will help the thing we are trying to do," most were less sanguine. "I think Long and Coughlin have the jump on any progressive movement," Norman Thomas wrote to his friend Amlie; and Amlie himself spoke ominously of the possibility of this "new mass movement" being "directed by the Longs, the Coughlins, and other essentially anti-democratic elements." How to appeal to the followers of these men without embracing the men themselves was a problem for which there was no ready solution.[43]

There was for a time a lively debate within the Federation over including Long and Coughlin in some of the organization's activities. At a meeting of the State Executive Committee in Minnesota early in April 1935, the "question as to our attitude and cooperation with Senator Huey Long, Father Coughlin and Townsend groups" was the leading item on the agenda. In Washington several weeks later, a meeting of the national leadership, gathered to make plans for the Chicago convention that summer, argued at length about whether to invite Long and Coughlin to speak. Time and again, the decision was to keep both men at arm's length—to bar them from Federation meetings and to express no open support for their views. Time and again, however, the subject resurfaced for further debate, and it was clear that opinion within the organization remained divided. The issue would continue to haunt the new movement for the rest of its brief existence.[44]

V

WHILE MOST of the Midwestern insurgent leaders were keeping a certain distance from Long and Coughlin, there was one notable exception. Milo Reno, the aging head of the Iowa-based Farm Holiday Association, welcomed them with open arms.

Born in 1866 in Agency, Iowa, Reno grew up in a family imbued with the ideas of the Grangers, the Greenbackers, and the Populists; and as an adult, he moved naturally into both farming and farm politics. In 1921, on the basis of his flamboyant speeches at a state convention, he won election as president of the Iowa Farmers' Union. And although he resigned the office nine years later (to devote more time to running the Union's lucrative insurance business), he dominated the organization until his death in 1936. Under Reno, the Union's membership grew to a robust 10,000 by the end of the twenties (still far less than the more conservative Farm Bureau Federation, but enough to be influential); and at his urging, it endorsed the demands of its more radical faction (from which Reno himself had emerged) for "cost of production" pricing, the right of farmers to determine the prices of their own produce and to guarantee themselves a return that at least matched their investment.[45]

By 1932, the ravages of the Depression had added an almost desperate urgency to these demands. Huge surpluses, intolerable prices, increasing bankruptcies and foreclosures—all helped push the long-festering rage and frustration of struggling farmers toward open expression. Many looked at first to Congress, where the once powerful "farm bloc" was working for passage of agricultural-relief legislation. But when a National Farmers' Union delegation returned from a visit to Washington in February to report that prospects for government assistance were bleak, all patience seemed exhausted.

Milo Reno was ready. Five years earlier, he had issued a stern warning: "If we cannot obtain justice by legislation, the time will have arrived when no other course remains than organized refusal to deliver the products of the farm at less than production costs." Now he began to translate his words into action. In Des Moines on May 3, Reno presided over a meeting of 2,000 farmers, most of them representing local units of the Iowa Farmers' Union but some from neighboring states and a few from as far away as Oklahoma and Montana. The delegates approved the formation of a new organization, an adjunct of the Union, to be known as the Farmers' Holiday Association. Its president would be Milo Reno, and its goal would be a national strike by farmers, beginning later that summer, to bring production to a halt and force action to raise agricultural prices. Suffused with crusading militancy, the new members returned to their homes to begin the work of peaceful revolution.[46]

The results were decidedly mixed. There was indeed a farmers' strike that summer. It began early in August, and it displayed notable vigor and not inconsiderable violence. But while some startled observers claimed at first that "This movement threatens to sweep the Midwest like wildfire," the strike in fact never extended much beyond the counties in western Iowa where it began. Divisions within the leadership, disagreement over tactics, forceful opposition from local authorities, and disillusionment over the increasing destructiveness of some participants brought the movement sputtering to a standstill by the beginning of September.[47]

Yet if the strike had failed in its stated goal, it had achieved unexpected results in other areas. Throughout the Midwest, politicians and farm leaders publicized and often supported the uprising. National political candidates, in the midst of their campaign, took notice of it and attempted to respond. President Hoover moved timidly to bolster farm prices through overseas sales, and Franklin Roosevelt expressed his commitment to federal farm relief (a frustratingly vague one, but a commitment nonetheless) during a visit to Iowa in September.[48]

The 1932 uprising may have been the high-water mark of the Farmers' Holiday Association's influence, but the organization remained an important force in agricultural politics in the following years. A threat by Reno of a second strike in the spring of 1933 helped spur the Congress and the Administration to speed action on the Agricultural Adjustment Act. It was not enough. After scattered local "holidays" during the summer, Reno finally ordered a new national strike, to begin in October 1933. Limited in impact and marred by violence, it did encourage new Administration efforts to mollify farmers. Henry Wallace, Hugh Johnson, and others toured the Middle West speaking on behalf of the Roosevelt policies, and the Agriculture Department quickly expanded its farm-loan program and put new production controls into operation, the combined effects of which helped bring the strike to an end by early December.[49]

The Farmers' Holiday Association had not produced the results Reno had envisioned, but its impact had been substantial enough to encourage hopes that it might endure. And so, in 1934, Reno began looking for ways to ensure the survival of his movement. At the age of sixty-eight, he undoubtedly realized that he had only a limited political future of his own (he died, in fact, in 1936). He decided, therefore, that his best course would be to ally his organization with other insurgent movements. He developed a limited relationship with such leaders as Olson, the La Follettes, Williams, and Bingham, but they considered him a relatively unimportant figure and treated him with some condescension. Undaunted, he turned his attention to Long and Coughlin.[50]

In the spring of 1934, Reno invited Coughlin to serve as the keynote speaker at the annual meeting of his association; and Coughlin, after prodding from Senator Burton K. Wheeler, agreed to attend. His appearance on May 3 was the highlight of the convention. Speaking to delegates who only moments earlier had voted almost unanimously to demand the resignation of Henry Wallace as Secretary of Agriculture, he delivered an unusually vitriolic attack upon the policies of the New Deal. Reno was particularly pleased at Coughlin's suggestion that Americans, denied their rights by a callous government, should "find a way in which the farmer and the laborer can join to give them back to us." Coughlin left Iowa with a host of new admirers.[51]

A year later, Reno's vision had grown, and he began to organize a

Farmers' Holiday Association convention that would bring together leading dissidents from throughout the nation. He made no secret of his hope that a new political party would emerge from the event. At first, it seemed that he might succeed. Coughlin, Long, Olson, and lesser dissident leaders announced their intention to attend. Disgruntled farmers took heart at the prospect of a new, more potent movement on their behalf. "Long, Coughlin and Reno are going to get together in May at a convention, as I heard announced," an Illinois man wrote enthusiastically to a small-town newspaper. "Then I expect to get a real common people's sensible organizing program. Then we will do some real organizing for happy living."[52]

Well before the meeting convened, however, the bright promise had faded. First Olson withdrew, under pressure from allies in Minnesota and elsewhere who feared even the appearance of cooperation with Long and Coughlin. Then Coughlin, apparently distressed at the possibility of losing the limelight to Long, announced that he, too, would be unable to attend. He assured Reno that he would send "representatives" as a sign of his interest and support, but later he canceled even this limited participation. (His attorney and another aide did attend, but Coughlin insisted that they were there in no official capacity.)[53]

Long, however, had no intention of backing out, particularly once it was apparent that, as one organizer put it a week before the event, "It's going to be a Huey Long party." And the prospect of his visit stirred both excitement and concern, as well as considerable confusion. The Des Moines *Register,* notably unsympathetic to Huey's program, nevertheless remarked calmly that it would be "good for Des Moines" to hear him. The legislature, however, was less composed. When several Republicans jokingly proposed that Huey be invited to address the lower house, Long's Democratic admirers took offense, brought the proposal to a vote, and resoundingly passed it. The Republicans were appalled. "He is a stench in the nostrils of political decency," one complained. "Why do you want to recognize this evil maniac?" But the Democrats were adamant, and they decisively defeated a motion to rescind the invitation. Iowa could "confer no greater honor upon that great commonwealth of Louisiana," one Representative insisted, "than by asking her illustrious senator to address this august body." His only reasons for hesitation, he added, were his doubts as to whether Long would "stoop to coming into a general assembly of the caliber of this." They were legitimate doubts; Long declined the invitation.[54]

Arriving in Des Moines on the day of the convention, Long looked slimmer and healthier than he had a year earlier, but no less flamboyant. He wore a blue double-breasted suit with red pinstripes, a dark bluish-purple shirt, and a purple-and-white tie; and he moved through the city with the frenetic energy that he seemed always to display on public occasions—"staccato, swagger, sharp and smart . . . everything clicked," one reporter described it.[55]

To the farmers gathered to hear him at the fairgrounds (a crowd estimated variously at from 10,000 to 18,000), Long was a sensation. His speech was little different from countless ones he had given before—lambasting Franklin Roosevelt, denouncing New Deal agricultural programs, and talking at length about the dangers of concentrated wealth. But the response was unusually warm and enthusiastic. When he asked the audience, "Do you believe in the Word of God?" almost everyone raised his hand. When he asked a few moments later, "Do you believe in the redistribution of wealth?" the response was unanimous. Huey was exhilarated. "That was one of the easiest audiences I ever won over," he told reporters that afternoon. "I could take this state like a whirlwind." Reno was equally pleased. After Long's speech, convention delegates voted overwhelmingly to endorse the idea of a third party in 1936. They chose no specific candidate or platform, but Long, clearly, would figure prominently in their plans.[56]

VI

THE LINES DIVIDING the various dissident movements in the 1930s were almost always thin and indistinct, and Long and Coughlin were usually happy to permit, at times even to encourage, the ambiguity. About one question, however, they were careful to leave no doubt. Neither was a communist, and neither was interested in any accommodation with the American Communist Party. For Coughlin, anti-communism had been a central element of his public message since his earliest radio sermons, and accusations of "Sovietism" or "Bolshevism" remained among the most damning weapons in his arsenal. He even established an Anti-Communist Club in the parish school in Royal Oak. Its object: "to teach the elements of communism and to show its fallacies." Long was less outspoken on the subject, perhaps, but no less adamant. Not the least important reason for adopting his Share Our Wealth Plan, he claimed, was to prevent the spread of communism.[57]

It was not surprising, then, that the attitude of the Communist Party toward Long and Coughlin was clear, public, unremitting hostility. The *Daily Worker* missed no opportunity to dismiss both men as fascists, demagogues, "the effluvia of the degeneration of capitalism." Party members published pamphlets, broadsides, and other literature detailing the fallacies of the Long and Coughlin programs. "Long says he wants to do away with concentration of wealth without doing away with capitalism," wrote Alex Bittelman, a party worker in New York. "This is humbug. This is fascist demagogy." Even the

Soviet press joined the chorus. Long's "buffoonish thunderings," said one Moscow paper, "show the extent of the charlatan demagogism of this Fascist prophet." Coughlin, it added, was Long's "twin." There was, clearly, little room for and little interest in rapprochement here.[58]

On the surface, the relationship of the Long and Coughlin movements to the Socialist Party would seem to have been much the same. Coughlin steadfastly denied that he had any more sympathy for socialism than for communism. They were, he said, virtually the same thing. Socialism, like communism, relied upon the teachings of Karl Marx, he explained. Socialism, like communism, pointed logically toward the abolition of all private property, even the right of a man to "possess his own home and children." Socialism, like communism, "professed atheism." Long, similarly, dismissed the socialists with open contempt. "We let Socialists lecture in Louisiana whenever we want," he boasted. "We let Communists speak, too. We don't pay any attention to them." There was no need to. "We haven't a Communist or Socialist in Louisiana. . . . They say that Huey P. Long is the greatest enemy that the Communists and Socialists have to deal with."[59]

For their part, Norman Thomas and the rest of the Socialist Party leadership denounced both Long and Coughlin as decided menaces, as the first manifestations of an American inclination toward fascism; and, like the Communists, Socialist Party members built the publication of anti-Long and anti-Coughlin literature into something like a cottage industry. In Illinois, the Cook County party organization purchased and distributed 5,000 pamphlets denouncing both men. In New York City, five branches of the party expressed interest in producing "a leaflet against Long and Coughlin." The American League Against War and Fascism, an organization allied with the Socialists, listed as one of its immediate "needs" the publication of new literature hostile to Long and Coughlin. In Buffalo, Philadelphia, Chicago, Lebanon, Pennsylvania, and elsewhere, units of the Socialist Party held public forums to discuss the "menace" of Huey Long and Father Coughlin.[60]

No one was more outspoken in his animosity than Norman Thomas, the Princeton graduate and former Presbyterian minister who had been both spiritual and political leader of the party (as well as its perennial Presidential candidate) since the early 1920s. Nothing so frightened Thomas as the specter of fascism, and in Long and Coughlin he saw that specter in ominous physical form. In 1934, he challenged Long to a public debate in New York on the future of capitalism. Long accepted, and Thomas used the occasion to make clear his belief that Huey's Share Our Wealth scheme was an insufficient and dangerous delusion. "It was that sort of talk, Senator Long, that Hitler fed the Germans," he snapped at one point, "and in my opinion it is positively dangerous because it fools the people."[61]

By 1935, Thomas had stepped up his attacks. After the Hugh Johnson speech in March, he issued a press release denouncing Long, Coughlin, and Johnson all as irrelevant to the real needs of the nation. In April, he publicly challenged both Long and Coughlin to another debate, this time on the subject of fascism, for which, he added, "you are preparing us." In June, he published an open letter to both men accusing them of disguising their real purpose: the importation of the programs of Mussolini and Hitler to America. And a month later, Thomas announced plans for a tour of Louisiana in October. He would, he promised, "expose the demagoguery of Huey Long's share-the-wealth program." (Long, when informed of the plan, dismissed it scornfully: "Mr. Thomas won't get three people to listen to him if he comes here.")[62]

Yet the lines dividing Long and Coughlin from the Socialist Party were by no means as clear as those dividing them from the communists. Both men admitted on occasion that socialism, in its American form at least, was not entirely incompatible with their own beliefs. "Socialism is predicated upon the fact that men will regard each other as brothers," Coughlin once wrote. "That is Christianity." And Long implicitly admitted that elements of his Share Our Wealth Plan smacked of socialism, and that he denied the connection for political rather than ideological reasons. "Will you please tell me what sense there is in running on a socialist ticket in America today?" he asked a reporter for the *Nation*. "What's the use of being right only to be defeated?"[63]

To Thomas, such statements brought little comfort, and he never expressed even limited public approval of either Long or Coughlin. (He did announce once that he was prepared to ask Long for help in a fight to "improve the lot of Arkansas share croppers," but he made it plain that he viewed the request as little better than making a deal with the Devil.) Other members of the party, however, were not always so certain. An Alabama man, for example, wrote Thomas in 1935 urging him to moderate his views on Huey Long. "Now I am a socialist," he explained, "have been for thirty five years. . . . [Long] is telling the people the things we have been telling them for a generation. They listen to him . . . while they thought we were fools." Nita Brunnon, a Socialist from Illinois, wrote a friend and fellow party member: "Say George, if possible, listen to Father Coughlin every Sunday afternoon. . . . He certainly is telling the people the straight of the thing." From California, one woman wrote Norman Thomas, "I can't make up my mind whether we who wish for the Cooperative Commonwealth will do better to support [Long] or to fight him. . . . if Long were elected, would it do our cause any harm?"[64]

This occasional evidence of uncertainty within party ranks was symptomatic of a larger problem: Long and Coughlin were winning the loyalties of the very people upon whom the future of the Socialist Party most depended. Men and women who might otherwise support the Socialists were gravitating instead toward the Share Our Wealth Clubs or the National Union for Social Justice. Nowhere was this more evident than among the tenant farmers and sharecroppers of the South. One of Thomas's strongest commitments in the 1930s was to the needs of these troubled people, and by 1935 he had committed the party openly and unequivocally to a new organization: the Southern Tenant Farmers' Union. Founded and led by H. L. Mitchell, a young Arkansas Socialist, the Union sought to organize poor farmers into an inter-racial coalition fighting for fundamental economic reform. From its start, the new organization was forced to deal with the popularity and influence of Huey Long.[65]

There is little evidence to suggest the character of the STFU members who gravitated to Long. On the surface, their admiration for him would seem to contradict the picture of his movement as predominantly middle-class, attracting largely men and women protecting marginal and imperiled middle-class status. Yet the two were not necessarily incompatible, for the agricultural crisis of the late 1920s and the 1930s had transformed many once-independent farm owners into tenants and sharecroppers; and such people, even when reduced to peonage, often retained the values and aspirations of the propertied. Whatever the explanation, however, the appeal of Huey Long to those whose support the Socialists coveted was both clear and troubling. Mitchell wrote Thomas in 1935 of a Share Our Wealth Club in Blytheville, Arkansas, led by men "who used to be Socialists." He was confident, he claimed, that the party could win them back; but on other occasions he was less certain. Long "can sure fool these southern farmers," he complained early in 1934. Months later, he was still worried. "Without organization and leadership," he warned in September, "the workers are just as apt to go [Long's] way as they are ours." The Share Our Wealth Clubs, he wrote in October, were more than ever threatening the new Union: "The people [in Arkansas] will either go Socialist or Huey Long."[66]

Time and again, Mitchell, Thomas, and other Socialist leaders were forced to confront a basic problem: the general unwillingness of even the most miserable Americans to countenance a genuinely radical economic program. Long's Share Our Wealth Plan, Coughlin's proposals for Social Justice, other dissident programs with limited goals: all offered the prospect of social uplift without the specter of excessively drastic change. Unlike the Communists, who could continue working patiently and (if necessary) covertly for revolution despite this opposition, the Socialists found such attitudes crippling. Their goal was fundamental change through peaceful and public efforts, and without widespread popular support they could do virtually nothing. It must have been with particular anguish, then, that they read messages such as the one the STFU received from Elmer Woods, an Alabama farmer, in the summer of 1935. Woods had read their literature and considered their proposals, and he had found much in them to admire. But in the end, his allegiances lay elsewhere. He said nothing in his letter about Huey Long or Father Coughlin, but it was undoubtedly of them that the Socialist leaders were thinking when they examined Woods's explanation:

> We has read your letter and we has studied over your program. We think the program is too radical. You all believe for equal rights for negras and you alls program sounds comoonist even if you all has kicked them out. . . . If we has looked at it wrongly or if there is some more to understand we would like to know. Otherwise I guess we won't be interested. We thank you for sending us your program, but we thinks it to radical. We think you all mean right but its to radical.[67]

VII

THE SPRING AND SUMMER OF 1935 were heady times for those awaiting a major political upheaval in America. For a moment, at least, almost anything seemed possible. Franklin Roosevelt and the New Deal were apparently floundering. The Republican opposition was weak and demoralized. Dissident movements were springing to life and gaining remarkable strength in virtually every region of the country. Talk of a new national party uniting the disparate "progressive" elements no longer seemed idle; newspapers carried reports almost every day of the latest effort to create an alliance of the discontented. As in the 1890s, the gathering clouds of political protest cast fear into the hearts of establishment politicians and raised brilliant hopes among the discontented. Once again, defiant Americans seemed to be rising up against the political establishment with impressive, organized strength.

No one seemed more likely to profit from the upsurge of dissidence than Huey Long and Father Coughlin. As interaction among dissident leaders increased in 1935, as the constituencies of particular movements began to overlap and coalesce, the possibilities for Long and Coughlin to expand their influence seemed limitless. The moment, apparently, was theirs.

In these months of expectant uncertainty, both men saw only hope, only possibilities. Yet, despite their optimism, the promise of greatness was an illusory one. The 1930s were not the 1890s; the insurgent fervor did not augur a revived and strengthened populist crusade. And neither Long nor Coughlin, looking to the future, could perceive the harsh realities or foresee the cruel events that would soon combine to put an end to their dreams.

11

The Last Phase

I N THE EUPHORIA of the moment, it seemed inconceivable that the Long and Coughlin movements would soon begin to crumble. But crumble they did. By the end of 1935, the prospects for an effective dissident challenge to the two major parties had faded considerably. By the late spring of 1936, the insurgent threat could no longer be taken seriously. And in November, Franklin Roosevelt roared to a victory in the Presidential election by the greatest margin in the nation's history. Huey Long and Father Coughlin had been powerless to stop him.

In part, the Long and Coughlin movements fell victims to fate, to developments they could neither foresee nor control. But they were victims as well of basic internal weaknesses. The weaknesses were less visible, perhaps, than their obvious strengths. But had Long and Coughlin looked carefully in 1935 at what they had built, they might have realized how formidable a task they still faced.

In retrospect, there were many features of both movements that should have appeared at least mildly troubling, and one in particular that portended disaster. Long and Coughlin had won the support of millions by promoting ideas and programs that combined a diffuse radicalism with a localistic conservatism. It remained to be seen whether their ideologies differed enough from those of more conventional politicians to be safe from co-optation. They had created personal organizations with local chapters scattered throughout the nation. But the organizations were diverse and shapeless, dominated more often than not by immediate local concerns. It was unclear how energetically members would respond to their leaders if called upon to do more than listen to the radio and write letters. Long and Coughlin had made inroads into the followings of dissident leaders everywhere and had watched as their constituencies began to overlap with those of Townsend, Olson, Reno, the La Follettes, and others. But no one could be certain that the interaction they had encouraged would ultimately redound to their own benefit.

Yet these weaknesses were not necessarily fatal. They were not necessarily weaknesses at all. The ideological fuzziness was in some ways a source of strength, allowing men and women of divergent views to gather under the same banner. The looseness of the organizations enabled Long and Coughlin to benefit indirectly from local community concerns. The interaction with other dissident movements offered not only the possibility of loss, but the opportunity for gain. In short, the heterogeneity and localism of the Long and Coughlin movements were obstacles, certainly, to the disciplined, anti-democratic, fascist challenge that many critics of both men feared. They did not, however, foreclose the possibility of an effective political campaign.

Far more troubling for the crusades Long and Coughlin were preparing was a single, debilitating weakness: inability to wean their followers from Franklin Roosevelt. It was no secret by the summer of 1935 that both men were contemplating a challenge to the President in the 1936 election. Yet even then, when their influence was at its peak, there were abundant indications that they could not be sure their supporters would follow them. The grip of Roosevelt on the American electorate was a powerful one, and neither Long nor Coughlin had found a way to break it. Both movements included opponents of the President, but they also included, apparently in much greater numbers, men and women who remained unwilling to turn their backs entirely upon the New Deal.

There was little question about Huey Long's feelings toward Franklin Roosevelt. Indeed, few other politicians of either party were as unremittingly hostile to the President and the New Deal in 1934 and 1935. Yet while some Long supporters shared that animosity, far more expressed ambivalence about, if not open enthusiasm for, the President. A few simply remained blithely unaware of the tensions between the two leaders and happily expressed support for both, such as the Milwaukee woman who wrote Roosevelt that "in [Long] you have a Staunch advocate"; the Georgia women's club that printed an editorial under the headline "God Save the President . . . and His Instrument, Huey Long"; or the nearly illiterate Long enthusiast from Tickfaw, Louisiana, who sent a scrawled note to the White House asking for money "to get me a car to go around" so he could sign up new members "for the Shear our Welt."[1]

More often, however, Long's admirers were all too aware of Huey's criticisms of the President and struggled to reconcile their admiration for Long with their continuing support of the New Deal. It was not an easy task. It produced tortured rationalizations, expressions of distress, anguish, and confusion. It did not, however, very often produce what Long himself would have liked: open repudiation of the New Deal.

Some responded by pleading with the two men to reconcile their differences. A Massachusetts man, for example, implored the President "from the
bottom of my hart" to "make up with your best freand Senator Long.... Why
not send for him to come to your office please." Others urged Roosevelt to
prove that Long's criticisms were unfounded by adopting the principles of the
Share Our Wealth Plan. To do so, a Texas man assured him, would be to
"complete the 'new deal' and you would be praised and made a hero.... We
sincerely hope you can see eye to eye with [Long] in this most important plan
of the hour." There was an air of near desperation in some such messages.
"Somehow I still believe that you are all for the poor, struggling masses,
despite considerable evidence to the contrary," a clearly anguished member
of a Maryland Share Our Wealth Club wrote Roosevelt. "I don't know why
you hesitate." Unwilling to repudiate Long, unable to abandon faith in Roosevelt, these men and women were performing a precarious balancing act,
struggling to maintain what would appear to have been two contradictory
commitments.[2]

For some Long supporters, perhaps for most, the struggle was still in
progress when Huey's death ended it. But many of those who made their
choices in 1935 indicated that it was Roosevelt, not Long, who was winning.
In the spring of that year, a friend of Jim Farley made a trip through parts
of the South and the Far West and sent his impressions to the Postmaster
General. "I talked with as many people as I could," he wrote. "My survey,
if survey you can call it, showed me ... that Huey is excessively popular with
the masses everywhere ... [but that they] can't understand why he has been
'messing in' with FDR in Washington ... that they would NOT vote for him
for President."[3]

Some Long supporters gave similar assurances directly to Roosevelt.
"Senator Long is a friend of the people of Louisiana and is the greatest leader
this state has ever been privileged to claim as its own," a group of Louisianans
wrote the President in 1935. But "We look upon you as the greatest leader of
the present generation and regard your Administration as almost a miracle."
A Share Our Wealth Club in Allston, Massachusetts, wrote Roosevelt only
days before Huey's death that it would support the President for re-election
in 1936 regardless of what Long decided to do.[4]

Father Coughlin faced an even more difficult dilemma. Having based so
much of his initial popularity upon his fervent support for the President, he
placed great strains upon the loyalties of his supporters when he began to
repudiate the New Deal in 1934 and 1935. Although Coughlin vacillated on
the subject of Roosevelt through much of that period, claiming intermittently
even as late as early 1936 that what he really wanted was to see the New Deal
succeed, it was scarcely possible after 1934 to take such protestations seriously

in light of his frequent and bitter tirades against the President. He hoped, of course, that his supporters would follow him into opposition; but more often than not, he hoped in vain.[5]

Either through wishful thinking or ignorance, some Coughlin admirers, like some Long supporters, simply refused to recognize that any serious rift had developed between the priest and the President; and Coughlin included just enough public assurances of support for Roosevelt to enable those who wanted to badly enough to maintain the delusion. His radio speech in response to the Hugh Johnson attack in March 1935, for example, was an important event for many such supporters. By far the greatest part of the address was a biting attack on Johnson, peppered with accusations that he and his allies had sabotaged the New Deal. But in his closing paragraphs, Coughlin added an important assurance: "I still proclaim to you that it is either 'Roosevelt or Ruin.' I support him today and will support him tomorrow."[6]

It had been many months since Coughlin's audience had heard such words, and anyone taking them in context would have recognized them for what they were: an aberration from the prevailing tone of his broadcasts, designed to give him an immediate tactical advantage. Indeed, in his very next sentence he added an important caveat, insisting that he was not "that type of false friend" who would "praise policies like N.R.A. when criticism is required or betray my millions of supporters throughout this nation by preaching to them the prostituted slogan of 'Peace, Peace,' when there is no peace." A week later, he seemed to have entirely forgotten his expressions of support and was once again voicing open antagonism toward the President.[7]

But even this modest expression of loyalty was enough to produce from some Coughlin supporters expressions of almost rapturous relief. "The reason for this letter," a young man in Springfield, Ohio, wrote the President, "is to state how happy I am tonight, after listening to the Reverend Charles E. Coughlin's reply to Gen. Johnson. I'm happy because I believe he still has a lot of faith in you." Another writer assured Roosevelt that, for him, the "high spot" of Coughlin's "masterful reply" to Johnson was "his tribute to yourself when he said that the only reason that your plans have not worked out as they were supposed to do is on account of the 'chiselers.' "[8]

Others in Coughlin's audience, of course, recognized his antagonism toward Roosevelt for what it was. And for them, the evidence of hostility between their leader and their President was the source of anguish, confusion, and at times even anger. Some were plagued by doubts about Roosevelt, and they attempted to resolve the painful conflict by begging the President to make his peace with Coughlin. "Our family have loved you, revered you, and wished you success," an Ohio woman wrote the White House shortly after having attended a Coughlin rally in Cleveland. "We will cooperate but, dear Mr.

Roosevelt . . . haven't you gotten away just a little?" Her distress was almost palpable. "Please do not alienate the masses from you," she pleaded. "They want to love you and have you lead them but a few more mistakes and they won't listen to you. Talk to us oftener. . . . You once gave the people courage and faith and I sincerely trust you will not fail us."[9]

Others were similarly troubled. "We just cannot bear to see our idol foresake us," a Pennsylvania woman wrote to Louis Howe after one Coughlin denunciation of the President. "Your ardent friend Charles E. Coughlin . . . is the man whom to take his ardent advice, the man who will never betray you," a barely literate Indiana man urged the President. "Many of your advisers are and is a Judas." And a Pittsburgh admirer wrote to Roosevelt: "The fact that I have always admired your humility, ability and courage prompts me to most respectfully ask you to think twice before you break with your true friend who is the outstanding mentor of the massess [sic]."[10]

But for every person who began to doubt Roosevelt because of Coughlin's attacks, there were two who began to doubt Coughlin himself. "I have been for you," one supporter gently prodded Father Coughlin in the fall of 1934, "but just now I think that if you can not help the plan F.D.R. is working out you better let him alone and give him a chance." A beautician in Lansing, Michigan, wrote the President at about the same time and asked a question that made clear where her first loyalty lay: "There are a lot of us here who would like to know whether or not we should join Father Coughlin's organiza- tion. . . . if it is to help you and our United States, we want to join. If not, we don't want anything to do with it."[11]

Others went even further. "I am for the President first, last and always until he has been proven absolutely wrong," one angry member of the Na- tional Union told Coughlin. "And I am sorry to say I couldn't under any consideration continue to support you if you feel it your duty to criticize him." When Coughlin took to the air in the fall of 1935 to say that he had erred in asking his supporters to back the President, a Chicago follower fired back an embittered reply that was typical of many Coughlin received: "It is better that I stand, with many of my friends before the people that we have asked to listen to your broadcasts and admit, humbly we have been wrong in asking them to support you."[12]

The more Coughlin criticized the President, in other words, the more support he lost. He continued to claim that he was attracting more new recruits than he was losing old ones (a claim with no basis in fact), but he was forced to admit when prodded by reporters that "thousands of members have written to say that if I criticize the policies and activities of the Roosevelt administration, they will withdraw from our ranks."[13]

There were many reasons for the durability of Roosevelt's popularity among Long and Coughlin supporters, most of them a result of the President's own political skill. The most obvious was the sudden flurry of New Deal legislative activity in the spring of 1935, the so-called Second New Deal, which many described as the Administration's "turn to the left." The new program was hardly radical; indeed, an argument can be made that it represented little substantive change in policy. Its political effect, however, was dramatic, for it strengthened the President's position among almost every group to whom the dissident spokesmen were attempting to appeal. The Social Security Act offered only inadequate pensions to limited groups of the elderly, but it helped to undercut the Townsend movement and the efforts of Long and Coughlin to draw support from its members. The National Labor Relations Act (better known as the Wagner Act) won passage over Roosevelt's initial objections, but the President nevertheless took credit for the crucial federal guarantees it gave to the right of workers to organize and bargain collectively. The Utilities Holding Company Act, which proposed to break up large utility combinations, and the so-called "Soak-the-Rich" tax bill, which raised levies on wealthy Americans, were more symbol than substance; but they indicated to Long and Coughlin supporters that Roosevelt, too, was concerned about the dangers of concentrated wealth and power.

The most conspicuous element, perhaps, of the "Second New Deal" in 1935 was the creation of the Works Progress Administration, a relief agency with a $5 billion budget that ultimately provided jobs for over three million people. Along with lesser New Deal relief efforts—the Public Works Administration, the Civilian Conservation Corps, and others—the WPA made the federal government, and more specifically the Administration of Franklin Roosevelt, a visible and valued presence in the lives of individual citizens. Even those who did not benefit directly from the programs (and there were more than seven million unemployed who did not) were aware of their existence and the possibilities they created. The New Deal, in short, had not ended the Depression or provided for the needs of all those in want; but the President had succeeded in creating great difficulties for those who, like Long and Coughlin, wished to portray him as a callous and reactionary friend of special privilege.[14]

Long and Coughlin attacked the Administration on other grounds as well, charging that the New Deal was endangering the autonomy of communities by centralizing too much authority in the federal government. Yet here, too, the President was less vulnerable to attack than he may at first have seemed. The Administration had, it was true, created a bewildering maze of new bureaucracies. But many of these new programs and agencies did not intrude profoundly upon local social and political structures. Studies of the effects of New Deal programs upon localities have shown repeatedly that, as one disappointed liberal observer wrote several years after Roosevelt's death, "The federal government has not encroached upon state government."[15]

Time and again, Roosevelt confronted a choice between battling local interests to achieve his goals or modifying his aims to appease community leaders. Time and again, he chose the latter. Many of the most important New Deal agencies were markedly decentralized in their operations, establishing broad policy directives in Washington, but leaving specific administrative decisions to local officials, who were usually natives of the communities in question. Even entrenched machines in industrial cities often found themselves not only unthreatened but actually strengthened by New Deal largesse. In Pittsburgh, Kansas City, and Chicago, for example, it was the local Democratic organizations that controlled a large proportion of the federal funds flowing into the communities, and with them much of the political credit for their effects. The Roosevelt Administration took care, moreover, to avoid involvement with issues particularly likely to inflame local sensibilities: questions of race, religion, and morals. Roosevelt remembered how destructive such social and cultural controversies had been to the Democratic Party in the 1920s. He had no wish to arouse them again.[16]

The New Deal was not always successful in maintaining this balance between federal and local interests. The power of the federal government was indeed growing; the national bureaucracy had indeed become larger and more intrusive. But the Administration had remained sensitive enough to local concerns to limit the damage of such changes, which in any case, often seemed a small price to pay for the economic benefits that accompanied them. In the process, the President had created for his dissident adversaries a troubling dilemma. Long and Coughlin had offered to the nation a vision of a sharply limited radicalism, fearing that more drastic positions would be politically untenable. But in appealing to the discontented, they were competing with a leader at least equal to them in political skill and vastly superior to them in public power, a President whose programs and rhetoric exerted a strong influence on the very people whose support Long and Coughlin most needed. In attempting to offer both change and continuity, they were occupying crowded ground. Their messages simply did not differ enough from that of Franklin Roosevelt to protect them from co-optation.

Long and Coughlin may have been aware of these difficulties in 1935, but neither man was ready to concede that they were insuperable ones. Each remained convinced that ultimately he could mount an effective challenge to the existing parties, that his dreams of national power could survive the defections of the moment. Coughlin was able to put his claims to the test in 1936. Long never had the chance.

II

HUEY LONG RETURNED to Louisiana early in September 1935 tired, grim, and determined. The day before, he had addressed an enthusiastic Labor Day crowd in Oklahoma City, denouncing Franklin Roosevelt and predicting the emergence of a new third party in 1936. But now there were the old battles to face. There were fiscal problems in New Orleans, political complications throughout the state (a result in part of Long's continuing battle with New Deal agencies in Louisiana), and, as always, murmurings of revolt from his sullen and embittered enemies. He hesitated for several days, but on September 7 he announced that Governor Allen had called a special session of the legislature to convene that night.[17]

By early the same evening, forty-two new bills lay awaiting enactment —most of them routine, but two of them startling even to legislators accustomed to the remarkable. One was a vague and threatening statute giving state officials the authority to fine and imprison anyone who interfered with the powers "reserved" to Louisiana under the Tenth Amendment to the Constitution. It was directed, clearly, at agents of the Roosevelt Administration in the state, a warning that they could challenge the Long regime only at their peril. ("I don't give a damn," Long replied when the lawyer he had chosen to draft the bill complained that it was plainly unconstitutional.)[18]

The second surprise was a direct affront to one of Long's oldest and most powerful remaining enemies—Judge Benjamin Pavy of St. Landry Parish, a seemingly impregnable figure after twenty-eight years on the bench. Huey knew he could not hope to unseat Pavy in St. Landry, so he proposed an elaborate scheme to gerrymander the Judge into a new district where the Long organization could control the next election. Such tactics were not new, but this proposal was so naked in its purpose that even some of Huey's allies protested.[19]

As usual, Long seemed to be everywhere as the legislators began their work—darting in and out of the House, meeting with associates, barking orders to his floor leaders, chatting with the press. No one, it seemed, could keep up with him—not his advisors, not his secretaries, not even his bodyguards. Shortly after nine o'clock, he left the House chamber and was striding rapidly down a corridor, his entourage trailing frantically behind, when a tall, thin, bespectacled young man stepped out from behind a pillar, raised his right hand, aimed a small pistol at Long's rib cage, and shot.[20]

Huey let out a surprised yelp, spun around, and tore down the hallway —"like a hit deer," one witness later recalled. His bodyguards grabbed the gunman, wrestled him to the floor, and shot him twice. Then, although he was clearly already dead, they stood over him and emptied their pistols. The crisp white suit was soon stained dark with blood, the body mutilated with more than fifty wounds, and the shiny marble wall of the state capitol Long had constructed for himself permanently scarred with bullet holes. At first, no one recognized the assailant; but finally a member of the nervous crowd that quickly gathered elbowed his way to the front, looked at the body, and identified the dead man as Carl Austin Weiss, a respected Baton Rouge physician and the son-in-law of Benjamin Pavy.[21]

Huey in the meantime had been rushed to a nearby hospital and wheeled into an operating room, where, surrounded by politicians jostling for position, doctors worked to repair the wound and stop the internal hemorrhaging. The damage appeared to be slight, and for a few hours it seemed that Long would recover. But by early the next morning, it was clear that the surgeons had hopelessly bungled it: they had failed to detect damage to the kidney. The bleeding continued, and Long was now too weak to survive a second operation. For twenty-four hours, he remained alive—at one moment unconscious, at the next delirious, at the next awake, alert, and talking politics. But he was clearly sinking. And early on the morning of September 10, with the family he had barely noticed through most of his life gathered around his bed, he died.[22]

In retrospect, it seemed almost inevitable that it would end this way— a career that had soared rapidly, dramatically, recklessly to unprecedented heights crashing suddenly in one appalling, violent moment. Yet, at the time, the event produced only shock, and those Huey left behind felt suddenly helpless and frightened. They managed to keep their composure long enough to stage a remarkable state funeral. A crowd of more than 100,000 gathered on the front lawn of the capitol to hear Gerald L. K. Smith deliver an emotional, even mawkish eulogy and to watch Long's copper-lined casket (Huey himself lying inside clad, incongruously, in evening clothes) lowered reverently into a grave less than a hundred yards from the scene of the assassination. Within weeks, however, the Long organization in Louisiana was dividing into bitter factions, squabbling over who would succeed Huey in the Senate, who would follow Allen in the statehouse, who would control the money (some of which could not be found, for Huey had died without revealing the location of the "deduct box").[23]

Despite it all, the Long forces continued to control Louisiana politics, at least for the moment. But there was one major casualty—the Share Our Wealth movement. Without Huey to lead them, few of his political heirs had any stomach for national heroics, and even fewer had any interest in continuing the feud with Franklin Roosevelt. Eager for New Deal funds, concerned about federal investigations into their taxes and other financial dealings, the Long forces quickly and quietly made their peace with the Administration. They would support the President in 1936; he would allow them access to patronage and would halt the investigations. It was, jaundiced observers remarked, "the second Louisiana Purchase."[24]

Gerald L. K. Smith, in the meantime, was becoming almost completely isolated. He had never been an intimate of Long's Louisiana allies; most had barely tolerated him, others had despised him. And once Huey himself was gone, he ensured that he would have no meaningful role in the state, first by allying himself publicly with the weaker of the two major competing factions, then by switching his allegiance to the victors at the last moment. In the end, neither group would have anything to do with him, and ultimately he had no choice but to leave Louisiana. He was, he claimed, the legitimate successor to Long as leader of the Share Our Wealth movement. But without funds, without a base of support, without the crucial mailing lists, without even an office or a secretary, he was a leader with nothing to lead. He moved about erratically for several months, at one moment trying to ingratiate himself with the Long family, at the next flirting briefly with Eugene Talmadge and his abortive new Grass Roots Party. Nothing seemed to help.

In May 1936, he showed up at a Congressional hearing in Washington to hear Francis Townsend testify, and he soon managed to ingratiate himself with the doctor and plant himself in the center of the Old Age Revolving Pensions movement, where the first of many new chapters in his career began. For more than three decades thereafter, Smith remained an active and increasingly sordid presence in American public life: a harsh religious fundamentalist, a vicious anti-Semite, and a rabid anti-communist. By the time of his death in 1976, he was living in Eureka, Arkansas, presiding sourly over a cluster of "sacred projects"—a gaudy religious tourist attraction whose highlight was a hideous seven-story statue of Jesus: the "Christ of the Ozarks."

Through all the twists and turns in Smith's distasteful career, he continued to revere the memory of his first political idol. He even wrote a brief biography entitled "Huey P. Long: A Summary of Greatness; The Political Genius of the Century; An American Martyr." Never, however, was Smith able to offer credible leadership to Long's national constituency. After 1935, the Share Our Wealth Society survived only in his own hopeful imagination.[25]

III

FOR COUGHLIN, the end was less swift and perhaps, ultimately, less kind. In many ways, he, too, was a victim of Carl Weiss's pistol, for Huey Long, despite the tension between them, had been his most valuable potential ally. Coughlin alone would have great difficulty sustaining an effective insurgent challenge in 1936. "With the death of Long," the *Nation* said reassuringly shortly after the assassination, "the field of demagoguery is left to Father Coughlin, of whom one need be much less afraid." There was even speculation that Coughlin was contemplating a return to the New Deal fold. It was not lost upon reporters that he visited the President in Hyde Park in September 1935, only hours after Long died—that he was present, in fact, when Roosevelt received (with mixed feelings, one suspects) the chilling news from Louisiana.[26]

What seemed clear to others, however, was not at all apparent to Coughlin. Long's death may have shaken him momentarily ("the most regrettable thing in modern history," he commented shortly after the shooting), but it caused no fundamental change in the trajectory of his career. The visit to Hyde Park marked no lasting peace with the President. Indeed, only two months later, in December 1935, Coughlin announced openly what had been implicit for over a year: his support for Franklin Roosevelt had come to an end. The principles of the National Union and those of the New Deal were, he told his radio audience, "unalterably opposed. . . . Today I humbly stand before the American public to admit that I have been in error." It was finally clear, he admitted, that Roosevelt had never intended to drive the "money changer . . . from the temple." Not for another seven months did he formally commit himself to defeating the President in 1936, and in the interim it remained barely possible for those Coughlin supporters who wished to badly enough to believe that he might still reconcile with the President. But the time for that was past. Coughlin had made the break, and neither he nor Roosevelt ever made any serious efforts to heal it.[27]

In December, he called for a reorganization of the National Union for Social Justice and the recruitment of "20,000 selected workers" to begin the work of purging Congress of "rubber-stamp" members. The new activists were to establish an elaborate system of local units, one in every Congressional district, which would support candidates without regard to party affiliation; the only criterion would be a candidate's willingness to endorse the principles of social justice. The Presidential election, Coughlin continued to insist, would be of no concern to him. But at the local level, he promised, the National Union would become a potent political force.[28]

In the first months of 1936, it appeared that it had. Coughlin's power seemed not only to have survived the death of Long and the break with Roosevelt, but to have expanded. New Coughlin organizations were springing up in great numbers in important states—Ohio, Massachusetts, Michigan, New Jersey, Pennsylvania, New York. And they played active roles in several Congressional primaries that spring, with apparently astonishing results. In Pennsylvania, the National Union supported thirty-two Congressional candidates; twelve of them won. In Ohio, Coughlin himself campaigned actively for some of the thirty-two men the Union had endorsed—speaking first in Toledo and later in Cleveland at a large rally in Municipal Stadium; fifteen of the Coughlin candidates emerged triumphant. The organization claimed credit as well for victories in Wisconsin, Michigan, Massachusetts, and Maine. All spring, reported the *New Republic*'s T.R.B., representatives were "straggling back" to Washington from the political wars "filled with tales of Father Coughlin."[29]

Yet this impressive performance was in part an illusion; for Coughlin had chosen his candidates carefully, and there was good reason to question whether his intervention had been the decisive factor in many of these contests. In Pennsylvania, for example, ten of the twelve victorious Coughlin candidates were incumbents, for most of whom re-election had already seemed likely. (The National Union apparently was an important factor in helping Michael J. Stack win renomination over the opposition of the Philadelphia Democratic machine; but even there, some believed, the outcome might have been the same without Coughlin.)[30]

It was in Ohio that Coughlin's influence had appeared strongest, and it was there that the illusory nature of that influence was most apparent. In Cleveland, for example, several National Union-sponsored candidates (including Coughlin's long-time ally Representative Martin Sweeney) won nomination, but political observers noted that the vote had reflected less love for Father Coughlin than disenchantment with the entrenched, conservative local machine. Nor did the outcome represent any genuine animosity toward the Roosevelt Administration. Most observers believed that New Deal candidates, if any had been available, would have triumphed in many of the contests; and to those who supported the President, almost anyone was preferable to the tired, corrupt, and myopic members of the local Democratic organization, whose hostility to Roosevelt had long been manifest. In Toledo, where men endorsed by the National Union triumphed in both the Republican and Democratic primaries, Coughlin's influence seemed to have been even stronger. But he profited there, unexpectedly, when local relief organizations suddenly ran out of money. Unemployed voters, desperate and angry, vented their frustrations at the polls.[31]

To Coughlin, however, the results were heartening; and while early in the year he had remained uncertain about whether to plunge into the Presidential contest, by late spring he was newly confident and ready to act. There is no reason to believe that he ever considered becoming a candidate himself; as a Catholic priest, he was, in effect, removed from consideration by definition. But there was nothing to stop him from choosing a surrogate, and nothing to keep him from playing a major, perhaps dominant role in a third-party campaign. The nature of the party and the identity of the candidate were not immediately evident even to Coughlin. But slowly a new political ally was intruding into his consciousness.[32]

William Lemke, a short, unprepossessing, second-term Congressman from North Dakota, was hardly one of the titans of American public life. He had, however, earned modest repute in the Midwest for his outspoken championing of agrarian dissidents. He had co-sponsored legislation in 1934 and again in 1935 to insure farmers against foreclosures on their property, legislation that the Roosevelt Administration had grudgingly accepted. And he had worked tirelessly in the early months of 1936 on behalf of a new and even more drastic measure: the Frazier-Lemke Act, a bill that provided for government refinancing of all farm mortgages and for a major inflation of the money supply. The President opposed him on the issue; and although Lemke seemed at first to have secured the votes necessary for passage, Administration pressure ultimately proved fatal. On the final roll call, the North Dakotan's support all but evaporated, and his bill suffered a humiliating defeat.[33]

Lemke emerged from the struggle with a deep and abiding hatred of Franklin Roosevelt. He emerged, too, as a compatriot of Father Coughlin. For Coughlin's enthusiastic support of the Frazier-Lemke Act, his angry criticisms of the President for opposing it, and his vicious denunciations of some Congressional adversaries of the bill had produced one of the most acrimonious controversies of his career. One Coughlin radio attack so enraged John J. O'Connor of New York, chairman of the House Rules Committee, who was attempting to prevent the measure from reaching the floor, that the Congressman issued a belligerent public challenge. Coughlin should appear in Washington and confront O'Connor personally, he demanded, and "I shall guarantee to kick you all the way from the Capitol to the White House, with clerical garb and all the silver in your pockets you got by speculating in Wall Street." (Coughlin intemperately accepted the challenge and announced he would arrive in the capital the next morning, but he soon thought better of it. His reluctance did not, however, prevent a small deluge of angry letters to the White House from his supporters demanding that the President "fire" O'Connor for his impudence and disrespect.)[34]

The Lemke relationship was, then, an alliance forged in combat; and early in May, Coughlin wrote the Congressman about his plans to establish a new political organization. It was to serve as a vehicle to unite all "progressive" opponents of the Administration; it was to nominate candidates for both state and national offices; and it was to be known as the Union Party. Lemke was to be its North Dakota chairman.

Lemke would soon become much more than that. On June 8, Coughlin casually informed him that "in due time, I will send you the name of our presidential candidate." Only a week later, he decided that the candidate was to be Lemke himself—a prospect the North Dakotan no doubt found startling, but one he happily accepted. On June 20, Lemke called a press conference to announce that he was entering the Presidential contest. (His running mate, he announced several days later, would be Thomas C. O'Brien, a lusterless Massachusetts lawyer whose greatest political distinction had been a single term as Boston district attorney.) There would, Lemke claimed, be a "mass convention" in Cleveland, probably in August, to formalize the new party and to make his nomination official. But his designation was by then as official as it needed to be. Reporters covering the announcement joked that Lemke had already held his nominating convention—in a phone booth, with Coughlin on the other end of the line. As if to prove them right, Coughlin took to the airwaves only six hours later to issue a formal endorsement of the Lemke candidacy. The Union Party was born.[35]

IV

ALMOST AT THE SAME TIME that Coughlin and Lemke were announcing their plans, Gerald L. K. Smith was holding a press conference in Chicago. The "Smith-Townsend" forces, as he called them, had reached a "loose working agreement" with the Union Party. He and Dr. Townsend would, he announced, support the Lemke candidacy.[36]

Coughlin would probably never have committed himself to the creation of a new party had he not been assured of at least that much additional support. His only hope for success, he realized, was to attract other dissident movements to the cause. Yet, from the beginning, his relationship with his new allies was fraught with difficulty, and it seemed at times as if Coughlin considered their participation in the campaign an unwelcome intrusion. Eager to exploit their strength, he was at the same time unwilling to share with them either control or acclaim.

The petty jealousy that underlay these relationships was evident at the national convention of the Townsend organization in Cleveland in mid-July. It was an impressive occasion. More than 11,000 elderly Townsendites flocked into the city from throughout the country, gathering not only to cheer their own leader and hear arguments for their own program, but also to endorse the national ticket of the new Union Party. Townsend, Smith, Lemke, and Coughlin were all to speak; it was to be, some reporters claimed, a great insurgent "love feast."[37]

It was anything but. The audiences were enthusiastic enough, but not always in ways the leadership found encouraging. When a speaker during the first session warmly praised Franklin Roosevelt, the delegates cheered lustily. When only hours later another delegate rose to excoriate the President, they cheered again. Townsend himself spoke on behalf of the Lemke candidacy, but without notable enthusiasm. And while the delegates obligingly voted to endorse the Union Party ticket, it was evident that their first concerns lay elsewhere. On the final morning of the convention, Lemke arrived at Cleveland's enormous Municipal Stadium to speak to what party organizers had hoped would be a crowd of 80,000 people. Only 5,000 showed up. Most of the Townsend delegates had already gone home.[38]

More disturbing to Coughlin, however, was a quite different problem: the prospect of sharing the limelight with Gerald L. K. Smith. Coughlin had arranged to be the final speaker at the last evening session; his was to be the climactic speech of the convention. But Smith spoke shortly before him, and he stirred the audience to such frenzied excitement that Coughlin, squirming uncomfortably at the back of the hall, began to feel decidedly upstaged. Determined not to be outdone, he rose to deliver the most intemperate speech he had ever made, in the course of which he removed first his coat, next his clerical collar, and then, standing in his shirtsleeves—no longer the commanding priest, but an ordinary, sweat-soaked crowd-pleaser—denounced the President in language that even his warmest admirers found shocking. Roosevelt was a "betrayer," a "liar," a "double-crosser," he said; and although the delegates once again shouted approval, Coughlin soon realized he had gone too far. It was one of the few statements for which he received a public rebuke from Bishop Gallagher, and several days later he humbly recanted.[39]

Reporters covering the Townsend convention called it an "exercise in confusion," an event that augured poorly for the future of the Union Party. The same could be said for the first annual meeting of Coughlin's own National Union for Social Justice a month later. Over 10,000 delegates gathered —again in Cleveland—for what was to be not only a paean to Father Coughlin but a demonstration of united support for the Lemke candidacy. As before, signs of jealousy and bickering among the Union Party leadership were conspicuous. Lemke, Townsend, and Smith were all again present. But Coughlin was clearly in command, and he did his best to ensure that this time he alone would be the center of attention. Other leaders were scheduled to speak at inauspicious moments, sandwiched in among nonentities from the National Union. And Smith was assigned to the dinner hour, at the end of a series of particularly boring addresses.[40]

Once again, however, Coughlin's careful maneuvering was to no avail. Although Smith appeared under the most unpromising of circumstances, facing a tired, hungry, and impatient crowd, he created an undeniable sensation, delivering what some reporters later called the finest "rabble-rousing oration" they had ever heard. He left his audience on its feet and screaming. Coughlin sat on the podium during the speech, grinning patronizingly, wiggling in his seat, and finally pretending to fall asleep. He was, however, well aware of the effect Smith had created, and of how much would be necessary for him to surpass it.

The next morning, Coughlin himself walked up to the podium, spoke for a few minutes in a calm, almost professorial tone, and then—in the midst of denouncing the New Deal as dangerous and "communistic"—stepped back from the microphone and collapsed. There was a stunned silence as aides rushed him to a hospital, and the shaken delegates quickly knelt to pray for their leader's recovery. They need not have worried. It was, doctors explained, simply a case of exhaustion; some were ungracious enough to suggest that it had been even less serious than that—a carefully staged attention-getting device. Whatever the explanation, it was evident that Coughlin was not entirely himself, that the frustrations of the campaign were taking their toll. The future was beginning to look grim.[41]

Grim indeed, for almost from its first moments, the Union Party crusade was a disaster. It was not only the squabbling among the party leaders, not only the colorlessness of the Presidential candidate, and not only the unwillingness of Dr. Townsend to evince any real enthusiasm for the cause (one reason, perhaps, why the promised Union Party convention never took place). Even more damaging was that other dissident leaders remained conspicuously aloof—either ignoring or openly repudiating the Lemke candidacy. Some of the most important—the La Follettes, Olson, Bingham, Amlie, Williams, Sinclair, and others—ultimately announced their support for the re-election of Franklin Roosevelt. The alternative, they warned, was a "fascist Republican." Coughlin was finding himself increasingly isolated, left alone with allies he neither liked nor respected, saddled with a candidate who was both lusterless and anonymous.[42]

Nothing, however, proved as devastating to Coughlin as the simple fact of his open opposition to Roosevelt. The animosity toward the Administration was not new, but the unequivocal support of another candidate was. Finally his followers faced a choice that until now many had tried to avoid. The alternatives were inescapable: they could support Coughlin, or they could support Roosevelt. No longer could they do both. In overwhelming numbers, they chose the President.[43]

The evidence was unmistakable. At the White House, the stream of letters to the President from men and women urging him to heed Father Coughlin's advice slowed and finally all but stopped. Once, there had been dozens of messages every day expressing support for the priest; now, several weeks often went by without a single such letter. From the American Catholic Church came howls of outrage. Before the Union Party announcement, most of Coughlin's fellow clergy had remained relatively mute about his political activities, not daring to incur his wrath. Now they denounced him openly— a Catholic laymen's league in New York, for example, demanding that Coughlin be "barred from further meddling in the affairs of the nation"; a bishop in Indiana angrily denying press reports that he had once been a Coughlin admirer; Cardinal Mundelein of Chicago calling together all the priests in his large and populous jurisdiction to decry Coughlin's actions.[44]

The national press greeted the Union Party crusade with a devastating indifference. Reports appeared in June explaining the new party and its candidate; but where once news of Coughlin had remained on the front pages for weeks on end, now most papers dropped the story almost immediately, as if it were too insignificant to merit serious attention. "The real threat of a new party passed away with the death of Long," the Nashville *Banner* condescendingly explained. Coughlin's activities were simply the flailings of a desperate man. "No demagogue of the first caliber, say Huey Long," the *Nation* argued, "would have joined forces with any other. . . . there is nothing so damaging to a panacea as another panacea on the same platform." Father Coughlin, by sharing the spotlight even if reluctantly, was vitiating his strength. He had, the magazine claimed, "lost caste."[45]

From the public, moreover, from whom Coughlin could once have expected an enthusiastic response no matter what the established press reported, the warmth and affection were visibly fading. As he traveled from city to city campaigning for Lemke and denouncing the President, crowds many times smaller and far less demonstrative than expected greeted him. There were occasional exceptions—an impressive gathering of nearly 100,000 in Chicago's Soldiers' Field in September, for example. But more typical was his experience in Cincinnati, long one of his most reliable strongholds. Union Party organizers worked frantically for weeks to bring out a crowd of 50,000 or more to hear Coughlin at Crosley Field. Hardly 10,000 showed up; and though Coughlin delivered an impressive and fiery speech, his audience seemed more concerned with keeping warm than expressing their approval. The disenchantment was spreading almost everywhere. An erstwhile supporter in California wrote Coughlin of a recent visit to a movie theater:

"Not a sentence of your newsreel speech can be heard for the hissing and booing of the people here who resent and are rebuking you for your attack against the President. The support of the people you worked so long to obtain is now lost."[46]

What remained was a small and unpromising segment of what had once been a vast constituency. Coughlin's critics had long dismissed his supporters as "chronic malcontents," "crackpots," or "ignorant illiterates." By the fall of 1936, such characterizations were, for the first time, reflecting the truth. Coughlin now retained only those relatively few supporters whose loyalty to him had been so intense, so single-minded, indeed, so fanatical that it could survive almost anything. At one time, such people had been a relatively small part of his constituency. Now they came close to constituting the whole. They were, by and large, less prosperous, less educated, less articulate than those who had deserted. They were also more uniformly Catholic, mainly Irish and Germans. And they tended to be men and women suffering deep personal anguish, people whose fears and frustrations were pushing them to the brink of irrationality.[47]

The character of this reduced constituency was evident at the National Union convention in August. The rapturous, fawning praise of Coughlin, the bitter, angry, even violent reactions to dissenting voices—all combined to suggest that here were men and women under great emotional stress, eager to immerse themselves in the anonymity of an all-embracing mass movement. "They indulged," one reporter observed, "in cries, shrieks, moans, rolling of the eyes and brandishing of the arms that—performed in their own family circles—would have caused their relatives to summon ambulances." In parades and demonstrations on the convention floor, delegates struggled with one another to reach the front of the center aisle—the point closest to Father Coughlin's seat. "Three hundreds of them would stand [there] from head to foot, until they were brushed aside by the ravenous idolators behind them." Speakers referred to Coughlin reverently simply as "Father"; and one delegate, "in the grip of almost unbearable emotion," rose to introduce a resolution "that we give thanks to the mother of the Reverend Charles E. Coughlin for bearing him." There were repeated attempts to identify Coughlin with Christ.[48]

The disturbing fanaticism of the gathering became uncomfortably clear during the perfunctory balloting on the endorsement of William Lemke. The vote was 8,152 to 1—with John H. O'Donnell, a stubborn alternate from Pennsylvania, raising the only dissenting voice. The crowd turned on him with a ferocity that even Coughlin found frightening, and convention officials quickly summoned armed policemen to escort O'Donnell to safety outside the hall. Enraged delegates screamed "Judas" and "traitor" as he left.[49]

Father John A. Ryan, the Catholic social reformer whose relations with Coughlin had been strained for more than a year, received additional evidence of the new character of the Coughlin constituency when he took to the air in September to denounce his fellow priest. Coughlin's criticisms of the President had, Ryan claimed, been "ugly, cowardly and flagrant calumnies." Catholics should pledge themselves to the re-election of Franklin Roosevelt. Almost immediately, Ryan was deluged with angry letters from outraged Coughlin supporters. But there was a striking difference between the messages he received and those that admirers of Coughlin had sent to public figures in earlier years. In 1934 and 1935, Coughlin followers—writing to the President, to members of Congress, to journalists, and others—had often produced neatly typed letters on printed stationery; now they were sending illegible and nearly illiterate scrawls on dime-store paper. Once they had exhibited a measure of realism, intelligence, and independence; now they spoke with frenzied voices —bitter, hostile, nearly irrational, and with an exaggerated devotion to their leader.[50]

A New Jersey woman, for example, claimed that she had postponed sending her letter for several weeks, and that now she was writing "not as I would have written [on the day of Ryan's speech] to tell you how much I hate you but tonite to tell you I feel sorry for what you have to answer before God for what you have done." A Coughlin supporter in Pittsburgh called Ryan "the personification of the modern Judas," and another angry listener described him as "a dirty dog mongrel." Coughlin, by contrast, such writers described as a figure almost divine: "the Greatest Leader since the time when Our Lord was on earth"; "the greatest teacher of all time, excepting Christ"; a man who "has given us all that his life is worth—his all." Such fanaticism may have been gratifying to a man who thrived on public acclaim. It was not, however, a promising base upon which to build a national campaign.[51]

The results of the Presidential election showed how unpromising. Long before the voting, the Union Party was in desperate trouble. In fourteen states, including California and New York, it was unable to secure enough signatures on petitions to win a place on the ballot. In seven more states, Lemke secured a listing only under labels other than that of the new party. And on election day, finally, the house of cards collapsed. While Franklin Roosevelt was storming to a dramatic victory by an unprecedented margin, William Lemke was taking a humiliating drubbing. Out of more than 45 million votes, the Union Party ticket received only 892,378—fewer than 2 percent of the total. Lemke had not come close to carrying a single state. He polled a vaguely respectable total in North Dakota, his home, where he received 13 percent of the ballots; but nowhere else did he receive even 7 percent of the vote. What had seemed his areas of greatest strength—Massachusetts, Minnesota, Ohio,

Wisconsin, Illinois, Michigan, Pennsylvania—provided him with no significant support, his vote there varying between 4 and 6.5 percent. "I don't know how many people told me that they voted for me and then I found out that I had no votes at all in their precincts," a stunned and confused Lemke told reporters. But few were listening. The Union Party had been exposed. Its leaders stood revealed as men of negligible political power.[52]

For Coughlin, the rebuke was shattering. Earlier in the summer, he had made a public promise: if he could not deliver at least nine million votes to William Lemke, he would retire from public life—resign from broadcasting and return to his parish. Now, with tears streaming down his cheeks, he admitted defeat. "President Roosevelt can be a dictator if he wants to," he barked shortly after hearing the returns. "I hope that God will bless him." Several days later, he took to the air for what he announced would be the last time. The National Union had been "thoroughly discredited," he admitted; it was time to disband the organization. As for himself: "I hereby withdraw from all radio activity in the best interests of the people. . . . I love my country and my church too much to become a stumbling block to those who have failed to understand. . . . Good by and God bless every one, friends and opponents. You are all friends tonight."[53]

V

HUEY LONG AND FATHER COUGHLIN faded so quickly from public prominence that it was easy in the ensuing years to forget how powerful and ominous they once had seemed. Yet their brief moment of prominence continues to deserve attention; for it revealed much not only about the nation's response to the Great Depression but about its long, painful, halting adjustment to the realities of modern industrial life. Long and Coughlin seized upon vague anxieties that had afflicted their society for many decades—the animosity toward concentrated power, the concern about the erosion of community and personal autonomy. They did more, however, than simply fan diffuse resentments. They turned the gaze of their troubled followers away from the cultural issues that had dominated the politics of the 1920s and toward the economic realities of the Great Depression. Rather than stressing questions of religion, ethnicity, race, or personal morality, they raised issues that only a few years before had seemed all but dead: issues of privilege, wealth, and centralized power, and of the failure of political institutions to deal with them. They gave evidence, in short, that the long tradition of opposition to large, inaccessible power centers, a tradition that stretched from the American Revolution to the populist revolt and beyond, continued to survive.

Yet Long and Coughlin displayed as well how greatly constricted that tradition had become. They spoke bravely at times of the possibilities of fundamental reform. But they lived in a society in which economic centralization was already so far advanced that the prospects for a genuine reversal appeared increasingly dim. Repeatedly, they gave evidence of the limits this reality had imposed upon their vision. Rather than confront the structure and process of economic consolidation, which was the true foundation of their laments, they railed against specific villains and peripheral problems. Rather than propose methods to revive the integrity of local institutions, they called for a major expansion in the power of the federal government. They failed, in short, to offer a convincing picture of how the kind of society they envisioned could be achieved.

It would be unfair to judge them too harshly for that failure. For if Long and Coughlin offered in the end an uncertain vision, they only reflected the uncertainty of the society in which they lived. They spoke to a people enchanted by the material fruits of industrialization but troubled by the inequalities of wealth and power that accompanied them; a people who had spent more than a century trying to devise ways to preserve the one and destroy the other; but a people whose search for solutions had grown more feeble and ineffectual with every passing decade. The quest for an answer to this dilemma continued in the 1930s; it would continue in one form or another in the years that followed. But the careers of Huey Long and Father Coughlin suggested, if nothing else, that the long struggle against the new economic order had already entered its twilight.

Epilogue

T HE INFLUENCE OF HUEY LONG in national politics all but vanished after 1935. In Louisiana, however, he remained nearly as potent a force in death as he had been in life. For more than two decades, his legacy survived as the central issue in virtually every political contest in the state. Even forty years later, Long cast a large shadow.

There was little question in the months following Long's assassination that the immediate political future, at least, belonged to his heirs. Oscar K. Allen, nearing the end of his term as governor, called tearfully upon his associates on the day of Huey's funeral to honor the memory of their martyred leader "by perpetuating ourselves in office." Allen himself died before he could fulfill the mission, causing momentary confusion; but the 1936 elections gave a resounding victory to a full slate of candidates strongly identified with the Long organization. Richard W. Leche, a state judge of minor note and modest talents, succeeded to the governorship; Earl Long, Huey's brother, became lieutenant governor; and Allen Ellender, an influential state legislator, assumed Long's Senate seat, which Huey's widow, Rose, had occupied briefly in the months before the voting. The principles and commitments of Huey Long, the new leadership promised, would guide their work.[1]

Long himself, however, had more accurately predicted the future when he once warned, "If those fellows ever try to use the powers I've given them without me to hold them down, they'll all land in the penitentiary." The Leche administration did attempt to use the powers Huey had bequeathed it—not to enact any substantial programs of social and economic reform (the new Governor moved quickly, rather, to appease the conservative opposition) but to plunder the state treasury with a brazen greediness that Long himself would never have tolerated. Leche admitted late in 1936 that he had an income of over $90,000 during his first year as governor, an office with a $7,500 annual salary. "When I took the oath as governor," he explained, "I didn't take any vow of poverty." James Monroe Smith, president of Louisiana State University, oversaw the transformation of his school from a monument to Long's grandiose aspirations into a funnel for channeling state funds to Huey's political heirs. Smith himself embezzled over $500,000 from the university in three years. The Leche regime not only continued the practice of deducting political contributions from the salaries of state employees, but it required every officeholder to sell (or himself purchase) up to ten subscriptions to the *American Progress*, which survived less as a propaganda organ than as a lucrative business enterprise. Within three years, according to some estimates, public officials had defrauded the state of $100 million.[2]

By 1939, graft had become so rampant and so blatant that even Louisiana, a state more tolerant than most of political corruption, could no longer ignore it. A series of state and federal investigations exposed a vast network of illegalities, popularly known simply as "the Scandals." And when all was done, the administration lay in shambles. Leche resigned in disgrace, was convicted of mail fraud and tax evasion, and was sentenced to ten years in prison. James Monroe Smith, who emerged from hiding to stand trial, was convicted of embezzlement by both state and federal courts and likewise served time in jail. Others followed: Seymour Weiss, one of the Long organization's most powerful figures; Abe Shushan, Huey's Levee Board president (the airport he had built was soon stripped of his name); the Conservation Commissioner; the LSU construction superintendent; and a host of others. Earl Long succeeded Leche in the governorship and did his best to disassociate himself from his predecessor. But the Scandals proved too devastating. In the February 1940 primary, Sam Houston Jones, an anti-Long candidate running on a promise of honest government, ousted Huey's brother from office. After twelve years of virtually unchallenged rule, the Long regime stood repudiated.[3]

The repudiation, however, was neither a convincing nor a lasting one. Jones won the 1940 contest by only a narrow margin, after a campaign in which he carefully avoided attacking the memory of Huey Long. His anti-Long successor, Jimmie Davis, a Public Service Commissioner (better known as a country singer and composer of "You Are My Sunshine"), won a similarly narrow mandate. And both Jones and Davis found themselves harried throughout their terms by a vicious and unrelenting pro-Long opposition, one that grew steadily stronger as for eight years the two administrations compiled ineffectual and generally conservative records. Jones himself had admitted in 1940 that the strength of the Long regime had been in large part a result of the old guard's unresponsiveness to the state's social needs. He may have recalled that warning when in 1948 he lost his bid to return to the statehouse by the largest margin in modern history. The victor was Earl Long.[4]

The Long forces in Louisiana did not regain their former hegemony, but their influence remained strong for years. Earl Long served his term as governor, retired briefly (he was barred by law from succeeding himself), and returned to the statehouse in 1956. In 1960, he became a candidate for Congress (having discharged himself from a mental institution to campaign), won the election, but died only a few days after the voting. His cousin Gillis Long won the seat two years later, only to lose it in 1964 to another cousin, Speedy Long. And of most significance, if not to Louisiana then to the nation, Russell Long, Huey's eldest son, entered the United States Senate in 1948 and remained there over thirty years later, having spent many of them as the chairman of the Senate Finance Committee and one of the most powerful figures in American government.

Long's political heirs benefited from their association with his name. They did not, however, always sustain the thrust of his policies. The Leche administration perfunctorily sold out to conservative interests in the state. Earl Long made a number of attempts during his years as governor to revive his brother's liberal economic programs, but, lacking Huey's political talents, achieved only modest success. Russell Long became, as the years passed and his father's memory dimmed, an effective friend of the oil industry and a man whom even Huey's bitterest foes viewed with approval and respect.

Yet the changes Long had wrought in Louisiana politics went far deeper than the survival in office of members of his family. The elevation of economic issues to the forefront of the state's public life was not an ephemeral accomplishment. Decades later, even in campaigns that involved no candidate intimately identified with the Longs, questions of wealth, of privilege, and of social reform repeatedly surfaced. A substantial number of Louisianans continued to seek leaders who asked, as Huey Long had done in 1928, for "the chance to dry the eyes of those who still weep."[5]

II

THE NATION HAD NOT HEARD the last of Father Coughlin when he canceled the "Golden Hour of the Little Flower" late in 1936, but his days as a serious political force were over. The remaining years of his public career were a time of steady deterioration, of a pathetic decline into bigotry and hysteria.

Coughlin did indeed retire from broadcasting after the debacle of the 1936 election—for six weeks. On New Year's Day 1937, he was back on the air with a holiday message. And a few weeks later, he announced he was resuming his weekly discourses. It was, he said, a response to overwhelming popular demand and to the last request of Bishop Michael Gallagher, who had died only days before.[6]

For a while, it seemed like old times. Coughlin continued to lambaste the Roosevelt Administration, to flay the "money changers" and the "international bankers," to draw large audiences and generate popular enthusiasm. A Gallup Poll early in 1938 showed that 10 percent of all families owning radios listened regularly to Coughlin's sermons (25 percent heard him occasionally), and that 83 percent of those who listened each week approved of what they heard. But it was not the same as the heady days of 1935 and before. Coughlin seemed to have lost some of the old fire, and increasingly his sermons displayed only a crude and embittered conservatism. His denunciations of the New Deal for its "dictatorial" and "communistic" policies were becoming virtually indistinguishable from those of the Liberty Leaguers and other right-wing critics. His appeals for progressive reform became both less frequent and less forceful.

And while he retained an audience, it was a different, less committed audience. No longer were there torrents of adoring letters and invitations to address public gatherings. No longer did crowds wait to glimpse him as he traveled to distant cities. Most importantly, perhaps, no longer was there money; and in the fall of 1937, charging "censorship" by his new archbishop, Edward Mooney, but more likely suffering from financial strain, he withdrew from the air.[7]

Early in 1938, he was back, filling his broadcasts and the columns of his newspaper with even direr warnings of the dangerous "radicalism" of the New Deal and of the anarchic possibilities of the increasingly militant labor movement. And in midsummer, finally, he crossed the line from embittered conservatism to open bigotry. An ugly anti-Semitism infected first his newspaper and then, beginning in November, his radio sermons, spreading like a dark stain until it had become the most conspicuous (although never the dominant) element of his rhetoric. *Social Justice* soon began to publish the spurious *Protocols of the Elders of Zion,* which allegedly exposed an ancient Jewish plot to impose financial slavery upon the world. Coughlin's own editorials spoke stridently of the "communistic Jews"; and in one, he plagiarized egregiously from a speech by Nazi propagandist Joseph Goebbels, lifting such passages as: "Almost without exception, the intellectual leaders—if not the foot and hand leaders—of Marxist atheism in Germany were Jews."[8]

At about the same time, Coughlin urged his supporters to organize into "Platoons," whose purpose he did not define but whose name suggested an ominous military quality. Months later, the movement had adopted a more explicit title: the Christian Front. Membership was always small (it peaked, according to most estimates, at about 1,200); and it remained concentrated in a very few cities—New York, Boston, Hartford, and others with large Catholic populations. But despite its modest size, the Christian Front managed in a short period of time to acquire a remarkably odious record. It attracted numerous violent and unstable members, many of whom bore substantial criminal-arrest records, and perhaps as a reflection of the nature of its constituency, it advocated force in its undefined struggle against "Jewish communism." One organizer established a "sports club" to train young men "how to take orders and accept discipline" and to prepare them "to go into the streets and protect their rights by force." Others met regularly for military "drills." In January 1940 an FBI raid on a New York branch of the Front uncovered a cache of weapons; J. Edgar Hoover claimed that the members had planned to "eliminate" Jews and Communists and "knock off about a dozen Congressmen." And on occasion, bullies and street toughs associated with the Christian Front smashed windows in stores owned by Jewish merchants and engaged in open, Nazi-like brawls with Jews.[9]

When war began in Europe in 1939, Coughlin became a strident advocate of American neutrality. Although he was not alone in this, his isolationism reflected more than diffuse animosity toward "internationalism" or the antipathy for Great Britain he had expressed in earlier years. It reflected, too, an explicit admiration for the German and Italian governments. In mid-1940, he praised the Hitler regime for imposing a new moral purity upon Germany, for reforming the nation's financial system, and for purging its politics of communists and subversives. "Had we Christians enforced the discipline and produced the good accomplished by the Nazis for a good end," he argued, "we would not be weeping at the wailing wall." On other occasions, he urged Americans to consider the virtues of the "corporate state."[10]

This deterioration not only dissipated much of the modest public support Coughlin retained; it also produced a storm of criticism—from Jewish organizations, from Catholic leaders, from the press. Archbishop Mooney rebuked him repeatedly; radio stations began to refuse to carry his broadcasts; newspapers and magazines portrayed him as a public menace. Coughlin struggled against the tide, but to no avail. Early in 1940, the National Association of Broadcasters adopted new codes sharply limiting the sale of radio time to "spokesmen of controversial public issues." Despite Coughlin's protests, by the end of the year he found himself with virtually no access to the air.

He continued, however, to speak through the pages of *Social Justice,* which was becoming ever more strident and pernicious. After Pearl Harbor, it occurred to the Roosevelt Administration that the publication might also be treasonous. Although Coughlin had written grudgingly after the declaration of war that "we submit to the will of the government," he continued to write of the superior strength of the Axis powers, of the dangers of associating with the "sleazy Britishers," and of the responsibility of American Jews for propelling the nation into the conflict. In the spring of 1942, finally, Postmaster General Frank Walker barred the publication from the mails, and Attorney General Francis Biddle warned Archbishop Mooney that Coughlin would face formal charges of sedition if his public activities did not cease. Early in May, Coughlin quietly announced that he had "bowed to orders from Church superiors," that he was severing his ties to *Social Justice* and ceasing all political activities.[11]

The man who had stirred millions returned without fanfare to his duties as parish priest at the Shrine of the Little Flower, where he remained for twenty-four more years. Occasionally he sent out circulars to his parishioners warning of the dangers of communism, or used his Sunday sermons to warn of subversion. For the most part, however, he was silent. The infrequent interviews he granted to scholars and journalists were usually less than frank, contradicting not only the historical record but each other. When a biographer asked him in 1970 how he would live his life if he had it to do again, he replied, "I would do it the same way." Two years later, he told another interviewer, "There is nothing I would do the same."[12]

In 1966, in response to pressure from the leaders of his diocese, he reluctantly retired, left to others the church his radio sermons had built, and settled in a comfortable home in a wealthy Detroit suburb. He was seventy-five years old. There he lived quietly until his death in 1979, saying mass each morning in a private chapel, observing the world he had tried to shape, and spending idle moments, perhaps, remembering better days.[13]

APPENDIX I

The Question of Anti-Semitism and the Problem of Fascism

THROUGHOUT THEIR PUBLIC CAREERS, both Long and Coughlin faced a plague of criticisms and accusations, not only from those who disagreed with their policies or disapproved of their tactics but from some whose objections were more fundamental and disturbing. Two accusations in particular have survived well beyond the 1930s: that Coughlin based a large part of his national popularity upon an appeal to anti-Semitism; and that Long and Coughlin both represented an incipient American fascism. Both charges are serious; both rest on a certain level of substance; and both, therefore, deserve discussion.

There can be little doubt about Coughlin's open and strident anti-Semitism after 1938. He always insisted that his attacks then upon particular Jews did not indicate hostility to the Jewish people as a group; but the anti-Semitic elements of his rhetoric—and the anti-Semitic activities of his organization—clearly suggested otherwise. By 1938, however, Coughlin could hardly be taken seriously as a major political force; and, aware of the dissolution of his power, he had become a harsh and embittered man. His retreat into bigotry and hysteria was largely an act of resentful desperation.

In Coughlin's earlier years, the years before 1936 when his political strength was at its peak, the story was somewhat different. It is difficult, knowing what Coughlin later became, to look at any period of his life without seeking signs of religious bigotry; and it is possible to find clues in Coughlin's early career of the hatred that later would nearly consume it. The important question, however, is whether the men and women who heard him then could detect such elements. Were they aware of and attracted by anti-Semitic elements in his message? The evidence suggests that they were not.

It is possible, even likely, that Coughlin harbored private anti-Semitic sentiments long before he became identified with them in public. One observer claimed in 1940 that Coughlin's associates had for years known him "to be personally anti-Semitic, possessor of an elaborate library on the subject." And while there is no visible substantiation for the charge, there is no particular reason to doubt it. A deep, if diffuse anti-Semitism had long been a part of the culture of the American Midwest, where Coughlin spent most of his adult life. It had surfaced on occasion as part of the populist movement in the 1890s and again, in more virulent form, with the rise of the Ku Klux Klan in the 1920s. The Catholic Church, moreover, had historically countenanced a vague anti-Semitism within its own theology by insisting upon the responsibility of the Jews for the death of Christ; and that a member of the clergy would translate that abstract animus into a personal and immediate one would be neither unusual nor surprising.[1]

Publicly, however, Coughlin said very little about Jews before 1936 or, indeed, before 1938; so the case for his anti-Semitism during that period has, of necessity, rested on a very few, usually passing remarks. In a 1930 sermon, for example, he referred briefly to Wall Street bankers as "modern Shylocks ... grown fat and wealthy." A year later, he compared the crass materialism of modern capitalism with the transgressions of the lost tribe of Israel: " ... in the midst of our glowing prosperity we, as did the Jews of old, deserted the principles of the God Who was so generous to us. We set up the golden calf of our cruel financial system." In 1934, defending his organization against charges of silver speculation, he made passing reference to the metal as "Gentile silver," a description he did not embellish and accompanied with no direct reference to Jews.[2]

More perplexing was Coughlin's frequently cited sermon of February 19, 1933, in which he chose, for no apparent reason, to engage in an extended discussion of Jewish history. For centuries after the age of Abraham, he explained, the Jew had suffered persecution and exile. Despised by other races, seldom permitted to settle permanently in any land, he dared not "enter into the natural business of farming because tearfully he remembered how his lands had been stolen." As a result, Jews turned to the only livelihood available to them: finance. Gold, they had learned "by bitter, cruel experience from every so-called Christian nation in Europe," was the only form of wealth "which they felt was secure in their possession." It was little wonder, then, "that there grew up that spirit of gold trading in the heart of the international Jew, as some have called him ignominiously. . . . They were forced into this position by the hatred of Christians."

"What has all this to do with the question of depression," Coughlin asked midway through the sermon, "with the question of gold and hoarding and starvation?" His answer was ambiguous at best. He wanted, he explained, to show that it had been "our Christian ancestors who forced the Jew to hoarding gold," and that there was no reason why "we Christians must continue upon the vicious policy of hatred" that had characterized earlier societies. On the contrary, Americans had come to learn that "the Jew has at last a home; has at last a nationality." He was "just as much a child of God as the best of you are. This is a democratic country where Jew and Gentile are equal."

The broadcast could be interpreted in several ways. Coughlin himself would have argued that it was an impassioned plea for religious toleration, a call for understanding and acceptance of Jews. He might also have claimed that the sermon was an attempt to show how the fallacy of considering gold as the basis of wealth had emerged, how it was a result not of any immutable economic laws but of the bigotry and cruelty of early Christians. "It was hate that gave birth to the idea that gold is wealth," he claimed. "Hate must give way to charity."

But while on the surface the sermon clearly called for an end to anti-Semitism, it also reinforced many of the stereotypes that had traditionally sustained the prejudice. It was an unquestioned assumption of the address, for example, that Jews were responsible for the tyranny of the gold standard. The theory that "gold is sacred, gold is wealth, gold is more precious than men and the homes in which they live" was "the theory of the European Jew." The phrases echoed the accusations most commonly leveled against Jews by populists and others in the 1890s, who complained frequently about Jewish control of international finance. There was also in Coughlin's sermon a clear implication that Jews maintained tribal loyalties to one another that superseded their loyalties to the nations in which they lived. Despite his hopeful statement that American Jews had finally found a home, he was clearly evoking the traditional, pejorative image of Jewish "internationalism," an image that had supported anti-Semitism for decades.[3]

It was, in short, a gratuitous sermon that worked at cross-purposes with itself. At the time, however, it evoked virtually no response. There is no record of public charges in 1933 that Coughlin was evoking anti-Semitism; there is no evidence that his followers seized upon the address to support anti-Jewish sentiments (indeed, letters written around the time of the broadcast made no mention of the subject); and Coughlin did not pursue the issue in any of his ensuing sermons.

It was not until a year later that Coughlin encountered any public accusations that he was encouraging anti-Semitism. In 1933, he had for the first time attacked his enemies, whom for years he had called only "money changers" or "international bankers," by name; and in 1934, it began to occur to some observers that a disproportionate number of the names were Jewish. The Rothschilds began to play a major role both in Coughlin's historical scenario and in his analysis of present conditions. Along with them came mention of such Jewish financial establishments as Kuhn-Loeb and Lazard Frères and of such Jewish financiers as Eugene Meyer and, above all, Bernard Baruch (to whom Coughlin occasionally made vituperative reference as "Bernard Manasses Baruch," as if, some believed, he were trying to emphasize the Jewishness of the name; Baruch's real middle name was "Mannes"). "Continuing his attack on the international bankers," the *Nation* noted after one public statement, "Father Coughlin named a few names, all of them Jewish, and called them 'Dillingers.' " It was, the journal argued, an effort to plant "an anti-Semitic seed in the fertile minds of millions of his followers." Stephen S. Wise, a prominent New York rabbi and a leader of the American Zionist movement, took note of a 1935 Coughlin sermon in which the priest listed six international banking firms, five of them Jewish. "Beware," Wise warned him publicly, "lest you lightly speak words that will feed and fan flames of anti-Jewish feeling. . . . Do you want to evoke anti-Semitism?"[4]

It was true, as Wise and others occasionally noted, that some Coughlin sermons did dwell upon Jewish far more than Christian financiers; but, as a rule, quite the opposite was the case. Throughout Coughlin's 1933 and 1934 sermons, reference to Christian (usually Protestant) bankers and financial establishments were nearly 50 percent more frequent than references to Jewish men or firms. Andrew Mellon, Ogden Mills, Thomas W. Lamont, and others received more consistent criticism than either the Rothschilds or Baruch; and if any one figure personified financial evil most clearly in the Coughlin litany, it was not a Jew, but J. P. Morgan. By 1935, the proportion of Jewish names in Coughlin's sermons was increasing; but never did those names constitute very much more than half the total, and never did Coughlin draw any special attention to their Jewishness. The most that can be said is that Coughlin may have implied that Jews made up a somewhat larger proportion of the international financial community than they actually did.[5]

More importantly, whatever Coughlin's intent, his statements seemed not to evoke any serious expressions of anti-Semitism from his followers. In the many letters members of his radio audience sent to Coughlin and to other public figures, almost never was there evidence of religious prejudice. There were carping references on occasion to Bernard Baruch and a few other Jewish financiers, but not nearly as often as there were attacks upon Morgan or Mellon or any number of other prominent Protestant bankers. One Coughlin follower complained to H. V. Kaltenborn in 1935 that he was "tired of being cleaned out financially by the Jewish bankers." And a critic of Coughlin wrote the President at about the same time, urging him to "disspell the terrific damage done by Coughlin. . . . When the liberty of the Jew is in danger, so is the liberty of every American." But such responses were rare. More typical was the 1935 statement by a Midwestern woman that "the question of race, color and religion does not enter into this affair." And most typical were the countless letters, cards, and wires that made no mention of race or religion at all.[6]

Even before 1938, Coughlin could hardly be termed a warm friend of the Jew. At best, his message in the early and mid-1930s was neutral on the subject. At worst, his rhetoric—with its excoriation of "international bankers" and its references to "money changers" and the "sin of usury"—may have worked in a diffuse way to evoke images and produce stereotypes that could be translated easily into hostility toward Jews. But Coughlin himself did little before 1938 to encourage such a translation. His rhetoric was not incompatible with some forms of anti-Semitism; and his excoriation of Jews after 1938 did not, therefore, emerge unnaturally from his earlier positions. Neither, however, did it emerge inevitably from them. Whatever Coughlin's private feelings about Jews, there is nothing to indicate that anti-Semitism played any appreciable role in building his early national popularity.

II

WHEN JAMES FARLEY met Benito Mussolini in Rome in the early 1930s, he looked at the Italian dictator and thought immediately, he later claimed, of Huey Long. Farley was neither the first nor the last to do so. Attempts to link both Long and Coughlin with fascism were widespread and relentless throughout their public careers; and neither Long's death nor Coughlin's retirement stilled the accusations.

The reasons are not difficult to identify. For Huey Long, charges of fascism stemmed naturally from his blatant accumulation of extraordinary powers in Louisiana, powers that earned him the widely accepted characterization of "dictator" and invited comparison with the totalitarian regimes emerging in Germany and Italy. For Father Coughlin, the charges emerged, like the accusations of anti-Semitism, from the excesses of his own later years, among which were open expressions of admiration for Hitler and Mussolini.[7]

Nevertheless, Long and Coughlin themselves both vehemently denied in the early and mid-1930s that they had any connection with or sympathy for fascism. Coughlin called repeatedly for "an America that will have no patience either with Nazism or Communism" and insisted even toward the end of the decade (when some of his other actions seemed to belie his words) "that Fascism and Nazism are outright tyrannies." In a 1935 sermon, he attacked the U.S. Chamber of Commerce for proposing to give Franklin Roosevelt "the power of a dictator, of a Mussolini"; and, beginning with his earliest political sermons and continuing for years, one of his most frequent demands was for the rejection of "communism, socialism, fascism, or any other 'ism.'" Long, similarly, grew angry at suggestions that he was comparable in any way to Adolf Hitler, sputtering to one reporter: "Don't liken me to that sonofabitch. Anybody that lets his public policies be mixed up with religious prejudice is a plain God-damned fool!" Like Coughlin, he accused others of fascism when he wanted to deliver a particularly forceful indictment. "The Roosevelt 'New Deal,' " complained the *American Progress* in 1935, "has finally come out in the open with an announcement of its ultimate hope . . . [of] setting up a Fascistic 'planning council' which would be more powerful even than the Supreme Court."[8]

Questions, however, remain. Neither Long nor Coughlin would have been likely to publicize fascist sympathies even if he had harbored them. Not a few critics have argued that both men carefully disguised their fascist leanings, that they permitted their real inclinations to bubble to the surface only occasionally. Some have even implied that they maintained quiet, illicit connections with fascist movements or regimes. Long and Coughlin might, moreover, have displayed fascist sympathies unwittingly. That, in fact, has been the most frequent charge leveled against them: that, whether they realized it or not, they were creating movements that closely resembled European fascism.

The first accusation can be answered simply. There is little to suggest that either Long or Coughlin maintained any sympathy for, or even interest in, fascism until Coughlin begin to discuss it in 1938. Those who have claimed otherwise have rested their arguments on casual statements attributed to the two men that are either apocryphal or subject to serious distortion. Long apparently never said that "when the United States gets fascism, it will call it anti-fascism"; but the remark has remained part of the folklore surrounding his life nevertheless. Coughlin did indeed say (although not until 1936) that America had been led to a "crossroads. One road leads to communism, the other to fascism." And he apparently also said, when a reporter asked him which of the two roads he would choose, "I take the road to fascism." What he meant, however, and what he went to great pains to explain when the remark surfaced again and again to haunt him, was only that he thought fascism a lesser evil than communism (an opinion with which many, perhaps most, Americans of the time would have agreed). The nation would, he hoped, turn away from the unattractive "crossroads" he had defined and choose instead his own formula for social justice, which was, he insisted, quite different.[9]

Nor were there any active connections with fascist movements or regimes. There is nothing to suggest that either man ever communicated with or even thought much about Hitler, Mussolini, or any other European fascist leader; and there is nothing to imply that the Europeans, for their part, were more than dimly aware of the existence of Long and Coughlin. The picture was only slightly different within the United States.

American fascists in the early 1930s were a motley group—men who expressed varying degrees of support for Hitler and Mussolini, who attempted to adapt the European systems to their own society, and who found few willing to listen to them. William Dudley Pelley, an open admirer of Hitler, did achieve modest success organizing SS-like "Silver Shirt" brigades in North Carolina, California, and elsewhere. A disturbed and vicious man, he enthusiastically emulated the Nazis in his militarism, supernationalism, and anti-Semitism. But he never became a genuinely important force in American politics. Art J. Smith, a former mercenary soldier, established a similar organization: the Khaki Shirts, composed largely of veterans and descended in a perverse way from the 1932 Bonus Expeditionary Force. Unlike Pelley, Smith was more a charlatan than a fanatic; and when a group of his followers brutally murdered a heckler during a Khaki Shirt rally in New York State, Smith took the money he had raised for the organization and disappeared. The Khaki Shirt movement quickly dissolved.[10]

Fascists of this stripe—activists attempting to organize popular movements on the German and Italian models—paid virtually no attention to Long and Coughlin except occasionally to denounce them. The Progressive Fascisti Party, a small Chicago-based group and one of the few such organizations to take any note of either man, harshly criticized Coughlin in 1935, accusing him of advocating "class war" and claiming that his program for social justice "cannot mean anything else but that the Church should dominate the State." Long and Coughlin, for their parts, did not give the native fascist organizations even passing notice. Neither man ever mentioned them.[11]

There were, however, other American fascists, men of a very different sort. Intelligent, educated, occasionally from distinguished backgrounds, they developed no popular followings of their own but looked to others as potential means to their ends. To some such men, Long and Coughlin seemed attractive indeed. Lawrence Dennis, Georgia born, Harvard educated, bright and literate, was perhaps the most prominent of such fascist "intellectuals." In several articulate books, he argued that capitalism was doomed by the pressures of modern society, and he claimed that fascism offered the only hope of saving America from communism. By 1935, he had decided that Coughlin and Long might become vehicles for the fulfillment of his dreams.

They were, he argued, "in far closer harmony with the logic of mass needs" than any other popular leaders. "I hail these movements and pressure groups," he added, "not because their members are as yet fascists or friends of fascism, but because they are making fascism the alternative to chaos or national disintegration." Long in particular he praised as "the nearest approach to a national fascist leader," explaining that "It takes a man like Long to lead the masses. I think Long's smarter than Hitler but he needs a good brain-trust." He left little doubt that he hoped himself to become the nucleus of that brain trust. He was deeply disappointed. Neither Long nor Coughlin ever paid him even the slightest attention.[12]

Dennis may have been the most prominent American fascist to express admiration for Long and Coughlin, but he was not the most active in courting their support. Late in 1934, two young intellectuals—Philip Johnson, later to become one of America's most distinguished architects, and Alan Blackburn, a member of the staff of the Museum of Modern Art—abandoned their New York careers and set off in search of political fulfillment. Admirers of their fellow Harvard alumnus Lawrence Dennis, they hoped to begin the work of building an American fascist movement; and they decided to travel first to Huey Long's Louisiana. Their purpose, they claimed, was to "study" Long's methods; but, while they did not say so, they evidently also expected to become allies of and advisors to the Long organization. Like Dennis, they were disappointed. Long and his associates showed no interest in them whatsoever. Two years later, still seeking an outlet for their political energies, they surfaced as supporters of Coughlin's Union Party; and Johnson, at least, apparently played briefly a minor role on Coughlin's staff. But once again, they found no one very interested in their own beliefs or plans.[13]

III

IT SEEMS CLEAR, then, that neither Long nor Coughlin openly approved of fascism or maintained any meaningful connection with fascist movements or thinkers. The more important question, however, and one that is more difficult to answer conclusively, is that of intangible connections. Did Long and Coughlin offer the American people a promise of fascism without admitting or even realizing it? Were their movements in fact, though not in name, the domestic counterparts of the movements of Hitler and Mussolini?

The difficulty begins with the ambiguity of the term itself. Neither in the 1930s nor at any time since have politicians or scholars reached anything remotely approaching agreement about what fascism was. No commonly accepted body of literature articulates a theory of fascism. There is no single, coherent set of social or economic policies common to all so-called fascist regimes; historians have had great difficulty finding common ground between even the two most celebrated fascist societies, Germany and Italy. Nor has there been agreement about the psychological characteristics of fascist leaders or their followers. "In our common scale of speech," an American journalist noted in 1936, "fascism has reached the stage where it is applied to almost any kind of thing or person one does not like." The same could be said decades later. "Perhaps the word fascism should be banned," a historian of the phenomenon suggested in 1968.[14]

But the term "fascism" cannot, of course, be banned. It retains a powerful, if imprecise meaning if only because it continues to evoke such strong, haunting images. And the question of the relationship of Long and Coughlin to fascism, therefore, cannot be quickly dismissed. To answer that question requires an examination of what some scholars have called a "fascist minimum"—a set of general characteristics common to all phenomena deserving of the label. In particular, it requires examining two broad categories: behavior and ideology. If the term "fascism" is to have any meaning, it must define a particular kind of relationship between a leader and his followers. Or it must suggest a particular set of ideas and programs, a vision of society distinct from that of other political philosophies.[15]

Thomas Mann produced a particularly vivid picture of what many have claimed is the special bond that existed between a fascist leader and his followers. His short story "Mario and the Magician," although it was published in 1931, well before either Hitler or Mussolini had worked their full horrors, created in the character of Cipolla an ominous portrait of the political climate to come. A man of indeterminate age, slightly deformed, vaguely preposterous in appearance, Cipolla appears one evening in an Italian resort town to perform what he claims will be a "magic show." His magic, however, consists not of conventional tricks, but of a brilliant manipulation of his audience through his own charismatic power. By the end of the evening, virtually everyone in the room is in his control, responding to his suggestions and commands even when their own inclinations would ordinarily have blocked their actions. One young man—Mario, a waiter in a hotel—becomes so crazed by the public humiliation that Cipolla inflicts upon him that he finally shoots and kills the magician.[16]

Few scholars would attribute to fascist political leaders precisely the same sort of power. Hitler, Mussolini, and others did not usually impel their supporters to do or think things that were in sharp conflict with their own inner beliefs. Hitler did not create a hatred of Jews among the German people out of thin air; anti-Semitism was deeply rooted in the nation's culture. The impulse toward martial splendor and national unity that Hitler and Mussolini both evoked was not an entirely new feature of either German or Italian society; both peoples had displayed the same impulse in earlier times.[17]

But Thomas Mann was describing, nevertheless, a characteristic of fascism that virtually any definition must include: the creation of an intense bond between a charismatic leader and his minions. Leni Riefenstahl's film *Tri-*

umph of the Will, a record of a massive Nazi Party rally in Nuremberg, shows how eagerly great masses of people engaged in behavior carefully orchestrated and manipulated by Hitler and his regime. And while the regimented passion of Nuremberg was scarcely indicative of the normal, daily existence of Nazi loyalists, there can be little doubt that glorification of and submission to Adolf Hitler became a central element of the political life of Nazi Germany, just as the glorification of Mussolini was central to the life of Italy. The simple, unadorned titles that both men adopted ("Fuhrer," "Duce"—Leader) was one indication of the extent to which they dominated their nations. So was the ease and brutal effectiveness with which they stifled dissent and emasculated the institutions of government that might have limited their power.[18]

Neither Long nor Coughlin approached wielding comparable influence or exercising comparable leadership. They had some passionately committed disciples to be sure; but it would be difficult to argue that the highly conditional loyalty they received from most of their supporters resembled the devotion that Hitler or Mussolini attracted from his multitudes; or that the flimsy, ephemeral organizations they produced were in any respect similar to the disciplined, hierarchical party organizations of the Nazis or the Italian Fascists. And although Long may have trampled upon some of the institutions of democratic government in Louisiana, he made no efforts to establish anything remotely resembling a totalitarian regime; he displayed no serious inclination toward suppressing individual dissent, controlling the press, or circumventing free elections. If, then, fascism is defined by the special character of the loyalties it produces, the definition is not applicable to the Long and Coughlin movements.

In the realm of ideas, however, the distinction is often less clear. In the early stages of fascism in particular—in Germany in the 1920s, when National Socialism was still a movement and not yet a regime; in Italy in the first years after World War I, when Mussolini was only beginning to consolidate his power—the similarities to the later Long and Coughlin movements were often striking. The rhetoric of fascism was laden with appeals to the idea of the traditional, rooted community and the special virtues of the common people. It reflected a deep ambivalence about the effects of industrial growth and technological progress. It warned constantly of the dangers posed by distant, hidden forces. It emphasized with special urgency the issue of money—of unstable or scarce currency, of tyrannical bankers, of usurious interest. And fascist rhetoric resounded, too, with hostility toward "internationalism" in politics and economics. All of these elements appeared in the messages of Long and Coughlin as well.[19]

It was not by design, and even less by coincidence, that such similarities existed. It was because fascism and the Long and Coughlin movements were products of similar social and economic crises and drew from similar political traditions. Fascist leaders appealed, like Long and Coughlin, to members of a troubled middle class uneasy about their eroding position in society and about their declining ability to control their own destinies. Such men and women were no more eager in Europe than in America for genuinely radical change. They aspired, instead, to a restoration of what they considered artificially disrupted social bonds. They embraced economic proposals that required no fundamental upheaval, no frontal assault upon class structure, only a set of limited reforms to restore balance and equity to their society.

In that, followers of fascism, no less than supporters of Long and Coughlin, were reviving the still potent tradition of late-nineteenth-century populism. German and Austrian populists had denounced "interest slavery" and "bankers' plots" in the 1890s. Italian dissidents had raised visions of occult financial conspiracies threatening to enslave the common man. Hitler and Mussolini themselves had grown to maturity in an environment laden with resentments of "financial parasites" and usurious moneylenders. The European anti-Semitic tradition, of which Hitler made such effective and terrible use, drew much of its strength from the general association of Jews in the 1890s with despised institutions of finance and thus with canny manipulation of the currency. There may have been few direct links between European and American populism; but there were many indirect connections, both in the conditions from which they emerged and in the ideas and images they employed. And it was perhaps unsurprising, therefore, that in the twentieth century, European fascists and American dissidents, drawing from similar political traditions, should revive many of the same sentiments.[20]

Most Americans in the 1930s were understandably reluctant to admit such associations, but not all. Ezra Pound, the celebrated poet, began openly to embrace fascism and less openly to descend into madness during his years of self-imposed exile in Europe. He nevertheless retained sufficient sanity to point out in 1935 what most of his countrymen now found too uncomfortable to admit: that Mussolini was making effective use of ideas and images deeply imbedded not only in European but also in American culture. In Pound's rambling, impassioned, often incoherent pamphlet *Jefferson and/or Mussolini*, he combined what can only be described as lunacy with occasionally persuasive evidence of the connections between Italian fascism and American political traditions. Like Jefferson, he explained, Mussolini was railing against the maldistribution of wealth and power in his society and evoking a vision of sturdy freeholders and self-reliant workers. Like Jefferson, he was defending the people against the powerful, central "interests." Like Andrew Jackson, who waged war against a powerful bank that was "milking the nation," Mussolini was attacking excessively powerful and despotic financiers. Long and Coughlin, although Pound did not say it, were doing so as well.[21]

In Coughlin's case, the connection with European ideas and traditions may have been more than a vague, unacknowledged relationship. Michael Gallagher, his beloved bishop in Detroit, had spent a portion of his youth in Austria, immersed in the anti-socialist, vaguely populistic activism of the Catholic clergy there. He had befriended Monsignor Ignaz Seipel, the Austrian priest who assumed control of his country's government in the troubled aftermath of World War I. He had brought back to America (and presumably to Coughlin) a belief not only in the duty of the clergy to take political stands, but in the European Catholic concept of "social justice"—which, like many other European ideologies of the same era, included hostility toward bankers and financiers.[22]

Coughlin also read widely, if not always well, in politics and economics; and although there is little evidence of precisely what he studied, it seems likely that he encountered the writings of such English Catholic thinkers as G. K. Chesterton and Hilaire Belloc. Their philosophies were ultimately influential in shaping the outlook of much of the British right, including England's own fascist leader Oswald Mosley; and their ideas of "distributism" resonated with many of the same financial assumptions that Coughlin espoused.[23]

Yet to say that these movements—Long's, Coughlin's, Hitler's, Mussolini's, and others—drew from many of the same political traditions and resonated with many of the same images is far from declaring that they represented identical or even fundamentally similar impulses. What defines a political movement is not just the intellectual currents it vaguely absorbs, but how it translates those currents into a message of immediate importance to its constituency. While there were many superficial similarities between the way fascist leaders accomplished that translation and the way Long and Coughlin did so, the comparison breaks down on the points of most fundamental importance.

One such point was obvious. Hitler and, to a lesser extent, Mussolini appealed openly to racial and religious hatred. Long and Coughlin, in their primes, did not. They encouraged animosity toward certain villains, certainly, but they did not invoke racism or anti-Semitism in any serious way until Coughlin began to do so in 1938. Another point of contrast is a matter of degree. Essential to fascism in virtually all its forms was a clearly stated, ardently preached opposition to communism; indeed, the rise to power of Hitler and Mussolini would have been almost inconceivable without the effective manipulation of anti-Bolshevist sentiments among their followers. Long and Coughlin, by contrast, relegated anti-communism to rather minor roles. Coughlin harped on the issue frequently in the first stages of his career and again in its last stages. During his most successful years, however, he spoke of communism only occasionally and in passing. And while Long never left any doubt that he opposed Bolshevism, and although he referred to his own programs on occasion as the only alternative to it, it would be difficult to argue that an active fear of communism played much of a role in his success.[24]

What most clearly distinguished the European fascists from Long and Coughlin, however, was what most distinguished fascism in general as an ideology. Hitler and Mussolini did, to be sure, employ populist rhetoric and evoke culturally comfortable images of a stable, rooted society. But such tactics were for the most part either shams or secondary concerns. Their principal commitment, almost from the beginning, was to a concept of organic social unity, to a sense of common national purpose. Ultimately, it became a commitment to a belligerent super-nationalism. Hitler attempted to awaken among Germans (as he made clear in *Mein Kampf,* published years before he seized power) a racial and cultural chauvinism. He and Mussolini both invoked luminous visions of a transcendent national destiny. And once in power, both men tried to create economic systems that reflected these goals: what Mussolini called the "corporate state," and what Hitler called "national socialism." At the heart of both was an attempt (never fully successful in practice) to harness the economy to a centrally conceived national goal without resorting to socialism or communism. The government would make the position of capitalists secure and provide certain guarantees to workers, farmers, and others. But while the state would avoid systematic attacks upon entrenched wealth (except, of course, among Jews), it would radically increase its control of the economy, coordinating production and directing investment according to national social aims. By the late 1930s, when the German and Italian regimes were becoming great war machines, state control of the economies of both nations was in some respects even more pervasive than in many socialist countries.

Central to any definition of fascism, therefore, is the idea of unity, the commitment to a society working as one on behalf of common goals. The idea found graphic expression in the symbol of the Italian Fascist Party: the old Roman fasces, a bundle of sticks bound tightly together around an ax. Fascist societies were to be bound tightly together around a centrally conceived national purpose.[25]

The loosely defined social philosophies of Long and Coughlin rested on fundamentally different concerns. At the center of their messages was a commitment to a major shift in the locus of economic power in America, not to the state, but to small community institutions and to individual citizens. Long and Coughlin contemplated a far more fundamental assault upon the "plutocrats" and "financial despots" than the European fascists ever attempted.

Hitler and Mussolini relied upon the great capitalists to underwrite many of the grandiose projects of their regimes; Long and Coughlin proposed not to impoverish or destroy the moguls, perhaps, but so to limit their wealth and power as to ensure that they would no longer wield disproportionate influence. At the same time, Long and Coughlin envisioned a far different and more limited role for the government than the fascists proposed. Its purpose would not be, as in Germany and Italy, to subordinate individual economic interests to the central goals of the nation. It would, rather, liberate individuals from the tyranny of the plutocrats, restore a small-scale, decentralized capitalism that would increase, not restrict, economic independence.

Long and Coughlin were not offering surging visions of national destiny. They were not appealing to the concept of a triumphant, collective Will, to a sense of the awesome power of a united *Volk*. Nazi Germany and Fascist Italy were to be nations tightly bound together, regimented, virtually militarized in pursuit of great common goals. America, as Long and Coughlin envisioned it, was to be a small man's paradise, a society in which wealth, power, and influence would not be concentrated in the hands of private interests or the government, but widely shared among all. To the extent that they advocated collectivism at all, it was a mild, localistic, almost neighborly version—a vision of benign and limited cooperation within communities to promote individual fulfillment.[26]

Long and Coughlin shared with the fascists certain anxieties, ideas, and images and drew from similar political traditions; they were not, however, fascists in any meaningful sense of the term. Why, then, has the label clung so tenaciously to them both? In part, it has been a result of the ambiguities in the concept of fascism; in larger part, perhaps, it has been because of the difficulties in finding any other political label that seems appropriate for Long and Coughlin. They occupied a murky realm that belonged clearly to no single conventional category. At times they sounded like spokesmen for the left, with their denunciations of entrenched wealth and power, their defense of the common man against the "special interests," and their insistence upon the duty of society to provide for the minimal needs of its citizens. At other times, they seemed to resonate with the themes of the right, with their opposition to socialism, communism, and statism, their emphasis upon a few hidden enemies rather than an unjust economic system, their concern with control of money rather than ownership of the means of production.

This casual mingling of themes commonly associated with opposite political poles did not originate with the Long and Coughlin movements; nor did it end with them. The populists, from whom both men derived so much ideological strength, had exhibited similar contradictions; so did later political phenomena: the George Wallace movement of the 1960s and the New Right of the 1980s, which combined populist rhetoric with cultural conservatism. Nor are the similarities surprising. Underlying all such movements in varying degrees has been a common impulse: the fear of concentrated power, the traditional American resistance to being governed—whether by private interests or by public institutions. It is an impulse that can, under different circumstances, lead either to the left or to the right. Or it can—as it did in the cases of Huey Long and Father Coughlin—lead to both simultaneously. As long as this fear of distant power remained the basis of a movement rather than the foundation of a regime, it was easy to avoid the contradictions. But had Long and Coughlin ever gained power, the conflicts within their beliefs would have become far more painful. How they might have resolved them we can only guess.

APPENDIX II

The 1935 Democratic National Committee Poll

LITTLE EVIDENCE SURVIVES to suggest what techniques Emil Hurja and his colleagues used to conduct the Democratic National Committee's Presidential preference poll in the spring of 1935. Its reliability, therefore, cannot be confirmed. It is clear, however, that the Hurja poll was far more scientific, far less biased in its sample, than such popular-opinion surveys of the time as the *Literary Digest* poll. Like the *Literary Digest,* the DNC conducted its poll by mail, and it asked respondents to send their ballots to a magazine (the mythical "National Inquirer"). But there was a crucial difference. Hurja chose members of his sample in advance and mailed ballots directly to them; the *Literary Digest,* in effect, simply polled its readership. How Hurja selected his sample is unclear; but the form in which he tabulated the results suggests that he attempted to ensure both regional and economic diversity.

The tables below summarize the results of the poll. Table 1 is a compilation by region of totals for all survey respondents. Table 2 shows the responses for the thirteen major cities in which results were tabulated separately. Table 3 shows the results by region for those respondents identified as relief recipients.

TABLE 1

1935 Democratic National Committee Poll:
Regional Totals (All Ballots)

Region	FDR Vote	%	GOP Vote	%	Long Vote	%	Coughlin Vote	%	Others Vote	%	Total
South	2,952	71.3	432	10.4	601	14.5	0	0	156	3.8	4,141
Border	1,827	61.4	735	24.7	303	10.2	14	0.5	97	3.3	2,976

(Table 1, cont.)

Region	FDR Vote	%	GOP Vote	%	Long Vote	%	Coughlin Vote	%	Others Vote	%	Total
Mid-Atlantic	3,721	50.7	2,623	35.7	564	7.8	93	1.3	344	4.7	7,345
New England	737	37.7	947	48.4	157	8.0	44	2.2	72	3.7	1,957
Great Lakes	4,067	51.5	2,446	30.9	989	12.5	109	1.4	293	3.7	7,904
Farm Belt	1,410	51.1	949	34.4	272	9.9	18	0.7	110	4.0	2,759
Mountain	407	52.1	222	28.4	106	13.6	0	0	46	5.9	781
Pacific	1,652	53.9	811	26.5	372	12.1	6	0.2	222	7.2	3,063
TOTALS	16,773	54.2	9,162	29.6	3,365	10.9	280	0.9	1,344	2.1	30,924

Source: Emil Hurja MSS, Franklin D. Roosevelt Library.

TABLE 2

1935 Democratic National Committee Poll:
City Totals (All Ballots)

City	FDR Vote	%	GOP Vote	%	Long Vote	%	Coughlin Vote	%	Others Vote	%	Total
*Baltimore	58	49.2	43	36.4	11	9.3	2	1.7	4	3.4	118
Boston	75	46.3	53	32.7	21	13.0	3	1.9	10	6.2	162
Brooklyn	389	61.3	163	25.7	37	5.8	8	1.3	38	6.0	635
Buffalo	88	36.5	99	41.1	31	12.9	9	3.7	14	5.8	241
Chicago	929	53.7	510	29.5	204	11.8	32	1.8	56	3.2	1,731
Cincinnati	207	57.7	93	25.9	48	13.4	2	0.6	9	2.5	359
Cleveland	354	60.7	101	17.3	95	16.3	12	2.1	21	3.6	583
Detroit	283	60.3	101	21.5	57	12.2	8	1.7	20	4.3	469
*Indianapolis	48	44.9	46	43.0	8	7.5	1	0.9	4	3.7	107
New York City	754	57.1	387	29.3	82	6.6	11	0.8	87	6.6	1,321
Philadelphia	509	61.3	230	27.7	45	5.4	16	1.9	30	3.6	830
Pittsburgh	356	63.3	119	21.2	60	10.7	9	1.6	18	3.2	562
*St. Louis	109	47.8	84	36.8	22	9.6	3	1.3	10	4.4	228
TOTALS	4,159	56.6	2,026	27.6	721	9.8	116	1.6	321	4.4	7,346

Source: Emil Hurja MSS, Franklin D. Roosevelt Library.
*No relief recipients polled.

TABLE 3

1935 Democratic National Committee Poll:
Regional Totals (Relief Recipients)

Region	FDR Vote	%	GOP Vote	%	Long Vote	%	Coughlin Vote	%	Others Vote	%	Total
South	1,379	70.5	117	6.0	390	20.0	0	0	70	3.6	1,956
Border	814	73.1	117	10.5	154	13.8	5	.5	24	2.2	1,114
Mid-Atlantic	1,651	69.2	281	11.8	290	12.2	41	1.72	122	5.2	2,385
New England	297	59.4	74	14.8	84	16.8	26	5.2	19	3.8	500
Great Lakes	2,015	65.2	324	10.5	571	18.5	63	2.0	117	3.8	3,090
Farm Belt	192	67.4	43	15.1	239	13.7	3	1.1	8	2.8	285
Mountain	145	60.2	21	8.7	52	21.6	0	0	23	9.5	241
Pacific	681	64.3	87	8.2	192	18.1	3	.3	96	9.1	1,059
TOTALS	7,174	67.5	1,061	10.0	1,773	16.7	137	1.3	483	4.6	10,628

Source: Emil Hurja MSS, Franklin D. Roosevelt Library.

APPENDIX III

Father Coughlin's Preamble and Principles of the National Union for Social Justice

ESTABLISHING MY PRINCIPLES upon this preamble, namely, that we are all creatures of a beneficent God, made to love and serve Him in this world and to enjoy Him forever in the next; and that all this world's wealth of field and forest, of mine and river has been bestowed upon us by a kind Father, therefore, I believe that wealth as we know it originates from the natural resources and from the labor which the sons of God expend upon these resources. It is all ours except for the harsh, cruel and grasping ways of wicked men who first concentrated wealth into the hands of a few, then dominated states and finally commenced to pit state against state in the frightful catastrophes of commercial warfare.

With this as a preamble, then, these following shall be the principles of social justice towards whose realization we must strive.

1. I believe in the right of liberty of conscience and liberty of education, not permitting the state to dictate either my worship to my God or my chosen avocation in life.

2. I believe that every citizen willing to work and capable of working shall receive a just and living annual wage which will enable him to maintain and educate his family according to the standards of American decency.

3. I believe in nationalizing those public necessities which by their very nature are too important to be held in the control of private individuals. By these I mean banking, credit and currency, power, light, oil and natural gas and our God-given natural resources.

4. I believe in private ownership of all other property.

5. I believe in upholding the right to private property yet in controlling it for the public good.

6. I believe in the abolition of the privately owned Federal Reserve Banking system and in the establishment of a Government owned Central Bank.

7. I believe in rescuing from the hands of private owners the right to coin and regulate the value of money, which right must be restored to Congress where it belongs.

8. I believe that one of the chief duties of this Government owned Central Bank is to maintain the cost of living on an even keel and the repayment of dollar debts with equal value dollars.

9. I believe in the cost of production plus a fair profit for the farmer.

10. I believe not only in the right of the laboring man to organize in unions but also in the duty of the Government which that laboring man supports to facilitate and to protect these organizations against the vested interests of wealth and of intellect.

11. I believe in the recall of all non-productive bonds and thereby in the alleviation of taxation.

12. I believe in the abolition of tax-exempt bonds.

13. I believe in the broadening of the base of taxation founded upon the ownership of wealth and the capacity to pay.

14. I believe in the simplification of government, and the further lifting of crushing taxation from the slender revenues of the laboring class.

15. I believe that in the event of a war for the defense of our nation and its liberties, there shall be a conscription of wealth as well as a conscription of men.

16. I believe in preferring the sanctity of human rights to the sanctity of property rights. I believe that the chief concern of government shall be for the poor because, as it is witnessed, the rich have ample means of their own to care for themselves.

These are my beliefs. These are the fundamentals of the organization which I present to you under the name of the NATIONAL UNION FOR SOCIAL JUSTICE. It is your privilege to reject or accept my beliefs; to follow me or repudiate me.

NOTES

Preface

1. Robert Penn Warren always denied that his character Willie Stark was intended to represent Huey Long. But there can be little doubt that Warren's experiences in Louisiana during the Long era helped shape his portrayal of Stark. Warren, *All the King's Men* (Harcourt, Brace, 1946).

2. Suspicion of mass behavior has been a constant theme of many American intellectuals since the 1920s. Walter Lippmann was among the first to express misgivings about the totalitarian implications of unbridled majoritarian politics: *Public Opinion* (Harcourt, Brace, 1922) and *The Phantom Public* (Macmillan, 1925). Confirmed, it seemed, by events in Europe, his concerns received more elaborate theoretical treatment from such social scientists as Harold Lasswell—e.g., "The Psychology of Hitlerism," *Political Science Quarterly* 4 (1933), 378–82; and later from a wide range of post-war critics. See Daniel Bell, ed., *The Radical Right* (Doubleday, 1963); T. W. Adorno et al., *The Authoritarian Personality* (W. W. Norton, 1969),

esp. R. Nevitt Sanford et al., "The Measurement of Implicit Antidemocratic Trends," pp. 222–80; Seymour Martin Lipset and Earl Raab, *The Politics of Unreason* (Harper & Row, 1970); and Edward Shils, *The Torment of Secrecy* (Free Press, 1956). A particularly heavy-handed indictment of mass behavior can be found in Eric Hoffer, *The True Believer: Thoughts on the Nature of Mass Movements* (Harper & Brothers, 1951). Indictments of the Long and Coughlin movements that make use of these views include Victor Ferkiss, "The Political and Economic Philosophy of American Fascism" (Ph.D. dissertation, University of Chicago, 1954), esp. pp. 131–38; Peter Viereck, "The Philosophical New Conservatism," in Bell, ed., *The Radical Right,* pp. 185–87; Lipset and Raab, *Politics of Unreason,* pp. 167–203; and, in more muted form, Arthur M. Schlesinger, Jr., *The Politics of Upheaval* (Houghton Mifflin, 1960), pp. 66–68, 96–97.

3. Revisionist views of mass behavior include Charles Tilly, "Collective Violence in European Perspective," in Hugh David Graham and Ted Robert Gurr, eds., *Violence in America* (Sage Publications, 1979), pp. 83–118; Ted Robert Gurr, "Political Protest and Rebellion in the 1960's: The United States in World Perspective" and "On the History of Violent Crime in Europe and America," in ibid., pp. 49–76, 353–74. See also E. P. Thompson, *The Making of the English Working Class* (Pantheon Books, 1963); and Eric Hobsbawm and George Rudé, *Captain Swing* (Pantheon Books, 1968). Margaret Canovan offers an overview of the debate over mass politics in *Populism* (Harcourt Brace Jovanovich, 1981), pp. 162–71. T. Harry Williams wrote without specific reference to any of the new theoretical or historical literature on mass politics, much of which had not yet appeared when he was at work on his biography. Curiously, he did employ the ideas of Eric Hoffer, the most intemperate critic of mass movements, avoiding Hoffer's hostility by drawing a distinction between "good" and "bad" mass leaders. Williams cited both Hoffer and Maritain in "The Gentleman from Louisiana: Demagogue or Democrat?" *Journal of Southern History* 26 (1960), 18–21; and his ideas about mass movements informed his biography *Huey Long* (Alfred A. Knopf, 1969), pp. 408–19 and passim. See also Jacques Maritain, *Man and the State* (University of Chicago Press, 1951), p. 141.

4. The tension between local autonomy and national consolidation received one of its classic discussions in Ferdinand Tönnies, *Gemeinschaft und Gesellschaft* (1887), trans. by Charles P. Loomis as *Community and Society* (Harper & Row, 1963). A recent theoretical overview of the issue is Thomas Bender, *Community and Social Change in America* (Rutgers University Press, 1978). Perhaps the most influential application of this theme to recent American history has been Robert Wiebe, *The Search for Order, 1877–1920* (Hill and Wang, 1967). See also Arthur J. Vidich and Joseph Bensman, *Small Town in Mass Society* (Princeton University Press, 1958; revised ed., 1968); Maurice R. Stein, *The Eclipse of Community* (Princeton University Press, 1960).

Prologue

1. "Cassandra Talking," *Time,* March 18, 1935, p. 13; Arthur M. Schlesinger, Jr., *The Politics of Upheaval* (Houghton Mifflin, 1960), pp. 1–2; James T. Patterson, *Congressional Conservatism and the New Deal* (University of Kentucky Press, 1967), pp. 32–76; Ellis W. Hawley, *The New Deal and the Problem of Monopoly* (Princeton University Press, 1966), pp. 72–129.

2. "Cassandra Talking," *Time,* p. 13; "Demagogues," *Newsweek,* March 16, 1935, p. 5; Washington *Post,* March 5, 1935.

3. Hugh S. Johnson, *Hell-Bent for War* (Bobbs-Merrill, 1941), passim; Arthur M. Schlesinger, Jr., *The Coming of the New Deal* (Houghton Mifflin, 1958), pp. 105–06, 114–18; Bernard

Bellush, *The Failure of the NRA* (W. W. Norton, 1975), pp. 36–48, 50–51; Hugh S. Johnson, *The Blue Eagle from Egg to Earth* (Doubleday, Doran, 1935), pp. 207–365, 366–408; William E. Leuchtenburg, *Franklin D. Roosevelt and the New Deal* (Harper & Row, 1963), pp. 67–69; "The Reminiscences of Henry A. Wallace," pp. 298–99, Oral History Project, Columbia University; Bellush, *Failure,* pp. 55–84, 146–57.

4. Washington *Post,* March 5, 1935; *New York Times,* February 21, 22, March 5, 10, 1935; New York *Herald Tribune,* March 5, 1935; Charles E. Coughlin, *A Series of Lectures on Social Justice* (Radio League of the Little Flower, 1935), pp. 193–206.

5. St. Louis *Post-Dispatch,* March 8, 1935; *New York Times,* March 6, 1935.

6. *Rocky Mountain News,* March 7, 1935; New York *Herald Tribune,* March 10, 1935; *New York Times,* March 8, 10, 1935; Raymond Gram Swing, "The Build-Up of Long and Coughlin," *Nation* 140 (March 20, 1935), 325. Ashmun Brown, a Washington correspondent for the Providence *Journal,* wrote privately, shortly after the speech, that Roosevelt had indeed been instrumental in getting Johnson to make the attack. As evidence, he cited the presence of Charles Michelson, a White House assistant, in New York with Johnson on the day before and the day after the address. "I told Charley that I did not detect his part in the phrasing of the speech, which was purely Johnsonian," Brown noted, "but Charley looked sly and intimated that he had considerable to do with it. . . . He was greatly rejoiced that the Johnson speech had turned attention from Farley for the time being, as well as from Roosevelt." See Ashmun Brown to Sevellon Brown, March 21, 1935, Post-Presidential Inventory, "Brown," Herbert Hoover Presidential Library. White House records, however, disclose no evidence of any role by Michelson or anyone else in the Administration in writing or encouraging the speech. Johnson himself explicitly denied that he was speaking at the request of the President.

7. During the first two weeks in March, in a sample of 28 daily newspapers throughout the country, the Long-Coughlin-Johnson controversy received an average of 30 stories per paper, far more than any other single topic during the same period. For the first week, moreover, nearly every paper displayed at least one story about the controversy (or about Long and Coughlin in general) on the front page each day. *Newsweek,* March 16, 1935; "The Pied Pipers," *Time,* March 18, 1935, pp. 14–16; Sara McGeady to H. V. Kaltenborn, n.d., Kaltenborn MSS, Wisconsin State Historical Society; *New York Times,* March 7, 1935; Long radio speech, March 7, 1935, U.S. Congress, *Congressional Record,* 74th Congress, 1st session (March 12, 1935), pp. 3436–39; Coughlin, *Series,* pp. 219–31.

8. Swing, "Build-Up," p. 325.

Chapter 1

1. Huey P. Long, *Every Man a King* (National Book Company, 1933), pp. 37–39.

2. T. Harry Williams, *Huey Long* (Alfred A. Knopf, 1969), p. 107.

3. *New York Times,* January 8, 1930; W. Adolphe Roberts, *Lake Pontchartrain* (Bobbs-Merrill, 1946), p. 333.

4. The most elaborate treatment of the Long assassination is Hermann B. Deutsch's *The Huey Long Murder Case* (Doubleday, 1963). See also Williams, *Huey Long,* pp. 867–72.

5. H. Dale Abadie, ed., "A Song of Huey Long," in "Notes and Documents," *Louisiana History* 101 (1970), 271–73.

6. Forrest Davis, *Huey Long: A Candid Biography* (Dodge Publishing Company, 1935), p. 22.

7. Williams, *Huey Long,* pp. 11–12; John Milton Price, "Slavery in Winn Parish," *Louisi-*

ana History 8 (1967), 137–42; Roger W. Shugg, *Origins of Class Struggle in Louisiana* (Louisiana State University Press, 1939), p. 327.

8. James Rorty, "Callie Long's Boy Huey," *Forum,* 94 (1935), 78–79, 126; Price, "Slavery in Winn Parish," p. 142; Harnett T. Kane, *Louisiana Hayride: The American Rehearsal for Dictatorship* (William Morrow, 1941), pp. 36–37.

9. William Ivy Hair, *Bourbonism and Agrarian Protest: Louisiana Politics, 1877–1900* (Louisiana State University Press, 1969), pp. 205–10; Melvin J. White, "Populism in Louisiana During the Nineties," *Mississippi Valley Historical Review* 5 (1918), 3–19; Perry Howard, *Political Tendencies in Louisiana, 1812–1852* (Louisiana State University Press, 1957), pp. 83–99.

10. Grady McWhiney, "Louisiana Socialists in the Early Twentieth Century: A Study of Rustic Radicalism," *Journal of Southern History* 20 (1954), 315–23, 333–35. For an excellent discussion of the nature of Southern agrarian socialism, see James R. Green, *Grass-Roots Socialism* (Louisiana State University Press, 1978).

11. Rorty, "Callie Long's Boy Huey," p. 78; Williams, *Huey Long,* pp. 16–24, 45.

12. Long, *Every Man a King,* pp. 2–6; Williams, *Huey Long,* pp. 25–40, 43; Roberts, *Lake Pontchartrain,* p. 329; *Christian Science Monitor,* September 11, 1935; Davis, *Huey Long,* p. 50.

13. Rose Lee, "Senator Long at Home," *New Republic* 79 (1934), 67; Long, *Every Man a King,* pp. 2–5.

14. Long, *Every Man a King,* pp. 8–14; Kane, *Louisiana Hayride,* pp. 41–44.

15. Long, *Every Man a King,* pp. 15–17; Carleton Beals, *The Story of Huey P. Long* (J. B. Lippincott, 1935), pp. 34–35; Williams, *Huey Long,* pp. 73–79.

16. Long, *Every Man a King,* pp. 18–23; Julius T. Long, "What I Know About My Brother, United States Senator Huey P. Long," *Real America,* September 1933, pp. 32–35.

17. Long, *Every Man a King,* pp. 23–25.

18. Ibid., p. 37; Williams, *Huey Long,* pp. 89–106.

19. Allan P. Sindler, *Huey Long's Louisiana: State Politics, 1920–1952* (Johns Hopkins University Press, 1956), pp. 5–26; Shugg, *Origins of Class Struggle,* pp. 234–73; Hodding Carter, "Huey Long: American Dictator," in Isabel Leighton, ed., *The Aspirin Age: 1919–1941* (Simon & Schuster, 1949), pp. 343–46; Harold Zink, *City Bosses in the United States* (Duke University Press, 1930), pp. 317–33; A. J. Liebling, *The Earl of Louisiana* (Simon & Schuster, 1961), p. 18; V. O. Key, Jr., *Southern Politics* (Alfred A. Knopf, 1949), pp. 157–60.

20. Sindler, *Huey Long's Louisiana,* pp. 21–26, 40, 45; Dale M. Robison, "From Tillman to Long: Some Striking Leaders of the Rural South," *Journal of Southern History* 3 (1937), 289–310; Gerald W. Johnson, "Live Demagogue or Dead Gentleman?," *Virginia Quarterly Review* 12 (1936), 3–4; Rupert B. Vance, "Rebels and Agrarians All: Studies in One-Party Politics," *Southern Review* 4 (1938), 26–44; Reinhard H. Luthin, "The Flowering of the Southern Demagogue," *American Scholar* 20 (1951), 185–95; W. J. Cash, *The Mind of the South* (Alfred A. Knopf, 1941), pp. 290–91.

21. Key, *Southern Politics,* pp. 157–60; Sindler, *Huey Long's Louisiana,* pp. 5–26.

22. Long, *Every Man a King,* pp. 25–28; Davis, *Huey Long,* pp. 68–70.

23. Long, *Every Man a King,* pp. 33–36; Davis, *Huey Long,* pp. 70–71; Hermann Deutsch, "The Kingdom of the Kingfish," New Orleans *Item,* July 19, 1939.

24. Long, *Every Man a King,* pp. 31, 39–41; Davis, *Huey Long,* pp. 73–76; *Rocky Mountain News,* March 17, 1935; Burton L. Hotaling, "Huey Pierce Long as Journalist and Propagandist," *Journalism Quarterly* 20 (1943), 21–23; Deutsch, "Kingdom," New Orleans *Item,* July 19, 1939.

25. Ibid., July 20, 1939; Williams, *Huey Long,* pp. 125–27, 153–80; Sindler, *Huey Long's Louisiana,* pp. 46–48; Floyd Martin Clay, *Coozan Dudley LeBlanc: From Huey Long to Hadacol* (Pelican, 1973), pp. 55–63.

26. Deutsch, "Kingdom," New Orleans *Item,* July 21, 25, 27, 30, 31, August 1, 1939; Williams, *Huey Long,* pp. 145–80; Long, *Every Man a King,* pp. 41–63; Davis, *Huey Long,* pp. 80–83.

27. Ibid., pp. 84–86; Williams, *Huey Long,* pp. 202–11; Hotaling, "Long as Journalist," pp. 21–26; Deutsch, "Kingdom," New Orleans *Item,* August 2, 3, 1939.

28. Ibid.; Sindler, *Huey Long's Louisiana,* pp. 48–50; Long, *Every Man a King,* pp. 70–78.

29. Sindler, *Huey Long's Louisiana,* pp. 50–54; Roberts, *Lake Pontchartrain,* pp. 331–32; George M. Reynolds, *Machine Politics in New Orleans, 1897–1926* (Columbia University Press, 1936), pp. 222–23.

30. Long, *Every Man a King,* pp. 97–98; Williams, *Huey Long,* pp. 248–49; New Orleans *Times-Picayune,* July 9, 1927.

31. Arthur M. Schlesinger, Jr., *The Politics of Upheaval* (Houghton Mifflin, 1966), pp. 45–46; Kane, *Louisiana Hayride,* pp. 54–57; Roberts, *Lake Pontchartrain,* pp. 331–32; Deutsch, "Kingdom," New Orleans *Item,* August 9, 1939.

32. Long, *Every Man a King,* p. 99.

33. Sindler, *Huey Long's Louisiana,* pp. 54–57; Howard, *Political Tendencies in Louisiana,* pp. 124–28; Russell B. Long interview, May 5, 1981.

34. Sindler, *Huey Long's Louisiana,* p. 57; Howard, *Political Tendencies in Louisiana,* pp. 98–102, 126–28; Hair, *Bourbonism and Agrarian Protest,* pp. 255–64.

35. Beals, *Story of Huey P. Long,* p. 83; Kane, *Louisiana Hayride,* p. 58; New Orleans *Times-Picayune,* January 18, 1928.

36. Williams, *Huey Long,* pp. 200–01, 267; Liebling, *Earl of Louisiana,* p. 8.

37. Schlesinger, *Politics of Upheaval,* p. 46; Long, *Every Man a King,* p. 87.

38. Williams, *Huey Long,* pp. 267, 280–81; Davis, *Huey Long,* pp. 55–56; New Orleans *Times-Picayune,* February 15–16, 1928.

39. Davis, *Huey Long,* p. 96; Kane, *Louisiana Hayride,* pp. 58–59; New Orleans *Times-Picayune,* May 22, 1928.

40. Long, *Every Man a King,* pp. 106–22; Sindler, *Huey Long's Louisiana,* pp. 57–61; Williams, *Huey Long,* pp. 281–346; Leslie Moses, "The Growth of Severance Taxation in Louisiana and Its Relation to the Oil and Gas Industry," *Tulane Law Review* 17 (1943), 602–19; Deutsch, "Kingdom," New Orleans *Item,* August 10, 13, 1939.

41. Long, *Every Man a King,* pp. 122–25; Beals, *Story of Huey P. Long,* pp. 109–15.

42. Ibid., pp. 116–21; Williams, *Huey Long,* pp. 356–64; Long, *Every Man a King,* pp. 139–47; Glen Jeansonne, *Leander Perez* (Louisiana State University Press, 1977), pp. 65–66.

43. Ibid., pp. 66–68; Williams, *Huey Long,* pp. 365–405; Newman F. Baker, "Some Legal Aspects of Impeachment in Louisiana," *Southwestern Political and Social Science Quarterly* 10 (1930), 359–87; Benjamin Stolberg, "Dr. Huey and Mr. Long," *Nation* 141 (September 18, 1935), 345–46; Long, *Every Man a King,* pp. 146–72.

44. Davis, *Huey Long,* p. 119.

45. Beals, *Story of Huey P. Long,* pp. 167–69; L. Vaughn Howard, *Civil Service Development in Louisiana,* volume 3 of *Tulane Studies in Political Science* (Tulane University Press, 1956), pp. 35–54; Williams, *Huey Long,* pp. 334–35, 484–85; *New York Times,* September 6, 7, 8, 11, 1930. For Irby's own account of the incident, see Sam Irby, "Kidnapped by the Kingfish" (New Orleans, 1932), pamphlet in Irby MSS, Duke University.

46. *Louisiana Progress,* July 24, 1930; Hotaling, "Long as Journalist," pp. 21–29.

47. Hermann B. Deutsch, "Huey Long of Louisiana," *New Republic* 78 (1931), 349–51; Julius Long, "What I Know About My Brother," p. 39.

48. Elmer Irey, *The Tax Dodgers* (Garden City Publishing Co., 1948), pp. 88–117; Williams, *Huey Long,* pp. 819–28.

49. Ibid., pp. 566–67; Schlesinger, *Politics of Upheaval,* p. 58; *Louisiana Progress,* July 17, 24, 1930, March 1931; Boston *Globe,* March 6, 1935.

50. *New York Times,* June 3, 1932; "Huey Long's Forty-four Laws," *New Republic* 81 (November 28, 1934), 63; Hodding Carter, "The Kingfish on His Way," ibid. (November 21, 1934), pp. 40–42; Williams, *Huey Long,* pp. 737–49; *Daily Worker,* March 12, 1935; New Orleans *Times-Picayune,* February 27, 28, March 1, July 5–6, September 7–8, 1935.

51. Hilda Phelps Hammond, *Let Freedom Ring* (Farrar & Rinehart, 1936), p. 102; *New York Times,* February 10, 1935.

52. Sindler, *Huey Long's Louisiana,* pp. 71–74, 77–78, 80–83.

53. Kane, *Louisiana Hayride,* p. 76; Davis, *Huey Long,* pp. 125–26; Hammond, *Let Freedom Ring,* passim; *New York Times,* January 17, 20, 24, 26, 30, February 1, 1935; Craddock Goins, "Huey Long and the Women's Committee of Louisiana," *Real America,* January 1935, pp. 36–37, 48, 56; Josiah Bailey to Hilda Phelps Hammond, April 11, 1935, Bailey MSS, Duke University.

54. Davis, *Huey Long,* pp. 12–13; T. Harry Williams, *Huey P. Long: An Inaugural Lecture Delivered Before the University of Oxford on 26 January 1967* (Oxford University Press, 1967), p. 14; St. Louis *Post-Dispatch,* March 3, 1935; Mrs. Katherine Blades to Franklin D. Roosevelt, OF 1403, FDRL; Miss Dorothy Collins to Roosevelt, August 6, 1934, ibid.; Paul Hutchinson, "Concerning Huey Long," *Christian Century* 52 (1935), 791–94.

55. George Gallup and Samuel Forbes Rae, *The Pulse of Democracy: The Public-Opinion Poll and How It Works* (Simon & Schuster, 1940), pp. 156–59; Jack Bass and Walter DeVries, *The Transformation of Southern Politics* (Basic Books, 1976), p. 161.

56. Jerome Beatty, "You Can't Laugh Him Off," *American Magazine* 115 (January 1933), 118; Kane, *Louisiana Hayride,* p. 72; F. Raymond Daniell, "Once More Huey Long Calls the Dance," *New York Times Magazine,* September 2, 1934, p. 3; Roberts, *Lake Pontchartrain,* pp. 338–39.

57. *Louisiana Progress,* April 24, 1930; John D. Klorer, ed., *The New Louisiana* (Official State Administration Inaugural Publication, 1936), pp. 12–17; T. Harry Williams, *Romance and Realism in Southern Politics* (Louisiana State University Press, 1966), pp. 76–77.

58. Klorer, *New Louisiana,* pp. 18–19, 165–66, 205–06; Tom Wallace series on Huey Long in Boston *Globe,* March 4–9, 1935; Roberts, *Lake Pontchartrain,* pp. 338–39; Stella O'Conner, "The Charity Hospital at New Orleans: An Administration and Financial History, 1736–1941," *Louisiana Historical Quarterly* 31 (1948), 86–93; Don Wharton, "Louisiana State University," *Scribner's* 102 (September 1937), 35–39; *New York Times,* October 28, December 18, 1934; *Louisiana Progress,* April 17, 1930; Schlesinger, *Politics of Upheaval,* pp. 59–60; Raymond Moley, *27 Masters of Politics in a Personal Perspective* (Funk & Wagnalls, 1949), p. 223.

59. Sindler, *Huey Long's Louisiana,* pp. 86–95, 102–16; Bass and DeVries, *Transformation,* p. 161.

60. Sindler, *Huey Long's Louisiana,* pp. 102–16. I am indebted to Glen Jeansonne, whose unpublished paper "Huey P. Long: A Post-Revisionist View" contributed to this evaluation of the Long record. Klorer, *New Louisiana,* pp. 18–19, 217–18; *Louisiana Progress,* April 17, August 14, 29, 1930; St. Louis *Post-Dispatch,* March 3, 1935; *New York Times,* March 3, 1935; Deutsch, "Huey Long of Louisiana," pp. 349–51; Hamilton Basso, "The Death and Legacy of Huey Long," *New Republic* 85 (January 1, 1936), 217; Hodding Carter, "How Come Huey Long? 1. Bogeyman—," *New Republic* 82 (February 13, 1935), 12.

61. John Dollard, *Caste and Class in a Southern Town* (Yale University Press, 1937), pp. 214, 218; Ralphe J. Bunche, *The Political Status of the Negro in the Age of FDR* (University of Chicago Press, 1973), p. 193.

62. Roy Wilkins, "Huey Long Says: An Interview with Louisiana's Kingfish," *Crisis* 42 (February 1935), 41, 52; Beals, *Story of Huey P. Long*, p. 351; Williams, *Huey Long*, p. 703; T. Harry Williams, "Huey Long and the Politics of Realism," in E. C. Barksdale, ed., *Essays on Recent Southern Politics* (University of Texas Press, 1970), p. 114.

63. Beals, *Story of Huey P. Long*, p. 351; Carleton Beals, "Louisiana's Black Utopia," *Nation* 141 (October 1935), 503–04; Wilkins, "Huey Long Says," p. 42; Glen Jeansonne, "Racism and Longism in Louisiana: The 1959–1960 Gubernatorial Elections," *Louisiana History* 11 (1970), 270; Jeansonne, "Huey P. Long," pp. 7–8; Riley E. Baker, "Negro Voter Registration in Louisiana, 1879–1969," *Louisiana Studies* 4 (1963), 338–39.

64. *Louisiana Progress*, September 4, 11, 1930, August 18, November 10, 1931; campaign circulars 53 and 38, n.d., Wisdom Collection, Tulane; Williams, *Huey Long*, p. 328.

65. U.S. Congress, *Congressional Record*, 73rd Congress, 2nd Session (June 16, 1934), p. 1941; Long radio address, March 7, 1935, in ibid., 74:1 (March 12, 1935), p. 3436.

66. Wilkins, "Huey Long Says," pp. 41, 52.

67. "Huey P. Long," *Crisis* 42 (October 1935), 305; Williams, "Huey Long and the Politics of Realism," pp. 110–14; Johnson, "Live Demagogue or Dead Gentleman?" pp. 1–14.

68. Roman Heleniak, "Local Reaction to the Great Depression in New Orleans, 1929–1933," *Louisiana History* 10 (1969), 289–306; John Robert Moore, "The New Deal in Louisiana," in John Braeman et al., eds., *The New Deal* (Ohio State University Press, 1975), II, 137–38.

69. *Louisiana Progress*, August 29, 1930; Mrs. Katherine Blades to Roosevelt, March 18, 1935, OF 1403, FDRL; Basso, "Death and Legacy," pp. 217–18.

Chapter 2

1. *New York Times*, March 4–5, 1930; Huey P. Long, *Every Man a King* (National Book Company, 1933), pp. 192–99.

2. *New York Times*, May 25, 1931, October 28, 1934, February 17–18, 1931; William F. Mugleston, "Cornpone and Potlikker: A Moment of Comic Relief in the Great Depression," *Louisiana History* 16 (1975), 279–88; Jerome Beatty, "You Can't Laugh Him Off," *American Magazine* 115 (January 1933), 116; Elliott Roosevelt, ed., *F.D.R.: His Personal Letters* (Duell, Sloan and Pearce, 1950), I, 176–77; Julius T. Long, "What I Know About My Brother, United States Senator Huey P. Long," *Real America*, September 1933, p. 30.

3. T. Harry Williams, *Huey Long* (Alfred A. Knopf, 1969), pp. 533–34.

4. C. Vann Woodward, *Origins of the New South, 1877–1913* (Louisiana State University Press, 1951), pp. 414–15; George B. Tindall, *The Emergence of the New South, 1913–1945* (Louisiana State University Press, 1967), pp. 112–13, 139, 354–55.

5. Montgomery *Advertiser*, August 18, 1931; *New York Times*, August 17, 1931; "The Reminiscences of Henry A. Wallace," Oral History Project, Columbia University, p. 297.

6. "Governor Long's Drop-a-Cotton Plan," *Literary Digest* 110 (September 19, 1931), 8–9.

7. *New York Times*, August 18, 1931; Montgomery *Advertiser*, August 22, 1931; Williams, *Huey Long*, p. 532; Walter George to Long, August 18, 1931, Theodore Bilbo to Long, August 13, 1931, Wright Patman to Long, August 18, 1931, all in Huey Long MSS, LSU; Scaramouche, "Senator Huey P. Long: Clown and Knave," *Real America*, July 1933, p. 12.

8. Ross Sterling to Long, August 21, 1931, Long MSS, LSU; Houston *Post*, September 12,

1931; Donald W. Whisenhunt, "Huey Long and the Texas Cotton Acreage Control Law of 1931," *Louisiana Studies* 13 (1974), 144–45, 148–49; Robert E. Snyder, "Huey Long and the Cotton Holiday Plan of 1931," *Louisiana History* 18 (1977), 133–60.

9. Ibid., pp. 144, 150–51; Houston *Post*, September 7, 9, 10, 12, 16, 1931; I. C. Blackwood, Governor of South Carolina, to Huey Long, September 18, 1931, Long to Blackwood, September 22, 1931, both in Long MSS, LSU.

10. *New York Times,* September 16, 1935; Houston *Post,* September 11, 1935.

11. Ibid., September 16, 17, 18, 1931; *New York Times,* September 17–18, 1931; "Statement of Governor Long," n.d., 1931, Long MSS, LSU; Tindall, *Emergence of the New South,* p. 354.

12. Letters to Huey Long, August-September 1931, Long MSS, LSU; M. McFountain to Long, September 4, 1931, ibid.; I. B. Rennyson to Long, September 3, 1931, ibid.

13. Whisenhunt, "Huey Long and the Texas Cotton Acreage Control Law of 1931," p. 148; Seth P. Storrs to Huey Long, September 11, 1931, Faber W. Kearse to Long, August 29, 1931, G. W. Willis and W. O. Wingate to Long, n.d., 1931, F. H. Watson to Long, August 30, 1931, G. B. Phillips to Long, September 5, 1931, Bill Graham et al. to Long, September 4, 1931, Scrap Chasm to Long, September 14, 1931, W. C. Coker to Long, September 7, 1931, Ben S. Mooney to Long, September 17, 1931, all in Long MSS, LSU.

14. Edgar W. Witt to Long, September 4, 1931, S. C. Bull to Long, September 4, 1931, both in Long MSS, LSU.

15. T. H. Abercrombie to Long, August 29, 1931, J. C. Anderson to Long, September 12, 1931, R. W. Brooks to Long, September 18, 1931, all in Long MSS, LSU.

16. Anonymous correspondent to Long, August 19, 1931, J. W. Buckley to Long, August 22, 1931, K. E. N. Cole to Long, October 5, 1931, all in Long MSS, LSU.

17. *Louisiana Progress,* December 1930 and 1931, passim.

18. Ibid., 1930–32, passim, and January, May, 1931.

19. M. L. Mott to Long, September 25, 1931, Long MSS, LSU.

20. Long, *Every Man a King* p. 290; M. S. Cushman, "Huey Long's First Session in the United States Senate (January 25 to July 16, 1932)," *Proceedings of the West Virginia Academy of Science* 11 (February 1938), 131.

21. "A Louisiana Kingfish in Washington," *Literary Digest* 112 (February 6, 1932), 7; Louis Cochran, "The Louisiana Kingfish," *American Mercury* 26 (1932), 287; Clinton W. Gilbert, "The Irrepressible Mr. Long," *Collier's* 89 (June 4, 1932), 24; *New York Times,* January 31, April 17, 1932.

22. "Louisiana Kingfish in Washington," p. 7; *New York Times,* January 28, April 8, May 17, 1932; A. J. Liebling, *The Earl of Louisiana* (Simon & Schuster, 1961), p. 8.

23. U.S. Congress, *Congressional Record,* 72nd Congress, 1st session (March 21, 1932), p. 6453.

24. Ibid. (April 29, 1932), pp. 9212–15.

25. Ibid. (May 12, 1932), pp. 10062–65; *New York Times,* May 13, 1932.

26. *Congr. Record,* 72:1 (March 18, 21, April 4, 1932), pp. 6452, 6541, 7372–77.

27. Gilbert, "Irrepressible Mr. Long," p. 24; Chicago *Tribune,* May 5, 1932; *Llano Colonist,* April 9, 1932, HLS.

28. *Congr. Record,* 72:1 (April 29, 1932), pp. 9214–15; Buffalo *Times,* May 14, 1932; New Orleans *Item,* May 4, 1932.

29. Jordan A. Schwarz, *The Inter-Regnum of Despair* (University of Illinois Press, 1970), pp. 78–141; *New York Times,* March 22, 1932; *Congr. Record,* 72:1 (March 21, 1932), pp. 6538–44.

30. *New York Times,* May 7, 1932; Frank Freidel, *Franklin D. Roosevelt: The Triumph*

(Little, Brown, 1956), p. 279; Burton K. Wheeler, *Yankee from the West* (Doubleday, 1962), p. 285; Long, *Every Man a King,* pp. 301–03.

31. Freidel, *Triumph,* p. 279; Wheeler, *Yankee,* p. 285.

32. *New York Times,* June 18, 26, 27, 29, 1932; James A. Farley, *Jim Farley's Story: The Roosevelt Years* (McGraw-Hill, 1948), p. 16; Raymond Moley, *27 Masters of Politics in a Personal Perspective* (Funk & Wagnalls, 1949), p. 221; Arthur F. Mullen, *Western Democrat* (Wilfred Funk, 1940), p. 264; Alben Barkley, *That Reminds Me* (Doubleday, 1954), p. 160; Robert J. Noel to Huey Long, July 9, 1932, HLS.

33. Freidel, *Triumph,* pp. 279, 306; Farley, *Story,* pp. 15–16; Lela Stiles, *The Man Behind Roosevelt: The Story of Louis McHenry Howe* (World, 1954), p. 171; Thomas L. Stokes, *Chip Off My Shoulder* (Princeton University Press, 1940), pp. 321–22; Edward J. Flynn, *You're the Boss* (Viking Press, 1947), p. 101; *New York Times,* June 26, 1932.

34. James A. Farley, *Behind the Ballots* (Harcourt, Brace, 1938), pp. 170–71.

35. Ibid.; George E. Sokolsky, "Huey Long," *Atlantic Monthly* 156 (1935), 529–30; Williams, *Huey Long,* p. 603; *New York Times,* October 16, 1932; Baton Rouge *State-Times,* October 27, 1932.

36. Hermann Deutsch, "Hattie and Huey," *Saturday Evening Post* 205 (October 15, 1932), 6–7.

37. Ibid., p. 88; Arkansas *Gazette,* August 12, 1933.

38. Wheeler, *Yankee,* pp. 280–81; Stuart Towns, "A Louisiana Medicine Show: The Kingfish Elects an Arkansas Senator," *Arkansas Historical Quarterly* 25 (1966), 119–22; *Congr. Record,* 72:1 (July 31, 1932), pp. 15192–93.

39. *New York Times,* July 31, 1932.

40. Deutsch, "Hattie and Huey," p. 88; "Speaking Announcements: Senator Hattie D. Caraway and Huey P. Long," n.d., Long form letter, July 19, 1932, "What the Re-election of Senator (Mrs.) Carraway Means to the People of America," circular, n.d., "A Letter from Uncle Trusty: Why the Financial Masters Oppose Senator Caraway," circular, n.d., all in William B. Wisdom Collection of Huey P. Long, Tulane University; *Labor,* August 2, 1932; Arkansas *Democrat,* August 1, 1932; New Orleans *Times-Picayune,* August 1, 1932.

41. Arkansas *Gazette,* August 1, 1932; T. Harry Williams interview with Murphy Roden, n.d., transcript in T. Harry Williams MSS, LSU.

42. Deutsch, "Hattie and Huey," p. 90.

43. Ibid.; Arkansas *Gazette,* August 2, 1932; "What the Re-election of Senator (Mrs.) Carraway Means . . . ," Wisdom Collection.

44. Deutsch, "Hattie and Huey," pp. 88–89; "Introduction of Senator Huey P. Long, Delivered at Camden, Arkansas, Monday, August 1st, 1932, by C. M. Martin," Huey Long MSS, LSU.

45. Arkansas *Gazette,* August 2–6, 9, 1932; Arkansas *Democrat,* August 3–4, 1932; Williams, *Huey Long,* p. 590.

46. Deutsch, "Hattie and Huey," p. 90.

47. Arkansas *Democrat,* August 6, 7, 9, 10, 1932; Arkansas *Gazette,* August 9, 10, 1932; Deutsch, "Hattie and Huey," p. 89.

48. *New York Times,* July 31, 1932; Arkansas *Gazette,* August 10, 1932.

49. Election returns as reported in Arkansas *Gazette,* August 15, 1932. Charles Seigel, "The Kingfish and 'The Little Woman Senator' " (B.A. thesis, University of Chicago, 1980), provides the most thorough analysis of the primary results. It concludes that Long's influence upon the result was substantial, but that Mrs. Caraway brought important strengths of her own to the contest.

Note for page 53

50. Percentage of Popular Vote Cast for Senator
Hattie Caraway in 1932 Arkansas Democratic
Primary, Listed by County in Order of Size
of Senator Caraway's Percentage

(Counties in which Huey Long campaigned are capitalized.)

County	Caraway %	County	Caraway %
1. QUACHITA	68.5	38. Grant	48.2
2. HOT SPRING	66.0	39. JACKSON	48.1
3. MISSISSIPPI	65.7	Clay	48.1
4. COLUMBIA	65.6	41. MONROE	46.2
CRAIGHEAD	65.6	42. LOGAN	45.9
6. LAWRENCE	65.4	43. Stone	45.5
7. ST. FRANCIS	64.8	44. PULASKI	44.5
8. JEFFERSON	63.1	45. Johnson	43.8
9. MONTGOMERY	61.7	46. WHITE	43.0
10. MILLER	61.4	47. Greene	42.6
11. CLARK	60.4	48. Lonoke	41.5
12. Perry	60.1	49. Cleburne	40.1
13. Calhoun	59.3	50. Fulton	40.0
14. Woodruff	59.1	51. Baxter	39.0
15. Pike	59.0	52. Ashley	34.8
16. IZARD	58.2	Randolph	34.8
17. Howard	57.9	54. Franklin	34.3
18. Sevier	56.9	55. Crawford	33.5
19. POLK	56.0	Yell	33.5
20. CROSS	55.6	57. Saline	32.2
21. LEE	55.2	58. Independence	31.7
22. POPE	54.2	59. SEBASTIEN	31.6
23. POINSETT	54.1	60. Scott	30.6
GARLAND	54.1	61. Carroll	30.3
25. PHILLIPS	53.7	62. Searcy	27.8
26. UNION	52.3	63. Faulkner	27.0
27. NEVADA	52.0	64. Conway	26.0
28. Lincoln	51.3	65. Marion	25.7
DALLAS	51.3	66. Drew	24.9
30. Desha	51.1	67. Benton	22.9
31. Van Buren	50.6	68. Bradley	22.6
LaFayette	50.6	69. CRITTENDEN	21.1
33. ARKANSAS	50.0	70. Washington	20.6
34. Prairie	49.6	71. Newton	17.3
35. Chicot	49.3	Boone	17.3
Little River	49.3	73. Madison	
37. HEMPSTEAD	49.1	Cleveland	returns unavailable
		Sharp	

Source: Arkansas *Gazette,* August 15, 1932.

51. *New York Times,* August 11, 1932; Arkansas *Gazette,* August 11, 1932; New Orleans *Times-Picayune,* August 11, 1932.

52. Arkansas *Democrat,* August 12, 1932.

53. *Congr. Record,* 72:2 (December 6, 1932), p. 56.

54. Ibid., pp. 57–58.

55. Ibid. (January 5, 10, 11, 12, 13, 1933), pp. 1330–33, 1451–70, 1573–81, 1624–36, 1646–48, 1749.

56. Ibid.; *New York Times,* January 10, 11, 13, 15, 1933.

57. *Congr. Record,* 72:2 (January 11, 1933), pp. 1580–81; *New York Times,* January 17, 1933.

58. Ibid.; *Congr. Record,* 72:2 (January 25, 1933), p. 2508.

Chapter 3

1. Washington *Sunday Star,* October 2, 1932.

2. Rexford G. Tugwell, *The Democratic Roosevelt* (Doubleday, 1957), pp. 348–50.

3. Grace Tully, *F.D.R. My Boss* (Charles Scribner's Sons, 1949), pp. 323–25; T. Harry Williams, *Huey Long* (Alfred A. Knopf, 1969), p. 602.

4. Arthur M. Schlesinger, Jr., *The Crisis of the Old Order* (Houghton Mifflin, 1957), p. 452.

5. *New York Times,* January 20, 1933; Huey Long to Franklin D. Roosevelt, January 31, 1933, PPF 2337, FDRL; Long form letter, January 28, 1933, Huey Long MSS, Duke University.

6. U.S. Congress, *Congressional Record,* 73rd Congress, 1st session (March 9, 1933), pp. 52–53.

7. Frank Freidel, *Franklin D. Roosevelt: Launching the New Deal* (Little, Brown, 1973), pp. 219–29; William E. Leuchtenburg, *Franklin D. Roosevelt and the New Deal* (Harper & Row, 1963), p. 43; Barton J. Bernstein, "The New Deal: The Conservative Achievements of Liberal Reform," in Bernstein, ed. *Towards a New Past* (Pantheon Books, 1968), pp. 267–68; *Congr. Record,* 73:1 (March 9, 1933), p. 59.

8. Ibid. (March 13, 15, 1933), pp. 274–75, 471.

9. Ibid. (April 11, 14, June 7, 1933), pp. 1477, 1484, 1741, 5178–79.

10. *New York Times,* May 27, 1933; *Congr. Record,* 73:1 (April 11, June 2, 1933), pp. 1473–74, 4830–43.

11. Ibid. (March 11, 15, 16, 30, 31, May 3, June 2, 6, 1933), pp. 186–91, 427, 625, 1042, 1091, 2780, 2808, 4840–44, 5085; *New York Times,* June 14, 1933; *American Progress,* August 24, 1933.

12. *Congr. Record,* 73:1 (March 30, June 9, 13, 1933), pp. 1038, 5424, 5861.

13. Ibid. (June 15, 1933), p. 6110.

14. Ibid. (March 10, 13, 1933), pp. 124, 275–76.

15. Huey Long, "How America Can Be Adjusted," radio address of March 17, 1933, William B. Wisdom Collection of Huey P. Long, Tulane University (reprint from *Congr. Record*); *Radio Guide,* March 2, 1935, HLS. Tape recordings of several of Long's NBC radio speeches are in the collections of the Museum of Broadcasting, New York, New York.

16. James A. Farley, *Behind the Ballots* (Harcourt, Brace, 1938), pp. 240–42.

17. Ibid.

18. Ibid., p. 243; Williams, *Huey Long,* pp. 638–39.

19. William F. Dombrow to Roosevelt, n.d., 1933, John J. Sarsfield, Secretary, Irish-American Independent Political Unit, Brooklyn, New York, to Roosevelt, April 21, 1933, both in OF 1403, FDRL.

20. Arthur M. Schlesinger, Jr., *The Politics of Upheaval* (Houghton Mifflin, 1960), p. 56; Harnett T. Kane, *Louisiana Hayride: The American Rehearsal for Dictatorship* (William Morrow, 1941), p. 101.

21. Elmer L. Irey, *The Tax Dodgers* (Garden City Publishing Company, 1948), pp. 90–101; John Morton Blum, *From the Morgenthau Diaries: Years of Crisis, 1928–1938* (Houghton Mifflin, 1959), p. 97; *Labor,* January 31, 1933; Joseph T. Robinson to James A. Farley, March 1, 1935, Farley to Robinson, March 4, 1935, both in Farley MSS, Library of Congress; Walter Davenport, "Catching Up with Huey," *Collier's* 92 (July 1, 1933), 12–13; Owen P. White, *The Autobiography of a Durable Sinner* (G. P. Putnam's Sons, 1942), pp. 273–76.

22. *Congr. Record,* 73:2 (January 30, February 2, 1934), pp. 1552–63, 1836–38; Tom Connally, *My Name Is Tom Connally* (Thomas Y. Crowell, 1954), pp. 167–68.

23. *New York Times,* August 19, September 3, 5, 21, 1933; Milwaukee *Journal,* August 28, 1933; Hodding Carter, "Kingfish to Crawfish," *New Republic* 77 (1934), 302–05; White, *Autobiography,* pp. 270–71.

24. Milwaukee *Journal,* August 29, 1933; Milwaukee *Sentinel,* August 29, 1933; *New York Times,* August 31, 1933.

25. Milwaukee *Sentinel,* August 29, 1933; New Orleans *Times-Picayune,* August 31, 1933.

26. "J. P. Morgan and Company Points Way for Capone's Release," circular, n.d., 1933, OF 1403, FDRL; *American Progress,* September 7, 1933.

27. *American Progress,* August 31, 1933; Burton L. Hotaling, "Huey Pierce Long as Journalist and Propagandist," *Journalism Quarterly* 20 (1943), 22; C. S. Wilkinson, letter to editor, Salt Lake City *Telegram,* n.d., HLS; Robert S. Lynd and Helen Merrell Lynd, *Middletown in Transition* (Harcourt, Brace, 1937), p. 497.

28. *New York Times,* November 11, 1933; New Orleans *Times-Picayune,* October 10, 1933; Williams, *Huey Long,* pp. 663–64; Schlesinger, *Politics of Upheaval,* pp. 58–59.

29. Carter, "Kingfish to Crawfish," pp. 302–05; *New York Times,* November 10, 1933.

30. Connally, *My Name Is Tom Connally,* pp. 167–68; Williams, *Huey Long,* pp. 682–87; "H.M.K." to Marvin McIntyre, December 11, 1934, OF 300 (LA-L), FDRL; Josiah Bailey to Tom Connally, April 30, 1935, Bailey MSS, Duke University.

31. Hodding Carter, "The Kingfish on His Way," *New Republic* 81 (November 21, 1934), 40–42; "Huey Long's Forty-four Laws," ibid. (November 28, 1934), 63; Arnold S. Fulton, "First Month of Dictator Long," *Nation* 141 (August 14, 1935), 179–81; "The New Orleans Political War," *Literary Digest* 120 (August 10, 1935), 8; Philadelphia *Evening Bulletin,* March 6, 1935; Des Moines *Register,* April 17, 1935; *New York Times,* January 24, 1935; Williams, *Huey Long,* p. 737.

32. Ibid., pp. 678–79; *New York Times,* December 16, 1933, November 26, 1934.

33. Huey Long, *Every Man a King* (National Book Company, 1933); *New York Times,* October 19, 1933; *New York Times Book Review,* December 17, 1933; Allan Nevins, "One of Our Conquerers," *Saturday Review of Literature* 10 (1933), 324; Hotaling, "Long as Journalist," pp. 27–28.

34. Ibid., pp. 23–29; *American Progress,* August 24, 1933, and passim; *Garden City Sun* (Baton Rouge), July 20, 1933.

35. John Francis Thorning, "Senator Long on Father Coughlin," *America* 53 (April 13, 1935), 8; Ernest Gordon Bormann, "A Rhetorical Analysis of the National Radio Broadcasts of Senator Huey P. Long" (Ph.D. dissertation, State University of Iowa, 1953), pp. 9–12.

36. Radio address, n.d., 1935, reprinted in *Congr. Record,* 74:1 (January 14, 1935), p. 412.

37. Long radio address, March 7, 1935, in ibid. (March 12, 1935), p. 3437; radio address, March 17, 1933, in ibid., 73:1 (March 23, 1933), p. 787; *American Progress,* September 28, 1933, February 1, 1935.

38. An earlier (1933) version of the codes had provided for a capital levy increased by only one percent for each million, so that a fortune would have to reach $100 million before the tax rate would become fully confiscatory; by 1934, however, Long had apparently decided that the rate was too moderate, and without fanfare he proposed a much higher one. *Congr. Record,* 73:1 (May 12, 1933), pp. 3318–20; ibid., 72:1 (April 29, 1932), p. 9202; Huey Long, "Huey P. Long Explains His 'Share-The-Wealth Plan,' " *Real America,* July 1935, p. 19; "The Long Plan to Spread the Wealth of the Country Among All the People!," leaflet in OF 1403, FDRL; *American Progress,* October 12, 1933.

39. This was, again, a change from 1933, when Long had been willing to allow inheritances of more than $5 million. "The Long Plan," OF 1403, FDRL; radio address, March 17, 1933, in *Congr. Record,* 73:1 (March 23, 1933), p. 786; "Huey P. Long Explains," p. 19; Rose Lee, "Senator Long at Home," *New Republic* 79 (1934), 66–68.

40. Long radio address, April 21, 1933, in *Congr. Record,* 73:1 (April 24, 1933), pp. 2211–12; radio address, February 23, 1934, in ibid., 73:2 (March 1, 1934), p. 3452; radio address, March 7, 1935, in ibid., 74:1 (March 12, 1935), p. 3439; radio address, January 19, 1935, in ibid. (January 23, 1935), p. 792; *American Progress,* February 1, January 11, 1934; "The Educational Program for Share Our Wealth Society," leaflet in Huey Long MSS, Duke University.

41. *Congr. Record,* 73:1 (May 12, 1933), p. 3321; *New York Times,* March 9, 1935; Williams, *Huey Long,* pp. 694–95.

42. Robert R. Doane, *The Measurement of American Wealth* (Harper & Brothers, 1933), p. 25; Long radio address, February 23, 1934, in *Congr. Record,* 73:2 (March 1, 1934), p. 3450; Buel W. Patch, "National Wealth and National Income," *Editorial Research Reports* 1 (April 20, 1935), 287–304.

43. Ibid.; H. L. Mencken, "The Glory of Louisiana," *Nation* 136 (1933), 507.

44. Martha Mays Schroeder, "Huey Pierce Long: The Kingfish of the Senate" (M.A. thesis, University of Texas, 1967), pp. 64–65.

45. *Congr. Record,* 73:2 (April 5, 1934), pp. 6081–82, 6092–96; William H. Harbaugh, *Lawyer's Lawyer: The Life of John W. Davis* (Oxford University Press, 1973), p. 360.

46. *New York Times,* January 16, 18, February 12, 15, 20–22, March 5, 1935; St. Louis *Post-Dispatch,* March 7, 1935; James A. Farley, *Jim Farley's Story* (McGraw-Hill, 1948), pp. 50–51; Harold Ickes, *The Secret Diary of Harold L. Ickes: The First Thousand Days, 1933–1936* (Simon & Schuster, 1953), pp. 294–99, 345–46; *Congr. Record,* 74:1 (January 7, February 11, 12, 14, 20, April 22, May 14, 1935), pp. 158, 1794–97, 1829–40, 1933–43, 2276–83, 6109–13, 7432–42; Long to Senate Judiciary Committee, March 6, 1935, Cummings MSS, University of Virginia.

47. *New York Times,* June 13, 15, 18, August 27, 1935; Washington *Post,* June 13, August 27, 1935; *Progressive,* August 31, 1935; *Congr. Record,* 74:1 (June 12, 14, 17, August 26, 1935), pp. 9091–175, 9291–97, 9428–37, 14718–52; Williams, *Huey Long,* pp. 832–36, 842.

48. During Long's first three sessions in the Senate (72:1, 72:2, 73:1—1932–33), he voted with the majority 83 times and with the minority 71. In his last two sessions (73:2, 74:1—1934–35), he cast 61 ballots with the majority, 58 with the minority. In 1934 (73:1), he voted with the majority on only 43 percent of the roll calls (21 times) and with the minority on 57 percent (27). Roll-call votes tabulated from the *Congr. Record,* 1932–35.

49. Burton K. Wheeler, *Yankee from the West* (Doubleday, 1962), p. 284; *New York Times,* March 12, 13, 1933, November 15, 1934; Glass to Dr. Ben H. Smith, February 6, 1933, James Hartley to Glass, May 30, 1933, Glass MSS, University of Virginia; *New York Times,* April 6, 1934.

50. Wheeler, *Yankee,* pp. 280–83; Ickes, *Secret Diary,* p. 313.

51.

Percentage of Senate Roll-call Votes Cast in Accord with Huey Long, 1932–35

	1932–33 (72:1, 2, 73:1)	1934–35 (73:2, 74:1)
William Borah (R—Ida.)	58	74
Bronson Cutting (R—N.M.)	65	69
Lynn Frazier (R—N.D.)	68	77
Robert La Follette (R/Progr.—Wis.)	63	67
George Norris (R—Neb.)	56	62
Gerald Nye (R—N.D.)	66	80
Henrik Shipstead (F-L—Minn.)	71	79
Elmer Thomas (R—Okla.)	64	63
Burton Wheeler (D—Mont.)	76	74

Source: U.S. Congress, *Congressional Record,* 72nd Congress, 1st session, through 74th Congress, 1st session (1932–35).

52. Long radio address of February 23, 1934, reprinted in *Congr. Record,* 73:2 (March 1, 1934), pp. 3450–53.

53. Washington *Daily News,* February 3, 1934.

54. *New York Times,* January 10, 1935.

55. Homer Cummings to Roosevelt, April 18, 1935, Roosevelt to Joseph Robinson, April 20, 1935, OF 1403, FDRL; Harold M. Stephens to Homer Cummings, September 7, 1934, Marvin McIntyre to Cummings, February 1, 1935, Cummings MSS, University of Virginia.

56. *New York Times,* January 10, 1935; New York *Sun,* March 4, 1935; "News and Comment from the National Capital," *Literary Digest* 119 (May 4, 1935), 13.

57. Schlesinger, *Politics of Upheaval,* pp. 325–38; *Congr. Record,* 74:1 (June 19, 1935), 9557–59; Chicago *Tribune,* June 21, 1935.

58. San Francisco *Examiner,* March 2, 1935.

59. "Spotlight Again Plays on Long," *Literary Digest* 120 (September 7, 1935), 8.

Chapter 4

1. Ruth Mugglebee, *Father Coughlin of the Shrine of the Little Flower* (Garden City, 1933), pp. 158–62.

2. Cleveland *Press,* May 9, 1935; Columbus *Evening Dispatch,* May 9, 1935.

3. Forrest Davis, "Father Coughlin," *Atlantic Monthly* 156 (1935), 660; New York *Daily*

News, November 29, 1935; *New York Times,* November 27, 1933, August 7, 1936, October 11, 1936; Boston *Globe,* August 13, 1935; David H. Bennett, *Demagogues in the Depression: American Radicals and the Union Party, 1932–1936* (Rutgers University Press, 1969), pp. 228, 230.

4. Boston *Globe,* August 13, 1935; Marquis Childs, "Father Coughlin: A Success Story of the Depression," *New Republic* 78 (May 2, 1934), 326–27.

5. "Three Priests Preach the Gospel of Social Justice," *Literary Digest* 116 (December 23, 1933), 21.

6. Mugglebee, *Father Coughlin,* pp. 6–7; Louis B. Ward, *Father Charles E. Coughlin: An Authorized Biography* (Tower Publications, 1933), p. 7.

7. J. F. Carter ("The Unofficial Observer"), *American Messiahs* (Simon & Schuster, 1935), pp. 36–37; John M. Carlisle, "Priest of a Parish of the Air Waves," *New York Times Magazine,* October 29, 1933, p. 8; *Rocky Mountain News,* March 15, 1935.

8. Mugglebee, *Father Coughlin,* pp. 3, 6.

9. Ibid., pp. 4–7, 9.

10. Ibid., pp. 11–26, 32–36; Ward, *Father Charles E. Coughlin,* pp. 9–10.

11. Peter A. Soderbergh, "The Rise of Father Coughlin," *Social Science* 42 (1967), 11; Mugglebee, *Father Coughlin,* pp. 45–55.

12. Ibid., pp. 56–80; Ward, *Father Charles E. Coughlin,* pp. 10–13.

13. Mugglebee, *Father Coughlin,* pp. 81–96; *New Catholic Encyclopedia,* 1967 ed., "Basilians," "Leo XIII," "Social Movements," "James Gibbons," *"Rerum Novarum"*; Leo XIII, "On the Condition of Workers," in *Two Basic Social Encyclicals* (Benziger Brothers, 1943), pp. 3–81; George Q. Flynn, *American Catholics and the Roosevelt Presidency* (University of Kentucky Press, 1968), pp. 22–35.

14. Leo XIII, "On the Condition," p. 29 and passim; Flynn, *American Catholics,* pp. 25–30.

15. Mugglebee, *Father Coughlin,* pp. 81–96; Ward, *Father Charles E. Coughlin,* pp. 13–15; Raymond Gram Swing, "Father Coughlin: I. The Wonder of Self Discovery," *Nation* 139 (1934), 731–33; George N. Shuster, "Radio Sky Pilot," *Review of Reviews* 141 (April 1935), p. 24.

16. Mugglebee, *Father Coughlin,* pp. 97–122.

17. Carlisle, "Priest of a Parish," p. 8; Carter, *American Messiahs,* p. 37; Mugglebee, *Father Coughlin,* pp. 123–39.

18. Ibid., pp. 140–47, 155.

19. "Father Coughlin," *Fortune* 9 (1934), p. 35; Soderbergh, "Rise of Father Coughlin," p. 11; Ward, *Father Charles E. Coughlin,* pp. 17–18; Kenneth T. Jackson, *The Ku Klux Klan in the City, 1915–1930* (Oxford University Press, 1967), pp. 127–43.

20. Mugglebee, *Father Coughlin,* pp. 164–66.

21. Ibid., pp. 148–57; Sheldon Marcus, *Father Coughlin: The Tumultuous Life of the Priest of the Little Flower* (Little, Brown, 1973), pp. 23–25; Shuster, "Radio Sky Pilot," p. 24.

22. Mugglebee, *Father Coughlin,* pp. 161–63; Soderbergh, "Rise of Father Coughlin," p. 15.

23. Mugglebee, *Father Coughlin,* pp. 164–66.

24. "Father Coughlin," *Fortune,* pp. 35–36; Edgar DeWitt Jones, "Radio Preacher Holds a Party," *Christian Century* 48 (1931), 883; John C. Calahan, Jr., "The Hour of Power," *Commonweal* 13 (1931), 343.

25. Raymond Gram Swing, *Forerunners of American Fascism* (Julian Messner, 1935), pp. 38–39; Mugglebee, *Father Coughlin,* pp. 170–71.

26. Ibid., pp. 170, 172–78.

27. "Father Coughlin," *Fortune,* pp. 34, 110; Carlisle, "Priest of a Parish," p. 8.

28. Wallace Stegner, "The Radio Priest and His Flock," in Isabel Leighton, ed., *The Aspirin Age: 1919–1941* (Simon & Schuster, 1949), p. 234. I am indebted to Mr. John Dunning for access to tape recordings in his possession of several of Father Coughlin's 1937 sermons. Earlier Coughlin sermons can heard on tape recordings in the collections of the Museum of Broadcasting, New York, New York.

29. "Father Coughlin," *Fortune,* pp. 35–36; Calahan, "Hour of Power," p. 343; Carter, *American Messiahs,* pp. 38–39; Ward, *Father Charles E. Coughlin,* pp. 28–29. Estimates of the size of Coughlin's radio audience vary markedly, in large part because there is no definitive evidence to support or refute such claims. Coughlin himself claimed a regular audience of forty-five million or more. Others have speculated that the number may have been many times lower than that. See, e.g., Gary Marx, *The Social Basis of the Support of a Depression Era Extremist: Father Coughlin* (Survey Research Center, University of California, 1962), p. 119.

30. Ibid., pp. 55–59.

31. Sidney Fine, *Frank Murphy: The Detroit Years* (University of Michigan Press, 1975), pp. 201–02; Wallace Stegner, "Pattern for Demagogues," *Pacific Spectator* 2 (1948), 399; William Haber, "Fluctuations in Employment in Detroit Factories, 1921–1931," *Journal of the American Statistical Association* 27 (June 1932), 141–52; William J. Norton, "The Relief Crisis in Detroit," *Social Science Review* 7 (March 1933), 1–10; Helen Hall, "When Detroit's Out of Gear," *Survey* 17 (April 1930), 9–14, 51–54.

32. Mugglebee, *Father Coughlin,* pp. 29–30; Charles J. Tull, *Father Coughlin and the New Deal* (Syracuse University Press, 1965), p. 9.

33. Marcus, *Father Coughlin,* p. 21; Shuster, "Radio Sky Pilot," p. 124; Davis, "Father Coughlin," pp. 661–63.

34. Ward, *Father Charles E. Coughlin,* pp. 56–58.

35. Ibid., pp. 59–68.

36. Charles E. Coughlin, *By the Sweat of Thy Brow* (Radio League of the Little Flower, 1931), p. 105 and passim.

37. Ibid., pp. 23–24, 34, 63; Charles E. Coughlin, *Father Coughlin's Radio Discourses: 1931–1932* (Radio League of the Little Flower, 1932), pp. 22, 133–38, 163.

38. Coughlin, *By the Sweat of Thy Brow,* pp. 55–57, and passim; Coughlin, *Radio Discourses,* pp. 28–74, 100–17, and passim.

39. See, for example, Albert U. Romasco, *The Poverty of Abundance: Hoover, the Nation, the Depression* (Oxford University Press, 1965), chapters 2, 3, 9; Elliot A. Rosen, *Hoover, Roosevelt, and the Brains Trust: From Depression to New Deal* (Columbia University Press, 1977), chapters 3, 11; David Burner, *Herbert Hoover: A Public Life* (Alfred A. Knopf, 1978), pp. 252–59, 297–305.

40. Carlisle, "Priest of a Parish," p. 8.

41. Coughlin, *Radio Discourses,* p. 72.

42. Ibid., p. 83.

43. Ibid., pp. 189–200, 207; Coughlin, *By the Sweat of Thy Brow,* pp. 33, 52–53, 127–36.

44. Ibid., pp. 75, 84, 95–96, 118.

45. Rev. Thomas E. Boorde to Herbert Hoover, July 18, 1932, PSF 508, Herbert Hoover Presidential Library; John C. Motton to Coughlin, February 15, 1932, ibid.; "Demagogy in the Pulpit," *Literary Digest* 113 (May 7, 1932), 18; *New York Times,* May 10, 1932.

46. The network's specific complaint was about Coughlin's plan to discuss the Treaty of Versailles in a January 4, 1931, sermon. How CBS found out about the proposed discourse is not clear; Coughlin's associate and authorized biographer, Louis B. Ward, claimed that the White House tapped a telephone call between Coughlin and Congressman Louis McFadden,

whom he was consulting. See Ward, *Father Charles E. Coughlin,* pp. 83–86; "Father Coughlin," *Fortune,* p. 37; St. Louis *Post-Dispatch,* January 5, 1931.

47. Ward, *Father Charles E. Coughlin,* p. 85; Washington *Evening Star,* January 5, 1931; "Father Coughlin," *Fortune,* p. 37.

48. Philadelphia *Evening Bulletin,* January 5, 1931; St. Louis *Post-Dispatch,* January 5, 1931; "Father Coughlin," *Fortune,* p. 37; Ward, *Father Charles E. Coughlin,* p. 86; *New York Times,* January 12, 1931; Coughlin, *By the Sweat of Thy Brow,* pp. 77–89.

49. Swing, *Forerunners,* pp. 41–42; Stegner, "Radio Priest," p. 237; Geoffrey S. Smith, *To Save a Nation: American Counter-Subversives, the New Deal, and the Coming of World War II* (Basic Books, 1973), pp. 15–16.

50. Ibid., pp. 15–16; Mugglebee, *Father Coughlin,* pp. 254–55; Tull, *Father Coughlin,* p. 9; Swing, *Forerunners,* p. 42.

51. Coughlin to Station WJR, April 23, 1929, Leo Fitzpatrick MSS, University of Michigan; "Father Coughlin," *Fortune,* p. 34; Calahan, "Hour of Power," p. 343; Davis, "Father Coughlin," p. 660; Jones, "Radio Preacher," p. 883. Mail to the Hoover White House about Coughlin was relatively light, although increasing in 1931–32; only about a third was favorable to Coughlin, as, for example, Paul Husted to Hoover, November 1, 1932, PSF 508, Hoover Library.

52. Ward, *Father Charles E. Coughlin,* pp. 42–43; Swing, *Forerunners,* p. 43; William V. Shannon, *The American Irish: A Social and Political Portrait* (Macmillan, 1966), p. 299.

53. Detroit *Free Press,* July 26, 1930; Mugglebee, *Father Coughlin,* pp. 192–96; Smith, *To Save a Nation,* p. 13; David O. Powell, "The Union Party of 1936" (Ph.D. dissertation, Ohio State University, 1962), p. 7.

54. Fine, *Frank Murphy,* pp. 254–55, 435–36, 451; Coughlin to Murphy, November 4, 1931, March 18, December 22, 1932, January 5, July 26, 1934, September 5, November 13, 1935, March 13, 1936, Arthur Maguire to Murphy, March 2, 1935, Murphy to Maguire, March 5, 1935, all in Frank Murphy MSS, University of Michigan; George Murphy to Coughlin, March 6, 1933, September 9, 1933, George Murphy MSS, University of Michigan.

55. "Father Coughlin," *Fortune,* pp. 37–38; Ward, *Father Charles E. Coughlin,* p. 107; Bennett, *Demagogues,* pp. 48–49.

56. Ward, *Father Charles E. Coughlin,* pp. 83–86; Smith, *To Save a Nation,* pp. 15, 191; Davis, "Father Coughlin," p. 664.

57. *New York Times,* April 27, 1931.

58. Shannon, *American Irish,* pp. 65, 144; Oscar Handlin, *Al Smith and His America* (Atlantic Monthly Press, 1958), pp. 73, 162; Gene Fowler, *Beau James: The Life and Times of Jimmy Walker* (Viking Press, 1949), pp. 274–302.

59. *New York Times,* April 27, 1931; Mugglebee, *Father Coughlin,* pp. 238–44.

60. *New York Times,* April 27, 1931; New York *Herald Tribune,* April 27, 1931.

61. Mugglebee, *Father Coughlin,* pp. 267–68; Davis, "Father Coughlin," p. 663; Detroit *Free Press,* October 12, 1931.

62. Ibid.; Mugglebee, *Father Coughlin,* p. 266.

Chapter 5

1. G. Hall Roosevelt to Franklin D. Roosevelt, May 5, 1931, Governor's Personal File 147, FDRL; Charles J. Tull, *Father Coughlin and the New Deal* (Syracuse University Press, 1965), p. 14.

2. Frank Freidel, *Franklin D. Roosevelt: The Triumph* (Little, Brown, 1956), p. 285;

Roosevelt to Charles E. Coughlin, July 29, 1932, in Elliott Roosevelt, ed., *F.D.R.: His Personal Letters* (Duell, Sloan and Pearce, 1950), I, 292.

3. *New York Times,* April 13, June 10, August 19, 1932; H. C. Batten to Herbert Hoover, July 31, 1932, PSF 508, Hoover Presidential Library; Tull, *Father Coughlin,* p. 45.

4. David S. Burner, *The Politics of Provincialism: The Democratic Party in Transition, 1918–1932* (Alfred A. Knopf, 1967), pp. 244–52; Roosevelt to Coughlin, July 29, August 21, 1932, in E. Roosevelt, ed., *Letters,* I, 292–93; Raymond Moley, *27 Masters of Politics in a Personal Perspective* (Funk & Wagnalls, 1949), pp. 208–11.

5. Tull, *Father Coughlin,* p. 18; Charles E. Coughlin, *Eight Discourses on the Gold Standard and Other Kindred Subjects* (Radio League of the Little Flower, 1933), pp. 45–64; Paul Husted to Herbert Hoover, November 1, 1932, PSF 508, Hoover Presidential Library; George Murphy to Coughlin, March 6, 1933, George Murphy MSS, University of Michigan.

6. Arthur M. Schlesinger, Jr., *The Politics of Upheaval* (Houghton Mifflin, 1960), p. 23; Charles E. Coughlin, *Driving Out the Money Changers* (Radio League of the Little Flower, 1933), p. 85.

7. Ibid., pp. 80, 85.

8. Coughlin to Marvin McIntyre, November 14, 1933, OF 306, FDRL; Coughlin to Roosevelt, October 23, 1933, ibid.; Coughlin to McIntyre, March 13, 1933, PSF 800B, FDRL.

9. Rexford G. Tugwell, *The Democratic Roosevelt* (Doubleday, 1957), pp. 349–50; Tull, *Father Coughlin,* p. 22.

10. Coughlin to McIntyre, November 14, 21, 1933, OF 306, FDRL; George Q. Flynn, *American Catholics and the Roosevelt Presidency, 1932–1936* (University of Kentucky Press, 1968), p. 48; "The Reminiscences of Henry Wallace," Oral History Project, Columbia University, pp. 192–94; McIntyre to Louis Howe, March 27, 1933, OF 306, FDRL.

11. Roosevelt wrote on one Coughlin wire, for example: "Mac—Prep. nice letter." Coughlin to Roosevelt, October 4, 1933, PSF 229, FDRL; Wrigley to W. W. Chaplin, November 28, 1933, OF 306, FDRL; McIntyre to Coughlin, n.d., 1933, PPF 2338, FDRL.

12. Coughlin, *Driving Out the Money Changers,* pp. 25, 43.

13. Coughlin, *Eight Discourses,* pp. 7, 13–19, 20, 30.

14. Frank Freidel, *Franklin D. Roosevelt: Launching the New Deal* (Little, Brown, 1973), pp. 320–39; Arthur M. Schlesinger, Jr., *The Coming of the New Deal* (Houghton Mifflin, 1958), pp. 238–42; Coughlin, *Driving Out the Money Changers,* pp. 74–79; Coughlin to Roosevelt, October 23, 1933, OF 306, FDRL.

15. Charles E. Coughlin, *The New Deal in Money* (Radio League of the Little Flower, 1933), pp. 38–52; James MacGregor Burns, *Roosevelt: The Lion and the Fox* (Harcourt, Brace, 1956), pp. 189–90; Freidel, *Launching the New Deal,* pp. 323–25, 337.

16. Coughlin, *New Deal,* pp. 43–52, 110–19; Coughlin, *Eight Lectures on Labor, Capital and Justice* (Radio League of the Little Flower, 1934), pp. 24–25, 111–14.

17. Schlesinger, *Coming of the New Deal,* pp. 248–52; Freidel, *Launching the New Deal,* pp. 323–25; Coughlin, *A Series of Lectures on Social Justice* (Radio League of the Little Flower, 1935), pp. 16–19.

18. Ibid., pp. 164, 166–75.

19. Ibid., pp. 162, 171–72.

20. Coughlin, *Eight Lectures,* p. 114; Baltimore *Sun,* March 13, 1935; Coughlin, *Eight Discourses,* p. 34.

21. Joseph F. Scheuer to Coughlin, October 31, 1933, OF 306, FDRL.

22. "Gentile Silver," *Nation* 138 (1934), 522.

23. Milton Friedman and Anna Jacobson Schwartz claimed in their "definitive" 1963

study of the "Great Contraction" that the shortsighted policies and subsequent collapse of the banking establishment were the most important immediate cause of the crisis. See Friedman and Schwartz, *A Monetary History of the United States, 1867–1960* (Princeton University Press, 1963), pp. 299–419. More recently, Peter Temin has disagreed, arguing that "it is more plausible to believe that the Depression was the result of a drop in autonomous expenditures, particularly consumption, than the result of autonomous bank failures." See Peter Temin, *Did Monetary Forces Cause the Great Depression?* (W. W. Norton, 1976), pp. 14–31, 178.

24. Coughlin to Roosevelt, July 21, October 4, 1933, OF 306, FDRL; Coughlin, *New Deal*, pp. 20, 37–38.

25. C. T. Kern to William Cardinal O'Connell, April 3, 1933, OF 306, FDRL; H. G. Wengert to Roosevelt, November 5, 1933, ibid.; C. C. Savers to Roosevelt, November 21, 1933, ibid.

26. Susan Estabrook Kennedy, "The Michigan Banking Crisis of 1933," *Michigan History* 17 (1973), 240–43.

27. Ibid.; "Father Coughlin," *Fortune* 9 (February 1934), 31; Sidney Fine, *Frank Murphy: The Detroit Years* (University of Michigan Press, 1975), pp. 373–75, 379–80.

28. Ibid., p. 374.

29. Kennedy, "Michigan Banking Crisis," pp. 240–43; "Memorandum" to McIntyre, March 23, 1933, PPF 2338, FDRL; Stephen Early to Homer Cummings, March 23, 1933, ibid.; McIntyre to Howe, March 27, 1933, OF 306, FDRL; Detroit *Free Press*, March 24, 1933.

30. Ibid., March 27, 1933.

31. *New York Times*, April 2, 1933; Detroit *Free Press*, March 28, 29, 30, April 3, 1933; *Rocky Mountain News*, March 17, 1935; Edgar DeWitt Jones, "Father Coughlin Flays Bankers," *Christian Century* 50 (1933), 468; Jones, "Paper Threatens Radio Priest," ibid., pp. 507–08; Angus McLean to McIntyre, March 27, 1933, PPF 2338, FDRL.

32. Fine, *Frank Murphy*, p. 375; Paul Rieker to Roosevelt, March 30, 1933, OF 306, FDRL; Tull, *Father Coughlin*, p. 29.

33. McIntyre to Louis Howe, March 27, 1933, OF 306, FDRL.

34. *New York Times*, August 14, 1933; Detroit *News*, August 23, 1933; Detroit *Free Press*, August 24, 25, 1933; J. Walter Drake to Hoover, August 30, 1933, Hoover Presidential Library; Hoover to Drake, September 4, 1933, ibid.

35. Schlesinger, *Politics of Upheaval*, p. 20; "Memorandum re Reverend Charles E. Coughlin's Special Network," OF 306, FDRL.

36. Marquis W. Childs, "Father Coughlin: A Success Story of the Depression," *New Republic* 78 (1934), 326–27; Francis Rufus Bellamy, "Priest of the Air," n.p., n.d., 1934, p. 17, Raymond Clapper MSS, Library of Congress; W. L. Slattery to James A. Farley, March 19, 1935, OF 306, FDRL.

37. *New York Times*, February 25, November 29, 1934; Coughlin to Carl M. Weideman, January 3, 1934, Weideman MSS, University of Michigan; Bellamy, "Priest of the Air," pp. 17–21.

38. OF 306, FDRL; handbill, November 27, 1933, Elmer Thomas MSS, University of Oklahoma; New York *Herald Tribune*, November 28, 1933; New York *Daily News*, November 29, 1933; *New York Times*, November 27, 1933; "Coughlin: Radio Priest Makes New Yorkers Hiss Their Hero," *Newsweek*, December 12, 1933, p. 32; "Dangers of Demagogy," *Commonweal* 19 (1933), 144; "Father Coughlin and Ex-Governor Smith," *Christian Century* 50 (1933), 1564; Eddie Dowling to Marguerite Lehand, November 29, 1933, PPF 827, FDRL.

39. "Reminiscences of Henry Wallace," pp. 194–95; Elmer Thomas to Coughlin, December 7, 1933, Thomas MSS; "The Reminiscences of James Warburg," Oral History Project,

Columbia University, pp. 500–01; Burton K. Wheeler, *Yankee from the West* (Doubleday, 1962), pp. 302–03; "The Reminiscences of Burton K. Wheeler," Oral History Project, Columbia University, pp. 20–21; William Borah to Coughlin, January 30, 1935, Borah MSS, Library of Congress; Washington *Evening Star,* March 8, 1935; Bronson Cutting to H. Phelps Putnam, April 22, 1934, Cutting MSS, Library of Congress; Elmer Thomas et al. to Roosevelt, June 9, 1933, OF 17, FDRL; Carl M. Weidman to Roosevelt, June 10, 1933, ibid.; *New York Times,* June 15, 1933; letters in OF 21-A, "Coughlin," FDRL.

40. Boston *Globe,* August 13, 1935; Charles H. Trout, *Boston: The Great Depression and the New Deal* (Oxford University Press, 1977), p. 289.

41. Coughlin to Howard Y. Williams, June 22, 1933, H. Y. Williams MSS, Minnesota Historical Society; Henry Wallace to J. H. Sexton, November 19, 1932, Wallace MSS, University of Iowa; Wallace to F. A. Pearson, January 4, 1956, ibid.; *New York Times,* January 5, 1934, September 14–15, 1935.

42. John M. Carlisle, "Priest of a Parish of the Air Waves," *New York Times Magazine,* October 29, 1933, p. 8; letter to editor from H. M. Berg, February 28, 1935, *Nation* 140 (1935), 333.

Chapter 6

1. Memorandum to Marvin McIntyre re Coughlin telephone call, November 24, 1933, OF 306, FDRL; Sheldon Marcus, *Father Coughlin: The Tumultuous Life of the Priest of the Little Flower* (Little, Brown, 1973), p. 60.

2. *New York Times,* April 29, 1934.

3. Ibid.; "Gentile Silver," *Nation* 138 (1934), 522; John L. Spivak, *Shrine of the Silver Dollar* (Modern Age Books, 1940), passim; Marcus, *Father Coughlin,* p. 70.

4. James P. Shenton, "The Coughlin Movement and the New Deal," *Political Science Quarterly* 73 (1958), 355–63.

5. Open letter to Martin S. Sweeney, in Cleveland *News,* January 20, 1934; *New York Times,* March 5, 1934.

6. Charles E. Coughlin, *Eight Discourses on the Gold Standard and Kindred Subjects* (Radio League of the Little Flower, 1933), passim; Coughlin, *Eight Lectures on Labor, Capital and Justice* (Radio League of the Little Flower, 1934), passim.

7. *New York Times,* November 12, 1934; Charles E. Coughlin, *A Series of Lectures on Social Justice* (Radio League of the Little Flower, 1935), pp. 8, 13; David Owen Powell, "The Union Party of 1936" (Ph.D. dissertation, Ohio State University, 1962), p. 21.

8. Coughlin to McIntyre, September 10, 1934, OF 306, FDRL; Roosevelt to the Assistant Secretary of the Navy, September 10, 1934, ibid.; McIntyre to Stephen Early, October 4, 1934, ibid.; *New York Times,* October 12, 1934; Arthur M. Schlesinger, Jr., *The Politics of Upheaval* (Houghton Mifflin, 1960), p. 24.

9. New York *Daily News,* March 5, 1934; *New York Times,* November 26, 1934; Coughlin, *Series,* pp. 34, 44.

10. "Reverend Charles E. Coughlin's special network," Memorandum, June 28, 1934, OF 306, FDRL; W. L. Slattery to James A. Farley, March 19, 1935, ibid.; Farley to Roosevelt, March 19, 1935, ibid.; D. W. McCormack to Louis Howe, January 22, 1934, ibid.

11. Detroit *News,* April 23, 1935.

12. New York *Daily News,* May 22, 1935; Charles J. Tull, *Father Coughlin and the New Deal* (Syracuse University Press, 1965), p. 235; "Our Forum," *Commonweal* 22 (April 26, 1935),

735; Father Tiernan to Roosevelt, April 24, 1935, OF 306, FDRL; *New York Times,* May 21, 1935.

13. "Father Coughlin Talks Back to a Cardinal," *Christian Century* 51 (1934), 1645; Tull, *Father Coughlin,* p. 15; *New York Times,* December 4, 1933; "Canonist vs. Coughlin," *Literary Digest* 120 (July 6, 1935), 23.

14. David J. O'Brien, *American Catholics and Social Reform: The New Deal Years* (Oxford University Press, 1968), pp. 17–21; Pius XI, *Quadragesimo Anno / Forty Years After on Reconstructing Social Order* (Benziger Brothers, 1943), pp. 20–24 and passim.

15. Coughlin to McIntyre, March 21, 1934, OF 306, FDRL; Coughlin to Roosevelt, March 21, 1934, ibid.; "Vatican Voices," *Time,* August 17, 1936, p. 30; Neil Betten, "Catholic Periodicals in Response to Two Divergent Decades," *Journalism Quarterly* 47 (1970), 303–08; *Catholic Worker,* May 1935, HLS.

16. George Q. Flynn, *American Catholics and the Roosevelt Presidency* (University of Kentucky Press, 1968), pp. 26–27, 30–31.

17. Irving Bernstein, *The Lean Years: A History of the American Worker, 1920–1933* (Houghton Mifflin, 1960), p. 432.

18. Flynn, *American Catholics,* pp. 37–38, 42.

19. O'Brien, *American Catholics,* pp. 120–49; "Three Priests Preach the Gospel of Social Justice," *Literary Digest* 116 (December 23, 1933), 21; *New York Times,* December 5, 1933; Raymond Gram Swing, "The Build-Up of Long and Coughlin," *Nation* 140 (March 20, 1935), 325–26. Father A. J. Hogan, president of Fordham University and another leading Catholic intellectual, remarked at about the same time that Ryan and Coughlin together had "prepared the way for acceptance of the New Deal by Catholics" by familiarizing the public with the encyclicals; Flynn, *American Catholics,* p. 45.

20. "Putting the Church in Her Place," *Commonweal* 21 (1935), 635; "Father Coughlin's Authority," ibid., 22 (1935), 113.

21. David Carl Colony, "Dictator Coughlin: Fascism Under the Cross," *Forum* 93 (1935), 196–201; "Our Rostrum," ibid. (May 1935), ix; ibid. (June 1935), xix.

22. St. Louis *Post-Dispatch,* December 10, 1934; *New York Times,* December 10, 1934; "Father Coughlin Talks Back," p. 1645.

23. Des Moines *Register,* April 22, 1935.

24. *Rocky Mountain News,* March 21, 1935; Flynn, *American Catholics,* p. 216.

25. Detroit *Free Press,* March 30, 1933; "Communications," *Commonweal* 21 (April 5, 1935), 656; *New York Times,* January 23, 1934.

26. Detroit *Free Press,* November 12, 1934; Coughlin, *Series,* p. 16.

27. Ibid., p. 22.

28. Ibid., pp. 109, 121, 199, 230; A. B. Magil, "Can Father Coughlin Come Back?," *New Republic* 87 (June 24, 1936), 197–98.

29. Geoffrey S. Smith, *To Save a Nation: American Counter-Subversives, the New Deal, and the Coming of World War II* (Basic Books, 1973), pp. 30–31.

30. Cordell Hull, *The Memoirs of Cordell Hull* (Macmillan, 1948), I, 389.

31. *New York Times,* January 21, 1935.

32. Coughlin, *Series,* pp. 122–36.

33. *New York Times,* January 28, 29, 1935; Herbert O'Brien to Louis Howe, January 28, 1935, OF 306, FDRL; A. D. Linch to George W. Norris, January 20, 1935, Norris MSS, Library of Congress.

34. Harold L. Ickes, *The Secret Diary of Harold L. Ickes: The First Thousand Days, 1933–1936* (Simon & Schuster, 1953), pp. 284–85; Roosevelt to Joseph T. Robinson, January

30, 1935, in Elliott Roosevelt, ed., *F.D.R.: His Personal Letters* (Duell, Sloan and Pearce, 1950), I, 450.

35. *New York Times,* January 29, 31, May 15, 1935; U.S. Congress, *Congressional Record,* 74th Congress, 1st Session (January 17, 1935), pp. 563–78; *People's Voice* (Cincinnati), February 1, 1935, HLS; W. A. Swanberg, *Citizen Hearst* (Charles Scribner's Sons, 1961), pp. 445–61, 473.

36. Roosevelt to Elihu Root, February 9, 1935, in E. Roosevelt, ed., *Letters,* I, 45; Tom Connally, *My Name Is Tom Connally* (Thomas Y. Crowell, 1954), p. 211; *New York Times,* January 30, February 3, 1935.

37. Ibid., January 30, 1935; Coughlin, *Series,* pp. 137–38.

38. Ibid., p. 140.

39. Chicago *Tribune,* March 6, 1935; Philadelphia *Evening Bulletin,* March 7, 1935; Coughlin, *Series,* p. 178.

40. Washington *Evening Star,* March 8, 1935; *New York Times,* March 18, May 20, 1935.

41. Schlesinger, *Politics of Upheaval,* pp. 10–11; St. Louis *Post-Dispatch,* May 6, 1935; *New York Times,* May 13, 1935.

42. Ibid., January 14, June 10, 1935; St. Louis *Post-Dispatch,* March 1, 1935; Ickes, *Secret Diary,* pp. 536–37.

43. T.R.B., "Washington Notes," *New Republic* 84 (August 21, 1935), 46.

44. Ibid.; Magil, "Can Father Coughlin Come Back?," pp. 197–98; *New York Times,* July 30, 1935.

45. Irving Bernstein, *Turbulent Years: A History of the American Worker, 1933–1941* (Houghton Mifflin, 1969), pp. 503–04; "The Reminiscences of R. J. Thomas," Oral History Project, Columbia University, II, 1–3; Peter Friedlander, *The Emergence of a UAW Local, 1936–1939* (University of Pittsburgh Press, 1975), p. 115; Alexander Cook, United Auto Workers Oral History, Wayne State University, p. 40; Richard Harris, ibid., pp. 13–14; John W. Anderson, ibid., pp. 30–31, 80; "President Frankensteen Appeals for Unity Giving Reasons and Facts," n.d., Harry Ross MSS, Wayne State University.

46. Detroit *Free Press,* April 25, 1935; *New York Times,* July 1, September 2, 1935; *The Progressive,* September 14, 1935; "First Year Book and History of the A.I.W.A.," December 14, 1935, Harry Ross MSS; "Reminiscences of R. J. Thomas," I, 33; Richard Frankensteen, UAW Oral History, p. 15; Mort Furay, ibid., p. 13; Joseph Hattley, ibid., pp. 9–10; Richard Harris, ibid., pp. 13–14; Alexander Cook, ibid., p. 40; John A. Zaremba, ibid., pp. 14–15; Neil Betten, *Catholic Activism and the Industrial Worker* (University Presses of Florida, 1976), pp. 90–99.

47. "First Year Book and History of the A.I.W.A.," Ross MSS; Betten, *Catholic Activism,* pp. 92–99; Friedlander, *Emergence,* p. 115; Richard Frankensteen, UAW Oral History, p. 15; Adam Poplawski, ibid., p. 6; Carl Haessler, ibid., pp. 5, 29; Michael J. Manning, ibid., pp. 23–24; Bernstein, *Turbulent Years,* pp. 503–04.

48. *Progressive,* September 14, 1935.

49. *New York Times,* May 6, June 14, 1935; Walter Davenport, "The Shepherd of Discontent," *Collier's* 95 (May 4, 1935), 60.

50. Boston *Evening Globe,* August 13, 1935; *New York Times,* October 17, November 4, 1935.

51. Magil, "Can Father Coughlin Come Back?," pp. 197–98; *New York Times,* June 14, 1935.

Chapter 7

1. See Max Weber, "The Sociology of Charismatic Authority," in H. H. Gerth and C. Wright Mills, eds., *From Max Weber* (Oxford University Press, 1946), p. 246.

2. Thomas Bender, among others, has offered a definition of community as "a social network characterized by a distinctive kind of human interaction," a definition that challenges the more conventional, specifically territorial image of community. Bender, *Community and Social Change in America* (Rutgers University Press, 1978), pp. 10–11.

3. Charles E. Coughlin, *A Series of Lectures on Social Justice* (Radio League of the Little Flower, 1935), pp. 30, 109; U.S. Congress, *Congressional Record,* 73rd Congress, 2nd Session (March 5, 1934), p. 3694; Coughlin, *By the Sweat of Thy Brow* (Radio League of the Little Flower, 1931), p. 26; Coughlin, *Eight Discourses on the Gold Standard and Other Kindred Subjects* (Radio League of the Little Flower, 1933), p. 43.

4. Long radio addresses, January 19, 1935, and n.d., 1935, in *Congr. Record,* 74:1 (January 14, 23, 1935), pp. 411, 792; Charles E. Coughlin, *Father Coughlin's Radio Discourses* (Radio League of the Little Flower, 1932), pp. 31–32, 230; Coughlin, *Eight Discourses,* p. 14; Coughlin, *Series,* p. 189; Coughlin, *Eight Lectures on Labor, Capital and Justice* (Radio League of the Little Flower, 1934), pp. 117–21.

5. Coughlin, *Radio Discourses,* p. 171; *American Progress,* August 10, 1933; Coughlin, *By the Sweat of Thy Brow,* p. 95.

6. Coughlin, *Series,* p. 185; *Social Justice,* March 13, 1946; F. N. Olry to Coughlin, February 18, 1935, OF 306, FDRL; Bazz Hitt, Jr., "Why Huey Long Should Be President," pamphlet, 1935, in William B. Wisdom Collection of Huey P. Long, Tulane University, New Orleans, pp. 13–14; *American Progress,* May 1935.

7. *Congr. Record,* 73:1 (May 12, 1933), p. 3321; ibid., 72:1 (March 21, 1932), p. 6541. The crucial role of the local merchant in the community was particularly evident in the post-bellum South, where, according to Thomas D. Clark, "His store was the hub of the local universe." See Roger L. Ransom and Richard Sutch, *One Kind of Freedom: The Economic Consequences of Emancipation* (Cambridge University Press, 1977), pp. 126–46; and Clark, *Pills, Petticoats, and Plows: The Southern Country Store* (Bobbs-Merrill, 1944), pp. vii–viii and passim. A more general description of how modern retailing affected the community store and the decline of "local man" appears in Daniel J. Boorstin, *The Americans: The Democratic Experience* (Random House, 1973), pp. 109–12.

8. Federal Writers' Project, *These Are Our Lives* (University of North Carolina Press, 1939), p. 285; Arthur J. Vidich and Joseph Bensman, *Small Town in Mass Society* (Princeton University Press, 1968), pp. 89–92; A. Mathis to Long, January 19, 1935, HLS; *Social Justice,* April 17, May 8, 1936.

9. Robert S. Lynd and Helen Merrell Lynd, *Middletown* (Harcourt, Brace, 1929), pp. 62–63; *American Progress,* August 31, 1933.

10. Lynd, *Middletown,* pp. 46–47; Federal Writers' Project, *These Are Our Lives,* pp. 285–86.

11. Robert S. Lynd and Helen Merrell Lynd, *Middletown in Transition* (Harcourt, Brace, 1937), pp. 70–71; *Social Justice,* May 8, 1936.

12. *Social Justice,* May 8, 1936.

13. Coughlin, *The New Deal in Money* (Radio League of the Little Flower, 1933), pp. 68–69, 71; Coughlin, *Series,* p. 73.

14. *American Progress,* March 29, 1934, January 4, 1935; "A Letter from Uncle Trusty," circular, 1932, Wisdom Collection.

15. *American Progress,* August 24, 1933; *Congr. Record,* 72:1 (May 24, 1932), p. 10981.

16. Hodding Carter, "How Come Huey Long? 1. Bogeyman—," *New Republic* 82 (February 13, 1935), 11.

17. *American Progress,* August 10, 1933; Coughlin, *By the Sweat of Thy Brow,* p. 95; Coughlin, *Eight Lectures,* pp. 131–32; Akron *Beacon-Journal,* n.d., HLS.

18. Coughlin, *New Deal,* pp. 39–40; Coughlin, *Radio Discourses,* pp. 162–66; Coughlin, *Driving Out the Money Changers* (Radio League of the Little Flower, 1933), pp. 39–40, 62; Coughlin, *Series,* pp. 75–76.

19. *American Progress,* September 21, October 5, 1933, January 25, February 15, 1934, April 1935; Coughlin, *Driving Out the Money Changers,* pp. 62–63; *Congr. Record,* 74:1 (January 17, 1935), p. 575; *New York Times,* May 15, 1935.

20. *American Progress,* December 14, 1933, March 29, 1935; Jennie M. Taylor to H. V. Kaltenborn [February 2, 1935], H. V. Kaltenborn MSS, State Historical Society of Wisconsin; Detroit *News,* April 28, 1935.

21. Coughlin, *By the Sweat of Thy Brow,* pp. 50, 53, 78–81; *Congr. Record,* 74:1 (January 17, 1935), p. 565; ibid., 73:2 (February 28, 1934), p. 3375; Coughlin, *Driving Out the Money Changers,* pp. 69–70; Coughlin, *Radio Discourses,* pp. 229–30.

22. J. H. Connery to Long, n.d., 1935, HLS; "A Hartford Listener" to H. V. Kaltenborn [March 21, 1935], Kaltenborn MSS.

23. Coughlin, *Eight Discourses,* pp. 57–64; Long radio address, March 17, 1933, in *Congr. Record,* 73:1 (March 23, 1933), p. 787; ibid., 73:2 (March 5, 1934), p. 3694; Coughlin, *By the Sweat of Thy Brow,* p. 33; Coughlin, *Driving Out the Money Changers,* pp. 71–72; Long radio address, March 17, 1933, in *Congr. Record,* 73:1 (March 23, 1933), p. 787; ibid., 72:2 (January 23, 1933), pp. 2263–64; Coughlin, *New Deal,* pp. 25–27; *New York Times,* February 4, 1935; *Congr. Record,* 72:1 (July 6, March 18, 1932), pp. 14650, 6452; *American Progress,* September 14, 1932; Coughlin, *New Deal,* p. 24.

24. *Congr. Record,* 73:1 (March 30, 1933), p. 1020; ibid., 74:1 (January 7, 1935), p. 158; Coughlin, *Eight Lectures,* pp. 13, 48; Coughlin, *New Deal,* pp. 70–71; *American Progress,* January 4, 1934; David N. C. Astenius to Harold Ickes, May 4, 1933, Ickes MSS, Library of Congress.

25. For detailed descriptions of the specific economic proposals of Long and Coughlin, see chapter 3 (Long) and chapter 5 (Coughlin).

26. Coughlin, *Radio Discourses,* p. 182; *Social Justice,* April 17, 1936; Long radio address, July (n.d.) 1935, in *Congr. Record,* 74:1 (July 22, 1935), p. 11517; Hitt, "Why Huey Long," p. 7.

27. Long radio address, May 7, 1935, in *Congr. Record,* 74:1 (March 12, 1935), p. 3437; *New York Times,* February 11, 1935.

28. H. W. Strong to Harold Ickes, April 17, 1935, Ickes MSS; Howard Wilson to Roosevelt, OF 1403 FDRL; *American Progress,* October 5, 1933.

29. Ibid., September 7, 1933, May 1935; Coughlin, *By the Sweat of Thy Brow,* p. 103; "A Constitutionalist" to Josiah Bailey, April 26, 1935, Bailey MSS, Duke University. Long, of course, had personal reasons to fear such changes. The expansion of federal programs threatened his own hegemony in Louisiana.

30. Robert Wiebe has discussed the movement of American society from a locally based culture to a nationally oriented one in two works: *The Search for Order, 1877–1920* (Hill and Wang, 1967), an overview of the period, and *The Segmented Society: An Introduction to the*

Meaning of America (Oxford University Press, 1975), a more theoretical discussion. Community studies that illuminate the transformation include Lynd *Middletown* and *Middletown in Transition,* and Vidich and Bensman, *Small Town in Mass Society* (which uses the vantage point of the 1950s). Maurice R. Stein, *The Eclipse of Community: An Interpretation of American Studies* (Princeton University Press, 1960) is a critical examination of community studies. Bender, *Community and Social Change in America* proposes a theoretical structure for the study of community. See also James Turner, "Understanding the Populists," *Journal of American History* 67 (1980), 370–73.

31. The development of the modern corporation receives brilliant examination in two works by Alfred D. Chandler, Jr.: *The Visible Hand: The Managerial Revolution in American Business* (Harvard University Press, 1977), and *Strategy and Structure: Chapters in the History of the American Industrial Enterprise* (M.I.T. Press, 1962).

32. Louis Galambos, *The Public Image of Big Business in America, 1880–1940* (Johns Hopkins University Press, 1975), argues that public attitudes toward the corporate culture underwent a gradual process of accommodation in the first four decades of the twentieth century, so that by 1940 resistance to consolidation had dramatically declined. He does, however, record a sharp if temporary rise in animosity in the first years of the Depression; see pp. 222–49.

33. *Social Justice,* March 27, 1936; Coughlin, *By the Sweat of Thy Brow,* p. 12; Long radio address, May 11, 1935, in *Congr. Record,* 74:1 (May 23, 1935), pp. 8039–43.

34. Coughlin, *By the Sweat of Thy Brow,* p. 37; Huey Pierce Long, *My First Days in the White House* (Telegraph Press, 1935), pp. 95–99.

35. Federal Writers' Project, *These Are Our Lives,* pp. 284–85.

36. Lynd, *Middletown,* pp. 46–47, discusses the increasing availability of credit in the 1920s. Ransom and Sutch, *One Kind of Freedom,* pp. 127–31, illustrates the tyrannical possibilities of a local credit monopoly.

37. Huey P. Long, *Every Man a King* (National Book Company, 1933), pp. 23–25; see chapter 6 for a discussion of the Detroit banking controversy.

38. Bernard Bailyn, *The Ideological Origins of the American Revolution* (Harvard University Press, 1967) is one of many studies to illustrate the importance of fears of concentrated power as a source of revolutionary fervor; see esp. chapter 4 and "A Note on Conspiracy," pp. 144–58. Leonard L. Richards, *"Gentlemen of Property and Standing"* (New York: Oxford University Press, 1970) discusses the uneasiness about centralization and standardization that pervaded the Jacksonian era; and Eric Foner, *Politics and Ideology in the Age of the Civil War* (Oxford University Press, 1980) examines the continuing influence of republicanism in the mid-nineteenth century; see esp. pp. 10–11, 57–76. Foner explores the early development of that concept in *Tom Paine and Revolutionary America* (Oxford University Press, 1976); he describes the growth of the ideology of the Republican Party in *Free Soil, Free Labor, Free Men* (Oxford University Press, 1970). On anti-Masonry and anti-Catholicism, see David Brion Davis, "Some Themes of Counter-Subversion: An Analysis of Anti-Masonic, Anti-Catholic, and Anti-Mormon Literature," *Mississippi Valley Historical Review* 47 (1960), 205–24.

39. Forrest Davis, *Huey Long: A Candid Biography* (Dodge Publishing Company, 1935), p. 22; Coughlin, *New Deal,* p. 107; Coughlin, *Eight Discourses,* pp. 175, 198; Coughlin, *Driving Out the Money Changers,* p. 73.

40. See Neil Betten, *Catholic Activism and the Industrial Worker* (University Presses of Florida, 1976), pp. 4–16; Thomas N. Brown, *Irish-American Nationalism* (J. B. Lippincott, 1966), pp. 52–54.

41. William Ivy Hair, *Bourbonism and Agrarian Protest: Louisiana Politics, 1877–1900* (Louisiana State University Press, 1969) discusses the rise of populism in Long's native Winn Parish, pp. 205–25. For a discussion of the links between populism and agrarian socialism, see James R. Green, *Grass-Roots Socialism: Radical Movements in the Southwest, 1895–1943* (Louisiana State University Press, 1978), esp. pp. 12–52, 79–86.

42. William H. Harvey, *Coin's Financial School* (1894; reprint ed., Harvard University Press, John Harvard Library, 1963), p. 215; Ignatius Donnelly, *Caesar's Column* (1890; reprint ed., Harvard University Press, John Harvard Library, 1960), p. 109.

43. George B. Tindall, ed., *A Populist Reader* (Harper & Row, 1966), pp. 90–91; Norman Pollack, ed., *The Populist Mind* (Bobbs-Merrill, 1969) p. 327; Richard Hofstadter, *The Age of Reform* (Alfred A. Knopf, 1954), pp. 66, 74–75.

44. "The People's Party Platform of 1892," in Tindall, ed., *Populist Reader,* pp. 90–91; Donnelly, *Caesar's Column,* p. 112.

45. It would be a mistake to exaggerate the differences between Southern and Western populism, or to attribute to them a rigidity and uniformity that did not exist. Many Western populists shared the views of their most radical Southern counterparts; and some Southern parties—notably those in North Carolina and Alabama—began quite early to emphasize the "money question" over the movement's broader demands. To compare the South and the Midwest is to compare emphases, not distinct ideologies. See Lawrence Goodwyn, *Democratic Promise: The Populist Moment in America* (Oxford University Press, 1976), pp. 87–107, 582–921, and Bruce Palmer, *"Man Over Money": The Southern Populist Critique of American Capitalism* (University of North Carolina Press, 1980), pp. xviii, 81–95, 126–37, 199–221. Richard Jensen, *The Winning of the Midwest: Social and Political Conflict, 1888–96* (University of Chicago Press, 1971) examines the background of Western populism; see esp. pp. 178–237, 269–308. Robert C. McMath, Jr., *Populist Vanguard: A History of the Southern Farmers' Alliance* (University of North Carolina Press, 1975) discusses the origins of Southern populism and its decline after its alliance with the West; see pp. 110–57.

46. McMath, *Populist Vanguard,* p. 74; Pollack, ed., *Populist Mind,* p. 19. Turner, "Understanding the Populists," discusses "isolation" as a cause of populist discontent; Turner refers primarily to geographical isolation, but he suggests ways in which perceived cultural isolation played a role in spawning resentments.

47. J. P. Stern has discussed the importance of familiarity to the appeal of a political message in a study of the popularity of Adolf Hitler; the effect of Hitler's speeches, he argues, depended "on an all but complete foreknowledge of their informational content." Stern, *Hitler: The Führer and the People* (Fontana/Collins, 1975), p. 37.

48. Tindall, ed., *Populist Reader,* p. 30; McMath, *Populist Vanguard,* p. 35.

49. Ibid., pp. 10–32, 48–76; Goodwyn, *Democratic Promise,* pp. 109–243 and passim.

50. Long, *My First Days,* pp. 93–115.

51. Coughlin, *Series,* p. 178; Chicago *Tribune,* March 6, 1935.

52. Goodwyn, *Democratic Promise,* pp. 544–45; George B. Tindall, *The Emergence of the New South, 1913–1945* (Louisiana State University Press, 1967), pp. 111–42, 391–432; United States National Emergency Council, *Report on Conditions of the South* (1938; reprint ed., Da Capo Press, 1972), pp. 37–52 and passim; T. B. Manny, "The Conditions of Rural Life," in William F. Ogburn, ed., *Social Changes During Depression and Recovery* (University of Chicago Press, 1935), pp. 720–28.

Chapter 8

1. Ernest G. Bormann, "A Rhetorical Analysis of the National Radio Broadcasts of Senator Huey P. Long" (Ph.D. dissertation, State University of Iowa, 1953), pp. 9, 11–12, 40–41, 283, 427; Washington *Sunday Star,* January 20, 1935; Raymond Gram Swing, "The Menace of Huey Long: III. His Bid for National Power," *Nation* 140 (1935), 98; stenographic copy of Long radio address, January 9, 1935, Huey Long MSS, LSU; Des Moines *Register,* March 11, 1935.

2. Atlanta *Journal,* February 5, 1935; Atlanta *Constitution,* February 6, 1935; *New York Times,* January 30, February 5, 15, 1935; Topeka *Daily Capital,* February 9, 1935; Arkansas *Gazette,* February 10, 1935; Philadelphia *Evening Bulletin,* March 14, 15, 1935; Philadelphia *Inquirer,* March 15, 1935; T. Harry Williams interview with Theophile Landry, July 10, 1957, T. H. Williams MSS, LSU; Michael F. Doyle to James A. Farley, OF 1403, FDRL.

3. Columbia *State,* March 15, 23, 24, 1935; William C. Grace to Stephen Early, March 27, 1935, OF 1403, FDRL.

4. Des Moines *Register,* April 28, 1935; Lester P. Barlow to Alfred N. Phillips, n.d., 1935, T. H. Williams MSS; Phillips to Barlow, June 20, 1935, ibid.; Barlow to Phillips, June 21, 1935, ibid.; Phillips to Roosevelt, July 12, 1935, PPF 2666, FDRL.

5. Barlow to T. Harry Williams, April 23, 1963, T. H. Williams MSS; unidentified clipping, June 20, 1935, HLS; *National E.P.I.A. News,* April 5, 1935, HLS; *Daily Oklahoman,* September 1, 1935; Los Angeles *Daily News,* April 4, 1935, HLS.

6. David Owen Powell, "The Union Party of 1936" (Ph.D. dissertation, Ohio State University, 1962), p. 46; David H. Bennett, *Demagogues in the Depression: American Radicals and the Union Party, 1932–1936* (Rutgers University Press, 1969), pp. 114–15. I am indebted to Glen Jeansonne for sharing with me some of the results of his research for an as yet unpublished biography of Gerald L. K. Smith.

7. Bennett, *Demagogues,* p. 116; Harnett T. Kane, *Louisiana Hayride: The American Rehearsal for Dictatorship* (1941; reprint ed., Pelican, 1971), pp. 150–51.

8. Kane, *Louisiana Hayride,* p. 151.

9. St. Louis *Post-Dispatch,* March 3, 1935; T. Harry Williams interview with Seymour Weiss, July 3, 1957, T. H. Williams MSS; Williams interview with Richard Leche, June 30, 1957, ibid. Smith later denied during an interview with Glen Jeansonne that he had ever slept on the floor in Long's bedroom.

10. Hodding Carter, "How Come Huey Long? 1. Bogeyman—," *New Republic* 82 (February 13, 1935), 11–14; Gerald L. K. Smith, "How Come Huey Long?—Or Superman?," ibid., pp. 14–15; St. Louis *Post-Dispatch,* March 3, 1935.

11. T. Harry Williams interview with Frank Odom, May 21, 1958, T. H. Williams MSS; T. Harry Williams, *Huey Long* (Alfred A. Knopf, 1969), p. 700.

12. St. Louis *Post-Dispatch,* March 3, 1935; Carter, "How Come," p. 11; Williams, *Huey Long,* p. 700; Bennett, *Demagogues,* p. 125.

13. Share Our Wealth Society handbill, n.d., OF 1403, FDRL; Atlanta *Constitution,* February 6, 7, 1935; Atlanta *Journal,* February 7, 1935; Baltimore *Sun,* March 14, 1935; Augusta *Chronicle,* April 22, 23, 1935; "News and Comment from the National Capital," *Literary Digest* 119 (March 16, 1935), 12.

14. Long radio address, February 23, 1934, in U.S. Congress, *Congressional Record,* 73rd Congress, 2nd session (March 1, 1934), p. 3452; Rose Lee, "Senator Long at Home," *New Republic* 79 (1934), 66–67; Philadelphia *Evening Bulletin,* March 8, 14, 1935.

15. T. Harry Williams interview with Theophile Landry, July 10, 1957, T. H. Williams MSS; Hodding Carter, "Huey Long's Louisiana Hayride," *American Mercury* 68 (1949), 442; [Monroe Sweetland], "The Student Movement and Huey Long: A Brief Interview," *Student Outlook* 3 (April 1935), 10; T. Harry Williams interview with Joe Cawthorn, May 5, 1960, T. H. Williams MSS; Los Angeles *Daily News,* April 4, 1935, HLS; *New York Times,* March 27, 1935; Boston *Evening Globe,* May 13, 1935; Des Moines *Register,* April 21, 1935; William Allen White to Harold Ickes, February 7, 1935, Ickes MSS, Library of Congress. The question of Long's relationship with conservative businessmen and other Republicans remains unresolved. There is no concrete evidence of any connection, financial or otherwise, but there are several suggestive references to the possibility. Frank Altschul, an official of Lazard Frères in New York, wrote Herbert Hoover in April 1935 and talked at length of his belief that a Republican victory in 1936 was essential to "the fate of civilization." And in the midst of the discussion, he referred pointedly to Long. "Without Huey Long," he wrote, "I would consider the chance [of a GOP victory] very slight; with Huey Long, there is a chance which it seems worth devoting all one's energies to bring to realization." There was nothing more specific than that. See Frank Altschul to Herbert Hoover, April 17, 1935, PPI, Hoover Presidential Library. Franklin Roosevelt, in any case, was all but convinced that Long had reached some understanding with the Republicans. In a letter to Colonel House in February, he outlined what he considered the "schools of thought" of the Republican opposition—the old-guard conservatives, the liberals, and the Progressives like La Follette, Cutting, and Nye; and he concluded: "All of these Republican elements are flirting with Huey Long and probably financing him. A third Progressive Republican ticket and a fourth 'Share the Wealth' ticket they believe would crush us and that then a free for all would result in which case anything might happen." See Roosevelt to Colonel House, February 16, 1935, PPF 222, FDRL.

16. *New York Times,* August 16, 1935.

17. Ibid.; Swing, "Menace of Huey Long," p. 98; *Evening Ledger* n.p., February 17, 1935, HLS; William Allen White to Harold Ickes, February 7, 1935, Ickes MSS, Library of Congress.

18. Myles M. Platt, "Father Charles E. Coughlin and the National Union for Social Justice" (M.A. thesis, Wayne State University, 1951), p. 72; Eleanor Paperno, "Father Coughlin: A Study in Domination" (M.A. thesis, Wayne State University, 1939), p. 63; Charles E. Coughlin, *A Series of Lectures on Social Justice* (Radio League of the Little Flower, 1935), pp. 7–19; *New York Times,* November 19, 1934.

19. Ibid., April 28, 1935; Des Moines *Register,* April 13, 1935.

20. Coughlin to Elmer Thomas, May 13, 1935, Thomas MSS, University of Oklahoma; Thomas to Coughlin, May 15, 1935, ibid.; Charles J. Tull, *Father Coughlin and the New Deal* (Syracuse University Press, 1965), pp. 93–94; St. Louis *Post-Dispatch,* April 25, 1935; Detroit *News,* April 25, 1935; Detroit *Free Press,* April 26, 1935.

21. Cleveland *Press,* May 8, 9, 1935; Columbus *Evening Dispatch,* May 9, 1935.

22. *New York Times,* May 23, 1935; New York *Herald Tribune,* May 22, 23, 1935; Hamilton Basso, "Radio Priest—in Person," *New Republic* 83 (June 5, 1935), 96.

23. Ibid., pp. 96–97; New York *Daily News,* May 23, 1935; *New York Times,* May 23, 1935; New York *Herald Tribune,* May 23, 1935.

24. Ibid., May 23, 24, 1935; *New York Times,* May 26, 1935; "Father Coughlin at the Garden," *Nation* 140 (1935), 644.

25. *New York Times,* April 28, May 22, July 30, 1935.

26. Tull, *Father Coughlin,* pp. 100–01; Boston *Globe,* August 13, 1935.

27. New York *Herald Tribune,* May 22, 1935; *Rocky Mountain News,* March 20, 1935; Walter Davenport, "The Shepherd of Discontent," *Collier's* 95 (May 4, 1935), 60.

28. *New York Times,* April 28, 1935.

29. Martha Mays Schroeder, "Huey Pierce Long: The Kingfish of the Senate" (M.A. thesis, University of Texas, 1967), pp. 157–79; Huey Long form letters, n.d., OF 1403, FDRL; Huey Long form letters, n.d., Long MSS, Duke University; "Share Our Wealth Society" handbill, n.d., OF 1403, FDRL; Burton L. Hotaling, "Huey Pierce Long as Journalist and Propagandist," *Journalism Quarterly* 20 (1943), 28; Lee, "Senator Long at Home," p. 66.

30. Baltimore *Sun,* March 14, 1935; Augusta *Chronicle,* April 23, 1935.

31. "News and Comment from the National Capital," *Literary Digest* 119 (March 16, 1935), 12; Swing, "Menace," p. 99.

32. Unidentified clipping (Stokes), December 3, 1934, HLS; Olla *Signal* (Louisiana), May 10, 1935, HLS; Circulars 78 and 81 (August 15, 1935), William B. Wisdom Collection of Huey P. Long, Tulane University.

33. Sarasota *Herald,* n.d., 1935, HLS; *Arkansas Democrat,* n.d., 1935, HLS. Ft. Myers *News Press,* n.d., HLS; D. P. Granberry to William Colmer, May 9, 1934, Colmer MSS, Southern Mississippi University.

34. *Florida Times-Union,* March 7, 1935, HLS; George B. Hills to James A. Farley, March 8, 1935, OF 1403, FDRL; Governor David Sholtz to Farley, January 9, 1935, ibid.; *Cracker* (Riviera, Texas), May 1935, HLS.

35. Joseph H. Price to Huey Long, n.d., 1935, HLS; Ft. Myers *News Press,* n.d., 1935, HLS; Robert Lloyd to Franklin D. Roosevelt, March 18, 1935, OF 1403, FDRL; Sarasota *Herald,* n.d., 1935, HLS; Meridian *Star,* March 18, 1934, HLS; Picayune *Item,* n.d., HLS.

36. *American Veteran,* April 25, 1935, HLS; T. Harry Williams interview with Mary B. Wall, February 20, 1961, T. H. Williams MSS, LSU; *American Progress,* March 15, 1934; unidentified clipping, February 13, 1934, HLS; Kensington *News* (Pennsylvania), n.d., HLS.

37. Edgar Norton to T. Harry Williams, September 26, 1956, October 10, 1956, T. H. Williams MSS.

38. St. Louis *Post-Dispatch* (miscellaneous clippings), n.d., 1935, HLS; J. M. Callaway to Long, February 20, 1935, HLS.

39. St. Louis *Post-Dispatch* (clippings), n.d., 1935, HLS.

40. *New York Times,* March 21, 1935.

41. Des Moines *Register,* April 28, 1935; unidentified clipping (by Carey McWilliams), April 27, 1935, HLS; *National EPIA News,* April 5, 1935, HLS; *Share the Wealth,* June 8, 1935, HLS; *Noble News,* n.d., 1935, HLS.

42. Unidentified handbill, n.d., 1935, HLS; *Post Record,* n.p., May 17, 1935, HLS; *Upton Sinclair's EPIC News,* May 20, 1935, HLS; *National EPIA News,* April 12, 1935, HLS; Tom R. Amlie to Harold Gilbert, April 22, 1935, Amlie MSS; Des Moines *Register,* April 28, 1935; unidentified clipping, n.d., 1935, HLS; Pismo *Times* (California), April 5, 1935, HLS.

43. *Share the Wealth,* June 8, 1935, HLS; *Uncle Sam, The People's Paper,* n.d., 1935, HLS; unidentified clipping, n.d., 1935, HLS; "Robert Noble," handbill, n.d., 1935, HLS.

44. *National EPIA News,* April 12, 1935, HLS; unidentified clipping, n.d., 1935, HLS; *Noble News,* n.d., 1935, HLS; Katherine de Core-Glazier to Roosevelt, February 10, 1935, OF 1403, FDRL.

45. William E. Akin, *Technocracy and the American Dream: The Technocrat Movement, 1900–1941* (University of California Press, 1977), passim; *Technocrat,* April 1935, HLS; *Western States Technocrat,* n.d., 1935, HLS; Pismo *Times,* April 5, 1935, HLS; *Uncle Sam,* n.d., 1935, HLS.

46. Des Moines *Register,* April 28, 1935.

47. A. B. Magil, "Can Father Coughlin Come Back?" *New Republic* 87 (June 24, 1936), 196; George A. Condon, "The Politics of the Social Justice Movement" (Ph.D. dissertation, University of Tennessee, 1962), p. 168.

48. Magil, "Can Father Coughlin," p. 196; Coughlin, *Series,* pp. 7–24; Coughlin to Robert T. Malone, November 19, 1934, January 14, 1935, Malone MSS, Nebraska State Historical Society; National Union for Social Justice membership application, OF 306, FDRL; Coughlin to Robert T. Malone, June 5, 1935, Malone MSS.

49. Brent Spence to Marvin McIntyre, February 23, 1935, OF 306, FDRL; "Petition to President Roosevelt," Dayton, Kentucky, ibid.; Robert T. Malone to Coughlin, n.d., Malone MSS; Mrs. M. M. Morrow to editor, Omaha *World Herald,* March 6, 1935, ibid.

50. *New York Times,* March 31, April 16, June 14, 1935.

51. Earle Edward Eubank, "Father Coughlin Triumphs in Cincinnati," *Christian Century* 52 (1935), 1514–15.

52. *People's Voice,* February 1, 8, 1935, HLS.

53. Eubank, "Father Coughlin Triumphs," pp. 1514–15; *People's Voice,* February 15, 1935, HLS.

54. Tull, *Father Coughlin,* pp. 113–16; *New York Times,* December 16, 1935, February 10, 1936.

55. *Social Justice,* April 24, May 8, 29, June 12, 1936.

56. Ibid., April 24, May 8, 15, 1936.

57. Ibid., March 29, April 3, 17, 24, 1936.

58. Robert C. McMath, Jr., *Populist Vanguard: A History of the Southern Farmers' Alliance* (University of North Carolina Press, 1975), pp. 12–14, 64–76; Lawrence Goodwyn, *Democratic Promise: The Populist Moment in America* (Oxford University Press, 1976), pp. 3–50 and passim.

59. See Marshall McLuhan, *Understanding Media: The Dimensions of Man* (McGraw-Hill, 1964), pp. 7–32, 297–307.

Chapter 9

1. William C. Schimpf to Roosevelt, n.d., Alphabetical File 8155, FDRL; Schimpf to Roosevelt, November 22, 1933, ibid.; *New York Times,* March 31, 1935.

2. Schimpf to Roosevelt, November 22, 1933, Alphabetical File 8155, FDRL; abstract of letter, Schimpf to Roosevelt, August 26, 1935, OF 306, FDRL; Schimpf to Roosevelt, September 11, 1934, Alphabetical File 8155, FDRL.

3. Schimpf to Roosevelt, n.d., 1934, June 29, 1934, November 22, 1933, ibid.; *New York Times,* March 31, 1935.

4. St. Louis *Post-Dispatch,* n.d., HLS.

5. A. R. Boley to Senator C. C. Dill, April 18, 1933, Long MSS, LSU; Boley to Senator William McAdoo, April 22, 1933, ibid.

6. Boley to Roosevelt, April 18, 1933, ibid.; Boley to Dill, May 24, 1933, ibid.; Dill to Boley, April 21, 1933, ibid.; Boley to Long, May 27, 1933, ibid.

7. James Zuccarelli to H. V. Kaltenborn, January 18, 1935, Kaltenborn MSS, Wisconsin State Historical Society; Paul Black to Huey Long, May 3, 1935, OF 1403, FDRL; Thomas Alessi to Roosevelt, November 5, 1933, OF 306, FDRL; W. E. Warren to Roosevelt, February 14, 1935, OF 1403, FDRL; Louis Howe to Roosevelt, February 21, 1935, ibid.; Lela McHenry Stiles, *The Man Behind Roosevelt: The Story of Louis McHenry Howe* (World, 1954), p. 285;

"Huey Long," *New Republic* 135 (December 18, 1935), 177; A. B. Magil, "Can Father Coughlin Come Back?" *New Republic* 87 (June 24, 1935), 196.

8. Des Moines *Register,* April 28, 1935; Stroud *Democrat: The Farmer's Weekly,* May 10, 1935, HLS; Isabella Greenway to Long, July 3, 1934, HLS; Oklahoma *Union Farmer,* n.d., HLS; E. J. Clarke to Long, n.d., HLS.

9. Des Moines *Register,* April 6, 1935; Carlyle *Union Banner,* February 8, 1935, HLS; *National Union Farmer,* March 15, 1935, HLS; John Kasmeier to Elmer Thomas, May 17, 1935, Thomas MSS, University of Oklahoma.

10. Neil Betten, *Catholic Activism and the Industrial Worker* (University Presses of Florida, 1976), pp. 92–93; *New York Times,* March 26, 1934; Charles E. Coughlin, *Eight Lectures on Labor, Capital and Justice* (Radio League of the Little Flower, 1934), pp. 120–132.

11. *Progressive,* September 14, 1935; Detroit *Free Press,* April 25, 1935; Alexander Cook, United Auto Workers Oral History, Wayne State University, p. 40.

12. *New York Times,* September 2, 1935; Richard Frankensteen, UAW Oral History, pp. 19–21; Irving Bernstein, *Turbulent Years: A History of the American Worker, 1933–1941* (Houghton Mifflin, 1971), pp. 503–04.

13. Green apparently resisted pressures from some elements within the AFL to repudiate Coughlin; and he told Coughlin in a letter that he considered him "most sympathetic and friendly to the organized labor movement." Betten, *Catholic Activism,* p. 92. John A. Zaremba, UAW Oral History, pp. 14–15; Bernstein, *Turbulent Years,* p. 509; Daniel J. Tobin to James A. Farley, April 23, 1935, OF 306, FDRL; *Progressive,* August 17, 1935; *New York Times,* December 3, 1935; Homer Martin to Coughlin, January 19, February 16, April 25, July 5, 1935, Martin MSS, Wayne State University; John W. Anderson, UAW Oral History, pp. 30–31, 80; *Social Justice,* February 8, 1937.

14. Letters from Coughlin supporters in OF 306, FDRL disclose a particularly large number of German and Irish names from industrial cities. See also James P. Shenton, "The Coughlin Movement and the New Deal," *Political Science Quarterly* 73 (1958), 360, 366; Samuel Lubell, *The Future of American Politics* (Harper & Row, 1965), pp. 143–44; Zaremba, UAW Oral History, pp. 14–15; Peter Friedlander, *The Emergence of a UAW Local, 1936–1939* (University of Pittsburgh Press, 1975), pp. 4, 115.

15. *Daily Worker,* March 19, 1935; T. Harry Williams interview with Richard Leche, June 30, 1957, T. H. Williams MSS, LSU.

16. *American Progress,* September 7, October 5, 11, 1933, May 1935; Clive Edgin et al. to Roosevelt, March 12, 1934, OF 1403, FDRL; clippings and leaflets in file 96, William Jett Lauck MSS, University of Virginia; James T. Gallagher to Huey Long, July 19, 1935, HLS; *New York Times,* August 15, 1935; *Labor,* January 26, June 28, 1935; "Comment," *Railroad Telegrapher,* March 1935, pp. 166–68, T. H. Williams MSS.

17. Ronald Schatz has argued that it was the skilled, relatively privileged workers within the mass production industries who spearheaded the drive for industrial unionism and became the early leaders of the C.I.O. His analysis of 35 "union pioneers" in one Westinghouse and three General Electric factories in the mid-1930s discloses that male organizers "were members of an elite stratum of the industry's work force." Many held positions in such areas as maintenance, landscaping, or plant construction that left them relatively autonomous, free from the rigid control of a foreman or supervisor. They displayed, in short, some of the same characteristics as Long and Coughlin followers. Schatz's findings support the thesis that workers of higher status with vaguely middle-class values are more likely to become politically active in times of stress than those who are more dependent and less affluent. His argument also suggests that not all such people were likely to channel their political activism in the direction of Long and

Coughlin. See "Union Pioneers: The Founders of Local Uhions at General Electric and West-inghouse, 1933–1937," *Journal of American History* 66 (1979), 586–602.

18. Louis Levand to Roosevelt, March 8, 1935, OF 1403, FDRL; Charles D. O'Brien to Roosevelt, September 9, 1934, OF 306, FDRL; Daytona Beach *News-Journal,* December 22, 1934, HLS; Los Angeles *Times,* March 13, 1935.

19. Philadelphia *Evening Bulletin,* March 11, 12, 1935; unidentified clipping, Stroudsburg, Pennsylvania, March 19, 1934, HLS; Philadelphia *Record,* March 12, 1935; New York *Sun,* April 4, 1935; Riverhead *News* (New York), March 22, 1935, HLS; Newark *Star Eagle,* June 6, 1934, HLS; Raritan *Independent,* n.d., 1934, HLS; unidentified clipping, Hoboken, New Jersey, February 13, 1934, HLS; unidentified clipping, Stamford, Connecticut, n.d., 1935, HLS; *American Progress,* March 1, 1934.

20. Dubuque *Telegraph Herald* (Iowa), March 29, 1935, HLS; *Kansas Cityan,* June 1935, HLS; John B. Moritz to Roosevelt, February 4, 1935, James A. Farley MSS, Library of Congress; Louis Howe to Roosevelt, February 12, 1935, ibid.; Roosevelt to Howe, February 13, 1935, ibid.; Howe to Farley, February 15, 1935, ibid.; Farley to William T. Kemper, February 21, 1935, ibid.; Indianapolis *Star,* March 12, 1935; Chippewa *Herald* (Wisconsin), January 18, 1935, HLS; John Cowles to Herbert Hoover, March 9, 1935, Post-Presidential Inventory 307, Hoover Presidential Library; St. Louis *Post-Dispatch,* March 11, 1935; J. M. Callaway to Huey Long, February 20, 1935, HLS; St. Louis *Star-Times,* February 26, 1935, HLS; G. H. Forge to Ewing Y. Mitchell, March 12, 1935, Mitchell MSS, University of Missouri.

21. Stephen Demmon to Harold Ickes, April 26, 1935, Ickes MSS, Library of Congress; Frank W. Joesten to Farley, February 26, 1935, OF 300, FDRL.

22. Arizona *Republic,* March 12, 1935; *Dunbar's Weekly* (Maricopa County, Arizona), n.d., 1935, HLS; *Progressive,* May 4, 1935; *Share the Wealth,* June 8, 1935, HLS; Seattle *Star,* March 8, 1935, HLS; Shelton *Independent* (Washington), March 25, 1935, HLS; *New York Times,* March 17, 1935; Portland *Journal,* March 8, 1935, HLS.

23. *American Progress,* August 24, 1933, April 1935; unidentified clipping, n.d., HLS; Oakland *Tribune,* June 26, 1935, HLS; San Francisco *Chronicle,* editorial, n.d., reprinted in *New York Times,* March 10, 1935; Carey McWilliams, unidentified clipping, April 27, 1935, HLS; William Jennings Bryan, Jr., to Farley, March 18, 1935, Farley MSS; Farley to Roosevelt, March 21, 1935, OF 1403, FDRL; M. S. Lehand to Farley, March 25, 1935, ibid.; San Francisco *News,* March 26, 1935, HLS; L. H. Bowlby to Roosevelt, March 8, 1935, OF 1403, FDRL; Louis Piro to Roosevelt, n.d., 1935, ibid.; Des Moines *Register,* April 28, 1935.

24. Results of a compilation of 616 letters to the editor of the *American Progress,* from its first issue in August 1933 until the death of Huey Long in September 1935.

25. Shenton, "Coughlin Movement," 353, 357, 360; Ashmun Brown to Herbert Hoover, April 4, 1934, Post-Presidential Inventory, Hoover Presidential Library; Springfield· *Union,* March 16, 1935, January 6, 1936; George A. Condon, "The Politics of the Social Justice Movement" (Ph.D. dissertation, University of Tennessee, 1962), p. 141; Baltimore *Sun,* March 3, 14, 1935; Coughlin to Carl Weideman, December 29, 1934, Weideman MSS, University of Michigan; Des Moines *Register,* April 6, 28, 30, 1935; Earle Edward Eubank, "Father Coughlin Triumphs in Cincinnati," *Christian Century* 52 (1935), 1514–16.

26. Sample of 78 letters to the editor of *Social Justice,* March–June 1936.

27. George Gallup and Samuel Forbes Rae, *The Pulse of Democracy: The Public Opinion Poll and How It Works* (Simon & Schuster, 1940), p. 45; Harold L. Ickes, *The Secret Diary of Harold Ickes: The First Thousand Days, 1933–1936* (Simon & Schuster, 1953), p. 462.

28. Poll results derived from data in Emil Hurja MSS, FDRL; a somewhat different analysis of the poll is available in Seymour Martin Lipset and Earl Raab, *The Politics of*

Unreason: Right-Wing Extremism in America, 1790–1970 (Harper & Row, 1970), pp. 191–94.

29. T. Harry Williams interview with Earle Christenberry, July 11, 1957, T. H. Williams MSS, LSU; "News and Comment from the National Capital," *Literary Digest* 119 (February 9, 1935), 13; Williams interview with James F. O'Connor, June 28, 1957, T. H. Williams MSS; U.S. Congress, *Congressional Record*, 74th Congress, 1st Session (March 5, 1935), pp. 2935–36; Des Moines *Register*, April 27, 1935.

30. Philadelphia *Bulletin*, March 15, 1935; Philadelphia *Inquirer*, March 15, 1935; David Carl Colony, "Dictator Coughlin: Fascism Under the Cross," *Forum* 93 (1935), 201; Benjamin Stolberg, "Dr. Huey and Mr. Long," *Nation* 141 (September 18, 1935), 344.

31. *New York Times*, April 27, 28, 1935; Walter Davenport, "The Shepherd of Discontent," *Collier's* 95 (May 4, 1935), 13; Arthur M. Schlesinger, Jr., *The Politics of Upheaval* (Houghton Mifflin, 1960), p. 248.

32. Letter to editor from H. M. Berg, *Nation* 140 (1935), 332; *New York Times*, April 27, 28, 1935.

33. John Francis Thorning, "Senator Long on Father Coughlin," *America* 53 (April 13, 1935), 8–9; Detroit *News*, April 25, 1935.

34. *Congr. Record*, 72:2 (January 3, 10, 1933), pp. 1184, 1451–70; ibid., 72:1 (April 8, 29, 1932), pp. 7767, 9215; ibid., 73:1 (April 17, 1933), p. 1818; Long radio address, April 21, 1933, in ibid., 73:1 (April 24, 1933), p. 2211; *American Progress*, September 28, October 29, 1933; Victor C. Ferkiss, "The Political and Economic Philosophy of American Fascism" (Ph.D. dissertation, University of Chicago, 1954), pp. 190–91.

35. Huey Pierce Long, *My First Days in the White House* (Telegraph Press, 1935), pp. 34–38.

36. Charles E. Coughlin, *A Series of Lectures on Social Justice* (Radio League of the Little Flower, 1935), pp. 18, 28, 51; New York *Herald Tribune*, May 23, 1935.

37. Charles E. Coughlin, *Eight Discourses on the Gold Standard and Other Kindred Subjects* (Radio League of the Little Flower, 1933), pp. 37–38; Coughlin, *By the Sweat of Thy Brow* (Radio League of the Little Flower, 1931), p. 14; *New York Times*, May 7, 1935; Coughlin, *Father Coughlin's Radio Discourses, 1931–1932* (Radio League of the Little Flower, 1932), pp. 157–58; *Congr. Record*, 74:1 (May 2, 1935), pp. 6776–82; ibid., 73:1 (March 30, April 11, 27, May 3, 1933), pp. 1038, 1473–75, 2456–59, 2780; Coughlin, *Driving Out the Money Changers* (Radio League of the Little Flower, 1933), p. 47; *American Progress*, May 1935; Condon, "Politics," pp. 185–88; Coughlin, *Series*, pp. 68, 76, 146, 149–50; Des Moines *Register*, April 28, 1935; Long radio address, May 11, 1935, in *Congr. Record*, 74:1 (May 23, 1935), pp. 8039, 8042; radio address, February 10, 1935, in ibid. (March 4, 1935), p. 2833.

38. J. B. Rudert to Long, January 22, 1932, Huey Long MSS, LSU; Harry C. Brodbeck to Roosevelt, November 15, 1933, OF 306, FDRL; Odus Ray to Josiah Bailey, February 3, 1935, Bailey MSS, Duke University; Paul D. Back to Roosevelt, November 14, 1933, OF 306, FDRL; D. H. Kilby to Coughlin, February 26, 1935, ibid.

39. Davenport, "Shepherd," p. 13; Nashville *Banner*, February 15, 1935; "Demagogues," *Newsweek*, March 16, 1935, p. 5; Des Moines *Register*, April 28, 1935; Raymond Gram Swing, "The Build-Up of Long and Coughlin," *Nation* 140 (March 20, 1935), 325.

40. Daniel Woodward to Harold Ickes, April 20, 1935, Ickes MSS, Library of Congress; Walter Clinedinst to H. V. Kaltenborn, May 25, 1935, Kaltenborn MSS, Wisconsin State Historical Society; Hartford *Courant*, March 15, 1935.

41. New Orleans *Item*, June 14, 1935, HLS; Springfield *Union*, n.d., 1935, HLS; *People's Voice*, February 15, 1935, HLS.

42. Elzey Roberts to Roosevelt, March 16, 1935, PPF 2293, FDRL; Richard Roper to

William Bankhead, November 20, 1934, Bankhead MSS, Alabama Department of Archives and History.

Chapter 10

1. George B. Tindall, *The Emergence of the New South, 1913–1945* (Louisiana State University Press, 1967), pp. 615–17; Reinhard Luthin, *American Demagogues* (Beacon Press, 1954), pp. 182–94; William Anderson, *The Wild Man from Sugar Creek: The Political Career of Eugene Talmadge* (Louisiana State University Press, 1975), pp. 16–123.

2. Atlanta *Constitution,* February 6, April 23, 1935; Atlanta *Journal,* April 22, 1935; Augusta *Chronicle,* April 23, 1935; *New York Times,* May 19, 1935; Anderson, *Wild Man,* p. 118.

3. Ibid., pp. 118–19; Atlanta *Constitution,* February 6, 1935; Atlanta *Journal,* February 6, 1935.

4. Des Moines *Register,* April 9, 1935; Eugene Dodd to Herbert Hoover, April 6, 1935, Post-Presidential Inventory 316, Hoover Presidential Library; Atlanta *Constitution,* March 7, 1935.

5. Tindall, *Emergence,* pp. 23–24; William Alexander Percy, *Lanterns on the Levee* (Alfred A. Knopf, 1941), p. 148; Luthin, *American Demagogues,* pp. 44–64; Robert J. Bailey, "Theodore G. Bilbo and the Senate Election of 1934," *Southern Quarterly* 10 (1971), 91–94; A. Wigfall Green, *The Man Bilbo* (Louisiana State University Press, 1963), pp. 9–97.

6. Robert J. Bailey, "Theodore G. Bilbo: Prelude to a Senate Career, 1932–1934" (M.A. thesis, University of Southern Mississippi, 1971), p. 29; Bailey, "Bilbo and Senate Election," p. 94; Raymond Gram Swing, *Forerunners of American Fascism* (Julian Messner, 1935), p. 111; "Theodore Bilbo and Huey Long," *Literary Digest* 119 (February 9, 1935), 7.

7. John M. Quarles to Bilbo, May 16, 1934, Bilbo MSS, University of Southern Mississippi; T. A. Hartley to J. G. Burkett, April 21, 1934, ibid.; Ethel Sanford to Bilbo, May 16, 1934, ibid.; Malcolm Hudnall to Bilbo, April 25, 1934, ibid.

8. G. D. Anderson to Bilbo, May 30, 1934, ibid.; Xavier A. Kramer to Lula Wimberly, August 1, 1934, ibid.; A. B. Schauber to Lula Wimberly, June 19, 1934, ibid.; Archibald S. Coody to Bilbo, May 19, 1935, Coody MSS, LSU; Thomas A. Hartley to Bilbo, May 3, 1934, Bilbo MSS.

9. Bailey, "Bilbo and Senate Election," p. 94; Bailey, "Bilbo: Prelude," p. 56; Luthin, *American Demagogues,* p. 64; J. L. Peavey to Bilbo, April 9, 1934, Bilbo MSS; Thad F. Buckley to Hollis Rawls, June 20, 1934, ibid.

10. Bilbo to John Green, August 31, 1934, ibid.; Meridian *Star* (Mississippi), March 7, 14, 1935; J. Bush to William Colmer, April 18, 1934, Colmer MSS, University of Southern Mississippi; A. S. Coody to Bilbo, May 5, 19, 1935, Bilbo MSS; *New York Times,* September 30, 1934; Green, *The Man Bilbo,* p. 91; Atlanta *Constitution,* March 7, 1935; Otto L. Rogers to Bilbo, April 21, 1934, Bilbo MSS.

11. Bilbo to Joseph Robinson, August 18, 1935, OF 1403, FDRL; Bilbo to Roosevelt, August 18, 1935, ibid.; Boston *Evening Globe,* August 13, 1935; Bilbo to Roosevelt, August 28, 1935, PPF 2184, FDRL; G. S. Agee to Bilbo, September 11, 1935, Bilbo MSS.

12. W. D. Archer to Harold Ickes, April 22, 1935, Ickes MSS; unidentified clipping, August 9, 1935, HLS; New Orleans *Times-Picayune,* August 6, 1935; Baton Rouge *Morning Advocate,* August 14, 1935; A. S. Coody to Allan McCants, July 25, 1935, Coody MSS; Swing, *Forerunners,* pp. 119–20.

13. *New York Times,* January 30, 1936; Anderson, *Wild Man,* pp. 136–40; Green, *The Man Bilbo,* pp. 98–121.

14. David H. Bennett, *Demagogues in the Depression: American Radicals and the Union Party, 1932–1936* (Rutgers University Press, 1969), pp. 149–50; [J. F. Carter] "The Unofficial Observer," *American Messiahs* (Simon & Schuster, 1935), pp. 77–80; Swing, *Forerunners,* pp. 124–26; Arthur M. Schlesinger, Jr., *The Politics of Upheaval* (Houghton Mifflin, 1960), pp. 30–31.

15. Abraham Holtzman, *The Townsend Movement: A Political Study* (Bookman Associates, 1963), pp. 32–33.

16. Ibid., pp. 33–40.

17. Ibid., p. 34; Bennett, *Demagogues,* pp. 152–54.

18. Ibid., pp. 154–55; [Carter], *Messiahs,* pp. 80–81.

19. Holtzman, *Townsend,* pp. 86–100; Bennett, *Demagogues,* p. 155; Frank Peterson to Frank Dyer, January 10, 1935, C. Jasper Bell MSS, University of Missouri; [Carter], *Messiahs,* pp. 84–86.

20. Schlesinger, *Politics of Upheaval,* p. 39; Bennett, *Demagogues,* pp. 176–78; David H. Bennett, "The Year of the Old Folks' Revolt," *American Heritage* 16 (December 1964), 102.

21. Tom Amlie to O. T. Babcock, January 10, 1935, Amlie MSS, Wisconsin State Historical Society.

22. *Townsend Weekly,* March 25, April 15, May 6, 1935. The newspaper of the Townsend organization experienced frequent (and inexplicable) name changes. Founded as the *Townsend National Weekly,* it was published at various times as the *Official Townsend Weekly,* the *Townsend Weekly,* and others. For purposes of clarity, all references to it here are to the *Townsend Weekly,* whatever version of the title the particular issue cited bears.

23. Frank Peterson to Frank Dyer, January 10, 1935, C. Jasper Bell MSS; *New York Times,* November 25, 1935; Charles J. Tull, *Father Coughlin and the New Deal* (Syracuse University Press, 1965), p. 105.

24. *Townsend Weekly,* January 18, March 18, 25, April 8, 22, June 16, November 18, 1935; San Diego *Union,* February 27, 1935, HLS.

25. Unidentified clipping (Associated Press), January 11, 1935, HLS; unidentified clipping (United Press), July 30, 1935, HLS; Long radio address, February 10, 1935, in U.S. Congress, *Congressional Record,* 74th Congress, 1st session (March 4, 1935), p. 2833; Long to S. J. Willis, March 23, 1935 (form letter), William B. Wisdom Collection of Huey P. Long, Tulane University; *New York Times,* March 22, November 25, 1935.

26. Los Angeles *Daily News,* February 28, 1935, HLS; *Valley Press,* Syracuse, New York, n.d., 1935, HLS; unidentified clippings, n.d., 1935, HLS.

27. Swing, *Forerunners,* p. 132.

28. [Carter], *Messiahs,* p. 134.

29. Ibid., pp. 89–95; Donald R. McCoy, *Angry Voices: Left-of-Center Politics in the New Deal Era* (University of Kansas Press, 1958), p. 55; Schlesinger, *Politics of Upheaval,* pp. 96–100; Everett E. Luoma, *The Farmer Takes a Holiday* (Exposition Press, 1967), pp. 67–79.

30. McCoy, *Angry Voices,* pp. 56–58, 97; Schlesinger, *Politics of Upheaval,* pp. 101–02.

31. Ibid., pp. 105–06; [Carter], *Messiahs,* pp. 104–14.

32. Patrick J. Maney, *"Young Bob" La Follette: A Biography of Robert M. La Follette, Jr., 1895–1953* (University of Missouri Press, 1978), pp. 133–48; McCoy, *Angry Voices,* pp. 44–48, 52; Donald R. McCoy, "The Formation of the Wisconsin Progressive Party in 1934," *The Historian* 14 (1951), 76–78; Schlesinger, *Politics of Upheaval,* pp. 106–07.

33. Maney, *"Young Bob,"* pp. 29–31, 38–40, 53–75, 110–32; Schlesinger, *Politics of Upheaval,* p. 105; [Carter], *Messiahs,* pp. 105–14; Harold L. Ickes, *The Secret Diary of Harold L. Ickes: The First Thousand Days, 1933–1936* (Simon & Schuster, 1953), p. 363.

34. Charles Herbert Backstrom, "The Progressive Party of Wisconsin, 1934–1936" (Ph.D. dissertation, University of Wisconsin, 1956), pp. 96–98; *Progressive,* January 26, February 2, March 16, 1935; [Carter], *Messiahs,* pp. 103, 114; John Edward Miller, "Governor Philip F. La Follette, the Wisconsin Progressives, and the New Deal, 1930–1939" (Ph.D. dissertation, University of Wisconsin, 1973), pp. 63–66, 74–83.

35. R. Alan Lawson, *The Failure of Independent Liberalism, 1930–1941* (G. P. Putnam's Sons, 1971), pp. 39–46; Alfred M. Bingham, *Insurgent America: Revolt of the Middle Classes* (Harper & Brothers, 1935), pp. 175–228; Schlesinger, *Politics of Upheaval,* pp. 144–46; Backstrom, "Progressive Party," pp. 114–16; McCoy, *Angry Voices,* pp. 38–49, 54–58; Alfred Bingham to Howard Y. Williams, April 18, 1935, H. Y. Williams MSS, Minnesota State Historical Society.

36. Alfred Bingham to Tom Amlie, March 18, 1935, Amlie MSS; McCoy, *Angry Voices,* pp. 80–82; Hugh T. Lovin, "The Fall of Farmer-Labor Parties, 1936–1938," *Pacific Northwest Quarterly* 62 (1971), 16; *New York Times,* July 5–7, 1935; Robert Morss Lovett, "A Party in Embryo," *New Republic* 83 (July 24, 1935), 292–95.

37. Tom Amlie to Paul Boyd, March 7, 1935, Amlie MSS; H. Y. Williams to R. D. Linton, May 8, 1935, H. Y. Williams MSS; *Progressive,* March 2, 1935; Alfred Bingham to H. Y. Williams, April 4, 1935, H. Y. Williams MSS; Tom Amlie to Daniel McCormack, March 25, 1933, Amlie MSS; H. Y. Williams to Amlie, April 2, 1935, H. Y. Williams MSS; Amlie to Paul Boyd, March 7, 1935, Amlie MSS; Amlie to Harry Peterson, June 20, 1935, ibid.; Schlesinger, *Politics of Upheaval,* p. 97.

38. *Progressive,* March 23, April 13, 1935; Miller, "Governor Philip F. La Follette," pp. 173–78; Donald P. Fina to Amlie, March 2, 1935, Amlie MSS; C. S. Perring to Farmer-Labor Convention, March 26, 1935, Farmer-Labor Association MSS, Minnesota State Historical Society; *Progressive,* September 7, 1935; William Douville to H. Y. Williams, July 1, 1935, H. Y. Williams MSS.

39. M. L. Williams to H. Y. Williams, April 13, 1935, ibid.; notes for county executive meetings, n.d., Farmer-Labor Party in Michigan MSS, University of Michigan; George F. Burash to H. Y. Williams, April 11, 1935, H. Y. Williams MSS; H. Y. Williams to Tom Amlie, April 2, 1935, ibid.; J. W. Bissell to H. Y. Williams, March 7, June 18, 1935, ibid.; C. E. Wharton to H. Y. Williams, n.d., ibid.

40. August Nelson to H. Y. Williams, June 12, 1935, ibid.

41. *Progressive,* January 26, February 2, 16, March 16, May 4, June 29, September 7, 1935; Miller, "Governor Philip F. La Follette," pp. 173–78; Des Moines *Register,* April 3, 1935; H. Y. Williams to Alfred Bingham, April 16, September 23, 1935, H. Y. Williams MSS; Robert Morss Lovett, "Hue [sic] Long Invades the Middle West," *New Republic* 83 (May 15, 1935), 10–11; Tom Amlie to H. Y. Williams, April 24, 1935, H. Y. Williams MSS; Bingham to H. Y. Williams, April 4, 1935, ibid.

42. Ibid.; Paul Douglas to Tom Amlie, April 22, 1935, Amlie MSS.

43. Tom Amlie to Samuel Sigman, March 14, 1935, Sigman MSS, Wisconsin State Historical Society; H. Y. Williams to Bingham, March 18, 1935, Amlie MSS; Norman Thomas to Amlie, April 27, 1935, ibid.; Amlie to Thomas, April 23, 1935, ibid.; Amlie to Selden Rodman, April 3, 1935, ibid.

44. H. Y. Williams to State Executive Committee, April 4, 1935, H. Y. Williams MSS; H. Y. Williams to G. F. Burash, April 16, 1935, ibid.

45. John L. Shover, *Cornbelt Rebellion: The Farmers' Holiday Association* (University of Illinois Press, 1965), pp. 25–27; [Carter], *Messiahs,* pp. 149–50.

46. Luoma, *Farmer Takes a Holiday,* pp. 26–28; Shover, *Cornbelt Rebellion,* pp. 27, 34–38.

47. Ibid., pp. 41–55; Luoma, *Farmer Takes a Holiday,* pp. 29–66; Theodore Saloutos, *Agricultural Discontent in the Middle West* (University of Wisconsin Press, 1951), pp. 435–51.

48. [Carter], *Messiahs,* pp. 150–54; Shover, *Cornbelt Rebellion,* pp. 55–57.

49. McCoy, *Angry Voices,* pp. 33–36; Shover, *Cornbelt Rebellion,* pp. 154–60; Saloutos, *Agricultural Discontent,* pp. 485–87.

50. H. Y. Williams to Tom Amlie, April 2, 1935, ibid.; H. Y. Williams to Alfred Bingham, April 16, 1935, ibid.; Milo Reno to William Hirth, April 23, 1933, Reno MSS, University of Iowa; *New York Times,* April 23, 1935.

51. Raymond Benjamin to Herbert Hoover, May 7, 1934, Post-Presidential Inventory, Hoover Presidential Library; Des Moines *Register,* May 3, 4, 1934.

52. Ibid., May 3, 1935; *New York Times,* April 23, 1935; Tom Amlie to Selden Rodman, April 17, 1935; Amlie MSS; H. Y. Williams to Amlie, April 2, 1935, ibid.; Freeport *Journal-Standard* (Illinois), April 4, 1935, HLS.

53. H. Y. Williams to Alfred Bingham, April 23, 1935, H. Y. Williams MSS; Des Moines *Register,* April 19, 26, 27, 1935.

54. Ibid., April 21, 27, 1935; Detroit *News,* April 22, 1935.

55. Ibid., April 28, 1935; Lovett, "Hue Long," pp. 10–11.

56. Des Moines *Register,* April 28, 29, 1935; Augusta *Chronicle,* April 28, 1935; Lovett, "Hue Long," pp. 10–11.

57. *New York Times,* September 18, 1935.

58. *Daily Worker,* March 6, 13, 14, 19, 1935; Alex Bittelman, "How Can We Share the Wealth? The Communist Way Versus Huey Long," Wisdom Collection; *New York Times,* June 2, 1935; "Moscow on Father Coughlin," *Living Age* 348 (1935), 86–87.

59. Coughlin to Sam Verne, November 26, 1934, Socialist Party of America MSS, Duke University; Benjamin Stolberg, "Dr. Huey, and Mr. Long," *Nation* 141 (September 18, 1935), 344–45; Columbia *State* (South Carolina), March 23, 1935.

60. Arthur G. McDowell to "Comrade Secretary," June 18, 1935, Socialist Party MSS; Mary Hunter to Norman Thomas, March 13, 1935, Thomas MSS, New York Public Library; *New York Times,* March 25, November 1, 1935; handbill, West Philadelphia Socialist Party, May 24, 1935, HLS; Richard B. Whitten, "Huey P. Long and the Working Class Movement," *The Socialist Appeal,* n.d., T. H. Williams MSS.

61. W. A. Swanberg, *Norman Thomas: The Last Idealist* (Charles Scribner's Sons, 1976), p. 134; Harry Fleischman, *Norman Thomas: A Biography* (W. W. Norton, 1964), p. 140; New York *Herald Tribune,* May 3, 1934; *New York Times,* May 3, 1934.

62. Press release, April 3, 1935, Norman Thomas MSS; *New York Times,* April 8, July 14, 15, 1935; Thomas to Huey Long, Charles E. Coughlin, June 1935, Socialist Party MSS; Thomas to "Mr. Van Dusen," March 29, 1935, Thomas MSS.

63. Coughlin to Sam Verne, November 26, 1934, Socialist Party MSS; Stolberg, "Dr. Huey," pp. 344–45.

64. Meridian *Star,* March 13, 1935; C. S. Hickey to Norman Thomas, July 15, 1935, Thomas MSS; Nita Brunnon to George Pickett, December 6, 1933, Pickett MSS, LSU; Fredrica Nuding to Thomas, April 6, 1935, Thomas MSS.

65. Swanberg, *Norman Thomas,* pp. 158–60; J. P. Butler to Thomas, May 20, 1935, Southern Tenant Farmers Union MSS, University of North Carolina; M. S. Venkataramani,

"Norman Thomas, Arkansas Sharecroppers, and the Roosevelt Agricultural Policies, 1933–1937," *Mississippi Valley Historical Review* 47 (1960), 226–44; Bernard K. Johnpoll, *Pacifist's Progress: Norman Thomas and the Decline of American Socialism* (Quadrangle Books, 1970), p. 148.

66. H. L. Mitchell to Norman Thomas, July 4, 1934, Thomas MSS; Mitchell to Thomas, February 21, September 5, 1934, ibid.

67. Elmer Woods to "Green," August 20, 1935, Southern Tenant Farmers Union MSS.

Chapter 11

1. Lucy Harrington to Roosevelt, March 8, 1935, OF 1403, FDRL; *Georgia Women's World,* n.d., 1935, HLS; Robert Loyd to Roosevelt, OF 1403, FDRL.

2. Walter Campbell to Roosevelt, June 18, 1935, ibid.; L. L. Braude to Roosevelt, March 11, 1935, ibid.; Garland Markovich to Roosevelt, March 18, 1933, Democratic National Committee MSS, 300 La. XYZ, FDRL; George C. Hart to Roosevelt, June 6, 1935, OF 1403, FDRL.

3. "Neil" to Farley, April 12, 1935, PPF 104, FDRL.

4. Frank J. Manning to Roosevelt, August 29, 1935, OF 1403, FDRL; John L. McInnis et al. to Roosevelt, January 19, 1935, Homer Cummings MSS, University of Virginia.

5. As late as January 29, 1936, Coughlin gave evidence of his residual loyalties to the Administration. In a telegram to Joseph P. Kennedy on that date, he warned that "the boss" was "getting the living hell batted out of him" by newspapers in Detroit. But the expression of solicitude was clearly self-serving. In the next sentence, Coughlin lobbied to have an acquaintance appointed to a vacant federal judgeship in Michigan, justifying the request by claiming that his candidate was "willing and desires [sic] of wringing the necks of the administration's enemy." Coughlin to Kennedy, January 29, 1936, FDRL.

6. Charles E. Coughlin, *A Series of Lectures on Social Justice* (Radio League of the Little Flower, 1935), p. 230.

7. Ibid., pp. 230, 232–44.

8. Stuart Simpson to Roosevelt, n.d., 1935, OF 1403, FDRL; (unsigned) to Roosevelt, n.d., 1935, OF 306, FDRL.

9. Clyde M. Hamel to Roosevelt, May 9, 1935, ibid.; Mary Harris to Louis Howe, March 8, 1935, ibid.

10. M. W. Yencer to Roosevelt, March 12, 1935, ibid.; R. Bucheit to Roosevelt, April 16, 1934, ibid.; John Jackson to Roosevelt, November 10, 1935, ibid.

11. Hugh Fraser to Coughlin, September 8, 1934, ibid.; Mrs. O. D. Little to Roosevelt, November 27, 1934, ibid.

12. Mary Bopp to Coughlin, September 21, 1934, ibid.; *New York Times,* November 18, 1935; "The Presidency," *Time,* November 25, 1935, p. 13; Charles H. Phelps to Coughlin, November 19, 1935, OF 306, FDRL.

13. Eleanor Paperno, "Father Coughlin: A Study in Domination" (M.A. thesis, Wayne University, 1939), pp. 61–62.

14. See, e.g., William E. Leuchtenburg, *Franklin D. Roosevelt and the New Deal* (Harper & Row, 1963); Henry H. Adams, *Harry Hopkins* (G. P. Putnam's Sons, 1977), pp. 67–109; Frank Freidel, *Franklin D. Roosevelt: Launching the New Deal* (Little, Brown, 1973), esp. chapters 6, 15, 25; Paul E. Mertz, *New Deal Policy and Southern Rural Poverty* (Louisiana State University Press, 1978); Charles H. Trout, *Boston: The Great Depression and the New Deal*

(Oxford University Press, 1977); Ellis W. Hawley, *The New Deal and the Problem of Monopoly* (Princeton University Press, 1966).

15. James T. Patterson, *The New Deal and the States: Federalism in Transition* (Princeton University Press, 1969), p. 195.

16. Ibid., passim; Trout, *Boston,* chapters 7, 11, 12; Harold Gorvine, "The New Deal in Massachusetts," in John Braeman et al., eds., *The New Deal* (Ohio State University Press, 1975), II, 3–44; Robert F. Hunter, "Virginia and the New Deal," in ibid., II, 103–36; James F. Wickens, "Depression and New Deal in Colorado," in ibid., II, 269–310; David J. Maurer, "Relief Problems and Politics in Ohio," in ibid., II, 77–102; Bruce M. Stave, *The New Deal and the Last Hurrah: Pittsburgh Machine Politics* (University of Pittsburgh Press, 1970); Lyle W. Dorsett, *Franklin D. Roosevelt and the City Bosses* (Kennikat Press, 1977); David S. Burner, *The Politics of Provincialism* (W. W. Norton, 1967), pp. 244–52 and passim.

17. *Daily Oklahoman,* September 3, 1935; T. Harry Williams, *Huey Long* (Alfred A. Knopf, 1969), pp. 859–60.

18. Ibid., pp. 860–61.

19. Ibid., pp. 861–62; Harnett T. Kane, *Louisiana Hayride: The American Rehearsal for Dictatorship* (1941; reprint ed., Pelican, 1971), p. 133.

20. Williams, *Huey Long,* pp. 863–66; New Orleans *Times-Picayune,* September 9, 1935.

21. A. J. Liebling, *The Earl of Louisiana* (Simon & Schuster, 1961), pp. 13–14; New Orleans *Times-Picayune,* September 9, 10, 1935; Williams, *Huey Long,* pp. 865–68.

22. Ibid., pp. 873–76; Liebling, *Earl of Louisiana,* p. 14; New Orleans *Times-Picayune,* September 10, 11, 1935.

23. "Louisiana: Death of a Dictator," *Time,* September 16, 1935, p. 15; "Louisiana: Mourners, Heirs, Foes," ibid., September 23, 1935, pp. 14–16; Hamilton Basso, "The Kingfish: In Memoriam," *New Republic* 84 (December 18, 1935), 177; *New York Times,* September 13, 23, 1935; "Funeral Oration Delivered Over the Grave of Huey Pierce Long, September 12, 1935," William B. Wisdom Collection of Huey P. Long, Tulane University; *American Progress,* September 1935; Allan P. Sindler, *Huey Long's Louisiana: State Politics, 1920–1952* (Johns Hopkins University Press, 1956), pp. 117–22.

24. Ibid., pp. 126–37; *New York Times,* February 23, June 24, 1936; Thomas L. Stokes, *Chip Off My Shoulder* (Princeton University Press, 1940), p. 404.

25. "Schism Among Long's Political Heirs," *Literary Digest,* September 28, 1935, p. 8; Sindler, *Huey Long's Louisiana,* pp. 117–22; David H. Bennett, *Demagogues in the Depression: American Radicals and the Union Party, 1932–1936* (Rutgers University Press, 1969), pp. 131–36, 138–41; *New York Times,* January 25, 27, 29, 30, February 8, May 23, 31, June 1, 2, September 15, 1936; Hamilton Basso, "The Death and Legacy of Huey Long," *New Republic* 85 (January 1, 1936), 217; Gerald L. K. Smith, "Huey P. Long: A Summary of Greatness," unpublished pamphlet, n.d. (I am indebted to Glen Jeansonne for a copy of this essay); Leo P. Ribuffo, "The Making of an Anti-Semite: Gerald L. K. Smith, 'Extremism,' and the 'Paranoid Style,' " unpublished essay, n.d. (I am indebted to the author for making the paper available to me).

26. *Nation* 141 (September 18, 1935), 309; *New York Times,* September 12, 1935; Sheldon Marcus, *Father Coughlin: The Tumultuous Life of the Priest of the Little Flower* (Little, Brown, 1973), pp. 98–99.

27. "After Huey Long: What?" *Literary Digest,* September 21, 1935, p. 3; *New York Times,* September 18, 1935; "The Presidency," *Time,* November 25, 1935, p. 13.

28. Charles J. Tull, *Father Coughlin and the New Deal* (Syracuse University Press, 1965), pp. 113–16; *New York Times,* December 16, 1935, February 10, 1936.

29. Ibid., June 14, 1936; Tull, *Father Coughlin,* pp. 113–16; T.R.B., "Washington Notes," *New Republic* 87 (June 3, 1936), 100–01.

30. Bennett, *Demagogues,* p. 82; Tull, *Father Coughlin,* pp. 117–18; *New York Times,* May 1, June 14, 1936.

31. T.R.B., "Washington Notes" (June 3, 1936), pp. 100–01; Tull, *Father Coughlin,* pp. 118–20; Bennett, *Demagogues,* pp. 82–83; *New York Times,* May 11, 14, 27, 1936.

32. Peter A. Soderbergh, "The Rise of Father Coughlin, 1891–1930," *Social Science* 62 (1967), 17; *New York Times,* April 6, May 28, 1936.

33. Bennett, *Demagogues,* pp. 96–101.

34. Ibid., pp. 190–91; *New York Times,* February 17, 18, 24, May 10, 1936. Typical of the letters to the White House in response to the O'Connor controversy was one to the President from A. J. Glasser of Corona, New York, who wrote: "Remove or impeach Mr. OConner as Chairmen [sic] of the Ways & Means Committee at once or lose 14 votes at the next election," n.d., OF 306, FDRL.

35. *New York Times,* June 20, 22, 1936; Bennett, *Demagogues,* pp. 191–92.

36. Ibid., pp. 198–200; *New York Times,* June 22, 1936.

37. Ibid., July 17, 18, 1936; Harry T. Moore, "Just Folks in Utopia," *New Republic* 85 (November 13, 1935), 10.

38. *New York Times,* July 15, 20, 1936; Bennett, *Demagogues,* pp. 9–11.

39. *Townsend Weekly,* July 27, 1936; *New York Times,* July 16, 17, 19, 1936.

40. Ibid., July 19, August 13, 14, 16, 1936; Bennett, *Demagogues,* pp. 16–18.

41. Ibid., pp. 17–21; Jonathan Mitchell, "Father Coughlin's Children," *New Republic* 88 (August 26, 1936), 74; Wallace Stegner, "Pattern for Demagogues," *Pacific Spectator* 2 (1948), 406; *New York Times,* August 17, 1936.

42. *Townsend Weekly,* July 14, August 17, November 3, 1936; Charles Herbert Backstrom, "The Progressive Party of Wisconsin" (Ph.D. dissertation, University of Wisconsin, 1956), pp. 331–33; *Progressive,* July 11, November 7, 1936; *New York Times,* June 18, September 11, 1936; Donald R. McCoy, "The Progressive National Committee of 1936," *Western Political Quarterly* 9 (1956), 459; Hugh T. Lovin, "The Fall of Farmer-Labor Parties, 1936–1938," *Pacific Northwest Quarterly* 62 (1971), 18–19; Donald R. McCoy, *Angry Voices: Left-of-Center Politics in the New Deal Era* (University of Kansas Press, 1958), p. 107.

43. The effects on the Coughlin movement of the break with Roosevelt are skillfully described in James P. Shenton, "The Coughlin Movement and the New Deal," *Political Science Quarterly* 73 (1958), 362–71.

44. See OF 306 (1936), FDRL; Robert V. Daly to Roosevelt, November 11, 1936, ibid.; John F. Null to James McMullin, October 28, 1936, ibid.; Stephen Early to Roosevelt, September 30, 1936, PPF 3960, FDRL.

45. A. B. Magil, "Can Father Coughlin Come Back?" *New Republic* 87 (June 24, 1936), 198; David Owen Powell, "The Union Party of 1936" (Ph.D. dissertation, Ohio State University, 1962), pp. 108–09; Early to Marvin McIntyre, October 13, 1936, OF 306, FDRL; "Father Coughlin Walks Again," *Nation* 143 (August 22, 1936), 201–02.

46. *New York Times,* August 7, 12, September 7, 1936; Cincinnati *Times Star,* September 25, 1936, OF 306, FDRL; Farley to Roosevelt, October 6, 1936, ibid.; R. C. Scott to Coughlin, August 12, 1936, ibid.

47. Shenton, "Coughlin Movement," pp. 365–67.

48. Mitchell, "Father Coughlin's Children," pp. 72–74.

49. Ibid.; *New York Times,* August 16, 1936; Stegner, "Pattern for Demagogues," p. 406.

50. *New York Times,* October 9, 1936; Shenton, "Coughlin Movement," pp. 366–70;

letters of October–November 1936, John A. Ryan MSS, Catholic University of America.

51. Mrs. Rosate Muichella to John A. Ryan, November 9, 1936, ibid.; Mrs. M. Connell to Ryan, November 8, 1936, ibid.; Ambrose Tenure to Ryan, November 16, 1936, ibid.; J. A. Lanx to Ryan, November 12, 1936, ibid.; Clement Smolen to Ryan, November 24, 1936, ibid.; Viola Fasullo to Ryan, October 25, 1936, ibid.

52. *New York Times,* November 4, 5, 1936; Bennett, *Demagogues,* pp. 263–68. See also Michael Rogin, *The Intellectuals and McCarthy: The Radical Specter* (M.I.T. Press, 1967), pp. 102–03, 105, 131–33, 213–15.

53. Ibid., pp. 263–65; "Coughlin Drive: He Promises to Swing 9,000,000 Votes to Lemke," *Literary Digest,* August 22, 1936, p. 4; *New York Times,* November 5, 8, 1936.

Epilogue

1. Harnett T. Kane, *Louisiana Hayride: The American Rehearsal for Dictatorship* (1941; reprint ed., Pelican, 1971), p. 136; Allan P. Sindler, *Huey Long's Louisiana: State Politics, 1920–1952* (Johns Hopkins University Press, 1956), pp. 117–22; Caddo Parish campaign pamphlet, January 1, 1936, LSU; Earle Christenberry to Josiah Bailey, January 10, 1936, Bailey MSS, Duke University.

2. Stan Opotowsky, *The Longs of Louisiana* (E. P. Dutton, 1960), pp. 109–33; "Soaking the Poor Again," leaflet, September 1936, William B. Wisdom Collection of Huey P. Long, Tulane University; Kane, *Louisiana Hayride,* p. 236; Sindler, *Huey Long's Louisiana,* pp. 137–39; V. O. Key, Jr., *Southern Politics* (Alfred A. Knopf, 1949), p. 156.

3. Kane, *Louisiana Hayride,* pp. 263–316; Sindler, *Huey Long's Louisiana,* pp. 137–52.

4. Ibid., pp. 154–207; Key, *Southern Politics,* pp. 164–68.

5. Jack Bass and Walter DeVries, *The Transformation of Southern Politics* (Basic Books, 1976), pp. 161–85; Key, *Southern Politics,* pp. 167–82; A. J. Liebling, *The Earl of Louisiana* (Simon and Schuster, 1961); Sindler, *Huey Long's Louisiana,* pp. 208–47; Marshall Frady, *Southerners* (New American Library, 1980), pp. 41–43; Huey P. Long, *Every Man a King* (National Book Company, 1933), p. 99.

6. Sheldon Marcus, *Father Coughlin: The Tumultuous Life of the Priest of the Little Flower* (Little, Brown, 1973), pp. 139–40; Charles J. Tull, *Father Coughlin and the New Deal* (Syracuse University Press, 1965), pp. 173–74.

7. Coughlin's radio sermons in 1937 were reprinted each week in *Social Justice.* His sermons for the first four months of 1938 were published in *Sixteen Radio Lectures* (Radio League of the Little Flower, 1938). George H. Gallup, *The Gallup Poll: Public Opinion 1935–1971* (Random House, 1972), I, 100–01; David H. Bennett, *Demagogues in the Depression: American Radicals and the Union Party, 1932–1936* (Rutgers University Press, 1969), pp. 278–79. See also Gary Marx, *The Social Basis of the Support of a Depression Era Extremist: Father Coughlin* (Survey Research Center, University of California, 1962).

8. Coughlin denied until the end of his life that he had ever been an anti-Semite; and even in 1938 and 1939, he was always careful to distinguish between "good Jews" and "bad Jews," separating himself from the Nazi argument of an inherent racial evil in Jewishness. It was also true that discussion of Jews never occupied nearly as large a proportion of Coughlin's rhetoric as it did those of some of his more venomous followers. Nevertheless, Coughlin maintained almost total control over the contents of *Social Justice,* and substantial control over the activities of many of his supporters at this time; and if he was unhappy about the blatant anti-Semitism being preached in his name, he never put a stop to it. See *Social Justice,*

December 5, 1938, July 24, 1939. Coughlin's sermons from November 1938 through the end of 1939 were collected in *Am I an Anti-Semite?* and *Why Leave Our Own?*, both published by his Radio League of the Little Flower in 1939. Subsequent sermons were published in the pages of *Social Justice*. See also Donald S. Strong, *Organized Anti-Semitism in America: The Rise of Group Prejudice During the Decade 1930–1940* (American Council on Public Affairs, 1941), pp. 59–63. The fullest study of *Social Justice* and its anti-Semitism is Marcus, *Father Coughlin*, pp. 139–224, 243–57.

9. Ibid., pp. 63–70. Ronald H. Bayor, *Neighbors in Conflict* (Johns Hopkins University Press, 1978) includes an excellent description of the activities of the Christian Front in New York. See pp. 173–238.

10. Marcus, *Father Coughlin*, p. 201.

11. Ibid., pp. 208–24; Tull, *Father Coughlin*, pp. 230–38; Bennett, *Demagogues*, pp. 279–82; *Social Justice*, e.g., March 30, 1942.

12. Coughlin continued to send out form letters to his parishioners as late as 1972 discussing political subjects. His Christmas letter that year, for example, began: "Christmas of 1972 will be remembered as the day the free world surrendered to Marxism." Coughlin form letter, December 10, 1972, Coughlin "Drop File," Michigan Historical Collections, University of Michigan. Interviews with Father Coughlin appear in Robert S. Gallagher, "The Radio Priest," *American Heritage* 23 (1972), 39–41, 100–09; George A. Condon, "The Politics of the Social Justice Movement" (Ph.D. dissertation, University of Tennessee, 1962), pp. 296–301; Marcus, *Father Coughlin*, p. 232. Coughlin to "Subscriber," June 1942, Hoover Presidential Library, Pegler Papers.

13. Gallagher, "Radio Priest," p. 39; Boston *Globe*, October 12, 1976; *New York Times*, October 28, 1979. Coughlin suffered a series of coronaries in his last years and finally died of heart failure, two days after his eighty-eighth birthday.

Appendix I

1. Dale Kramer, "The American Fascists," *Harper's* 181 (September 1940), 390. Richard Hofstadter discusses (and perhaps exaggerates) the role of anti-Semitism in populist ideology in *The Age of Reform* (Alfred A. Knopf, 1954), pp. 77–82. A more muted view of turn-of-the-century anti-Semitism is Oscar Handlin, "American Views of the Jew at the Opening of the Twentieth Century," *Publications of the American Jewish Historical Society* 40 (1951), 323–44. John Higham reconsiders the issue in "Anti-Semitism in the Gilded Age: A Reinterpretation," *Mississippi Valley Historical Review* 43 (1957), 559–78. See also Richard Hofstadter, *The Paranoid Style in American Politics* (Alfred A. Knopf, 1965), pp. 61, 300–02, a work that includes as well a brief and somewhat distorted discussion of Coughlin's own anti-Semitism.

2. Charles E. Coughlin, *By the Sweat of Thy Brow* (Radio League of the Little Flower, 1931), p. 35; Coughlin, *Father Coughlin's Radio Discourses, 1931–32* (Radio League of the Little Flower, 1932), p. 123; "Gentile Silver," *Nation* 138 (1934), 522.

3. Charles E. Coughlin, *Driving Out the Money Changers* (Radio League of the Little Flower, 1933), pp. 56–59; Handlin, "American Views of the Jew," pp. 329–35. Coughlin's elaborate discussion of Jews as an honorable people shamefully persecuted and thus perverted into worshipping the gold standard echoed almost precisely the account in Ignatius Donnelly's populist Utopian novel of the Jewish descent into "merciless" money-getting. Donnelly, *Caesar's Column* (1890; reprint ed., Harvard University Press, John Harvard Library, 1960), pp. 36–38, 111–12.

4. Charles E. Coughlin, *The New Deal in Money* (Radio League of the Little Flower, 1933), pp. 68–83; Coughlin, *A Series of Lectures on Social Justice* (Radio League of the Little Flower, 1935), pp. 72–83, 225; "Gentile Silver," p. 522; Philadelphia *Bulletin,* March 14, 1935.

5. John J. Loftus, "From One Who Really 'Thinks' " (letter to the editor), *Nation* 138 (1934), 650.

6. "A follower of Father Coughlin" to H. V. Kaltenborn, n.d., 1935, Kaltenborn MSS, Wisconsin State Historical Society; Mrs. Samuel Lichtenberg to Roosevelt, March 12, 1935, OF 306, FDRL.

7. James A. Farley, *Jim Farley's Story: The Roosevelt Years* (McGraw-Hill, 1948), p. 45; Raymond Gram Swing, "Father Coughlin: II. The Phase of Action," *Nation* 140 (1935), 9–11; Washington *Evening Star,* March 11, 1935; James P. Shenton, "Fascism and Father Coughlin," *Wisconsin Magazine of History* 44 (1960), 7; *Social Justice,* September 19, 1938; Sheldon Marcus, *Father Coughlin: The Tumultuous Life of the Priest of the Little Flower* (Little, Brown, 1973), pp. 180–207, 297–99; Donald S. Strong, *Organized Anti-Semitism in America: The Rise of Group Prejudice During the Decade 1930–1940* (Washington: American Council on Public Affairs, 1941), pp. 57–70; Ronald H. Bayor, *Neighbors in Conflict* (Johns Hopkins University Press, 1978), pp. 97–102; John P. Diggins, *Mussolini and Fascism: The View from America* (Princeton University Press, 1972), pp. 183–84, 321.

8. Shenton, "Fascism," p. 8; Institute for Propaganda Analysis, *The Fine Art of Propaganda: A Study of Father Coughlin's Speeches* (Harcourt, Brace, 1939), p. 51; Coughlin, *A Series of Lectures on Social Justice,* p. 88; Allan A. Michie and Frank Rhylick, *Dixie Demagogues* (Vanguard Press, 1939), p. 112; *American Progress,* May 1935.

9. Arthur M. Schlesinger, Jr., *The Politics of Upheaval* (Houghton Mifflin, 1960), p. 67; Kramer, "American Fascists," p. 390.

10. Geoffrey S. Smith, *To Save a Nation: American Counter-Subversives, the New Deal, and the Coming of World War II* (Basic Books, 1973), pp. 53–65; Schlesinger, *Politics of Upheaval,* pp. 79–80.

11. J. F. de Villard to Josiah Bailey, April 27, 1935, Bailey MSS, Duke University.

12. Lawrence Dennis, *The Coming American Fascism* (Harper & Brothers, 1936), pp. 49–50, 105–06, 163–87, and passim; Schlesinger, *Politics of Upheaval,* pp. 74–78.

13. Ibid., p. 72; *New York Times,* December 18, 1934; David H. Bennett, *Demagogues in the Depression: American Radicals and the Union Party, 1932–1936* (Rutgers University Press, 1969), pp. 4, 248.

14. Shenton, "Fascism," p. 7; S. J. Woolf, in Gilbert Allardyce, "What Fascism Is Not: Thoughts on the Deflation of a Concept," *American Historical Review* 84 (1979), 367.

15. Ernst Nolte discusses the idea of a "fascist minimum" in *Three Faces of Fascism* (Holt, Rinehart and Winston, 1965), p. 24, 39–40.

16. Thomas Mann, *Mario and the Magician* (Alfred A. Knopf, 1931).

17. J. P. Stern, *Hitler: The Führer and the People* (Fontana/Collins, 1975), pp. 27–37, 67–68.

18. Stern, *Hitler,* p. 110; Nolte, *Three Faces,* pp. 273, 281–90, 427–32, 513–22.

19. One of the early influences upon Adolf Hitler was Gottfried Feder, a German publicist who spoke out frequently against the "interest yoke" and denounced tyrannical financial institutions. Mussolini's attacks upon "financial parasites" and Freemasonry were similarly important in the early rise of Italian fascism. See Nolte, *Three Faces,* pp. 236–39, 411–13; Salvatore Saladino, "Italy," in Hans Rogger and Eugen Weber, eds., *The European Right* (University of California Press, 1965), pp. 242–44, 254, 257–58; Ernst Nolte, "Germany," in ibid., pp. 298–300.

20. Stern, *Hitler,* pp. 16–17, 113–15; Nolte, "Germany," pp. 289–90; Saladino, "Italy," pp. 224–27; Margaret Canovan, *Populism* (Harcourt Brace Jovanovich, 1981), pp. 103, 149, 229–30, 292.

21. Ezra Pound, *Jefferson and/or Mussolini* (Liveright, 1935), pp. 61, 65, 79–80, 104, 122–23.

22. Schlesinger, *Politics of Upheaval,* p. 18; Bennett, *Demagogues,* p. 60; Andrew Whiteside, "Austria," in Rogger and Weber, eds., *European Right,* pp. 332–38.

23. J. R. Jones, "England," in ibid., pp. 54–57, 58–66; Canovan, *Populism,* pp. 316, 336.

24. Nolte, *Three Faces,* p. 40.

25. Nolte, "Germany," p. 300; Allardyce, "What Fascism Is Not," passim; Adrian Lyttelton, "Italian Fascism," in Walter Laqueur, ed., *Fascism* (University of California Press, 1976), pp. 135–43; Hans Mommsen, "National Socialism: Continuity and Change," in ibid., pp. 179–210; Alan S. Milward, "Fascism and the Economy," in ibid., pp. 379–412; Zeev Sternhell, "Fascist Ideology," in ibid., pp. 315–60; Eugen Weber, "The Right," in Rogger and Weber, eds., *European Right,* pp. 24–26; Stern, *Hitler,* pp. 50–52.

26. Ibid., pp. 52, 68–80.

Locations of
Manuscript Collections

Thomas R. Amlie Papers	State Historical Society of Wisconsin, Madison, Wisconsin
Josiah Bailey Papers	Perkins Library, Duke University, Durham, North Carolina
William B. Bankhead Papers	State of Alabama Department of Archives and History, Montgomery, Alabama
Thomas Swain Barclay Oral History	Herbert Hoover Presidential Library, West Branch, Iowa
C. Jasper Bell Papers	Western Historical Manuscripts Collection, University of Missouri, Columbia, Missouri
Theodore G. Bilbo Papers	University of Southern Mississippi Library, Hattiesburg, Mississippi
William Borah Papers	Library of Congress, Washington, D.C.
Reuben D. Bowen Papers	Perkins Library, Duke
Edward Fullerton Brown Papers	Minnesota Historical Society, St. Paul, Minnesota
Eleanor Bumgardner Papers	Michigan Historical Collections, Bentley Historical Library, University of Michigan, Ann Arbor, Michigan
Father Raymond S. Clancy Papers	Archives of Labor and Urban Affairs, Walter P. Reuther Library, Wayne State University, Detroit, Michigan
Raymond Clapper Papers	Library of Congress
William M. Colmer Papers	University of Southern Mississippi Library
Columbia Oral History Project	Butler Library, Columbia University, New York, New York

Tom Connally Papers	Library of Congress
Archibald S. Coody Papers	Louisiana State University Library, Baton Rouge, Louisiana
Homer S. Cummings Papers	University of Virginia Library, Charlottesville, Virginia
Bronson Cutting Papers	Library of Congress
Democratic National Committee Papers	Franklin D. Roosevelt Library, Hyde Park, New York
Frederick C. Edwards Papers	Perkins Library, Duke
James A. Farley Papers	Library of Congress
Farmer-Labor Association of Minnesota Papers	Minnesota Historical Society
Farmer-Labor Party in Michigan Papers	Michigan Historical Collections
Frank D. Fitzgerald Papers	Michigan Historical Collections
Leo J. Fitzpatrick Papers	Michigan Historical Collections
Carter Glass Papers	University of Virginia Library
Herbert Hoover Post-Presidential Papers	Hoover Presidential Library
Herbert Hoover Presidential Papers	Hoover Presidential Library
Emil Hurja Papers	Franklin D. Roosevelt Library
Harold Ickes Papers	Library of Congress
Sam Irby Papers	Perkins Library, Duke
Jewish Community Relations Council of Minnesota Papers	Minnesota Historical Society
George F. Johnson Papers	George Arents Research Library, Syracuse University, Syracuse, New York
H. V. Kaltenborn Papers	State Historical Society of Wisconsin, Madison, Wisconsin
La Follette Family Papers	Library of Congress
William Jett Lauck Papers	University of Virginia Library
Richard W. Leche Papers	Louisiana State University Library
Huey P. Long Papers	Perkins Library, Duke
Huey P. Long Papers	Louisiana State University Library
Huey P. Long Scrapbooks	Louisiana State University Library

Robert T. Malone Papers	Nebraska State Historical Society, Lincoln, Nebraska
Homer Martin Papers	Archives of Labor and Urban Affairs
E. Y. Mitchell, Jr., Papers	Western Historical Manuscripts Collection, University of Missouri
Frank Murphy Papers	Michigan Historical Collections
George Murphy Papers	Michigan Historical Collections
George W. Norris Papers	Library of Congress
Westbrook Pegler Papers	Hoover Presidential Library
George T. Pickett Papers	Louisiana State University Library
Milo Reno Papers	University of Iowa Libraries, Iowa City, Iowa
Franklin D. Roosevelt Pre-Presidential Papers	Franklin D. Roosevelt Library
Franklin D. Roosevelt Presidential Papers	Franklin D. Roosevelt Library
Harry Ross Papers	Archives of Labor and Urban Affairs, Wayne State
John A. Ryan Papers	Catholic University of America Library, Washington, D.C.
Samuel Sigman Papers	State Historical Society of Wisconsin
John H. Small Papers	Perkins Library, Duke
Socialist Party of America Papers	Perkins Library, Duke
Southern Tenant Farmers Union Papers	University of North Carolina Library, Chapel Hill, North Carolina
John Nathan Sparks Papers	Western Historical Manuscripts Collection, University of Missouri
Lloyd C. Stark Papers	Western Historical Manuscripts Collection, University of Missouri
Elmer Thomas Papers	Western History Collection, University of Oklahoma Library, Norman, Oklahoma
Norman Thomas Papers	New York Public Library, New York, New York
United Auto Workers Oral History	Archives of Labor and Urban Affairs, Wayne State
George Sylvester Viereck Papers	University of Iowa Libraries
Henry A. Wallace Papers	University of Iowa Libraries
Carl M. Weidemann Papers	Michigan Historical Collections

Howard Y. Williams Papers	Minnesota Historical Society
T. Harry Williams Papers	Louisiana State University Library
William B. Wisdom Collection of Huey P. Long Materials	Tulane University Library, New Orleans, Louisiana

INDEX

About the Author

Alan Brinkley graduated from Princeton University in 1971, and received his M.A. and Ph.D. degrees from Harvard University. He is currently an assistant professor of history at M.I.T.

A Note on the Type

The text of this book was set via computer-driven cathode ray
tube in a face called Times Roman, designed by Stanley
Morison for *The Times* (London) and first introduced by that
newspaper in 1932.
Among typographers and designers of the twentieth
century, Stanley Morison has been a strong forming influence,
as a typographical adviser to the English Monotype
Corporation, as a director of two distinguished English
publishing houses, and as a writer of sensibility, erudition, and
keen practical sense.

Composed by The Haddon Craftsmen, Inc., ComCom Division,
Allentown, Pennsylvania. Printed and bound by the Haddon
Craftsmen, Inc.,
Scranton, Pennsylvania

Designed by Virginia Tan